ADVANCE PRAISE FOR

The White Educators' Guide to Equity

"*The White Educators' Guide to Equity* is a vital contribution to the literature on how to create racial equity in college settings—and, importantly, in the setting of community colleges, where such work is more important than ever, but often ignored. A must-read for all educators, but particularly those in community colleges looking to transform their institutions."

—Tim Wise, Author, *White Like Me: Reflections on Race from a Privileged Son*

"Given the disproportionate number of white faculty in the community system in comparison to the student population, this book is essential in providing the necessary guidance and tools that will allow white teachers to effectively teach students of color. Moreover, this text recognizes that if the community system is going to improve outcomes for students of color that white faculty have obligation to be equipped to have greater understanding of race and racism that would impact what and how they teach."

—Edward Bush, President, Cosumnes River College

"Improving outcomes for community college students begins with improving one's understanding of race and racism. The first-person perspective of engaging in anti-racist work in this book calls to our core values as community college educators. This book provides guidance, evokes critical self-reflection, and highlights practical tools to effectively educate historically minoritized students, especially for an educational system whose teaching faculty is predominantly white."

—Angelica Garcia, President, Berkeley City College

The White Educators' Guide to Equity

Educational Equity in Community Colleges

Jeremiah J. Sims and Lasana O. Hotep
General Editors

Vol. 2

The Educational Equity in Community Colleges series
is part of the Peter Lang Education list.
Every volume is peer reviewed and meets
the highest quality standards for content and production.

PETER LANG
New York • Berlin • Brussels • Lausanne • Oxford

Jeramy Wallace and Jeremiah J. Sims

The White Educators' Guide to Equity

Teaching for Justice in Community Colleges

Jeremiah J. Sims and
Lasana O. Hotep, Editors

PETER LANG
New York • Berlin • Brussels • Lausanne • Oxford

Library of Congress Cataloging-in-Publication Control Number: 2022039006

Bibliographic information published by **Die Deutsche Nationalbibliothek**.
Die Deutsche Nationalbibliothek lists this publication in the "Deutsche
Nationalbibliografie"; detailed bibliographic data are available
on the Internet at http://dnb.d-nb.de/.

ISSN 2690-4438 (print)
ISSN 2690-4446 (online)
ISBN 978-1-4331-9694-2 (hardcover)
ISBN 978-1-4331-9856-4 (paperback)
ISBN 978-1-4331-9854-0 (ebook pdf)
ISBN 978-1-4331-9855-7 (epub)
DOI 10.3726/b19966

Peter Lang Publishing, Inc., New York
80 Broad Street, 5th floor, New York, NY 10004
www.peterlang.com

This book is dedicated to all the critical community college educators who refuse to maintain the status quo and instead fight for educational justice.

Table of Contents

Acknowledgments

Jeramy Wallace

I would like to dedicate this work to my family – Sara, Anabella, Avery, and Charlie – for their support during this book's creation and for being the most amazing, beautiful family a man can ask for; to my parents and siblings for providing the childhood that has shaped me into the educator I am today; to my editor and coauthor Jeremiah J. Sims for your support and wisdom; to my mentor James and my friends/colleagues Fred, Jennifer, Jon, Mick, Robbie, Teresa, Gwen, Roniqua, Griselda, Patrice, Tabitha, and Aaron for sharing your wisdom and for expanding my understanding of social justice; and to all the students who *taught me* how to be a more compassionate, critical educator, but especially Dontario, Walter, Brandi, Jazzmin, Devante, Taylor, Briana, Hannah, and Aaliyah.

Jeremiah J. Sims

I dedicate this book to all of the people that have been and continue to be marginalized and dehumanized by our educational system. You are not powerless; in fact, you are filled with power. The power to change the status quo. That's why the prevailing system of the day is seeking to extinguish your light – they know their time is short. Thank you for showing up. I thank my Redeemer, my Lord, Savior, and best friend, Jesus. He has brought me from a mighty long way. And, I have to thank my partner, my soul mate, Rachel Eve Sims. I love you, babe! And, I have to thank our boys, Judah, Malachi, Zion, Freedom, and Jehu. Daddy loves y'all! Shout out to my mom, Denise and my brothers Joseph and Tosh. My nephews, JoJo, Elijah, Blue, Malique, Ozias; my nieces, Zoe, Yaelle, and Zhara. And my family in love, Henry, Sylvia, Tim, Shyra, Shobab, Sarah, Phil, and Liza. I love y'all! And, my brothers from another mother, Sepehr, Lasana, Kenyatta, Codey, Tunde, Solomon, and Vanson as well as my sisters, Jennifer (JTM), Tabitha, Jackie, and Malathi – you brilliant scholars inspire me! Shout out to the IDEAL Fellows and Kristi. And, last but not least, I have to thank my amazing coauthor, Jeramy Wallace. I appreciate you, brother. Thank you for inviting me to contribute to this important work!

Editor's Note

Community colleges are ideal sites for the disruption of the American educational system. This is the premise upon which Dr. Jeremiah J. Sims, and I decided to embark on this journey to co-edit a series of transformative texts written by community college researchers and practitioners. Being based in the Oakland/San Francisco Bay area, the hub of Silicon Valley, the idea of disruption is not only ubiquitous but, in many circles, sacrosanct. But when it comes to the field of education, there is a significant number of faculty, classified professionals, and administrators wedded to the status quo.

So herein lies the paradox. Do we interpret the outcomes data that shows minoritized students consistently disproportionately impacted as purely a representation of the capacity of the individual student or as a reflection of the policies, practices, procedures, and pedagogies/androgies of the educational institution and its agents? If it is the latter rather than the former, it is clear that the status quo is not only untenable but demonstrates a commitment to the unnecessary suffering of our students. Therefore, it is a prime candidate for disruption and disruptors.

Poor, Ethno-Racially Minoritized Students of Color (PERMSC) begin their college journey at community colleges at higher rates than their peers. Community colleges, unlike research universities, primary mission is instruction.

Student support services at community colleges are braided into cohorted programs and learning communities. Institutional success is measured by successful completion of all courses, transfer-level math, and english, certificate or degree and transferring to a four-year institution. Classroom sizes tend to be smaller. Faculty are allocated resources to support the professional learning experiences of their peers. The above reasons and dozens more are reasons why community colleges are prime for the work of disruptors of the status quo.

During our engagement of our community college colleagues over the past decade, we have had the honor and privilege to encounter thousands of disruptors at districts and campuses across that nation. One of the themes we have observed from our encounters is that these communities of disruptors are not only seeking out kindred spirits but also tools to deploy at their various sites to bring about equitable outcomes for our most marginalized students. Dr. Sims and I instinctively knew that it would be virtually impossible to provide all of the necessary tools in one singular tome, therefore we joined forces and partnered with Peter Lang Publishing to establish a series.

The Educational Equity in Community Colleges (EECC) series is a contribution to not only the disruption but also the reimagining of post-secondary education broadly and community college specifically. Our series defines and redefines, criticizes, and critiques, packs and unpacks, most importantly, imagines and reimagines. Our contributors take the time to lay the foundation by examining the historical origins of inequality and inequity, not because we are "stuck in the past" but because we understand that what we are looking at in terms of outcomes data, campus climate, and culture is the effect and not the cause. We take time in each volume to define terms, not because we believe that our work in an exercise in semantics but precisely because we understand how terms have been coopted and weaponized against equity-advancing practitioners. Lastly, our writers do not pull recommendations and solutions out of thin air but are rooted in years of practice, critical self-reflection, research, and application.

Some disruptors are genuinely shocked when their advocacy is met with resistance. It is imperative for our colleagues to embrace the reality that it is impossible to be equity-advancing and risk-averse. It is in some ways naive to believe that colleagues who have found solace in the current system and have zero desire to enact radical change. Others are merely afraid of the failure they might experience in engaging in new approaches while others desire transformative change yet lack the consciousness, tools, and supports to bring about an anti-racist, anti-sexist, and student-ready institution. Taking risk doesn't mean being bombastic or condescending to your colleagues who may not be on board with an equity agenda. It means being intentional and deliberate in developing relationships and mapping out ways to move the institution toward more equitable outcomes.

One of the most disappointing developments in this work has been the co-optation of the equity work by colleagues centering themselves as faculty, administrators, or classified professionals as the primary focus of the educational equity agenda. There has been a consistent trend of conflating labor issues with student equity issues by creating false equivalencies and strawman arguments. Yes, there are labor issues that need to be addressed by all constituent groups, but to stymie the efforts of our most vulnerable student populations to make your point is problematic. Our student equity agenda can no longer afford to be held hostage by our colleagues who are not able to address any institutional challenge beyond employee grievances, petty personality conflicts, and personal financial gain.

When I deliver public addresses, rather in person or virtually, one of the most consistent questions I get is about how to "get the people who really need to be here..." or some variation of solidifying "buy-in." Buy-in is a worthwhile endeavor if we are engaging colleagues dealing in good faith; however, it is a stall tactic at best and a disingenuous strategy to maintain the status quo at worst when dealing with bad actors. Far too many institution's equity efforts have plunged into an abyss of centering the comfort of our colleagues over the suffering of our students. Our series aims to remedy that tendency.

Therefore, the Educational Equity in Community College series is about pivoting from the performative to the transformative. We whole-heartedly believe in radical love and its power to transform the lives of individuals and communities; however, it must be paired with an equity-minded consciousness and transformative policies, practices, and procedures to truly disrupt and reimagine our community colleges and our college community.

Lasana O. Hotep
November 2021
Dallas, Texas

Introduction by Jeremiah J. Sims

Part One: Laying the groundwork

"There comes a point where we need to stop just pulling people out of the River we need to go upstream and find out why they're falling in."

– Desmond Tutu

Jumping in feet first

I don't know what prompted me to jump in with both feet. Perhaps it had to do with the unshakable feeling that the sun had hitched a ride on my back. It was hot, hot. And, if I am being honest, the heat was not the only motivating factor: I had been boxing for months; my body was changing. The softness of my 13-year-old body was being transformed before my very eyes. In retrospect, though I can't be totally sure, maybe I wanted to show off my (muscle) gains. I was in a place that'd I'd never been before. There were some familiar familial faces; however, they were sparingly interspersed amongst a sea of unfamiliar – albeit – friendly (white) faces. There were smiles everywhere. My unfamiliarity with this particular backyard and the faces occupying it, however, did not stop me from launching myself into the cooling waters of the host family's pool. In fact, if my memory serves, I remember being the first one in the pool. The feel of the liquid coolness, the liquid relief, was a welcome sensation; it provided an immediate respite from the Sacramento summer heat. I am from the East (San Francisco) Bay Area. I wasn't used to, nor was I built for Sacramento heat. As much as I wanted to show off my developing pecs, I have to believe that my desire to cool off was paramount. So far, this story is, admittedly, mundane. Lots of people swim when it's hot. Here's the thing: I knew that I could not swim, at least not well. But I figured that I would be fine because the water went no higher than my shoulder. Plus, the backyard was filled with people. If I got to a place where I was in trouble, one of the friendly faces surrounding me would surely reach in to help me out. Or so I thought.

This was a family pool; it did not have depth markings. Nevertheless, I did not really know anyone at this pool party except my cousins that I arrived with. I was interested in avoiding any and all conversations that held the potential to turn me back into a pumpkin. I was from the "hood"; this was not the hood. I felt out of place. For me, the pool was not only an escape from Sacramento's insidious heat, but it also seemed to be a safe haven from the conversations that would reveal that I was far more urban than I was urbane. Up until this point in my life, I'd never seen so many blonde people congregating in one place. I am from Richmond, California; suffice it to say, this was not my normal crowd. My cousins grew up in spaces like this. I did not. As the hum of the conversations – which seemingly enveloped the pool – grew louder, I decided to recommit to my watery refuge. Party goers were discussing things that were altogether foreign to me, like ski trips and planned European vacations. I went back and forth between pretending that I could swim and flopping around like a fish. All I knew was that as long as I was in the pool, I was relatively safe from questions about where I was from. What I did not know upon entering the pool, however, is that the pool floor was a gradual decline. I did not swim much. I had no access to backyard pools in my social circle, and despite the best efforts of the City of Richmond's Parks and Recreation folks, our city pool was notoriously filthy. So, in retrospect, it should come as no surprise that I found myself, rather abruptly, in over my head.

I was attempting to move away from a group of people that had congregated near the edge of the pool closest to me. It was clear in their eyes, their inquisitive, friendly eyes, that they wanted to get to know me better, which was perfectly understandable as I may very well have been in their backyard. As they approached, I feigned interest in swimming to the other side of the pool. I let loose with a few strokes, even though my feet were still firmly planted on the ground. As I advanced toward the other, completely unoccupied, part of the pool, to my horror, I soon faced the realization that there was no ground underneath my feet. I tried not to panic because I knew from G.I. Joe cartoons that panicking would not help my situation (and, if I am being completely honest, I did not want to be embarrassed for my inability to swim). Thinking back, knowing what I now know, it's clear that even at my young age, I was concerned with confirming the stereotypes around Black peoples' inability to swim (Steele, 2011). I tried to swim back toward the shallow end of the pool where my safety lay. I could not do it. I began to bob up and down. I was quickly growing tired. Because even though I may not have been panicking on the outside, I was certainly panicking internally. By the time I knew I needed to ask for help, my voice was gone. It had been swallowed up by fear. It was like a nightmare: I attempted to call out for help, but I had no voice. Except, this was a real life and death situation. I bobbed up and down several times. I was looking around at all the friendly faces. I could not make eye contact with anyone. No one would look my way. It felt like they were looking away so as not to watch my embarrassment. I thought for sure this was it. I tried one last time to cry out for help, to no avail. As I began to go down again, in the midst of what felt like a slow-motion montage of my young life, I felt a hand on my arm. My older cousin who I had come to this backyard pool party with pulled me out of the water. It is not an exaggeration to say that he saved my life. (Thanks, Rudy!) It is, also, not an exaggeration to say that ambivalence and inattention (combined with my inability to swim) almost cost me my life. No one asked me if I could swim. No one asked me what I needed to be safe.

This situation is not appreciatively different then my first foray into Community College. I am the first in my family to go to college. The Community College environment, in many ways, is represented by the pool. Like the pool, I jumped into without a clear understanding of the depth. In fact, this is true for far too many Community College students that represent the first person in their family to go to college. Community colleges are surrounded by friendly faces, overwhelmingly, friendly white faces. However, just like my real-life situation in this particular backyard, sometimes those friendly faces are too consumed with whatever they're consumed with to notice that someone not 10 feet away from them is drowning. You see, legally, once a minor enters into a backyard, the homeowners are responsible for them. Had my cousin not saved me, there may have been repercussions for the family had I drown in their pool. Obviously, they did not want me to drown, and they were not the ones that forced me to get into the water. However, their inattention, their preoccupied ambivalence, which was made manifest by their unwillingness to question whether or not I was fully apprised of the potential traps (i.e., a descending pool floor) mirrors the experiences that many first-in-family poor, ethnoracially minoritized students of color (PERMSC) face when entering Community College spaces. And I need to take this up here because this is a very important point: the overwhelming majority of PERMSC students that are first-in-family to go to college start their college careers at community colleges.

In community college, just like in the pool, I was surrounded by friendly faces. Many community colleges are surrounded by friendly faces. But again, I will say this for the people in the back: this is not enough! It's never been enough! Good intentions are not enough. Committed educators must be willing to jump in. Without real justice-centered work, we will never advance equity. In order to serve students who are the first in their family to go to college, we have to be hypervigilant so that they understand the terrain that they are being forced to navigate. If we leave students in situations where they are forced to navigate unfamiliar terrain without properly informing them of the traps that lie ahead, we have failed to adequately prepare them to reach their fullest potential. Had I known that the pool floor's decline, that it went from 4 feet to 9 feet, I would have stayed in a place where I felt safe. And it may be that everyone in this crowd had a pool of their own, I cannot be sure. They may have understood how backyard family pools work. But this was the first time I had ever been in a backyard family pool. From my view, prior to jumping into the pool, I had no way of recognizing the declination of the pool's floor. You see, the people that filled this backyard barbecue assumed that, because I was in the pool, I must have known how to swim.

Often, the people that work in our community colleges assume that because students are in school, they, too, know how to swim. As evidenced from my own near-death experience, this is clearly not always the case. This begs the question: how do we create safe spaces for students, specifically for poor, ethnoracially minoritized students of color, who are brave enough to jump in with both feet? How do we create a safe and inclusive spaces that identify and work to mitigate the potential traps that lie ahead, so that these students – who are full of promising potential – can reach the highest of heights both intellectually and humanly? You see, I know how to swim now. I took lessons. My inability to swim in this instance was not indicative of an innate deficiency. I was not physically incapable of swimming. Rather, I had never been taught to swim. And, I had never been exposed to a backyard pool, so I did not understand the unfamiliar terrain that I was navigating up until that point. The issue was not about my ability. The issue had much more to do with the realities of racialized capitalism working in the interest of white supremacy (Nobel, 2018; Sims, Taylor-Mendoza, Hotep, Wallace, & Conaway, 2020; Wacquant, 2008). My reality, which was both formed and informed by racialized capitalism, and white supremacy was this: as a 14-year-old, inner-city Black youth, growing up in a single-parent, low-income home, I was not exposed to backyard swimming pools; and, I had not been in the position to swim or to take swimming lessons regularly. This is true of our students as well.

First-in-family, poor ethnoracially minoritized students of color (PERMSC) do struggle in community colleges, not because they are innately unable to be successful, not because they are not filled with promise and potential, but precisely because we have not done the work of clearly delineating the necessary markings on the "pool." Here it makes sense to operationalize these two concepts. Both racialized capitalism and white supremacy exist conceptually and analytically, and both also exist materially. In order to understand the relationship, which I have described elsewhere as an unholy, incestuous union (Sims et al., 2020), between these two conceptual-material realities, I will endeavor to define them here.

White Supremacy and Racialized Capitalism

White supremacy is impelled by a belief that peoples racialized as white are more valuable than non-white people. The concept of white supremacy was created for two primary purposes. The first purpose was to justify the dehumanization of Indigenous and African peoples so that they could be marked as physical "sites" of surplus value extraction. This means that their minds, bodies, and souls were used to create wealth for their oppressors, which is the function of racialized capitalism. Capitalism is inherently exploitative. White supremacy, simultaneously, determines and provides justification for who can be systemically and systematically exploited. The second reason is to drive a wedge between people who have the same/similar socioeconomic realities but different ethnoracial identities. That is to say, the concept of race is used to keep poor BIPOC people and poor white people (more accurately, people racialized as white) from working together, in solidarity, to overthrow capitalism.

Capitalism and racism are intractably knitted together. Capitalism, particularly as it came about in America, is not only racialized, but American racism is inherently capitalist in nature. They reinforce and uphold each other in a semi-coherent ecosystem (Sims et al., 2020). Capitalism requires a metric to demarcate what group/caste/class/ segment of society is exploited (Wilkerson, 2020). Race and racism quickly became the preferred tools to do so. While there could hypo-thetically be some other metric - height, weight, gender, etc. – race is entrenched as the primary metric. Race's utility as an othering mechanism to the capitalist system primarily comes from the at-a-glance "determination" of one's race based on physical features. Racism in this country, though not reducible to this metric, can rightfully be understood by using this heuristic: civility, culture, intelligence, and value are determined in contradistinction to proximity to or distance from whiteness (Sims, 2018).

What's Height Got To Do with It?

Just imagine, if you will, that there is a group of immigrants that immigrated to a new country in order to escape persecution in their home country. These immigrants found an environment that was suitable for their way of life. They began to build. They built buildings; they built schools, and they built hospitals. For whatever reason, no one in this group was shorter than 6 foot 2 inches. Why is this important? It's important because all of the buildings that they built, the infrastructure, which held access to upward social and economic mobility, was built to accommodate people 6 foot 2 or taller.

Not long after settling in this new environment, these settlers became aware that there were other, Indigenous, peoples on this land. Many of these people were shorter than 6 foot 2; however, there was also a large number of people who were over 6 foot 2. Everything that these people needed to reach their fullest potential was located within the buildings built by the new immigrant population. And, while the members of the newly immigrated group were gregarious and benev-olent, the fact remained that everyone under 6 foot 2 had an incredibly difficult time accessing the opportunities built into these structures. It wasn't impossible, per say. In fact, there were people under 6 foot 2 that succeeded in spite of the height-supremacists-based inequity built into the system. (These individuals were routinely lionized and held up as exemplars or models meritocracy.) However, these successes do not change the fact that success was much harder to attain because these structures were not built to accommodate people under 6' 2".

Now, it's worth noting that the newly immigrated group did not consider themselves, necessarily, "heightists" or "height supremacists." And, if pressed, they would deny that height supremacy factored into the design of the structures they developed. Some of them even argued that they "don't even see heigh". And what is more, they roundly eschew the unearned height-privilege conferred to them because these structures were developed with them in mind. In fact, they claim to be height-blind. They maintain that their forefathers that developed this colony had never seen a person under 6 foot 2. So, understandably, the city that they built was not built to accommodate people under 6 foot 2; it was simply built to accommodate people who were 6 foot 2 or taller. They maintain that this is proof that there is no malicious design, no systemic heightism – and, consequently, no such thing as height supremacy.

As these two groups of people began to intermarry, heights began to vary. The original framers and builders of this city now had grandchildren that were both under and over 6 foot 2. Eventually, the original builders began to die out. This meant that the group of people that had previously had a minimum height of 6 foot 2 were almost completely gone. Now there was a diverse group of heights represented within this colony. Eventually people that were under 6 foot 2 began to oversee the structures that were built. These people certainly were not heightest, as they were of mixed height themselves. Nevertheless, people under 6 foot 2 still found it incredibly difficult to navigate these spaces because the things that they need to be successful, e.g., books, tools, seeds, etc., were placed on shelves that were simply out of reach to anyone under 6 foot 2. This is what is so pernicious about structuralized inequity: it still penalizes hypermarginalized peoples even if the intent of the people running these structures are not malicious. More specifically, it is just about individuals' views on height. It is always a macrostructural issue. Even if there is no one over 6-foot 2 left, the structures that they built were still developed to privilege people no shorter than 6 foot 2, and by default, penalize anyone under 6 foot 2. This is how racialized capitalism and white supremacy work, in concert, to create structures that privilege capital and whiteness while, simultaneously, penalizing non-whiteness.

We Have To Take a Systems Approach

Like any metaphor, the one outlined above fails to fully capture the complexity of the phenomena it describes. In this case, while helpful, this metaphor stops short of truly capturing how racial and economic inequity function in this country. Racism, in this country, has often been positioned as an individual problem. That is to say, if individuals would stop being racist, then, racism would, simply, cease to exist. And while it is true that individual racism is problematic and should be condemned, the reality is that individual racism is problematic precisely because structural and institutionalized racism are foundational to American life. That's the point of the metaphor detailed above. Even if, sticking to the metaphor, the individuals who created the systems and structures that allow for upward social mobility weren't heightest, even if they didn't think less of people that were shorter than them, nevertheless, the structures that they built were built to accommodate them, and by default, they do not accommodate people who are not like them.

This example doesn't get to the heart of white supremacy and racialized capitalism (Sims et al., 2020) and its particular manifestations here in the Land of the Free. But it doesn't have to. The point is clear, in order to move toward a more just society we cannot simply focus on individual acts. Rather, we have to focus on the systems, structures, policies, practices, and procedures that create and maintain structural and institutionalized inequity. Our institutions are made up of individuals. Individuals must begin (again) to radically reimagine their roles in supporting or challenging the institutional culture of their respective colleges so that they become increasingly and unmistakably justice-centered, and equity-advancing. There has been an influx of diversity, equity, and inclusion conversations, symbols, and platitudes in light of the purported racial reckoning that began in 2020. However, at the same time, there has been very little substantive change for poor, ethnoracially minoritized students of color. We need to walk the talk. We cannot simply be caught up in the mercurial wave of equity work that is, largely, spurred by what can only be described as a collective, white liberal desire to assuage any feelings of guilt fomented by the events of 2020. Equity is not cyclical, nor is it episodic. It's enduring and deeply-entrenched. Our work has to focus on changing these realities, or it's anemic, powerless, and ineffective.

Reimagining the Pool

Returning to the story I opened with, above, this near-death experience scarred me. As I sat down to write about it, I felt as though I was re-living it – not in the same way I "re-lived" it in the days and weeks after the incident – but the viscerality is still pervasive some 30 years removed. There was real trauma there. For a couple of months after this harrowing experience, I had nightmares about drowning. I avoided any swimming pool over 5 feet, for years, after this incident. This was my experience at community college, too. My first attempt to be a successful community college student was very similar to this backyard pool party, except in community college, not all of the white faces were quite as friendly. In my last book, *Minding the obligation gap in community colleges: Theory and practice in achieving equity* (Sims et al., 2020), I wrote extensively about my first few forays into community college. Thus, I will not go into great detail here. But I will say, as I began to figure out what it meant to be a successful community college student, I drowned over and over again even though I was surrounded by faces that seemed to have not only the ability but also the goodwill necessary to function as lifeguards. But they did not move; they did not react. This is ambivalence. In real justice work, there is no room for ambivalence. Educators that want to advance equity and justice cannot sit on the proverbial fence of ambivalence. Unchecked (white) ambivalence will eventually permutate and transmogrify into (white) apathy. If we are apathetic institutionally, our students are lost. We have to be impelled by love if we ever hope to achieve justice. According to Professor Cornel West, we must "Never forget that justice is what love looks like in public." (Selby & Terry, 2019, p. 344)

Why "a Guide"?

This book is somewhat unconventional in that it is written in two distinct yet interrelated parts. My contribution to this book, these first two chapters, is cross between a kind of Editor's note and an extended preface. My final contribution, the epilogue, speaks to the lessons I learned in centering radical love as praxis in 2021. My hope is to provide a lay of the land, so to speak. Jeramy carefully and painstakingly created and curated the heart of this book. At his invitation and commensurate with the suggestion of the good folks at Peter Lang Publishing, I contributed to this work. It is my honor. This book is fashioned as a guide for community college educators, especially white educators – because full-time, tenured community college faculty are overwhelmingly white (Sims et al., 2020). Nevertheless, this guide is for educators – irrespective of ethnoracial identity – that are ready and willing to commit to justice-centered pedagogies. Jeramy Wallace has been meticulously crafting this guide for some time now. Much of his work is informed by his experiences as a white educator that works to create space for Black, Indigenous, and other Peoples of Color (BIPOC) students to realize their fullest educational potential. He has had many successes, and he will be the first to tell you that he has also identified opportunities for further pedagogical growth. The same is true for me. I am an administrator now, but I have never strayed far from the classroom. I currently teach in two programs that I designed. One that centers praxis in enacting critical-reality pedagogy (Sims, 2018) in community college spaces, for faculty, staff, and administration. And, I currently work with a group of 30-plus community college students in a program designed to help them critically assess, and subsequently audit, the institutionalized policies, practices, procedures, and pedagogies of their respective community colleges. Like Jeramy, like many of you reading this book, I have had successes; I have also identified ample opportunity for personal, pedagogical growth.

Educational Equity in Community Colleges

This book is the second book in my series on Peter Lang titled, *Educational Equity in Community Colleges*. This series centers theory and practice in enacting educational equity, and, ultimately, educational justice at the administrative, institutional/programmatic, governance, and pedagogical levels of community colleges and other institutions of higher learning (Nevarez & Wood, 2010; Woods & Harris, 2016). There is a corpus of literature on the pernicious effects of oppressive pedagogy at the K-12 level, especially for traditionally marginalized, minoritized students (Delpit, 2012; Leonardo, 2010; Nasir, 2011). However, this is not the case at the community college level even though these same traditionally marginalized, minoritized students overwhelming start their college careers in two-year community colleges. Frankly, though there are many valuable contributions to community college education, overall, there is a dearth of literature on critical, justice-centered pedagogy, theory, and practice (i.e., praxis) within community college administration, governance, programming, and pedagogy.

Many community college practitioners are interested in enacting educational equity. However, there is little community college-specific literature for them to use to reimagine and, ultimately, reconstruct their administrative, programmatic, and pedagogical practices so that these institutionalized practices become commensurate with educational equity and justice (Tuck & Yang, 2018). Therefore, the goal of this series is to blend the work of university researchers and community college practitioners to illuminate best practices in achieving educational equity and justice via a critical-reality pedagogical framework (Emdin, 2017; Giroux, 2004; Sims, 2018). This series aims to highlight work that illuminates both the successes and struggles in developing institutionalized practices that positively impact poor ethnoracially minoritized students of color. Therefore, we will be looking at pedagogies, policies, and practices that are intentionally developed, curated, and sustained by committed educators, administrators, and staff at their respective college campuses that work to ensure just learning conditions for all students.

This guide is true to the mission of this series. We do not contend that it is *the* guide for white educators committed to equity-advancing work. Rather, this book is a guide amongst many other worthwhile guides that illuminate and even recommend praxis that is critical, liberatory, and justice-centered. That said, this particular guide has a very particular focus. In this book, our goal is to discuss the exigency, potency, and transformational power of liberatory pedagogy while, simultaneously, inviting educators to enter in to or go deeper in work that holds the potential to disrupt deeply-entrenched macrostructural inequity in community colleges (Sims et al., 2020).

To *guide*, in verb form, is defined as the act of "showing or indicating the way to; directing or having an influence on the course of an action." Our goal in this book is to present a cogent and compelling argument that rests on a kind of justice-centered, syllogistic reasoning. Our primary premise is this: we have to do something different if we hope to positively impact poor ethnoracially minoritized students of color (PERMSC); and we have to do it starting right now. If we stand pat, if we remain on the fence, PERMSC will continue to suffer, disproportionately, and they will continue to, disproportionately, fall short of reaching their fullest potential due to macrostructural/institutionalized bulwarks of inequity that have become institutionalized on our campuses. These bulwarks of inequity, irrespective of whether they are institutionalized polices, practices, procedures, and/or pedagogies, serve racialized capitalistic interests, which in turn, feed both the ubiquity and justification for and of white supremacy. In order to do this work, we have to assume and, ultimately, embody an antiracist theoretical and conceptual posture. To do this to commit ourselves to learning how race, whiteness, and capitalism work in concert to create inequitably stratified opportunity constructs (Mahiri & Sims, 2016.

Why all the Fuss? Critical Race Theory and White Guilt

If 2020 brought any one question to bear, I believe it was this: How did we get here? The answer is: we were always here. Right here. The United States of America, as an experiment in democracy, has always been racialized (Glaude, 2020). This is an inescapable reality, even though much effort has been put into reconceptualizing and, consequently, rewriting this Nation's sordid history. The emerging furor around Critical Race Theory (CRT) is evidence of a move to defang a race-centered critique of not only this Nation's white supremacist's history – but also, and perhaps more perniciously – this Nation's white supremacist present. Many people – let's be clear here – many people racialized as white, want to quash CRT in education and in industry because, well, it makes them feel bad. It activates white guilt. Many right-leaning white people decry CRT as an apparatus that teaches people to hate white people, as a mechanism that inculcates students in a way that may cause them to question or even doubt the prevailing Europocentric (i.e., whitewashed) retelling of our Nation's HIStory. These critics are not wrong on this point. CRT encourages students (broadly defined) to question Europocentric metanarratives. But that is only part of the problem for exponents of CRT. The bigger problem for them is that wherever CRT is taught, the current inculcative force of white supremacy is interrogated and, potentially, if we do this work well, interrupted. You see, there is already an inculcative/indoctrinating force at work in education and greater society. The force of our standardized, Europocentric (i.e., white supremacist) National ideology/ethos. There is no liminal space. We either create opportunities for our students to engage in a racialized analysis that not only incorporates but also centers the voices of minoritized peoples, which is the focus of CRT, or we force our students to engage in a racialized analysis that privileges whiteness (while denigrating non-whiteness). There is always a racialized analysis at play. However, for an analysis of our history and present (and the intersections therein), an analysis that starts and stops with race will always be insufficient.

It was Never Just About Race: Racialized Capitalism and White Supremacy

When we discuss racism, we have to understand that racism is the progeny of racialized capitalism and white supremacy (Sims, 2018; Sims et al., 2020). Racialized capitalism gave birth to white supremacy precisely because the enslavement and dehumanization of Indigenous and African peoples in a purportedly democratic, free country, was a social and moral contradiction (Glaude, 2020). Therefore, in order to justify the systemic, systematic extraction of surplus value from the very cells of Indigenous and Black peoples, white supremacy was posited as the rationale. The twisted logic is as follows: because the manifest destiny of European American peoples is predetermined by God, they are a supreme, sovereign people that should rule over inferior, i.e., more melanated peoples. To this point, James Baldwin said:

> [T]here was a day, and not really a very distant day, when Americans were scarcely Americans at all but discontented Europeans, facing a great unconquered continent and strolling, say, into a marketplace and seeing black men for the first time. The shock this spectacle afforded is suggested, surely, by the promptness with which they decided that these black men were not really men but cattle. It is true that the necessity on the part of the settlers of the New World of reconciling their moral assumptions with the fact—and the necessity—of slavery enhanced immensely the charm of this idea, and it is also true that this idea expresses, with a truly American bluntness, the attitude which to varying extents all masters have had toward all slaves. (Field, 2009, p. 53)

The notion of white supremacy was born out of this conceptual non sequitur. If my formulation is correct, and White supremacy is the progeny of racialized capitalism, then it follows that the notion of race is the descendant of white supremacy. For to understand white supremacy, to understand whiteness as the thesis, an antithesis is necessary. Elsewhere, I wrote about it in this way:

> Racism, which is predicated on a delusional and perverse notion of white supremacy [...] rests upon a pernicious, manufactured and patently false dialectical relationship with whiteness positioned as the thesis, and, Blackness, seemingly forever positioned as its antithesis. This negative reification of Blackness is convenient for white supremacy's capitalistic endeavors as well: Black males are sadistically over-represented in the multi-billion-dollar prison industrial complex. Whiteness determines the value of other commodities, in this case of other cultural commodities. It is also able to determine what qualifies as valuable and invaluable. In our society, whiteness has the power to determine what does and what does not count as currency, as capital, by either recognizing or ignoring forms of cultural capital based on their proximity to whiteness. (Sims, 2018, p. 27)

My secondary premise is impelled by the reality that the majority of community college educators are people that identify and/or are racialized as white (henceforth, European American). So, rhetorically, the syllogism works like this: if new, liberatory, justice-centered pedagogies are necessary if community college educators hope to truly reach PERMSC's; and the majority of tenured faculty in community college faculty are European American; then, in order to serve as many PERMSC's as possible, European American faculty need to adopt and employ new, liberatory, justice-centered pedagogies. Of course, there are many European American educators already doing this; and there are Black, Indigenous, and other Peoples of Color (BIPOC) faculty that also need to adopt and employ new, liberatory, justice-centered pedagogies. Still, we know from disproportional students learning outcomes and other academic metrics that PERMSCs are not reaching their fullest academic potential at comparable rates to their Asian and European American counter parts (Mahiri & Sims, 2016). We also (should) know that PERMSCs are not innately less capable, so something else must be afoot. In this book, we contend that "something else" has a great deal to do with institutionalized pedagogies that (perhaps unknowingly) enshrine whiteness while, simultaneously, upholding white supremacy.

This guide takes up whiteness in order to deconstruct it. This move is designed to aid European American educators in deepening their understanding of how whiteness not only pathologizes and penalizes non-whites, but also how

European Americans are conscripted into a system, if they do not actively fight against it, that functions to limit their pedagogical efficacy in a way that decenters justice and equity. This systemic decentering serves to reify, concretize, and subsequently institutionalize injustice and inequity. As I wrote elsewhere,

> It is important to note that these structural institutionalized bulwarks of inequity are not accidental any more than the genocidal land theft and peripheralizing of Indigenous peoples is. Rather, [these macrostructural barriers] are designed to ensure a material dowry…while they simultaneously uphold the unholy marriage between white supremacy and perverse racialized capitalism. This material and corporeal dowry is accrued on the backs of people of color precisely because in this country capitalism was built atop a foundation of white supremacy, which is inextricably an inescapably anti-Black. (Sims et al., 2020, p. 77)

I will return to the fence metaphor throughout this chapter. For now, suffice it to say, we cannot be on the fence when it comes to justice. If this book does nothing else, it is my hope that it can help some European American educators eschew ambivalence by getting of the fence and getting to work radically reimaging their pedagogy, so that is justice-centered and liberatory. Precisely because sitting on the fence will only render it immovable. There is no liminal space in this work (Sims, 2018). Schooling in this country is inequitable by design. It is inherently anti-Black and anti-BIPOC. Much of my time in this work is spent trying to help folks (educators, broadly defined) understand that schooling in this country is racialized not simply for the sake of classificatory differentiation, but rather, so that the roles necessary to support racialized capitalism are clearly and obdurately defined. In this chapter, I am operationalizing racialized capitalism in this way:

> In racialized capitalism, capital is accrued by extracting surplus-value from the mind, bodies, and spirits of poor, ethno-racially minoritized peoples. This is true of immigrant populations that traverse dangerous material and political terrain in order to achieve their American Dream. This is true of Black and Brown peoples that are used a frontline fodder for the military industrial complex. This is also true of the Black and Brown peoples that are entrenched in the prison industrial complex. This is also true of Black and Brown women and children that are ensnared in human trafficking. (Sims et al., 2020, p. 73)

As educators, we are either working toward justice, or we are upholding a system – based on racialized capitalism and white supremacy – that disproportionally punishes PERMSCs. Here is what I mean when I argue that there is no liminal space in this work: Everything that we do positively impacts some of our students and negatively impacts others. Equity efforts alone won't fix this. We need justice. We need to love justice to the point that we are willing to fight for it. Equity is not enough (Sims et al., 2020); it is just the first step in a long journey toward actual, tangible (social) justice. The fences that ambivalent educators sit on is nothing more than an additional obstacle for PERMSCs (Sims, 2018), which is why it must be torn down.

2020 – Reflecting on the Longest Year

As 2020 ended, it became abundantly clear that the events of 2020 will not soon be forgotten. We saw civil unrest, protest, acts of state-sanctioned violence, natural and manmade calamity, andl seemingly just below our collective consciousness, the exponential growth of the wealth gap. 2020, in many ways, pulled back the proverbial curtain regarding the two interrelated pandemics that poor, ethnoracially minoritized students of color (PERMSC) are forced to navigate. One pandemic, COVID-19, has fundamentally changed the way that many colleges function. Additionally, COVID-19 has, simultaneously, highlighted and worsened many of the systemic inequities that are baked into the ways in which institutions of higher learning do business. The other, much older pandemic, racialized capitalism working in the interest of White Supremacy, has been (disproportionately) wreaking havoc on Black, Indigenous, and Other Peoples of Color (BIPOC) for centuries. We know that we have to make changes. Institutionally, we have to start by interrogating our quotidian policies, practices, procedures, and pedagogies (i.e., our institutional culture). These institutionalized ways of being have gone unquestioned for far too long. If we actually desire to work in solidarity alongside our student body to ensure that our campus climates are welcoming, inclusive, and safe for all of the students that we serve, we have to work to create justice-centered, equity-advancing institutional cultures. What does an equity-advancing institutional culture look like? An equity-centered institutional culture is invested in and committed to identifying, interrogating, and ultimately interrupting (institutionalized) policies, procedures, and pedagogies that produce, maintain, and institutionalize structuralized inequities based on race, gender, sexual orientation, socioeconomic status, religion, (perceived) ability, religion as well as any other component of peoples' intersectional identities.

Simply put, an equity-centered institutional culture is radically inclusive!

Though not new to far too many people of color, this past year was characterized by a wanton disregard for Black life. We saw George Floyd's life, the very air that sustained him, be forcibly extracted from his body through extrajudicial violence. It was almost like he was the pawn of a murderous, sadistic magician whose disappearing act had gone awry. Magic is predicated on sleight of hand and optical illusions. The murder or George Floyd, however – which was predicated on white supremacy – was unfortunately very real. This is a microcosm of the ways in which racialized capitalism slowly and sadistically extracts capital – via the very life blood – of BIPOC peoples. Breanna Taylor was murdered in her sleep. Just think about that for a moment – there is no posture that can be less threatening than being prone, being fast asleep. Still, she was not safe from state-sanctioned violence operating in the interest of racialized capitalism and white supremacy. She was not safe while sleeping in her own home. COVID-19 also illuminated the health disparities that exist between poor, ethnoracially minoritized students of color (PERMSC) and non-PERMSCs. Poor Black, Indigenous, and Other Peoples of Color (BIPOC) peoples, including our PERMSCs, were disproportionately impacted by COVID-19 precisely because poverty is a comorbidity, and BIPOC peoples are disproportionately poor. Of course, these realities predate 2020, in some cases by centuries. Nevertheless, in many ways, 2020 serves as a microcosmic example of the realities that PERMSC's are forced to navigate in our schools and in our society, writ large.

But there is hope. There is always hope, no matter how fleeting. Impelled by Black, Indigenous, and Other Peoples of Color (BIPOC) activist-leaders, there were global demonstrations that made the truth plain: justice-minded peoples had had enough of white supremacy terrorizing BIPOC peoples in the interest of serving racialized capitalism. Still, like many folks who have been invested in this work for some time, I knew that the righteous indignation made manifest in global protests would eventually die down. Platitudes by corporations, schools, and other enterprises, like equity statements or increased representation in advertising, are and always have been enough for some social justice warriors. This is why it felt like the presidential election on November 3, 2020, represented a trial of sorts, but not just any trial – the soul of this country and the so-called democracy that purportedly undergirds and animates it was on trial.

The Trial of the Century: Fighting for the Soul of Democracy

If the election of 2020 was a trial, we were not exonerated. The despotic, homegrown face of fascism was excised, but not before more than 77 million Americans fought, prayed, and voted to keep him in office. We have work to do. Trump is a mirror, an instantiation of this country's soul. He's not especially racist or cruel, though he is both. He is also less politically refined and thus more overt than more polished politicians. However, he is not altogether different than his predecessors in that he does what this inequitable, anti-Black system allows him to do: he supports, champions, and upholds racialized capitalism. The term "Racialized Capitalism" is somewhat tautological. Capitalism, from its inception here in the U.S.A., has been inextricably tied to race and White supremacy. The peculiar institution of American Chattel Slavery birthed, necessitated, and worked to uphold capitalism (Beckert & Rockman, 2016; Sims et al., 2020). By now, these truths should be self-evident. However, they are not because this country has invested mightily in hiding, though not atoning for her sins. One need look no further than our standardized history curricula, which espouses the virtue of Western Expansion while, simultaneously offering excuses and platitudes for the purportedly anomalous instances of genocidal violence, land theft, and racism that this country is founded upon. To this point, Eddie S. Glaude, Jr., invoking James Baldwin, offers a stern warning: James Baldwin's words haunt: "People who shut their eyes to reality simply invite their own destruction, and anyone who insists on remaining in a state of innocence long after that innocence is dead turns himself into a monster." Are we a nation of monsters? (Glaude, 2020, p. 38)

Trump appealed to White Nationalism, white supremacy, xenophobia, anti-Asian/API rhetoric, and division with aplomb – with a sadistic, celebratory gusto. Yet, the results are the same. This country is Anti-Black and Anti-BIPOC. It is no wonder that Trump appeals to both outspoken and closeted racists. It seems insufficient to write that Trump is polarizing. That is a given. However, from my outsider's perspective, that he is so polarizing for white people is fascinating. Trump reminds liberal white America that systemic racism is a reality here in the Land O' the Free. He also reminds them that this country is founded upon and predicated upon a racialized, capitalistic value gap that holds that white lives are more valuable than non-white lives (Glaude, 2020). He's not different than Reagan or many others. Equity-advancing allies and advocates should and do find his particular brand of divisive nationalism repugnant. But there is more to this story. Trump also upsets white feminist because of his misogynistic, androcentric positionality, which causes understandable and legitimate angst. But I find it incredibly difficult to shake the feeling that some of the angst he causes some white women is derived from their collective incredulity in being treated in ways that are commonplace--ways that have been traditionally limited--to Black women and other women of color. Please do not miss my point here. All of this is terrible, irrespective of the varied emotional catalyst. Dehumanizing rhetoric paired with dehumanizing policy is always bad. Another point of clarification is due. I am in no way making excuses from our now-ousted demagogue. From all indications, he is a despicable human being. However, I believe that some of my brothers and sisters in white (liberal) America despise him so much because he is a living, breathing peek into the (capitalistic, white supremacist) soul of this country, and the soul of this country is crafted for and by racialized capitalism and white supremacy to benefit white people – no matter who they voted for.

Even with the outcome of our presidential election decided, there was still a fight to ensure that our now former despotic president would stay in power, no matter what. This fight to delegitimize the results of the election and the pseudo-democracy that many people feel this country is founded upon reached a boiling point on January 6th, when a huge cosplay of violent white supremacy erupted on our nation's capital. The riotous protesters that sought to subvert the will of the people, based not only on their own belief systems but also on the prodding of the now former president, stormed the United States Capitol. Many of these rioters expressed hopes of either seizing power so that it could be maintained by Trump, or at the very least, stalling the transition that the majority of Americans voted for.

These types of violent, even murderous white supremacist tantrums are not new, nor are they unprecedented. Normally, they are visited upon peoples of color, on Chinese people who experienced more success panning for gold than white 49ers, on entrepreneurial, free Black people that developed Black Wall Street, on Indigenous peoples for simply living on and cultivating their own land. White supremacist violence is not new. When we treat these instances, these clear demonstrations of white supremacy's unwillingness to cede any modicum of power to non-whiteness, as aberrant, we elide both the systematicity and his-toricity of whiteness (Sims, 2018). According to Glaude,

> White fear can be understood as something anticipatory, a fear just waiting to be expressed. It isn't based in any actual threat of harm. Instead, the idea of black violence or crime does all the work. The mere possibility of danger is enough to motivate us to act as if we are in immediate danger. (Glaude 2020, p. 22)

Like an angry volcano, whiteness erupts when it perceives a worthwhile chal-lenge. If we act as though January 6th is anomalous, we are necessarily defang-ing the insidious genocidal, violent manifestations of white supremacy that have occurred throughout this country's history. If we do this, we are lying to our-selves about who we are as a country and the role that whiteness plays in the formation and formulation of our so-called democracy (Glaude, 2020). The riot-ous peoples that fought to maintain the previous political regime on January

6th are people who are seemingly indifferent, ambivalent, or wholly apathetic with regard to race-based inequity. President Joe Biden, though the author and supporter of problematic, anti-Black legislation, does not seem as hateful as the president that preceded him. Nevertheless, President Biden, like all of the presidents that preceded him, is working within a system that serves a two-headed chimera: white supremacy (working at the behest of and in the interest of) and racialized capitalism.

Trump is the byproduct of a particular iteration of the white imagination. Still, we have to be honest if we hope to move forward. It is not only white nationalists that elected Trump. His presidency is the direct result of white fragility, or what Glaude (2020) refers to as white fear and rage.

> The American idea is indeed in trouble. It should be. We have told ourselves a story that secures our virtue and protects us from our vices. But today we confront the ugliness of who we are—our darker angels reign. That ugliness isn't just Donald Trump or murderous police officers or loud racists screaming horrible things. It is the image of children in cages with mucus-smeared shirts and soiled pants glaring back at us. Fourteen-year-old girls forced to take care of two-year-old children they do not even know. It is sleep-deprived babies in rooms where the lights never go off, crying for loved ones who risked everything to come here only because they believed the idea. It is Oscar Alberto Martinez Ramirez and his twenty-three-month-old daughter facedown, washed up on the banks of our border. Reality can be hard and heartless. (Glaude, 2020, p. 45)

Trump epitomizes whiteness; however, he is merely a symptom of a much larger chronic disease. White people, especially liberal white people, despise Trump not only for his racist, retrograde policies; but also because he reminds them that they are willingly participating in a system that simultaneously privileges them while penalizing PERMSCs. Herein lies a seemingly irreconcilable conundrum precisely because the fascists that Trump seemingly reawakened and the liberal white allies that oppose them all benefit from the same system. There is no easy way out of this. According to Glaude (2020), "To make that decision, we will have to avoid the trap of placing the burden of our national sins on the shoulders of Donald Trump. We need to look inward. Trump is us. Or better, Trump is you (Glaude, 2020, p.37)."

Attempts by white people to come to terms with the privileges conferred to them because of their skin color are admirable and necessary. But the work cannot stop there; it cannot be purely introspective. There has to be action. This profound quote by Rev. Dr. Martin Luther King, Jr. (henceforth, MLK) perfectly captures this exhortation: "An individual has not started living until he can rise above the narrow confines of his individualistic concerns to the broader concerns of all humanity." This is why we have to work to be anti-oppression, anti-fascism, anti-racist/sexist/homophobic/transphobic. Simply being non-racist (Kendi, 2019), for example, is an insufficient frame. If we want to do real equity-advancing work, we have to be anti-racist. In order to be anti-racist, we have to eschew ambivalence. In its place, we have to welcome commitment, solidarity, and work to develop a love for justice. Before we can commit to this work, we have to be honest about where we are individually, where we are institutionally, and where we are nationally. Put simply, we have to be willing to tell the truth.

Truth Be Told: Capitalism has Always Been Racialized

Capitalism is always racial capitalism; that is to say, capitalism is racialized in this country. The two, racialized capitalism and white supremacy, form a symbiosis that works in a concerted way, parasitically, to extract surplus value from poor ethnoracially minoritized peoples of color (PERMPOC). Therefore, any potentially liberatory (I use liberatory and emancipatory interchangeably), critical analysis of race must also be imbued with a critique of (racialized)capitalism. A racial analysis absents a concomitant analysis of capitalism (and the intersections of violence created by this insidious coupling) and is similar to an analysis of the health of a forest's ecosystem while purposely ignoring the role that trees and undergrowth play. The state is fully invested in advancing racial inequity and violence in order to maintain our Nation's hegemonic, white supremacist status quo which, for centuries, has marked out PERMPOC as corporeal sites of surplus value extraction and accrual. When we uncritically and haphazardly view the (racial) state as benevolent or neutral, we exculpate it for the role that it plays in catalyzing, reifying, and codifying (macrostructural) harm for poor, ethnoracially minoritized peoples of color. To this point, Ture and Hamilton (1992) write:

> If a white man wants to Lynch me, that's his problem if a white man has the power to list me that's my problem. Racism is not a question of attitude It's a question of power. Racism gets its power from capitalism. Thus, if you are antiracist, even if you don't know it, you must also be anti-capitalist The power for racism, the power for sexism, comes from capitalism, not an attitude. Kwame Ture

This pellucid quote from professor and freedom fighter Kwame Ture and Hamilton (1992) captures the intertwined relationship between white supremacy and racialized capitalism. As I have written elsewhere, this relationship can be likened to an incestuous relationship precisely because racialized capitalism birthed white supremacy, and now the two have essentially become one flesh so that it is nearly impossible to decipher where one begins and the other one ends (Sims, 2018; Sims et al., 2020). Racialized capitalism necessitates white supremacy, but white supremacy also feeds racialized capitalism. In education, we are just now getting to the point where white supremacy has been identified as the culprit. We have spent years, even decades, trying to mitigate the achievement gap. The achievement gap was never the actual issue. The achievement gap is the progeny, the offspring, of the unholy union between racialized capitalism and white supremacy (Sims, 2018). The achievement gap is like a weed. In order to properly address a weed problem, the weeds have to be killed at the root. Precisely because the root is what produces and carries the nutrients necessary for the weed live. The achievement gap can be likened to the end of the weed. It is simply a byproduct of a root that is deeply embedded into the soil of our educational system. We have to be ready and willing to treat the symptoms of this union. At the same time, however, we have to be laser-focused on destroying the root system that supplies sustenance, support, and justification for the achievement gap (Mahiri & Sims, 2016). If the root (causes) system is destroyed, then what it is that the root produces (in this instance, the achievement gap) is also destroyed.

The Half has not Been Told: The Afterlife of Chattel Slavery

Slavery was indispensable to the American economy. It is the foundational American institution (Beckert & Rockman, 2016). The combined capital within the very flesh, skeletal structures, and hearts and minds of African slaves exceeded all railroads and steel. In this instance, Black people were transmogrified into actual human capital. This inhuman process had to be precipitated by mass dehumanization. As I wrote elsewhere,

> In these contexts, domination, and hegemony, respectively, Black peoples have been cruelly denied any claims of agency or personhood. This is because slavery and colonization necessitate the dehumanizing denial of Black peoples' agency; they have to be essentialized and viewed as subhuman, non-agents in order for their maltreatment to be justifiable. According to Sartre, racist institutions like slavery and colonialism, require "…the Other to be falsely seen as an object". (Sims, 2018, p. 34)

Revisionist slavery/plantation lore positions the North as the great emancipator. However, the north was a ready partner in insidious capitalism that arose in order to commodify (African) human flesh. In essence, Chattel Slavery was the nursing mother of the profits of the north (Beckert & Rockman, 2016). Slavery was a huge serpent; the head may have been in the south, but the body extended throughout the New World. Slavery was the engine that drove the American economy. The North created the instruments used in the cultivation of cotton. Slavery played a central, indisputable role in the development of American capitalism. According to Beckert and Rockman (2016), at one point, one-fifth of all capital in the United States was housed, transported, evaluated, and enveloped within the very skin of enslaved Africans. This is true of England as well. The profits from sugar, cultivated through slave labor, underwrote the industrial advancement of the British revolution. The labor regime, instantiated by Chattel Slavery, created a political economy that was and still is distinctly racialized.

We have the challenge the mythology of slavery as a localized institution. It was anything but. Slavery is the interstate highway of the American past. It is not aberrational; it is who we are. It is our history. The origin of the capital built, the capital that propelled the United States into its position as a world power, can be traced to the exploitation of stolen African peoples. The financial windfall of American Chattel Slavery was not limited to the South. Northern industry during this time was wholly predicated on slavery as the commodities developed were in support of this insidious, inhuman enterprise. For a Yoruba person to become a slave took more than just violent theft of their corporal bodies; they had to become commodified. There had to be a system created in order to assign an exchange value to the limbs of little Black babies as well as older children and men and women. In capitalism the exchange value is necessary to determine value and ultimately surplus value, which is the false-god that capitalism worships. The stark reality of this enterprise is this: Black women's reproductive labor was the fundamental mechanism of wealth production for white slave holders. These women were transmogrified into pseudo-factories. This stolen wealth has been passed on from generation to generation, which is a direct explanation for the income inequity that we see now.

This system created an erstwhile unknow technology. Slaves were repacked as consumer goods via steamboats. They were essential property regimes in Baltimore, MD, and Richmond, VA, respectively. They were sold on credit to burgeoning cotton farmers miles away. We are talking about human beings! Wealth was stored, transferred, collateralized, and bequeathed in the bodies of Black women, children, and Black men. Make no mistake, plantations were the first big business – the first corporations. Torture was used to increase cotton picking more than 400 percent (Beckert & Rockman, 2016). The whip was the most transformative technology introduced in American Chattel Slavery. How sick is this? This is what our country was founded on; moreover, this level of abject, sadistic inequity it is still what our country is predicated on.

Enslaved peoples were purchased on credit, the same way that one might purchase a washing machine or dishwasher. This underwrote and undergirded American banking in the 19th century. Vast amounts of capital were stored in the bodies of slaves; slaves were also used as collateral. Slave owners could take out second mortgages from the enslaved bodies and souls of enslaved African peoples. This was more lucrative than the actual cotton produced for slave holders, at least initially. Often mortgages were taken out on children in order to accrue surplus value because to do so would allow slave owners to get paid twice. A mortgage would be taken out on a child because slave owners knew that their value would appreciate with the onset of puberty. So, they could pay off the loan for the money they received, immediately, with the future value of these African girls and boys. Enslaved peoples were a form of capital before they were born. And even after their deaths, too, precisely because slave owners could make legal claims to value lost by slave death – even if they caused the death. All of America's biggest banks used cotton profits and slaves as collateral. This history is important because it represents truths about the formation of this country. Racialized capitalism has an explanatory power that buoys racialized analysis. For example, the question as to why Black peoples are disproportionately incarcerated in this country can be explained away via a racialized analysis. We can reasonably surmise that is Black peoples are disproportionately incarcerated in this country because there are race-based policies and laws in place that target them. But why? Racial animus is not able to fully explain this phenomenon. However, when we consider that the carceral system, the prison industrial complex (PIC) is profitable in that it produces surplus value for investors, then the picture becomes clearer. Black peoples have been prefigured as cites of capital extraction in this country because of their distance from whiteness. This happened first through Chattel Slavery on through Jim Crow, and now we are still sites of surplus-vale (capital) extraction within the PIC as an underpaid, enslaved workforce.

Capitalism is a system that requires a universal equivalent to compare, commoditize, and ultimately gain surplus value from a product. Capitalism at its core is exploitive precisely because surplus value is only accrued through exploitation. In a capitalist system like ours, the people who own the modes of production are in the best position to extract surplus value from the very bodies of exploited people (Sims et al., 2020). Examples of this are easy to find. We need look no further than itinerant, immigrant farmworkers. Recently in California, as if 2020 was crazy enough, we had a spate of wildfires. The air quality was abysmal. But, because immigrant farmworkers' work is hand to mouth and because they, typically, do not have access to high-quality health care, they worked nonstop in heat that exceeded 100 degrees in California's Central Valley. These precious human beings toiled in places where the air quality index was three times that of what is considered to be safe. This is a form of racialized capitalism. The present carceral system, which many have described as a new form of slavery (Alexander, 2010), is a form of racialized capitalism. Capitalism by nature is exploitative and dehumanizing; it reduces people to consumers and producers. This is especially true for (people racialized as) Black peoples,

> This is the reality that many Black males face; and, instead of providing safe-haven from these exigent and dangerous realities, schools that are made up of predominately low-income Black students often reproduce these macro and micro-level aggressions (Sue, 2010). This should come as no surprise according to Duncan-Andrade and Morrell (2008): they argue that our national education system was designed to underserve (or in their words, fail) hyper-marginalized students. Racism is far from dead in this country (Leonardo, 2009). (Sims, 2018, p. 44)

When the same kinds of people are being exploited due to their ethnoracial identity, in order to accrue surplus value for people that own the modes of production, this is racialized capitalism. Education is a mirror of larger society. If we fail to center justice, we inevitably replicate the very same inequities that disproportionately impact PERMSC in greater society. We have to be honest about not only our history but also about present-day circumstances. There is no real, transformational justice work without honesty.

Part Two: *Love is what justice looks like in public...* – Prof. Cornel West

Only the Truth with Set Us Free: Baldwin and King, Jr.

Like Baldwin argued, this country's ethos positions it as a country that is wholly invested in democracy and justice and as such any deviation from that aim can be summarily dismissed as a bump in the road on the way to a more perfect union (Glaude, 2020). In many ways, institutions of higher learning take this same approach. This is a revisionist history that functions to exculpate the institution-alized policies, practices, procedures, and pedagogies that have historically and systematically penalized poor ethnoracially minoritized students of color (Sims et al., 2020). If we want to make real change, if we want to truly be equity-advancing, we have to confront the lies that have become axiomatic within our institutions:

> We must remove our mask to call attention to white advantage. That may help us understand one another a bit better. It may bridge divides, disrupt assumptions and stereotypes that block empathy and get in the way of serious efforts to achieve our country. As it stands, we don't really talk frankly about race. And too many people are too damn scared to say so. (Glaude, 2018)

Reverend Dr. Martin Luther King, Jr., is, perhaps, the most famous civil rights champion in this nation's history. I have seen Dr. King invoked by both sides of the proverbial isle. For me, it is important to set the record straight: Dr. King was not opposed to civil disobedience or civil unrest; however, he was vehemently opposed to violence as he felt violence was morally wrong (Shelby & Terry, 2020). Dr. King, Jr., was a radical anti-capitalist, anti-war, anti-racist Christian thinker, and social justice love warrior. Dr. King is integral to the struggle for justice in this country and, at the same time, he is emblematic of the intentional deradical-ization of this very same struggle. The whitewashing of King, Jr., is purposeful. On the one hand, sanitizing Dr. King defangs his critique of capitalism, white supremacy, and whiteness. And, on the other hand – especially in our current moment – it creates a space for him and (decontextualized readings of) his mes-sage to be weaponized against radical cries for economic and racial justice. Both Baldwin and King, Jr., contemporaries, and co-conspirators, held that this coun-try was underachieving because it continuously failed to deliver on its promise of democracy for all. Suturing our national identify to a lie has created a tense, ten-uous relationship between (American) history and reality. According to Baldwin,

> It is not really a "Negro revolution" that is upsetting the country. What is upset-ting the country is a sense of its own identity. If, for example, one managed to change the curriculum in all the schools so that Negroes learned more about themselves and their real contributions to this culture, you would be liberating not only Negroes, you'd be liberating white people who know nothing about their own history. And the reason is that if you are compelled to lie about one aspect of anybody's history, you must lie about it all. If you have to lie about my real role here, if you have to pretend that I hoed all that cotton just because I loved

you, then you have done something to yourself. You are mad. (James Baldwin Speech, 1963)

If we want to be true to this work, if we want to be allies and love warriors, we must be honest about not only the conditions faced by our disproportionally impacted students but also by the root causes and our contributions to and complicity in these inequitable conditions. The fetishization of surplus value, which both catalyzed and necessitated racialized capitalism, produced white supremacy, which then produced the concept of race in order to prove its "superior" positionality. Racism, then, is the naturally progression or more accurately digression of an unjust society. And, while this explains the genesis of structuralized inequity, its unchangeableness is impelled by something else entirely – a collective lack of love, or what Dr. Cornel West refers to as a "spiritual blackout".

We Must be Motivated by Love

Darkness cannot drive out darkness; only light can do that. Hate cannot drive out hate; only love can do that.

– Rev. Dr. Martin Luther King, Jr.

I have physically intervened in instances of domestic violence on more than one occasion. I have also alerted authorities when my intervention held the potential to escalate tensions. (I spent part of my young life in a battered women's shelter because of an abusive stepfather.) I abhor misogynistic violence. I am not simply non-misogynistic violence; in that I do not do it myself. Rather, I am opposed to it wherever it is, no matter who is doing it, which is why I have willingly put myself in harm's way to stamp it out. Domestic violence is unjust. I despise injustice because I love its obverse – justice. We have to love justice to do equity-advancing work. Love is the antithesis of apathy. If we hope to do work that is antiracist, we must abhor anti-Blackness and other forms of racism. I am not suggesting that we hate people, even if they have been willingly or unknowingly swept away by racist ideas. I agree with Dr. King's assertion that "Hate is too great a burden to bear." On the contrary, I am arguing that our love for people, our love for justice, should impel us to do the necessary reflexive, introspective work of challenging our own idiosyncratic worldviews so that we can work in solidarity with people that are doing the same. Centering equity requires love. As I wrote elsewhere,

Centering equity encourages us to constantly be reflective and reflexive in our practices so that our service to students builds them up instead of tearing them down. Equity-centeredness serves as a constant reminder that there is nothing wrong with PERMSCs. On the contrary, it is the lack of equitable educational opportunities that limits PERMSCs' socio-educational ascent. Absent an equity-centered analytical paradigm, we run the risk recriminating PERMSCs and, subsequently, blaming them for their own academic struggles. (Sims et al., 2020, p. 230)

Often, difficulty finding a starting point precludes European American educators from doing this work in solidarity with each other and with their BIPOC peers. The work of decentering ourselves, which of course, seems somewhat contradictory in that I have shared personal stories in this chapter, must take primacy over the discomfort that accompanies conversations that inhere around racial, gendered, and socioeconomic injustice.

This has everything to do with taking responsibility. Eddie S. Glaude (2020), quoted a beautiful line from James Baldwin: "Not everything is lost. Responsibility cannot be lost, it can only be abdicated if one refuses abdication, one begins again." We can begin again. We must begin again. Wherever you are right now in your progression toward what I have termed an antiracist growth mindset, you can begin again. This does not mean that you forget about prior, harmful behavior. Absolutely not. If you have caused harm, it is not sufficient to just do no further harm. Rather, you need to take a restorative justice frame in order to repair the relationships that you have compromised via ignorance and or outright malice. Real, authentic allyship necessitates the decentering of one's idiosyncratic worldview as well as the simultaneous abdication of ego to truly work in solidarity with hypermarginalized peoples. I am a cisgender, straight Black man. As a Black man in this country, I face obstacles that other ethnoracial groups do not. Nevertheless, working in solidarity with my LGBTQ+ and womyn comrades requires me to decenter my positionality while acknowledging my privilege within our cis-heteronormative/heteropatriarchal society. I have to employ an intersectional lens (Crenshaw, 2005). My starting point must be this: I know that I am fully capable of loosing the tentacles of toxic masculinity that I have learned and even nurtured (albeit unknowingly) over the years. Therefore, I have to be hypervigilant in order to ensure that, firstly, I am doing everything in my power to rid myself of these problematic traits. And secondly, while embarking on this journey to rid myself of toxic masculinity, if I unintentionally do harm, I need to immediately take accountability by working toward restoration. There is freedom in real love-fueled, justice-centered accountability.

If my goal is to be a true ally, then I do not get to determine the terms of the restoration. I want to make what I believe to be an important point here: I am not making nor am I supporting an erroneous conflation between Black masculinity and toxic masculinity. All masculinity has the potential to be toxic. Black men are not more predisposed to toxic masculinity than any other group (Curry, 2017). Just like European American educators have to be mindful of their positionality within a system designed to uphold and privilege whiteness, educators that identify as (cis)men must also be hypervigilant with regards to our own positionality within a cis-heteropatriarchal system that privileges us over womyn. Justice work is never wholly exogeneous or wholly intrinsic. It is always a combination of both. In the following section, I will outline a merger between a growth mindset (Dweck, 2006) and an antiracist educational paradigm (DuBois, 1920, 1968; Kendi, 2019) that, for me, represents a starting point for all educators committed to justice-centered pedagogy.

Getting Ready: The Difference Between a Growth Mindset and an Antiracist Growth Mindset

The antiracist growth mindset represents an intentional amalgamation between the work of Kendi and many others, on antiracism, Dweck (2016), on growth mindset, and Boaler (2017) on neuroplasticity. A move toward an antiracist growth mindset is necessary precisely because there is no middle ground in this work. If we are not wholly committed to antiracist work, the overwhelming likelihood—if not inevitability—is that we are contributing to work that is built to uphold, affirm, and feed white supremacy and racialized capitalism (Sims, 2018; Sims et al., 2020):

> Baldwin saw clearly what he was up against; he fully understood the power of the American lie. It is the engine that moves this place. It transforms facts and events that do not quite fit our self-understanding into the details of American greatness or features of our never-ending journey to perfection. The lie is the story that warps reality in this country, which means that resisting it involves telling in each moment a truer story, one that casts the lie into relief, showing it for what it is. (Glaude, 2020, p. 45)

In this country, there is a racialized value gap (Glaude, 2020) that undergirds our National ethos as well as the very structure of our society. This gap is predicated on the belief and upheld by concomitant policies, practices, procedures, and pedagogies that demonstrate that white lives are more valuable than non-white lives. I described this gap, thusly, elsewhere,

> Cultures that are commensurate with Europocentric values of "democracy," meritocracy, free trade, often Judeo-Christian and or Protestant aesthetics are of much more value than cultures that are incommensurate with these Europocentric, heteronormative, patriarchal ideals. Culture that is different from or perceived to be in opposition to whiteness is dismissed, denigrated, and sometimes destroyed (see the panoply of African and Indigenous cultures destroyed throughout our history) with only palatable vestiges left to be appropriated and exploited. (Sims, 2018, p. 19)

According to Glaude (2020), "[...] in the end, we have to allow this "innocent" idea of white America to die if we ever hope to bridge this seemingly intractable gap. For Glaude this metanarrative regarding America's innocence is irredeemable, but he contends that that does not mean we are too (p. 27). The lie that holds that every American is endowed with the inalienable rights to life, liberty, and the pursuit of happiness has been exposed over and over. Yet, somehow, it has been explained away – as bumps on a road that, ultimately, leads to justice for all. BIPOC peoples are still waiting for the road map for their pursuits of justice, liberty, and happiness.

We Have to Walk the Talk: The Antiracist Growth Mindset

Dweck's (2006) work on growth mindset was groundbreaking in that it offered challenges to purportedly axiomatic beliefs about how the human mind works. In her work, Dweck (2006) identifies two diametrically opposed mindsets: a fixed mindset, which is intractable, myopic, and static vis-à-vis a growth mindset, which is malleable, teachable, and dynamic. She made these arguments concrete by buoying them with neuroscience. Boaler (2019) extends Dweck's work while simultaneously narrowing the level of specificity. Boaler deconstructs arguments about perceived mathematical brains, and/or gifted and differently-abled learners. In *Limitless Mind*, Boaler using the concept of neuroplasticity – the ability of the human brain to physically reform in order to apprehend new content – argues that anyone can learn.

In conjoining, then, extending the arguments put forth by these three authors, I have developed the concept of the antiracist growth mindset (which I will take up in fine detail in my forthcoming book, *Towards liberation: Antiracism and the redesign of college redesign*). A racist mindset is the epitome of a fixed mindset. Racism necessitates the adoption of essentialized, stereotypical beliefs about individual people based on their ethnoracial identity. In order to remain racist, one must hold tightly to these fixed notions (consciously or non-consciously). This is an extension of Dweck's work as her work did not center race. To be clear, Kendi is arguing for a kind of antiracist growth mindset; however, he does not explicitly name it. There is power in naming, which is why I have taken this up here.

So, if an anti-racist growth mindset seems familiar, quite frankly it should. I felt the need to join these two important concepts. Antiracism, which is different from being non-racist, or racism averse. Antiracism, that is to be an antiracist, is to take the first position that systemic, macrostructural racism is rampant within our society. Concomitantly, an antiracist positionality demands that people working toward the realization of an antiracist educational system must work to not only identify but also mitigate and eventually eradicate the negative effects of racism on poor ethnoracially minority students of color (PERMSC). An antiracist educational paradigm is action-oriented. Simply being a non-racist still allows for a kind of ambivalence that will never lead to wholesale equity and justice.

A growth mindset, according to Dweck (2006), is diametrically opposed to a fixed mindset. A fixed mindset is intractable, immovable, and non-pliable. Dweck's work was initially geared toward industry; however, the principles were taking taken up wholesale in education because there is an organic crossover there. A growth mindset, in contradistinction to a fixed mindset is pliable, tractable, and dynamic. A racist mindset is the epitome of a fixed mindset. In order to essentialize another human being based solely on phenotypical characteristics, one would have to have fixed certain connections to these phenotypical characteristics.

So then, if in a racist mindset is a fixed mindset, it would follow that the antithesis to racist mindset, i.e., an anti-racist mindset, then epitomizes a growth mindset. Antiracist approaches are not new. We can trace this type of ethos all the way back to Frederick Douglass' Autobiography of a Former Slave., and W.E.B. DuBois in the Souls of White People, and its rejoinder the Souls of Black people. Both Douglass and DuBois, respectively, were writing about and actually doing antiracist work. (Abolition work is antiracist work.) That said, for many, the notion of antiracism was inaugurated by the indispensable scholarly contributions of Professor Ibram X. Kendi's in his bestselling book, *How to be an antiracist* (2019).

Kendi's contributions to generative discussions about race, racism, and the development of antiracist orientation are invaluable. Nevertheless, I disagree with

Kendi's assertion that we can all be racist. In community college spaces the term antiracist is gaining momentum daily, which is a good thing. However, for many of the people now using this term, Kendi's work is their only point of reference. Kendi is clear that he did not create antiracism, though I would argue that he should be credited, because of his commercial success, for introducing the term to the mainstream. I know that many of you have reading this book, have heard him speak, and/or read his work, which is great. There is immense value in his work. He has a lot of smart things to say. And, he is clearly a brilliant scholar, which is why his book has sparked book clubs throughout educational spaces including community colleges. I would argue, however, that part of his appeal can be directly attributed to the reality that his work, by and large, assuages white guilt. I do not want to replicate that here. I want all readers to feel safe. At the same time, I want all readers to understand that we all have a role to play, and that our roles differ based on who we are. People of color cannot tear down white supremacy alone; our white brothers and sisters have to join us if we hope to truly radically reimagine our schools so that they are commensurate with justice.

There is always a balance when writing to European American educators about race. If I am not careful, if I am not diligent, my contributions to this book can rightly be viewed as pandering to and or pleading with ambivalent white educators to simply do their jobs. This is not my goal. My goal in contributing to this book is to underscore the exigency of this work precisely because racialized capitalism and white supremacy, working in concert to uphold whiteness, are drowning our PERMSC students. If you are someone that identifies as white, if you are a European American educator, and you are not actively fighting against these realities, then, you are necessarily supporting them. I want to be very clear about this point. My goal is not to center whiteness; rather, my goal is to center justice. If we want to achieve educational justice, we have to first understand that the symptoms we see, like racialized, differential student learning outcomes, for example, or the so-called achievement gap, are produced by the unholy marriage between racialized capitalism and white supremacy. European American educators, you have an indispensable part to play. I am not letting anyone off the hook. You are either working toward emancipation, or you are continuing the unjust penalization and pathologizing of poor, ethnoracially minoritized students of color.

This is why I differ from Kendi on this particular point. I think that there is a nuanced difference between racism and bigotry – even if the outcomes are eerily similar. My wife, Rachel, and I have five rambunctious little boys (Judah, 11; Malachi, 8; Zion, 6; Freedom, 4; and, Jehu, 20 months). Sometimes when we need some time for quiet reflection or contemplation, so, we will put on a movie for "the squad." The other day we were watching the Incredibles (for the ump-teenth time) with the boys. The movies' antagonist, Syndrome, after seemingly vanquishing the protagonists, Mr. Incredible, and his family, said something that reminded me of Kendi's assertion regarding racism. Syndrome revealed that his ultimate goal was to use the technological advancements he created to make everyone a superhero because: "if everyone is super, then, no one is super." This rhetorical chiasmus can be used to reframe and interpret Kendi's argument: if everyone is racist, then no one is racist. This position is dangerous. Kendi claims that everyone can be racist if they support racist ideas. I wholeheartedly disagree with this assertion. Sure, anyone can be a hateful bigot, but racism is different. Racism requires institutional, hegemonic power (Gramsci, 1971).

Furthermore, saying everyone can be racist is analogous to arguing that any-one can be antisemitic, which on the surface is true. But not everyone could do what Hitler did because he had the power to systemically exterminate Jewish peoples and other POCs. Even if Kendi's position is true, technically, which I dis-agree with, the results are so different that the veracity of the statement – anyone can be racist, is rendered meaningless. Kendi's line of argumentation is akin to arguing that anyone can be an abuser when discussing child abuse. Whether or not children can be abusive is insignificant – they may have the propensity, even the desire, but they cannot abuse adults systemically. They are not supported by the power of the institution.

There is no doubt that toxic masculinity and its progeny, rape culture (and misogynoir), are incredibly problematic not only because of the individual acts of violence visited on womxn, but because these individual acts of violence are the result of an asymmetrical power relationship. Men have oppressed and con-tinue to oppress women individually and systemically, with impunity, because we are backed by a cis-heteropatriarchal, asymmetrical power structure. Saying that everyone can be racist is analogous to responding to the preceding paragraph with this refrain: womxn can be rapist, too, right? And, while this is true, this is an entirely different argument because womxn abusers are not armed with and by systemic, asymmetrical power that suggests and even concretizes the notion that their lives are of greater value than men's lives. (Jeramy Wallace will take this up in full force throughout the remainder of this book.) So, while the antiracist growth mindset is a kind of "call-in", it is not exculpatory.

Personal Note

In my work as an equity director, author, and Race, Equity, and Inclusion (REI) trainer/coach/consultant, I often come across well-meaning educators that want to positively impact PERMSC students. However, many of the people that attend my workshops and/or book talks express an uncertainty with their place in this work, even if they agree it is necessary. In my personal experience, the majority of people that prematurely disqualify themselves from contributing to justice work express a nearly uniform feeling that they lack the necessary knowledge, life experiences, and (accredited) training to be of any use. As a result, many of these people end up doing nothing while, simultaneously, lamenting their lack of commitment. They are paralyzed by a fear of getting it wrong, which is impelled by a fear of being seen or, in some cases, exposed as racist. For many of them, their inaction pains them; and their inaction contributes to and, in many cases, exacerbates the very issues that they felt impelled to address in the first place. It also leads to a kind of stasis.

Therefore, the antiracist growth mindset was developed to help educators understand that irrespective of where they are in their relative understanding of inequity, justice, white supremacy, racialized capitalism, etc., if they are open to shifting their mindsets toward justice, then they are fully capable of adopting and employing an antiracist growth mindset. They simply need to believe that their minds can make new (synaptic) connections (Boaler, 2019). I do not want to oversimplify the complexity of this important work. Not everyone will become a Race Scholar by adopting this mindset. As my colleague and co-editor, Lasana Hotep likes to say, "we all have teeth, but we are not all dentists." Nevertheless, now is as good a time as any to get started. I, we, invite you to jump in with both feet. It is our hope that this book will encourage, empower, and equip committed educators to insist on and even fight for real, transformational justice. If your college is like our college, the notion of a college redesign has come up. I agree that for most community colleges redesign is necessary. However, I would argue that the ways that we conceptualize redesign are not radical enough. We have to radically reimagine college redesign – that is to say, we have to *redesign* college redesign. Obviously, redesigning redesign is a monumental task. So is justice. We cannot be deterred. The next logical question for committed educators is: where do we start? In my opinion, any worthwhile college redesign must be predicated on an antiracist educational paradigm.

A Word on Redesigning College Redesign

People who are well-trained and conversant in race scholarship as well as people that have very little training in race scholarship can benefit by better understanding just how an antiracist growth mindset can be developed and employed in the interest of redesigning college redesign. This work will require us to radically reimaging institutionalized policies, practices, procedures, and pedagogies. The goal of redesigning redesign is to make this argument clear: we need a redo. We cannot continue to iterate on a model that is predicated on white supremacy and racialized capitalism. No matter how much we work to dress up the veneer of the institution, eventually this rotted foundation will fail. Therefore, we need to rethink redesign. I am suggesting that we must use the antiracist growth mindset as a foundational framework if we hope to realize real change. For educators, this means that while radically reimagining, and, subsequently, redesigning our curricula and pedagogy, we must also advocate for shifts in the many institutionalized policies that perpetuate inequity. We cannot merely stick to the classroom.

Furthermore, we have to become conversant and adroit in calling out and deconstructing normalized, quotidian educational policies/practices/procedures/pedagogies that are anti-Black (and racist in other ways, too). Many of these policies have successfully hidden in plain sight, for decades. Unless individuals and the institutions they work within are actively anti-racist, the reality is that racist ideas as well as institutionalized racist policies/practices/procedures/pedagogies become axiomatic. These racist, institutionalized policies/practices/procedures/pedagogies, if not excised, are inherited institutionally like a cursed family heirloom, passed down from generation to generation.

Racism necessitates macrostructural/institutional power and control over the upward mobility and very lives of subjugated, racialized/minoritized peoples. In this country, only white peoples have this level of "power" because this country is predicated on white supremacy. Of course, not all white people have the same level of power. And this is not to suggest that white people don't also face societal constraints and systemic barriers – but, these barriers are the byproduct of capitalism, not race. Now, anyone can be prejudice, hateful, bigoted, xenophobic, etc., but racism necessitates institutional power. Real discrimination necessitates the ability to include and exclude people from equitable opportunities. In my work I have conversed with many community college practitioners who want to move beyond race in discussing disproportional student achievement. However, for Black peoples in particular, we cannot simply move on from over four-hundred years of oppression, disenfranchisement, genocidal violence, rape, and sadistic, cold-blooded murder. That is like telling a victim of serial abuse to just get over it. Just get over the trauma. No one in their right mind would say that; just like no one in their right mind tells Jewish peoples to just get over the Jewish Holocaust. And, this cannot be overstated, for PERMSCs, this oppression is ongoing. It is impossible to get beyond something that is still happening.

Our Students are Drowning: We Can Be Lifelines

Racialized inequity has long been at pandemic levels. This new pandemic, COVID-19, is yet another source of hurt, of trauma. We are in an unprecedented time filled with, seemingly, ever-increasing uncertainty. However, unfortunately, there are some things that we can be certain of. The equity gaps that poor ethnoracially minoritized students of color (PERMSC) are forced to navigate have been exacerbated by this pandemic. The disparities in health outcomes for Black peoples, for example, are enough to throw even the most promising semester into turmoil. What is more, based on a survey conducted in 2018 (with more than 40,000 student respondents from 57 community colleges), 62 percent of Black students experience pernicious and constant food insecurities. Thirty-two percent of these students also faced housing insecurities. Chronic hunger can and does stultify even the brightest of minds. Couple this with the reality that many of these students are being forced to navigate an altogether new (and unprecedented) educational environment. And, as if this was not trying enough, many of these students are endeavoring to reach their fullest academic potential while they are disproportionately sick, hungry, homeless, and suffering through the loss of loved ones. COVID-19 is bad, but it is much worse for our PERMSCs because of preexisting societal and educational inequity.

In order to positively impact the marginalized of the marginalized, we must make every effort to advocate for our PERMSCs. Limited access to necessary technology, both hardware and software, is especially prominent within PERMSC student groups. Black students, for example, are disproportionately unemployed, too. This was true prior to COVID-19; it will only be exacerbated in light of the shuttering of many of the jobs that employed Black as well as other PERMSCs. More importantly, the loss of loved ones, of guardians, of caretakers – because Black peoples and other PERMSC groups are dying disproportionately from this sinister virus – ensures that these students will come back to school with trauma long after COVID-19 has been stamped out. Therefore, we have to reimagine the role of the educator and of the institution. If we are truly invested in educational equity; all of us must function as unrelenting advocates for our PERMSCs.

And our institutional commitment cannot be in word only: our resource allocation, that is to say our institutional budgets, must reflect this commitment, too.
Otherwise, our allyship is inauthentic and performative. Our redoubled commitment to PERMSC students cannot be in word only, like in revised mission
statements or altogether new statements of solidarity. Rather, our commitment
must be concrete. We have to change policies, practices, and pedagogies so that
they are commensurate with justice. And, we have to commit funding so that
monetary resources function as levers for social justice.

Our Budgets are Our Value Statements: Equitable Resource Allocation

When we talk about equity work, the aim – the "why" – for equity is fairly clear.
Equity advocates are opposed to injustice. However, often times, the "how" is
where people run into issues. In community colleges, we know that striving for
equity is important. The question of how to efficaciously "do" transformative
equity work has been much harder pen down. I would never be so bold as to
claim that I have *the* answer to this conundrum. But I have had some success
doing equity work while showing other people how to do equity in a meaningful way. I think that this work has to start with an intersectional analysis of
inequity and injustice. In this work the opposition, at least in name, changes. It
transmogrifies. Nowadays, the rightful object of our justice-centered ire is white
supremacy. The weapon that we now yield is antiracism. I want to be clear: white
supremacy is a problem, and antiracism as a policy/practice/pedagogical analytical frame is a real weapon against it. For example, in my community college
district, we now have both college level as well as district lead antiracism councils
or committees. This is a good start. It undoubtedly behooves equity practitioners
to identify a clear focus for equity-advancing work. At the same time, this focus
must be intersectional. We have to look at race. Here's the thing: race is both the
progeny of and a disguise for (racialized) capitalism. We must work to identify,
call out, and work to redress institutionalized inequity in our policies, practices,
procedures, and pedagogies. And in so doing we must look at the role that racialized capitalism plays in supporting, upholding, and even necessitating White
supremacy, and by default race and racism.

White supremacy and racialized capitalism are intractably bound, seemingly,
in perpetuity. What does this look like for us? There is no simple answer. However,
we need to start with this question: Does our resource allocation line up with the
spirit of the work that we're trying to undertake? Our institutional budgets are

our institutional value statements. Put simply, a budget is both a contract and an admission of the priorities of a given institution. Therefore, our justice work cannot be in word only; rather, our philosophically positionality must be made manifest in our deeds; that is, in the ways that we allocate resources as well.

Equitable resource allocation, i.e., putting our money where our mouths are, is an integral part of radically reimaging what an institution can actually look like, feel like, and how it can work in paradigm shifting ways to transform the educational experiences for all students. For this to work, we must start from a place that acknowledges that while race and racism are incredibly problematic, they do not happen in a vacuum. Race and racism are the byproducts of white supremacy. White supremacy works in the interest of and is arguably produced by racialized capitalistic interest (Nobel, 2017; Sims et al., 2020). Therefore, any analytical frame worth its' salt must be critical and intersectional. This means that we look at the ways in which race, racism, gender, sexual orientation, citizenship, and socioeconomic status inform, infract, and interact with each other to produce varied levels of inequity for PERMSCs. The component realities of this intersectional are now happenstantial. They are intentionally designed to produce a class of workers that are easily exploitable. Capitalism necessitates exploitation in order to accrue surplus value; racialized capitalism describes not only the impetus of capitalism but also the peoples that have been prefigured as cites human capital, i.e., as cites of surplus value extraction. We must be clear about the sources of inequity if we ever hope to overcome them. This is why an anti-racist growth mindset is integral, precisely because this mindset is undergirded by an analytical frame that functions to identify the conjoined roles of white supremacy and racialized capitalism and how they work in concert to delimit the opportunities afforded to PERMSCs.

Time to Get to Work

The pursuit of equity and justice is important to me because it is morally right. It is also important to me for deeply personal reasons. I grew up in a dire situation: I was homeless because of an abusive stepfather. I lived in a battered women's shelter with my mother and my younger brother. I lived in a neighborhood that boasted one of the highest murder rates, per capita, in the entire United States while I was in Middle School and High School. I grew up as a poor Black boy in America. Yet, somehow, I was able to achieve a level of academic success that was beyond my wildest dreams and the wildest dreams of my community in Richmond, California. I am the first one in my family to go to college. I went from student who was told that he would never amount to anything to a student that earned a (B.A., M.A., and) Ph.D., from the nation's preeminent Public University, the University of California, Berkeley. One could understand if I was an adherent to the myth of meritocracy. This mythology around merit and meritocracy is ubiquitous and pernicious. It holds that if you just work hard, you can achieve anything.

The most deceptive lies always hold at least some modicum of truth – the concept of meritocracy is no different. Some people are allowed to "do anything they put their minds to," while others – specifically poor ethnoracially minoritized students of color – are made to run a gauntlet of educational obstacles that are produced by an unholy marriage between racialized capitalism and white Supremacy (Sims et al., 2020). PERMSCs do achieve their goals, but, often, we are forced to achieve them in spite of the systems that we are made to navigate – not because of them. Simply put, meritocracy does not work for poor ethoracially minoritized students of color. This work is necessary precisely because this country and the educational systems it produces are predicated on a value gap that holds that white lives are more valuable than non-white lives (Glaude, 2020). White lives are imbued with innate merit; Black lives and the lives of other peoples of color are not.

Nevertheless, students that come from hyperghettoes as well as students that come broken, abusive home environments do succeed. The myth of meritocracy holds that everyone has boots and bootstraps to pull themselves up by. Rev. Dr. Martin Luther King, Jr., said that the cruelest thing that anyone can tell a bootless, disenfranchised person is that the world is theirs so long as they are willing to pull themselves up by the bootstraps. There is no crueler irony. This is why this work is necessary. We have to call out and work to ameliorate the cruelty of racialized capitalism, white supremacy, settler-colonialism, homophobia, misogyny, anti-Black and other forms or racism, cis-heteropatriarchy, Nationalism, xenophobia – the list goes on and on. Nevertheless, there is hope. At our own campus, we have experienced real paradigm shifts in our campus environment. We have not fully arrived. However, the number of people that are committing to and redoubling their efforts in order to achieve substantive equity-advancing work is growing. We are working toward educational equity. I know that this work is worthwhile and equally as important, I know that this work can be accomplished. I am convinced that educational equity, even if growth is incremental, is a worthwhile pursuit.

For educational equity (Darling-Hammond & Banks, 2010; Sims, 2018) to be far-reaching, long-lasting, and sustainable it must be arrived at thoughtfully and systemically. It must be preceded by positive shifts in cultural understanding at the institutional level and by the adoption of equitable pedagogical practices. To be clear, equitable education is not simply about leveling the proverbial playing field. I defined educational equity elsewhere as:

> Educational equity must be achieved via intentional work towards the creation of positive, nurturing educational spaces that actively combat structural and institutionalized inequity so that all students are empowered, encouraged, and equipped to succeed academically precisely because they have been afforded rigorous and rich educational opportunities that allow them work towards the realization of their full academic and human potential. (Sims, 2018, p.26)

Simply leveling the playing field will not do. Leveling the playing field usually results in equality. Equality is very different from equity, though the two terms/ concepts are often confused and or conflated. Put simply: equality is achieved when everyone has the same thing, irrespective of their specific needs or lack thereof. Equity, on the other hand, is achieved when the varied needs of people are considered when developing programming, policies, and pedagogies. Equality is often deployed in the interests of placation and pacification. Equity, conversely, is, well, at least it should be deployed in the interest of social justice – that is, in the interest of empowerment for traditionally disempowered peoples. According to Tuck and Yang (2018), there are, for all intents and purposes, no worthwhile emancipatory educational or equity-centered educational approaches that do not center social justice (Sims, 2018; Sims et al., 2020).

I want to be clear on this: it is important to note that equity, then, is not the end goal. Equity, if we are honest, is just the first step in the long road toward (social) justice. Working for justice, unlike equity, fixates on chronic diseases like white supremacy, settler colonialism, cis-heteropatriarchy, etc., and not just the symptoms produced by these systems of power accrual and differentiation. So, what is the difference between equity and justice? As previously mentioned, equity takes the first position that things are not fair – not unequal, but not fair. Justice-centered analysis, on the other hand, seeks to demystify the malevolent design that catalyzes and systematizes the injustices suffered by PMERSCs. Equity, especially in community college spaces, is celebrated as some kind of Holy Grail, some end goal; but it is not that. It is simply a recognition that some students face obstacles due to nothing more than the families that they were born in to. It is also true that the concept of equity has currency precisely because here in the United States our lives are impacted, infracted, and indissolubly informed by capitalism. Therefore, we must work to break the yoke that the marriage of racialized capitalism and white supremacy has placed around the necks of poor, ethnoracially minoritized students of color. Our focus can no longer be primarily in support the institution, or the district; rather, our renewed focus must produce opportunities for generative, justice-centered analysis of our institutionalize policies, practices, procedures, and pedagogies. A radically reimagined focus is exigent if we hope to positively impact all of the students we serve. In order to do this heart-work, we must uncover and, ultimately, deconstruct the rotting foundation that our educational system is built on.

This Old House: Uncovering the Racist Foundation this Country was Founded On

According to Isabel Wilkerson in her bestselling book, *Caste,*

> America is an old house. We can never declare the work over. Wind, flood, drought, and human upheavals batter a structure that is already fighting whatever flaws were left unattended in the original foundation. When you live in an old house, you may not want to go into the basement after a storm to see what the rains have wrought. Choose not to look, however, at your own peril. (Wilkerson, 2020, p. 22)

Wilkerson (2020) argues that we are living in a racialized caste system here in the Land of the Free.

The caste system in India is religion-based. Wilkerson argues that this is not unlike our own system here. All division is hierarchical. Wilkerson opens this book by retelling a harrowing, real-life (and death) story of Willie James. James wrote a note to a female co-worker. The note itself was nothing more than an innocuous Christmas greeting. However, James was Black; his co-worker was white. Clearly, James did not understand his forced subaltern positionality as an untouchable, as a Black Dalit. Because James transgressed the rigidified, racialized caste superstructure that exist here in the Land of the Free, Willie James was made to jump to his death while his father was forced to watch, for simply daring to sully the manufactured concept of white women's' virginal purity. He did this by simply writing a Christmas note. He was a child. He was murdered because he had the audacity to express his care for a white woman. Much of the violence visited on Black men, during Jim Crow, was predicated on a wholly manufactured united front designed to protect the purity of the virginal white women (Sims, 2018).

This caste system dehumanizes Black, Indigenous, and other Peoples of Color. We have to remember that it was not all that long ago that schools would close early so that the children could accompany their parents in reveling in the sadistic, deprived destruction of Black skin via lynching, tar, feathering, boiling, and any number of depraved torture techniques. This was conditioning for white people as much as it was for Black people. Over time white people came to understand that Blackness is not only not equal to whiteness but also not even equal to the life of the family pet. These same white people would not dare lynch, castrate, or boil their dog alive for perceived malfeasance. Yet, they did all these things and more to their fellow man. They did these sadistic things to human beings. And then they celebrated the torture. Let that sink in. This is dehumanization. Livingstone Smith's (2021) definition of dehumanization is especially helpful here,

> My conception of dehumanization is simple. We dehumanize others when we conceive of them as subhuman creatures. These creatures might be nonhuman animals such as lice, rats, snakes, or wolves, or they might be fictional or supernatural beings such as demons and monsters. But in all cases, they are, in a sense that I will explain later on, "beneath" the human, even if, as is often the case, they are thought to possess greater-than-human powers. On my account, then, dehumanization is a kind of attitude. It is something that happens inside people's heads. (Smith, 2021, p. 9)

For Livingstone Smith dehumanization requires human beings to think of other human beings as not human – not less human, which is what Jeshion (2018) defines as "weak" dehumanization, but actually non-human. This is America's history. Our country is a racialized hierarchy, defined, enforced, and concretized by an inequitable, white supremacist legal infrastructure. There was a legal framework for this up until the 1960s. From the 1960's until now constitutes a very short period of time of Black peoples being considered fully human. Let that sink in, please. Race is the tool of caste; it is the signifier of caste. The caste system is the underlying hierarchy that undergirds our National identity. Wilkerson claims the caste system is a skeleton that you cannot see. Wilkerson (2020) offers a heuristic to understand the important distinction between class and caste: if you can act your way out of it, it's class; if you cannot, it's caste.

If we fail to account for the foundation that our democratic experiment is built upon, that is, if we fail to tell the truth, we cannot feign surprise when this experiment fails to deliver on its promises. This was what Baldwin, Malcolm X, and King, Jr., lamented – America's unwillingness to deliver on its promise of freedom and justice for all. The thing is, this promise was never meant for non-white peoples. They had to know that. I believe they continued to hope because to abdicate hope is analogous to willingly descending into nihilistic despair. But all is not lost. We can change the way that we do college in service of PERMSCs. But, if we are going to actually transform our institutions, which are formed by the policies, practices, procedures, and pedagogies enacted by individuals, we cannot continue to rely on anachronistic educational paradigms. We need to redesign the ways that we conceive of college redesign.

The foundation is broken. If we continue to add new levels to this superstructure in the form of (even well-intentioned) new initiatives, yet fail to address the rotting, decrepit foundation that our colleges are building atop, we are doomed to fail PERMSCs. Committing to developing antiracist growth mindset is not only helpful, but it is indispensable in order to do antiracist, justice-centered equity work. Any college redesign predicated on equity and justice must be antiracist. Our National history has, by and large, institutionalized a simulacrum. Our canonical history curriculum has sought to gloss over the real history of this Country. This is our story; this is our song. America, the Land of the Free, is a lie. Glaude in speaking to James Baldwin's unmistakable contributions to the conversations of the day, talks about the "lie" that tormented Baldwin. This same lie torments the American psyche. This lie holds that America is a land of opportunity, a more "perfect" union. Any malfeasance on the way to a more perfect union must be ignored. In fact, the prevailing ethos is that innocence must be presumed and extended because the so-called mission of democracy is just. This is a lie. What's the truth? According to Wilkerson (2020), the truth is this: American is a caste system. It always has been. This is the lie that we have agreed upon. These lies have become commonsensical (Gramsci, 1971). I have to be clear: the Perfect Union that drives American democracy never included people that were considered only 60 percent (3/5) human. These obstacles are worrisome and deeply entrenched, but they are not immovable. This book outlines many of the obstacles to emancipatory pedagogy, because knowing the enemy is important. However, this book is filled with hope, audacious hope (Duncan Andrade, 2011). But hope alone will not suffice. In order to reach PERMSCs, we have to radically reimagine how we do college, including how we teach.

What is Critical Pedagogy

Critical pedagogy (CP) is a philosophy of education described by Henry Giroux as an "educational movement, guided by passion and principle, to help students develop consciousness of freedom, recognize authoritarian tendencies, and connect knowledge to power and the ability to take constructive action." PERMSCs are routinely limited with regard to available identities. As a result, the ability for them to re-create and actualize (Freire & Macedo, 1987) themselves and in so doing develop positive academic identities is constrained. Self-actualization is a hallmark of critical pedagogy. Critical pedagogy is vitally concerned with equipping students with the necessary analytic tools so that they can become increasingly conversant in critically interrogating the new and emerging technologies that exercise pedagogical influence over them (Giroux, 2011).

Likewise, according to Giroux, Critical Pedagogy is a language of hope, struggle, and possibility; and, as such, it must teach students to negotiate difference and make the mission of making knowledge relevant, meaningful, and transformative. Precisely because unlike mainstream students, whose cultural and linguistic repertoires are consistent with schooling culture, PERMSCs are largely thought to come from cultures that are purportedly antithetical to scholastic success (Sims, 2018). This erroneous thinking lends itself to deficit model thinking, which results in low educational expectations and, subsequently and unsurprisingly, inequitable educational outcomes.

Freire and the Pedagogy of the Oppressed

In his book entitled, *Literacy: reading the word and the world*, Paulo Freire (2017) argues that "Literacy becomes a meaningful construct to the degree that it is viewed as a set of practices that functions to either empower or dis-empower people (p. 155)". He goes on to write, "In the larger sense, literacy is analyzed according to whether it serves to reproduce existing social formations or serves a set of cultural practices that promotes democratic and emancipatory change (p. 156)." The primary tenet of his argument is that critical literacy should be predicated on critical pedagogy. And, concomitantly, Freire argues that CP must be a tool used for the construction of critical world-making. For Freire, this must be the ontological vocation of an emancipatory education. He also argues that for traditionally marginalized, or in his words "oppressed" students, critical literacy can only be fully developed once their respective languages and cultures have currency within the educational spaces that they inhabit (Freire, 2017).

According to Freire (and many others) schools are a battleground of sorts where the quest for and subsequent denial of personhood, of agency, plays out over and over again. Schools function as political sites in which class, gender, and racial inequities are both produced and reproduced.

In essence, the colonial educational structure served to inculcate the African natives with myths and beliefs that denied and belittled their lived experiences, their history, their culture, and their language [...] The schools were seen as purifying fountains where Africans could be saved from their deep-rooted ignorance, their savage culture, and their bastardized language, which according to some Portuguese scholars, was a corrupted form of Portuguese without grammatical rules. (Freire & Macedo, 2017, p. 156)

What Freire (2017) describes in the above quote is not limited to Brazil; in truth, this very same phenomenon exists here in the United States as well. And, just as in the abovementioned Brazilian context, our educational current system, with its overreliance and insistence on Standardized English (Mallinson, Charity Hudley, Strickling, & Figa, 2011), especially for linguistic minorities, "reproduce[s] in children and youth the profile that the colonial ideology itself had created for them, namely that of inferior beings, lacking in all ability." (p. 158)

Applying Freire

To be clear, Freire's conception of literacy is not limited to language arts education; rather, it is applicable irrespective of discipline. Freire is interested in a critical education that considers student's subjectivities, life experience as a priori knowledge, while simultaneously stoking their epistemological curiosity (Freire, 2017). What is more, Freire (2017) argues that the only way to extricate marginalized, oppressed students from an education that systematically disallows them from reaching their ontological vocation, i.e., to become more fully human, is to provide a radically emancipatory education, predicated on critical pedagogy. Freire argues that it is this kind of emancipatory pedagogy that will equip them to create and re-create their world through it. For Freire, emancipatory education must include, incorporate, and perhaps most importantly, welcome the language and culture of PERMSCs.

Freire's (2017) prescription for both potential liberation fighters and leaders of the people is as follows: their impetus must be love; they must see themselves as one with the oppressed, not one who is outside, no matter how benevolent their intent. This is true of educators as well. The teacher must eschew the role cast on her by the banking model of education, she must abdicate the lofty throne of the (all) knower, and the student can no longer be viewed as merely a blank slate that requires a deposit. On the contrary, the student and the teacher, the (former) oppressor and the oppressed, respectively, must work together in order to better the student's quest to become more fully human. And, in so doing the educator will find her or his humanity fuller as well (Freire, 2017). Freire makes this point clear,

> No pedagogy which is truly liberating can remain distant from the oppressed by treating them as unfortunates and by presenting for their emulation models from among the oppressors. The oppressed must be their own example in the struggle for their redemption. (Freire, 2017, p. 164)

Freire argues that the implementation of a critical, emancipatory education is one of the primary ways that the oppressed can begin to experience liberation. And, because this is so important, Freire argues that "radical" action is necessary. Educators must develop radical pedagogical structures that provide students with the opportunity to use their own reality as a basis for literacy. This includes, obviously, the language they bring to the classroom. To do otherwise is to deny students the rights that lie at the core of an emancipatory literacy (p. 166). What Freire is arguing for is a decolonization of the mind (Darder, 2018); that is, a critical education that encourages the oppressed to cast of the psychological shackles that torment and imprison them. Like I mentioned above, Freire (2017) argues that any pedagogy that seeks to be critical must incorporate the oppressed's worldview, and in order to do this it must incorporate their language and culture. To this point he cautions, "The failure to base a literacy program on the native language means that oppositional forces can neutralize the efforts of educators and political leaders to achieve decolonization of the mind (p. 168)." Educators must recognize that "language is inevitably one of the major preoccupations of a society, which, liberating itself from colonialism and refusing to be drawn into neo-colonialism searches for its own recreation. In the struggle to re-create a society, the re-conquest by the people of their own world becomes a fundamental factor (p. 166).

To be clear, Freire is not setting forth an unrealistic ask that would require all educators to be polyglots. Here, he is not speaking to actual dialects and languages so much as he is speaking to the language of the unheard. What Freire is asking educators to do is to inquire of students what it is that speaks to them so that teacher and student can begin co-constructing a meaningful, shared language. If students want to discuss white supremacy in math, for example, incorporating student's language would require educators to create opportunities for critical dialogue regarding white supremacy and math. A math teacher, in this example, need not be an expert on critical race theory in order to facilitate this conversation. However, this hypothetical math teacher would need to do the necessary work of positioning herself to fully participate in conversations that may be uncomfortable. This is emancipatory for students and teachers alike.

Freire goes on to write, "It is of tantamount importance that the incorporation of the students' language [and culture] as the primary language [mode] of instruction in literacy be given top priority. It is through their own language that they will be able to reconstruct their history and their culture (p. 166)." Furthermore, Freire argues that "the students' language is the only means by which they can develop their own voice, a prerequisite to the development of positive self-worth (p. 167). Student's language, in this context, is not simply that which they speak at home; rather, it incorporates and accounts for the variegated discourse communities that our students participate in (digital language, Hip Hop Nation Language, Standardized English, AAVE, STEM language, etc.). Next, Freire quotes Giroux, who argues that the students' voice "is the discursive means to make themselves 'heard' and define themselves as active authors of their world.

The authorship of ones' own world, which would also imply one's own language has currency, is analogous to what Mikhail Bakhtin defines as "retelling a story in one's own words (p. 167)." The space to tell one's own story is important for human beings, writ large; however, I would argue that it takes on a special meaning for oppressed groups who have been effectively silenced, primarily because of their perceived distance from what is considered to be the standard (i.e., whiteness). The voice that they develop will also allow them to see themselves iteratively. That is to say, they will be able to see themselves as more than the stereotypes that they are often reduced to. It is our responsibility, even our obligation (Sims et al., 2020) to create and co-create agency-inciting opportunities for and with our students.

Making the Case for Critical Reality Pedagogy

In my 2018 book, *Revolutionary STEM education: Critical-reality pedagogy and social justice in STEM for Black males*, I conceptualized, operationalized and, subsequently, applied a new educational framework: critical-reality pedagogy (henceforth, CrP). As I wrote in this book, this educational framework was "... consciously and collaboratively instituted[...]as a deliberate way to develop the students' identities with and competencies in STEM as well as their capacities to conceptualize, develop, create, and test socially just applications of STEM (Sims, 2018, p. 9)." A critical-reality pedagogical framework or approach alloys the critical pedagogical work of Freire (1997), Giroux (2011), Duncan-Andrade and Morrell (2008) and others with Emdin's (2010, 2016) work on reality pedagogy. In explicating the teleos of CrP, I often build on the metaphor used to explain critical thinking. As I wrote previously,

> To be considered a critical thinker—according to this metaphor—one must be willing to think outside of the confines/paradigm of the seemingly concretized box. However, a critical-reality metaphor goes further in that simply thinking outside of the "box" is not sufficient. Rather, a critical-reality pedagogical approach holds that students should not only be encouraged to think outside of the box, but, rather, that they should also be empowered, encouraged, and equipped to critically analyze the box (i.e., paradigm) to determine if its positionality is victimizing particular groups of people while, simultaneously, simultaneously, illuminating the beneficiaries of the box's positionality. The goal of this pedagogical approach is to (re)position students to use their knowledge and skills to deconstruct the box (i.e., white supremacist based structuralized inequity) in a way that is commensurate with social justice. (Sims, 2018, pp. 9–10)

CrP not only looks at macrolevel injustices, ala critical pedagogical, but it also positions students to understand, identify, and began to deconstruct and subsequently redress individualized issues while also helping students realize that the individualized, localized injustices that inform their lived experiences are part and parcel of a larger, macrostructural system of oppression. This system is impelled by and reliant on racialized capitalism and white supremacy. This unholy union is disproportionately injurious to PERMSCs. And while both critical and reality pedagogies emphasize student voice and student empowerment, the primary goal of critical-reality pedagogy extends beyond just creating safespaces. And it goes further than just equipping students with critical analytical tools. Rather, a critical-reality pedagogical approach is primarily concerned with action.

Reality pedagogy is concerned with action, too. That said, there is an indispensable tenet that critical-reality pedagogy espouses: while creating opportunities for students to co-create knowledge in a classroom/educative space is indispensable to efficacious, equitable pedagogy, students must also be empowered, encouraged, and equipped to take their classroom learning out of the classroom and apply it to issues that are important to them. This is key. The goal of critical-reality pedagogical approach is to provide students with the necessary analytical tools to create access to power for traditionally marginalized students, like themselves, by deconstructing the current power structure and radically reimagining it. CrP does not stop here. Ultimately, the goal of CrP is to encourage, empower, and equip students to re-form the "box" so that it is commensurate with social justice (Sims, 2018). CrP demands that we work alongside our students, in solidarity. We do not simply (do the work) work for them, as though they are mere objects; and we cannot ever work against them. Instead, we have to work with them by creating opportunities for students to demonstrate their expertise. To do this, we must begin by inviting students' languages and cultures into our classroom spaces. We must encourage them to explore their epistemological curiosity by empowering them to co-construct knowledge and meaning with us. A CrP approach does this so that students can critically contextualize their learning by using it to actually – not just theoretically – demand and ensure socially just societal change.

The Importance of Equitable Educational Spaces

Jeramy Wallace will go into detail regarding the importance and exigency of creating equitable educational spaces. I simply want to take this opportunity to foreshadow the spirit of what he writes. One of the gaps that I, along with my co-authors (including Wallace), illuminated in *Minding the Obligation gap in community colleges* (Sims et al., 2020) is the pedagogy gap. "Unlike K12 education, with few exceptions, community college faculty are not required to complete coursework on teaching and learning (i.e., pedagogy) prior to teaching. For us, this is a glaring gap – or what we referred to in this book as the "Pedagogy Gap." Liberatory pedagogy enables the creation and curation of equitable educational spaces. Equitable educational spaces afford students the opportunity to develop agency, to self-actualize. This process is important for all students. And it is especially important for poor ethnoracially minoritized students of color (PERMSC) because for much of their educational history, they have been told both implicitly and explicitly that who they are is antithetical to scholastic success (Steele, 2011). Creating spaces for self-actualization, i.e., the realization or fulfillment of one's talents and potentialities, is exigent for students that have been led to believe that scholastic success is unrealizable because of their ethnoracial identity, socioeconomic status, culture, home neighborhood, etc. (Sims et al., 2020).

Schooling in this country is designed for and still functions to maintain our Nation's white supremacist, hegemonic status quo (Sims, 2018). In order to positively impact PERMSCs, we have to radically reimagine and, ultimately, redesign the polices, practices, and pedagogies that have created an educative environment where racialized inequity is made to seem natural and endemic. We have to create agency-inciting opportunities for hypermarginalized students. If a college truly hopes to be equity-advancing, this work must be a concerted effort. At the same time, as educators, we cannot simply wait for everyone else to come on board. Rather, we must commit ourselves to, first, understanding and subsequently applying liberatory, agency-inciting pedagogies – irrespective of our discipline area. Good (i.e., emancipatory) pedagogies always center critical dialogue on perceived/manufactured human differences and how these differences are reified/concretized via asymmetric power relationships. Curriculum and pedagogy that is liberatory is, necessarily, agency-inciting. Agency-inciting pedagogy expands opportunities for self-actualization for all of the students we serve.

We Have to Account for Our Privilege: Self-Actualization and Critical Pedagogy

The pandemic catalyzed by the spread of COVID-19 caused us to change the ways that we do college. Most community colleges, like our four-year counterparts, transformed from primarily in-person learning institutions into primarily virtual (and in some cases hybridized) learning institutions in days or weeks. This new educational paradigm and concomitant modality caused us to think through new questions about pedagogy. Namely, what does critical, liberatory pedagogy look online? I do not have a one size fits all answer to this question. In fact, I do not have an answer at all. However, I do know this: no matter what the educational modality is, self-actualization must be the goal. The process of self-actualization is a hallmark of critical pedagogy. Therefore, a question that underpins, even impels us in our new digital environment must be: how can we develop, hone, and protect the relationship (and potential intersection/s) between digitally mediated instruction and critical, emancipatory pedagogy? Critical pedagogy is vitally concerned with equipping students with the necessary analytical tools to interrogate, critically, the new and emerging technologies that exercise pedagogical influence over them (Giroux, 2011). Likewise, according to Giroux, Critical Pedagogy is a language of hope, struggle, and possibility; and, as such, it must teach students to negotiate differences and make the mission of making knowledge relevant, meaningful, and transformative.

Literature supports the reality that digitally-mediated virtual spaces for PERMSCs, if thoughtfully developed, can function as spaces where these students can confront, and re-configure their identities (Mahiri & Sims, 2016). Mahiri (2017) and others have argued that digitally-mediated instruction carries the potential to extricate poor, marginalized students from the pedagogy of the oppressed. Therefore, we want to take a closer look at the ways in which digitally-mediated, virtual (educational) space, through a lens that is fixed on critical/critical-reality pedagogy, has the potential to simultaneously allow for and encourage PERMSC students to reimagine the identities that have hitherto been severely constrained (and perhaps off-limits). (I do this, albeit briefly, in the Epilogue of this book.)

The goal should be to examine and identify the educational vistas created by digital instruction. More specifically, we have to work to identify the interplay of social justice and emancipatory (critical) pedagogy, by critically examining issues of power and equity that are both situated and concretized in the cross-section of language and literacy, STEM education, and technology. *Make no mistake: access to digitally-mediated instruction is a matter of social justice.* Precisely because unlike mainstream students, whose cultural and linguistic repertoires are consistent with schooling culture, poor ethnoracially minoritized students of color (PERMSC) are largely thought to come from cultures that are antithetical to scholastic success. Virtual instructional space is, by no means, an educational panacea. However, if we are committed to equity and justice, critical/critical-reality pedagogical approaches to online instruction hold the potential to afford these students (virtual) spaces to loosen the constraints that have limited their access to opportunities for self-actualization and agential development.

Frankly, I hope that we never simply go back to business as usual. Prior to COVID-19, our poor, ethnoracially minoritized students of color were still living through a white supremacist pandemic that served the interests of racialized capitalism. Put simply, the normal that some of us have pined for in the face of COVID-19 was already bad for PERMSC. We cannot simply go back. We have to move forward. Nevertheless, as we do inevitably move closer to what we had before, we have to consider all of the things that we've learned about ourselves during this time. We cannot, we must not, try to put new wine in old wineskins because the old wineskins will burst. So even though we may not be primarily virtual moving forward, we still need to figure out how to crystallize and, subsequently, incorporate the pedagogical practices that lead to emancipatory physical and hybridized-virtual educational spaces.

You Were Built for Such a Time as This!

This work is incredibly personal for me. I am the product of my environment for better or worse. I grew up in a fence-line community, which is a neighborhood that is plagued by poor air quality, ubiquitous fratricidal violence, little access to jobs that paid a living wage, and little to no access to healthy food. I grew up in what Wacquant (2008) termed a hyperghetto. Community College represented a way out for me. My community college journey was not without vicissitudes. Nevertheless, community college did prove to be a throughput for a life that was not expected for me or, if I am honest, a life that I did not even expect for myself. So, when I got the opportunity to work in community colleges, I jumped in. This was something of a pivot as I had been trained to work toward professorship in urban education. Nevertheless, I knew that this is the right move for me. As a graduate student, I worked closely with a program that served transfer students. I myself was a beneficiary of this program as an undergraduate. Now, I am a full-time Director of Equity in what I recently learned is the third-ranked Community College in the country, College of San Mateo. I have been blessed with opportunities to work with other colleges in order to help them think through making their college environment commensurate with justice and equity. And although I have come across many different educators, with beautifully varied experiences and expertise, there are some connective tissues that run through the experiences that I have had in service to these different colleges. For many, a move toward equity and justice seems fairly simple. But this not simple work. It is hard, heart-work. In order to embark on this journey, we have to come clean, so to speak. We need to be completely honest about the ways that white supremacy and racialized capitalism, in a kind of unholy an incestuous marriage (Sims et al., 2020), work in concert to concretize institutional inequities. We have to start here.

Once we are ready to have this conversation, we can begin to do some real substantive work. When I have these conversations with folks, whether it be in training sessions or workshops or in keynote address, the response is generally positive. People want to be able to do this work. At the same time, some of these very same people feel as though they have no entry point into this work. For a long time, I thought that this was simply a cop-out, a readymade excuse for people that just did not care enough to change. It seemed to me that an alarming number of my European American colleagues were either unwilling or incapable of grasping the reality that the foundations that our colleges are operating on our inequitable by design. This was a point of frustration for me for years. Why even have these conversations? Why even bring in people like me, if there are so many people who are wholly and even vehemently unwilling to be moved by an appeal to do what's right, to do what is just?

But I have had time to have conversations at a different levels with some of these same people based on some of the principles that came to the fore in my last book, *Minding the obligation gap in community colleges*. I along with my co-authors led a five-part Summer Learning Institute in the summer of 2020, in order to introduce (especially but not exclusively) community college practitioners to the principles, arguments, and best practices found within the book. As a result of the success of that book, I have had increased opportunities to have conversations with cross-representational groups on college campuses other than my own. Again, I started to feel as though there were people who were either unwilling or simply unable to understand how dire the situation was for many PERMSCs. Now to be clear, I am not expecting people to apply the principles of critical race scholarship or critical whiteness scholarship based on a couple of conversations or even shared book clubs. What I am talking about is a kind of resistance to or denial of the fact that there are systemic inequities in the first place.

What I realize now, though, for many of the people that I am writing about (and to) this is a defense mechanism. The person-to-person opportunities that I have been presented with has given me ample food for thought. Opportunities to sit down with people as individuals (and in small groups) made me reconsider my initial presupposition. Sure, there are far too many people that do not love justice, which is equal parts maddening and saddening. At the same time, however, I became convinced that there are many well-meaning, well-intentioned community college practitioners that want to do substantive equity and justice work. They just do not know how to get started, and/or they feel as though they are un/underqualified. So, for them it is easier to defer to experts. And, in truth much of professional development at the community college level is set up in this way. Experts are brought in. People are inspired by these erudite folks, and as a result are moved and want to act. But the speakers eventually go back to wherever they came from, and the college that they visited is left trying to figure out how to implement the material that was covered. This model is unsustainable; it's also impractical. I am not trying to shoot myself in the foot, so to speak. I appreciate every opportunity I am given to deliver keynote addresses or talks or workshops. But, if I am being honest, I know full well that this is not enough.

This work does not come without inherent challenges. My challenge is to speak the truth in love, to not be disingenuous, to adhere to the complexity of the work, while also creating entry points into this conversation for people irrespective of their a priori understanding of justice, equity, white supremacy, and racialized capitalism. This is no small task, which is why it made sense for me to pair an anti-racist educational paradigm with growth mindset. In my experience, people feel as though they understand both the concept and benefits of a growth mindset. So, my goal, then, is to help people understand antiracism conceptually, so that the benefits of adopting this educational paradigm will be clear. I made this point earlier on, but it bears repeating here: there is no liminal space in this work. There is no safe middle. Silence is violence. Apathy and ambivalence are also violence. A lack of love is violence.

I am not naïve, nor am I overly optimistic, though I do have hope. I believe that there are people that want to do this work. I believe that there are people that have been waiting to be put in the game, to be called in. I believe that the antiracist growth mindset represents a call-in. I have spent the majority of my scholarly career calling out white supremacy and more recently racialized capitalism. I don't plan to stop because these two, conjoined diseases continue to pathologize and penalize poor ethnoracially minorities students of color with impunity. This is because our society, by and large, is predicated on and also in support of these two realities. This is precisely why conversations around the brokenness of education are not particularly compelling for me. Our educational systems, K12 and higher education, are working as they were designed. That much we need to be clear about. In order for people to have these conversations, it takes introspective and reflective work on their part. If you want to do equity and justice work, you have to be comfortable with the idea of being uncomfortable, and you have to be willing to both tell and face the truth. There's no other way to move forward.

This is hard, heart-work. This is not a battle that can be wone overnight. Here I am reminded of revolutionary love warrior, John Lewis's pellucid quote:

> Ours is not the struggle of one day, one week, or one year. Ours is not the struggle of one judicial appointment or presidential term. Ours is the struggle of a lifetime, or maybe even many lifetimes, and each one of us in every generation must do our part.(***Lewis on movement building in Across That Bridge: A Vision for Change and the Future of America***)

We have to cling to hope because all is not lost; it never is. However, we have to be honest about where we are and who we are both individually and institutionally. There is no amount of professional development that can move people enough to cause them to fall in love with justice. This is something that they have to want. This reality makes the work even more daunting. This is why working in solidarity, irrespective of where a person is on the continuum of understanding and or expertise on equity and justice, holds the potential to help a person develop an antiracist growth mindset. Working toward an antiracist growth mindset is indispensable if we hope to create equitable educational spaces for PERMSC. You can do this work because, well, you have to.

*It is the Job of the Conscious to make the Unconscious Conscious,
Kwame Ture and Hamilton (1992).*

I am still learning. I will always and forever be still learning. Nevertheless, this book is in an attempt to raise the level of consciousness regarding the ubiquity, perniciousness, and normalcy of white supremacy and racialized capitalism in the way that education is conceptualized and (pre)determined, especially for poor ethnoracially minoritized students of color. In these two introductory sections, my goal is to invite you into this work while providing a rearticulation of the work. In the middle of this book, Jeramy Wallace will masterfully interweave critical race scholarship with his own experiences as a white educator committed to antiracism. Then, finally, I will speak about some of the lessons learned while writing this book in the Epilogue. Even though we are writing as individuals from different vantage points, we are uniformly convinced that if readers are ready to commit to doing the necessary reflexive, introspective work that justice calls for, you can be someone that advances equity on your campus. Consider this your official invitation to join us on this journey.

Keywords: Racialized capitalism, justice-centered, equity-advancing, white ambivalence, white apathy, poor ethnoracially minoritized students of color (PERMSC), white supremacy, antiracism, antiracist growth mindset, the lie, caste, hope, James Baldwin, Rev. Dr. Martin Luther King, Jr.

Review: In this the opening word for this book, my intention ways to provide a lay of the land in order to contextualize Jeramy Wallace's exhortation to all educators, and especially white educators to radically reimagine their pedagogy so that it is equity-advancing and justice-centered. In order for this to happen, educators must understand that the foundation that this country is built on is rotting right before our eyes, precisely because our national foundation is built on the lie that white lives matter, and non-white lives do not. The twin pandemics of 2020 made this clearer. This is the context in which our PERMSC students do school. If we want to positively impact PERMSCs, we have to do something different. We have to love (justice) more, we have to listen more attentively, and we have to teach more empathically. We have to adopt an antiracist growth mindset. If we do not, our work, our pedagogies – irrespective of our intentions – will continue to oppress PERMSC students.

References

Beckert, S., & Rockman, S. (2018). *Slavery's capitalism: A new history of American economic development (Early American Studies)*. Philadelphia, PA. University of Pennsylvania Press. Reprint.

Brad Bird, et al. (2004). The Incredibles.

Boaler, J. (2019). *Limitless mind: Learn, lead, and live without barriers*. New York, NY. HarperOne. Illustrated.

Crenshaw, K. (2005). Mapping the margins: Intersectionality, identity politics, and violence against women of color (1994). In R.K. Bergen, J.L. Edleson, & C.M. Renzetti (Eds.), *Violence against women: Classic papers* (pp. 282–313). New Zealand: Pearson Education.

Curry, T.J. (2017). *The man-not: Race, class, genre, and the dilemmas of Black manhood* (1st ed.). Philadelphia, PA. Temple University Press.

Darder, A. (2018). Decolonizing interpretive research: Subaltern sensibilities and the politics of voice. *Qualitative Research Journal*.

Darling-Hammond, L., & Banks, J. (2010). *The flat world and education: How America's commitment to equity will determine our future (Multicultural Education Series)*. (31752nd ed.). New York, NY. Teachers College Press.

DuBois, W.E.B. (1920). The souls of White folk. In Darkwater: Voices from within the veil. New York, NY: Washington Square Press.

DuBois, W.E.B. (1968). *The souls of Black folk; essays and sketches*. Chicago: A.G. McClurg, 1903. New York, NY: Johnson Reprint Corp.

Dweck, C.S. (2006). *Mindset: The new psychology of success*. New York, NY. Random House.

Field, D. (2009). *A historical guide to James Baldwin*. Oxford: Oxford University Press.

Freire, P. (2017). *Pedagogy of the oppressed*. Westminster, London, England. Penguin Classics.

Glaude, E.S. (2020). *Begin again: James Baldwin's America and its urgent lessons for our own*. New York, NY. Crown Books.

Gramsci, A, et al. (2011). *Prison notebooks* (Vols. 1–3). New York, NY. Columbia University Press.

Jeshion, R.B. (2018). Slurs, dehumanization, and the expression of contempt. In D. Sosa (Ed.), *Bad words: Philosophical perspectives on slurs* (p. 79). New York, NY: Oxford University Press.

Kendi, I.X. (2019). *How to be an antiracist*. London. One world.

Mahiri, J., & Sims, J.J. (2016). Engineering equity: A critical pedagogical approach to language and curriculum change for African American males in STEM. In *Curriculum change in language and STEM subjects as a right in education*. Rotterdam: Sense Publishing.

Mallinson, C., Charity Hudley, A., Strickling, L.R., & Figa, M. (2011). A conceptual framework for promoting linguistic and educational change. *Language and Linguistics Compass*, 5(7), 441–453.

Shelby, T., & Terry, B. (2020). *To shape a new world: Essays on the political Philosophy of Martin Luther King, Jr.* Reprint, Belknap Press. Cambridge, MA. An Imprint of Harvard University Press.

Sims, J.J. (2018). *Revolutionary STEM education: Critical-reality pedagogy and social justice in STEM for Black males*. New York, NY: Peter Lang.

Sims, J.J. (Forthcoming). *Towards liberation: Antiracism and the redesign of college redesign.* New York:, NY Peter Lang.

Sims, J.J., Taylor-Mendoza, J., Hotep, L.O., Wallace, J., & Conaway, T. (2020). *Minding the obligation gap in community colleges and beyond: Theory and practice in achieving educational equity. Educational Equity in Community Colleges.* New York, NY. Peter Lang Publishing Group.

Smith, D.L. (2021) *Making monsters.* London. Harvard University Press. Kindle Edition.

Ture, K., & Hamilton, C.V. (1992). *Black power: The politics of liberation.* Vintage.

Wacquant, L. (2008). *Urban outcasts: A comparative sociology of advanced marginality.* Cambridge, MA. Polity.

Wilkerson, I. (2020). *Caste (Oprah's Book Club): The origins of our discontents.* New York, NY. Random House.

1 | Introduction

While on a short trip to a state-wide academic senate conference, I was provided a small glimpse into whiteness in America. More specifically, I was witness to the beliefs of two white passengers on race, racism, and the political climate in the United States. At first, I resisted eavesdropping. I sat behind them working on my first book, *Minding the Obligation Gap*, which I was co-authoring with several of my colleagues, but I couldn't resist listening for two reasons – one, I was, at that moment, reflecting on race and racism in higher education for that book, and two, we were crammed on one of those tiny commuter planes that are only a dozen or so rows long and four seats across. In other words, the white woman in front of me was not only chatting about a topic that was academically (and personally) interesting to me, but she was basically sitting in my lap as she did so. I would also soon find out that these two individuals were traveling to the same conference as me, so they were likely community college educators and faculty leaders – one woman and one man, both white. As I typed away on how white community college leaders can create more equitable campuses, I was able to hear first-hand these leaders' views on race and racism.

It was in the fall of 2018, and like many conversations for the past two years, this one started with the Trump administration. What started with general disdain quickly veered into the politics of race. The woman sitting in front of me remarked that she was disgusted that the president had made "racism mainstream" after it had been, by-and-large, "snuffed out." Her male colleague quickly agreed and appealed to the reliable trope that the election of President Barack Obama was evidence that widespread and overt racism was dead. They continued to discuss some of the egregious instances of racism and ethnocentrism of the time – the detention centers at the U.S./Mexico border, which had been discovered just months before, the family separation policy that removed immigrant children from their parents and siblings, the ban on Arabic Muslims entering the country, and other anti-immigrant rhetoric. It was a "greatest hits" of all of America's abhorrent – and racist – policymaking, at least the most recent at the time.

Let me first express my delightful surprise that these two white folks were even discussing race and racism in the first place. While their premises were shaky, they were struggling to understand the clear injustices and human rights abuses that they were witnessing in the newspapers, on the television, and in social media. This one act – talking about race – is a difficult one for those of us (read: white folks) who are not impacted by the policies of discrimination and hatred enacted by our government, so I certainly laud these two educators. For a critical educator who is interested in the discourses of racial inequity, this conversation was heartening.

However, to be clear, this conversation was also very problematic for a number of reasons. While these two individuals would be hailed as progressive whites who denounce racism and hatred in all forms, it was also abundantly clear that they did not truly grasp how engrained racism is in our society, as the male colleague demonstrated in his comment about the election of President Obama. On the one hand, you did have a white woman who was genuinely disgusted by the rise in hate crimes and the racist rhetoric of the nation's most powerful leaders. It was clear that they did not share the president's values and that they were even repulsed by them, and her male colleague sincerely agreed with her. However, on the other hand, these were also two white, middle-class professionals who believed that racism had essentially disappeared from 2008 to 2016 because it wasn't "mainstream" and because we had an African American president. Did she believe this because the gatherings of racists, like the KKK, weren't televised in the same way that alt-right riots had been in recent years? Was it because Trump was overtly racist, such as when he called immigrants "rapists and thugs," rather than using the coded language of his predecessors, like "super predators," "welfare queens," or "war on drugs"? Had she not been paying attention when the so-called "Tea Party" gained traction on an anti-Obama platform, one tenet of which was the birther conspiracy theory? Had they forgotten the current president was the number one evangelist for that same racist conspiracy? What about the officer-involved shootings of Oscar Grant, James Crawford, Michael Brown, and Freddie Gray, and the murder of Trayvon Martin by a neighborhood watchman, all of which occurred during Obama's presidency? I could go on, but I think I have made my point. Nevertheless, I am always curious about how white folks, especially those who keep abreast of the socio-political climate of the country, can ignore the clear swelling of racial tensions during the presidency of President Obama that would eventually come to a head in the election of Donald Trump and his tumultuous, hate-filled presidency. Perhaps it was an inability to see the forest for the trees.

But as I sat on that small Embraer jet working on my first book about community college leadership, race, and social justice, I couldn't help but wonder how these two professors' attitudes about race impacted their teaching. Data bears out that the vast majority of professors in higher education are white (generally white men, but women are gaining some ground) and that the demographics for their student bodies are the inverse. More specifically, according to the National Center for Educational Statistics (NCES, 2016a), as of fall 2016, 76% of all college professors are white – 41% of the total being male and 35% of the total being female. When the demographics are disaggregated by academic rank, the numbers are even starker: 81% of all full professors are white (54% male/27% female); 76% are associate professors (41% male/35% female); 72% of all assistant professors are white (34% male/38% female); and 76% and 80% of instructors and lecturers are white, respectively. In other words, as of fall 2016, less than 30% of any rank of the college faculty were comprised of people of color. In community colleges, in particular, the 2008 NCES report *The Condition of Education* notes that 84% of all community college faculty are white (as cited in NCES, 2019).

Compare these numbers to the students' demographics and we can easily see why I was so concerned with how the socio-political views of my two fellow white travelers impact their teaching. The NCES report "Status and Trends in the Education of Racial and Ethnic Groups 2016" indicated that, nationwide, the students in higher education are becoming more and more racially diverse. For example, in fall 2017, there were 16.8 million undergraduate students in the United States (in both two- and four-year institutions): 8.9 million white students (53%), 3.3 Latinx students (20%), 2.2 African American students (13%), 1.1 Asian American/Pacific Islander (8%), and 124,000 Indigenous students (0.01%). In community colleges, more specifically, 49% of students nationwide are white, 22% are Latinx, 14% are African American, 5% are Asian American, and 10%

are "other" ("Trends in Community Colleges," p. 6). However, in California and Texas, the country's two largest systems, the student demographics are even more diverse. In California, 28% of students are white, 43% are Latinx, 7% are African American, 12% are Asian American, and 9% are "other." In Texas, we see very similar patterns: 36% are white, 39% are Latinx, 14% are African American, 4% are Asian American, and 6% are "other." Finally, according to data collected by the American Association of Community Colleges (AACC, 2019), 46.2% of community college students nationwide identify as white, a drop from 60% in 2001 (p. 8). The AACC also notes that the Latinx community college population has also doubled between 2001 and 2017 while the African American student population has decreased from 14.6% in 2011 to 12.7% in 2017 (p. 9). In fact, according to the same report, there are now less than 1 million African American students attending community colleges nationwide. The NCES found that only 28% of African American men and 36% of African American women aged between 18 and 24 enrolled in any institution of higher education between 2003 and 2013 (NCES, 2016b).

I share these numbers for a couple of reasons. First, and most importantly, this diversity is very exciting for our institutions. As the College Board (2016) reports, the majority of African American and Latinx students are enrolled in community colleges. For instance, in 2014, 44% of all African American undergraduate students were enrolled in a community college (as opposed to 29% for public four-year universities), and similarly, a whopping 56% of all Latinx undergraduate students were enrolled in a community college (29% for public four-year universities). For first-time, full-time African American students, 36% enroll in a community college, mirroring the 36% that enroll in a four-year university. For first-time, full-time Latinx students, 43% enroll in a community college while 37% enroll in a four-year university. Furthermore, while first-time, full-time students of color attend community colleges in large numbers, many of the African American and Latinx students that we see in our classrooms are considered "non-traditional." They may be working parents, part-time students who work full-time to make ends meet or contribute to their households, adult workers looking for retraining, or formerly incarcerated students looking for a fresh start. This leads me to my second point – we white community college faculty are, by and large, unprepared to work with these populations.

My goal in this book is to provide white community college educators with the tools to more effectively educate students of color (tools, I'll add, that are valuable for teaching any student). Every student who steps on our campuses is looking for the same thing – a supportive, intellectually demanding, and nurturing educational environment. And I know some of you are rolling your eyes at that claim; you may automatically imagine that student who shows up late every other day, who has an empty desk for the entire class period, and who seems utterly disengaged to the point of seeming tortured. But at this point in the book and for the duration of your engagement with it, I need you to give the students the benefit of the doubt. Understand that so many of our students – especially *our* students – come from traumatizing experiences in the K-12 system, personal hardships, and responsibilities that most of us couldn't fathom as undergraduates. The behaviors mentioned above are, in many cases, their defense mechanisms. They do not want to open up and engage or invest too much in their dreams in the event that they must drop out, or possibly worse, in the event that one of their professors publicly humiliates them. With that in mind, let's get started.

a. Why Race?: "The Canary in the Coal Mine"

The most common question I encounter as a critical educator, especially as one of European descent, is why focus so much on race? Why not on gender, sexual orientation, or a host of other identities? Why not just stick to what I was trained for – teaching postsecondary composition and literature? There are a number of answers, but the most important reason for me is that race, race-relations, and racism have been an important part of my life for almost as long as I've been alive. In other words, it is personal. When I was a young child, my parents separated and divorced; both would remarry, but for the sake of this book, it is important only to know that my mother married an African American man. My stepfather would come into my life early on, and he not only became my father, but the new family dynamic would open my eyes to a worldview that most people who look like me will never know.

The story of my childhood will inform much of this book, so it is important to describe a few aspects of it here. My stepfather (hereafter affectionately referred to as "Pops") is a college-educated, professional who has worked in the tech, insurance, and banking industries. I mention this not because I need to combat any potential stereotypes of African American men or because his bona fides are relevant, but because it had a tremendous impact on where I would spend my childhood and on the person I would grow up to be. My mother earned her Associate's degree before becoming a small business owner (before the divorce) and then a flight attendant (after), a job she would have for the rest of my childhood (she would change jobs again to realty when I was already off to college). In other words, I lived with two parents who were both employed, one in the white-collar professional world and the other in the hybrid transportation/hospitality industry. As a result, I would spend my childhood in the suburbs of Phoenix – in Mesa, to be exact – where the vast majority of my neighbors, classmates, teachers, and others looked like me, my mom, and my sister, but whose own careers would more closely mirror my Pops's.

If these demographics made my Pops uneasy, he never shared it with me. In fact, it wouldn't be until I became an academic and I started teaching and writing on issues of race, racism, and social justice that he would start to divulge some of the realities of growing up as a Black man in America and being in a biracial marriage in suburbia. Nevertheless, even though my family never explicitly discussed race in America, I still learned to navigate race relations at school, and I was invited into the local African American community via weekend get-togethers with my Pops's friends and bi-annual family reunions, where I learned not only about the Black community but also how to be comfortable being one of only a few white folks in these settings (and to be clear, neither the nature of my family, nor my experiences in predominantly Black spaces mean that I automatically recognized structural racism and white supremacy. In fact, as I will discuss in more detail later, this absolutely was not the case). I developed my ability to notice, to see, when there was only a handful of classmates of color in my grade or teachers of color working at my school. I didn't know it then, but I would learn as I grew into my professional career that these were the consequences of structural discrimination and of institutional racism. Everyone in this suburb was by and large white. And to be clear, neither the nature of my family nor my experiences in predominantly Black spaces mean that I automatically recognized structural racism and white supremacy. In fact, as I will discuss in more detail later, this absolutely was not the case.

In short, this book is about race because it's what I know. Am I expert? Heck no. In fact, it is slightly problematic for any of us white folks to claim expertise in race and racism. But as mentioned above, I have had the privilege and pleasure to experience an enriching childhood in which seeing, interacting, and loving people of color was the norm. And now – well into my adulthood – that I am aware of the intentionality of de facto segregation, mass incarceration, and other forms of oppression, which I will discuss later in this chapter and the next, I have made it my professional goal to at least fight racism within my own sphere of influence – higher education, and more specifically, community colleges. It is my hope that I can share the insights derived from my childhood so that you, my reader, can see the lived realities of people of color in the United States, and it is my hope that once you see the injustices that exist in higher education, you too will be compelled to implement some of the practices and lessons that follow in this book.

While my first reason for focusing on race is a personal one, there are also academic reasons, the most important of which is that the inequities experienced by people of color, particularly African Americans, are a microcosm of the larger social injustices that impact women, the LGBTQ+ community, immigrants, religious minorities, and other minoritized people – that is, those who are not male, straight, Protestant, and of European descent. As my colleague Dr. Jeremiah Sims (2018) writes, African Americans, especially men, "represent the proverbial canary in the mineshaft in this country" (p. 4). In other words, the lived experiences of racism and structural discrimination and the oppression of African Americans and other people of color can help us uncover the oppression and injustices experienced by other marginalized groups. Furthermore, the legacies of discrimination experienced by the historically marginalized and oppressed peoples are so unique and so different, it'd be nearly impossible to write a book that adequately discusses them all. It will be difficult enough to be inclusive of all people of color in this book. With that being said, if you are able to use the theories, practices, and concepts in this book to work towards social justice for your students of color, you can more easily strive for social justice for other oppressed people. For example, if you read this book, and you are able to critique your whiteness, to identify white supremacy in higher education, and to take steps to eradicate it within your spheres of influence, you also have the tools to critique the privilege derived from your heterosexuality, identify homophobia and transantagonism in higher education, and to take steps to eliminate them from your spheres of influence. Note that I say "tools." It is up to you to do your research on the community – the history of their oppression, the prejudice they experience in education and society writ large, and of course, what they have identified as needs in pursuing social justice for their community.

Now, you might be thinking, "Wow, Jeramy, this is way too much! White supremacy? C'mon." I get it. Many of the ideas in this book are difficult to grapple with (they were for me, too). Many readers may not even want to acknowledge that these types of prejudices exist in higher education. Professors should be, after all, colorblind, right? As you will discover in this book, colorblindness is easier to pay lip service to than to adopt as an ideology. In fact, colorblindness is so often claimed by white folks that it is has become a parody. Scholars have even discovered that colorblindness has become a sort of new racism (see Bonilla-Silva, 2017).

I hope it might provide some relief to know that I had a very similar outlook early in my career. Race and racism were almost never discussed in my family, so it was very easy for me to believe the common narrative that racism was on the decline and racists were relegated to remote regions of the United States where they dressed in old bed sheets and burned crosses. The neighborhood where I lived was fairly homogenous and race simply didn't come up. To me, everything seemed fine. This perspective was further strengthened when I moved to the San Francisco Bay Area for college. I was suddenly dropped into spaces where the majority of the people around me were people of color, a stark contrast to my suburb in Arizona. However, this new contingency fortified my beliefs in a so-called "post-racial" society. It seemed to me that people in the Bay Area of all backgrounds were coexisting in harmony. I would go as far as to adopt this perspective early in my career as a community college educator.

In my first semester teaching at the College of San Mateo, my mentor, James Carranza, moved into a new role as the college's academic senate president, and I was offered his course in a learning community called "Voice of a Stranger." The learning community was comprised of three sections, one of which I taught and the other two of which were taught by two of my colleagues. Course topics included race and racism, immigration, drug addiction, and the human toll of war, and we read texts from significant authors, including Brent Staples, August Wilson, Tim O'Brien, and Laila Lalami. In my effort to "enlighten" my college students, I wanted to hit them first with the heaviest topic I could muster – race and racism. We would start with Brent Staples' seminal essay "Black Men in Public Space"... and I would absolutely bungle it.

Staples' essay was published in 1986, but he draws from personal experiences with stereotypes and racism in mid-1970s Chicago. An insomniac who frequently took late-night strolls, Staples found that he could "alter public space in ugly ways" (p. 19). He became "familiar with the language of fear" and accustomed to the thud of door locks, the clenching of purses, and the hostility of strangers who stereotyped him as a mugger. One woman even ran away from him while screaming. While my assignment focused more on Staples' response to these strangers – whistling Vivaldi's *Four Seasons* to seem less threatening – we had many discussions about stereotypes in general, particularly whether the types of racism experienced by Staples was still a problem. The class, with my tacit endorsement, concluded that it was no longer a major problem, and if it was, it only happened in places like the American South. I cannot recall, but I suspect that the students came to this conclusion because of something I said. I can't imagine what some of my students of color – those who had experienced these types of stereotypes in the 2010s – were thinking as I espoused these beliefs. I imagine my African American students were dumbfounded by me. However, my point is that we make mistakes as educators, and while we can't let ourselves off the hook for possibly causing trauma in our classrooms, we can learn from these mistakes. In fact, we must. And in many ways, this book is documentation of my journey from that ill-fated semester to now. And, again, to be clear, I am still learning!

Finally, nationwide student success data bears out the focus on race. In 2016, the NCES reported that the 6-year graduation rates for African American, Latinx, Pacific Islander, and Indigenous students were much lower than their Asian American and white peers. African American and Indigenous students, for example, had a 6-year graduation rate of just 41% as compared to Asian Americans (71%) and whites (63%). Latinx students and Pacific Islander students, meanwhile, had graduation rates of 53% and 50%, respectively. Unfortunately, graduation rates are a little more problematic for community colleges because many students are able to transfer to a four-year university without earning an Associate's degree and tracking students once they leave the community college system is fraught with obstacles and bureaucracy.

Nonetheless, it is certainly worth investigating community college completion data that illuminate racialized outcomes. From a broader perspective, when aggregated, less than 15% of students "complete" community college within two years. In fact, less than 30% of students even "complete" community college within four years (Kraemer, n.d.). Racialized patterns also emerge when we look closely at how many students complete a Bachelor's degree after leaving the community college system. Shapiro et al. (2018) tracked a fall 2012 cohort in order to determine the six-year completion rate of two-year college students. Of the entire cohort of 750,000 students, 27.9% of the students had completed their studies at the two-year college while only 8.1% of the students had completed their Bachelor's degrees within six years, 39.3% of the students in the study had either completed their Associate's degrees or transferred out, and sadly, only 14.6% were still enrolled in their "starting institution." Most surprising, however, was that 46.2% of the students were no longer enrolled in any institution. They had simply dropped out. When disaggregated, the numbers are even more concerning. Only 5.3% of the African American students and 6% of the Latinx students in the study had completed a Bachelor's degree within six years as compared to 14.9% for the Asian students and 10.5% for the white students. In fact, only 19% of the African American students and 25.8% of the Latinx students had completed community college and were either still enrolled in a four-year institution or had finished a terminal Associate's degree program (as opposed to 30.6% for Asian and 33.9% for white students). Unfortunately, the dropout rate between African American and Latinx students and their Asian and white peers is even more pronounced. Shapiro et al. found that a whopping 54.6% of African American students and 42.8% of Latinx students had stopped attending college altogether, which, when compared to Asian American students at 29.1% and whites at 39.1%, is extremely concerning. It is obvious that community colleges and other two-year colleges are not serving their Black and Brown students effectively.

Furthermore, African American and Latinx students have lower persistence rates – the percentage of students that re-enroll in college year after year – than their white and Asian American peers. According to the National Student Clearinghouse (2018), 74.1% of Asian American students and 67.6% of white students had a one-year persistence rate as opposed to 62.7% of Latinx and 56% of African American students. These are staggering inequities, and the logical question is why do so many Latinx and African American students simply stop attending community college? Again, it is worth noting that while four-year universities generally have higher persistence rates overall, these gaps are mirrored when disaggregated for race and ethnicity. For example, at the university level, Asian American and white students have persistence rates of 91.9% and 86.1%, respectively, while Latinx and African American students are at 81.3% and 79.7%, respectively. We can speculate as to why four-year universities are able to retain their students more effectively than community colleges, but I am more curious about the consistent gaps between Latinx and African American students and their white and Asian American counterparts, regardless of the type of institution. What is it about higher education that is creating these inequities at all levels?

Unfortunately, the above data suggest some sort of division between African American, Indigenous, Latinx, and Pacific Islander and their European American *and* Asian American classmates, as if the latter two are identical. This type of division in the data gives the impression that Asian American students are doing just fine in higher education, a consequence of what has become known as the "model minority" myth (Suzuki, 1977). One of the earliest allusions to the "model minority myth" was in William Petersen's January 9th, 1966 *New York Times* article "Success Story, Japanese-American Style." In this article, Petersen, a professor of sociology at the University of California at Berkeley, quite bluntly stated that Japanese Americans are:

a minority that has risen above even prejudiced criticism. By any criterion of good citizenship that we choose, the Japanese Americans are better than any other group in our society, including native-born whites. They have established this remarkable record, moreover, by their own almost totally unaided effort. Every attempt to hamper their progress resulted only in enhancing their determination to succeed. (p. 180)

Unfortunately, this statement is out of touch with the reality that Japanese Americans have and continue to experience racism, discrimination, nativism, and Ethnocentrism, the latter of which Petersen taps into: "The Japanese on the contrary, could climb over the highest barriers our racists were able to fashion in part because of their meaningful links with an alien culture. Pride in their heritage and shame for any reduction in its only partly legendary glory – these were sufficient to carry the group through its travail" (p. 191). This is a narrative that would eventually encompass Asian American ethnic groups, such as the Chinese and Indians, and it would eventually be blanketly applied to all peoples of Asian descent.

Conversely, the mythology of the "model minority" critiques this claim of exceptionalism. Suzuki observed that this myth came into prominence during the African American Civil Rights movement, indicating that this rise to prominence was more a reaction to the unrest in the African American community than anything grounded in objective reality. Furthermore, as Chang (1993) notes, "Asian Americans are portrayed as 'hardworking, intelligent, and successful.' This description represents a sharp break from past stereotypes of Asian as 'sneaky, obsequious, or inscrutable'... But, the dominant culture's belief in the 'model minority' allows it to justify ignoring the unique discrimination faced by Asian Americans" (pp. 1258–1259). Indeed, even today, proponents of the "model minority" argument still point to data that suggest that Asian Americans have higher educational attainment and higher incomes than European Americans. However, this data can be misleading because it buries the lived experiences of Asian American subgroups, such as the Vietnamese, Hmong, Cambodian, Pacific Islander, and many, many more who experience overwhelming poverty, overt discrimination, and lack of access to education and resources. Even the discourse around the most noticeably "successful" subgroups – Chinese, Japanese, and Indian Americans – tends to ignore the fact that members of these ethnic groups also experience a great deal of poverty, racism, and marginalization (just think about the hate crimes against Chinese Americans during the SARS-CoV-2 pandemic). This is not to say that our Asian American students are not brilliant – they are – but the above is a testament to how race and white supremacy can be politicized in order to denigrate one group and to pit people of color against one another. As a result, this book rejects the "model minority" argument and seeks to help community college educators create curriculum and classroom practices (e.g. pedagogy) that empower all students of color, no matter their ethnic background.

Furthermore, many educators like to highlight poverty, in a general sense, as the culprit for educational inequities. Take, for example, the recent *Washington Post* headline, "Achievement gaps in schools driven by poverty, study finds" or the *Edsource* article on the same study entitled "Poverty levels in schools key determinant of achievement gaps, not racial or ethnic composition, study finds" (Freedberg, 2019; Meckler, 2019). Displayed triumphantly, the article starts with the pronouncement that "High concentrations of poverty, not racial segregation, entirely account for the racial achievement gap in U.S. schools." Furthermore, both articles point to the study's conclusion that the "achievement gap" has less to do with the race of a student's classmates and more to do with the resources available to the school (reardon, Weathers, Fahle, Jang, & Kalogrides, 2019). However, this isn't a groundbreaking finding for the educational community, as Kozol's (1992) seminal book, *Savage Inequalities*, had already demonstrated that poverty and a lack of investment in public schools were eviscerating the upward mobility of families of color (reardon et al. just provided expansive quantitative proof). Antiracist and equity-minded educators have always known that the problem isn't with the students or their classmates – it's with the institutions, from the politicians who have defunded public education and the de facto segregation practices that have resulted in less funded "majority-minority" schools and well-funded, suburban, majority-white schools.

These newspapers' headlines and our collective fetishizing of poverty have several negative implications for discussions of race and equity. First, these types of arguments allow policymakers and educators to focus solely on socioeconomics while simultaneously ignoring the racist origins of these economic inequalities. In other words, the focus on income and wealth obscures the fact that poverty exists in communities of color because of systemic racism. As Te-Nehisi Coates (2015) described, these impoverished, segregated neighborhoods are the intentional consequence of national policy. Second, this sole focus on poverty reinforces the racist notions that families of color are experiencing educational inequities because of their inability to climb out of poverty. If the neighborhoods and schools are so bad, they should just leave, right? This, again, ignores the intentionality of low-income communities that are the result of white flight, redlining by banks, racist realty practices, and governmental housing policy. And third, it ignores the reality of students of color in wealthier schools (or wealthy students of color in general) who are still struggling in their schools due to microaggressions, racism, and other identity-based barriers. To the credit of reardon and his associates, they do tackle the larger social forces that create these educational disparities: "If minority students are disproportionately concentrated in poorer school districts, their schools will have fewer resources" (p. 8). However, the reardon study doesn't address why students of color are "concentrated in poorer school districts" or why racialized testing gaps exist between Black and white students in wealthier schools, especially when the students come from similar economic backgrounds.

At this point, it is worth asking who this book is for. The title explicitly refers to "white educators," but it is worth unpacking this a bit, especially as it relates to white men versus white women. For example, white men, as a group, have benefitted most from this country's legacy of oppression. One needs to look no further than membership of the country's wealthiest citizens. And in my experience as a faculty leader, it is usually white men who have resisted conversations about race and equity the most. This book is also derived from my experience as a white, male community college educator who has undergone many of the struggles and learning that I describe in it. It is my hope that this book will help my colleagues across the country undergo similar journeys.

However, white men are not the only people who have benefitted from this legacy. While acknowledging that women are paid 82% of what men are, I want to also emphasize that white women have benefitted socially and economically from the discrimination and oppression of people of color as well. As bell hooks (2015) recounted, the women's rights movements for white and black women have had a tumultuous history dating all the way back to Sojourner Truth's famous 1851 "Ain't I a Woman" speech, which was given before a hostile crowd of white women in Indiana (pp. 159–160). As hooks bluntly stated, the women's rights movement has historically "barred [black women] from full participation in the movement. Furthermore, it served as a grave reminder that racism had to be eliminated before black women could be recognized as having an equal voice with white women on the issue of women's rights" (p. 161). In the decades that would follow, black women would find that the agenda for the white women's rights movement would differ significantly from the needs of black women: "We were disappointed and disillusioned when we discovered that white women in the movement had little knowledge or concern for the problems of lower class and poor women or the particular problems of non-white women from all classes" (p. 188). In part, this chasm was a product of two goals: for white women, the ultimate goal of the women's rights movement was economic equality in which, by and large, white women who were not represented in the workforce sought the equal education that would lead to gainful and equal employment in the workplace; on the other hand, black women, who were already represented in the workplace, fought against sexism in the Black community and racism in society, writ large. As Audre Lorde (1984) writes, Black women, particularly mothers, experience the intersection of their race and gender "in the supermarket, in the classroom, in the elevator, in the clinic and the schoolyard, from the plumber, the baker, the saleswoman, the bus driver, the bank teller, the waitress who does not serve us" (p. 119). In other words, hooks and Lorde articulate how the mainstream women's rights movement has traditionally failed to understand the unique needs of black women. It is with this understanding that I ask my female readers to resist equating gender and racial oppression and to instead understand that the experiences of women of color are vastly different than the needs of white women (Crenshaw, 1989).

b. Racism: Defined

The concept of race is difficult to grapple with for people of all ethno-racial backgrounds. However, it is particularly difficult for people of Anglo-European background precisely because most of us do not see ourselves as "raced" people. We are simply American, Californian, Texan, Southern, or another geo-political designation. We simply "are." This is a problematic existence, especially when we insist on assigning race to others. We see people as African American, Asian American, and so on, and many of us are perplexed when people of color try to "hyphenate" us as European-American. We become the only people who can reject our racial labels and ethnic identities in favor of a national one. Meanwhile, others subscribe to a "colorblind" ideology – some of us don't "see race." As I will discuss later in the book, this ideology can come from a well-intentioned place, yet it is important to understand that we live in a racialized society wherein people of color experience higher levels of poverty, greater health disparities, and starker educational inequity. Whether we want to acknowledge it or not, as Cornel West (1994) remarks, "race matters."

As a result, we need to understand race and racism conceptually and ideologically as both a system of privilege (Tatum, 1997) and as a system of oppression (Leonardo, 2009). Before delving into the nuances of each system, I'd like to preface this section by acknowledging that, in economic terms, many low-income whites may not feel "privileged" just as not all white folks are "oppressive." It is important to understand that we are talking about systems when we speak of racism from a socio-political perspective. As a whole group, whites enjoy numerous privileges despite their economic standing (McIntosh, 1989). Similarly, in aggregate, laws, traditions, and norms have been created that not only privilege white people but also actively harm people of color, and we need not be active supporters of these structures in order to benefit from them, making us, unfortunately, participants in the oppression of people of color. No matter our situations or beliefs, these structures are ecosystems that have taken on a life of their own. With that being said, let's look at each system in more detail.

Racism as a system of advantage

In her pivotal book on race in the education, Beverly Tatum (1997/2017) goes to lengths to differentiate racism from prejudice. In describing the latter, Tatum writes, "*Prejudice* is a preconceived judgment or opinion, based on limited information," which is formed "in an environment in which we are bombarded with stereotypical images in the media, are frequently exposed to the ethnic jokes of friends and family members, and are rarely informed of the accomplishments of oppressed groups" (p. 85, 86, emphasis in original). In other words, prejudice is simply a dislike of people based on a preponderance of stereotypes and a lack of information about their group membership. I'd also like to add that prejudice goes beyond race to include dislike and discrimination of women, religious minorities, members of the LGBTQ+ community, and other traditionally marginalized groups. And as Tatum affirms, anyone, regardless of their group membership, can be prejudicial – a Latina can hold prejudices about gay men, a gay man can hold prejudices about people with disabilities, a man with a disability can hold prejudices about women, and so on.

Racism, on the other hand, is a system that privileges people who identify or are labeled as white. Building on David Wellman's definition of racism as "a system of advantage based on race," Tatum argues that "Racism cannot be fully explained as an expression of prejudice alone" (p. 87). Instead, racism is "a system involving cultural messages and institutional policies and practices as well as the beliefs and actions of individuals... this system clearly operates to the advantage of Whites and to the disadvantage of people of color" (p. 87, emphasis in original). In defining racism in this way, Tatum is able to critique the notion that an important component of racism is the wielding of some great power over people of color (which I will talk about in the next section). For example, Tatum utilizes the example of housing discrimination in which a person of color is denied an apartment by a discriminatory landlord. This act of discrimination makes this apartment available to a white applicant, who is "knowingly or unknowingly, the beneficiary of racism, a system of advantage based on race" (pp. 88–89). In this way, many of the advantages enjoyed by white people are the direct result of the quotidian withholding of resources to people of color, often without our knowledge. This can come in the form of educational funding for predominantly white schools, better hospitals and clinics in predominantly white neighborhoods, lower interest rates on home and car loans, and a many other racially acquired perks.

Racism as a system of racial oppression

Leonardo (2009) expands Tatum's definition of racism as a system of privilege to include the maintenance of a "system of racial oppression" (p. 54). This system is centuries old with a foundation that includes the legacy of chattel slavery, Jim Crow, internment camps, colonialism, resettlement, mass incarceration, and other forms of oppression, and it is upheld through the perpetuation of racist beliefs. For Leonardo, racism as a system of racial oppression highlights "a general institutional arrangement created between whites and people of color" (p. 19). Furthermore, like Tatum, Leonardo notes that racism goes beyond prejudice and racial beliefs, noting that in surveys, whites continually see themselves as progressive in their views of race, including in the years before the Civil Rights movements. He argues, "defining racism as fundamentally a problem of attitude and prejudice fails to account for the material consequences of institutional racism, behaviors that produce unequal outcomes despite the transformation of racial attitudes, and the creation of policies" (p. 132). In other words, these racial attitudes are simply one component of this system of racism; racial oppression is embedded in the very fabric of our institutions, including our schools, colleges, and universities.

However, Leonardo differs from Tatum in one major way – who can be racist. In critiquing Tatum's definition, Leonardo notes that her paradigm "leaves underdeveloped or unexplained the responsibility and accountability of people of color who do not help the cause of racial emancipation, or worse, perpetuate racist relations" (p. 54). For Leonardo, anyone, regardless of skin color, can participate in and uphold racist attitudes and thus the system of racism. In making this assertion, Leonardo asserts that "racist discourses maintain a certain autonomy from the subjects who utter them" (p. 55). Said another way, racist attitudes are racist attitudes no matter the person who holds them. Nonetheless, I depart with Leonardo in his argument of who can be "racist." Leonardo, for example, suggests that any person who holds racist beliefs and promulgates racist actions perpetuates this system of racial oppression: "it is... possible to say that the *actions* of people of color are racist when they participate in the maintenance of a racist system" (p. 54, emphasis in original). To be clear, Leonardo does not label these individuals as racist or white supremacists; however, there is a certain degree of wordsmithing in this argument that disregards the power dynamic that characterizes this racial hierarchy. As a group and systematically, whites wield the power to oppress people of color economically and socially. People of color, no matter how organized, simply do not have the power to oppress whites as a whole or other people of color.

Furthermore, I contend that because those in power, from the political sphere to the country's commerce and industry, are generally white men, this system of oppression is meant only to benefit them. It has been this way for centuries. People of color simply cannot benefit from this system wholesale, so even if large numbers of individual persons of color are able to access the country's vast wealth, they become a small minority within their racial/ethnic group. Take Oprah Winfrey or Michael Jordan, for instance. They are two of the wealthiest Americans, regardless of race (Oprah is ranked by Forbes as the 319th richest American). Even with this vast wealth and influence, they wouldn't be able to eradicate the stranglehold white folks have over the wealth and power in this country, even if they banded together with the richest African Americans in the country (or with the richest people of color in the country). Regardless of Winfrey's and Jordan's financial situation, the vast majority of the African American community still lacks access to this wealth. In fact, the top 400 richest Americans are a mishmash of bankers, hedge fund managers, real estate moguls, and owners of the country's media outlets, retailers, and sports teams, and they are almost exclusively white.

To demonstrate my point further, I'd like to propose a scenario that demonstrates this racialized power hierarchy. Imagine for a moment that racism, as a system of oppression, is upheld by the racist beliefs of all people, no matter their race. This system is upheld equally by the racism that many whites have for people of color and that many people of color have for each other (e.g. anti-Blackness held by an Asian American). Now imagine that by some wave of the wand, we were able to eliminate all the prejudices that people of color have against other people of color. In other words, imagine that people of color were no longer able to have denigrating or prejudicial beliefs about others. Would this suddenly eliminate racism as a system of oppression? Would this new paradigm lead to a world in which racism and oppression no longer existed? I tend to think it would not. Every person of color in the country could instantly stop holding prejudicial beliefs about other people of color and the racialized social and economic hierarchy of the country would still exist because the resources, media, wealth, and politics would still be controlled by the white elite. Instead, it will take the eradication of racism in the white community to eliminate the racial hierarchy in this country.

Similarly, those who argue that people of color can be racist might point to a powerful person like Ben Carson, the 17th U.S. Secretary of Housing and Urban Development. Carson is an African American surgeon who was appointed to his secretary position by Donald Trump in 2017, and in this position, Carson had the power to negatively impact low-income urban residents, which includes many people of color. A literal interpretation of the above definition would make Ben Carson a racist when he implements policies that intentionally impact people of color. However, it is important to question how much power Ben Carson truly has as the HUD secretary. Undoubtedly, any racist policy that Ben Carson enacts would be under the umbrella of Trump's broader housing agenda, and as a result, Carson's power is derived from the power of the presidency. If Carson suddenly woke up as a social justice advocate and wanted to make changes at HUD that benefitted people of color, he would surely be ousted by President Trump, which begs the question, how much power does Ben Carson truly have? Furthermore, even when occupying the most powerful position in the world, President Barack Obama did not have complete power; he was continually hamstrung by a Congress, including members of his own party, that blocked many of his appointments and legislative agendas. So even if President Obama had wanted to, hypothetically, enact racist (or antiracist) policies, it would only have been at the pleasure of the House of Representatives and the Senate, which are dominated by white men (the latter chamber had even successfully blocked Obama's constitutional right to appoint to the Supreme Court in 2016).

This is not to say that Leonardo is letting people of color "off the hook." In fact, he notes, "This does not suddenly put people of color on par with white subjects because Euro-white atrocities toward the other is more comprehensive, far-reaching, and unparalleled... Also, attention to racist acts as opposed to racist people should not be confused as saying that all racists are the same" (pp. 54–55). Furthermore, Leonardo argues that high-profile people of color, such as Snoop Doggy Dogg or popular radio DJs, can just as easily spread racist beliefs through their spheres of influence. He notes, "Millions of students the Los Angeles basin inhale these negative messages as they do the smog in the air" (p. 55). In this instance, it may help to understand how racist beliefs are one pillar of this country's racialized institutions and how they differ from racist power.

Using a historical context, Ibram X. Kendi (2016), in his groundbreaking book *Stamped from the Beginning*, describes the centuries long history of racism, arguing that racism is a system that both benefits whites and oppresses people of color. Unlike Tatum, Kendi sees racism maintained through the power wielded by the richest, most politically connected people in the country (who are predominantly white men). Kendi remembers, "I was taught the popular folktale of racism: that ignorant and hateful people had produced racist ideas, and that these racist people had instituted racist policies. But when I learned of the motives behind the production of many of America's most influentially racist ideas, it became quite obvious that this folktale, though sensible, was not based on a firm footing of historical evidence" (p. 9). For Kendi, then, racial discrimination is the father, not the son, of hatred: "racial discrimination led to racist ideas which led to ignorance and hate." This racial discrimination, according to Kendi, is in the service of economic, social, and political gains, and over the centuries, this racial hierarchy has necessitated an entire system of racist beliefs as its foundation. In other words, it is "self-interest" that necessitated racist ideas and policies: "self-interest leads to racist policies, which lead to racist ideas leading to all the ignorance and hate. Racist policies were created out of self-interest... Power cannot be persuaded away from its self-interest. Power cannot be educated away from its self-interest. Those who have the power to abolish racial discrimination have not done so thus far, and they will never be persuaded or educated to do so as long as racism benefits them in some way" (p. 506, 508). Again, we need to consider who wields this power; as argued above, it is the rich, white men who control the nation's media, enterprises, communication systems, and political power.

More importantly, Kendi describes how, historically, racist beliefs have maintained systems of racial oppression. As he writes, "Racism is a marriage of racist policies and racist ideas that produces and normalizes racial inequities" (p. 18). In other words, Kendi brings together racism as a system of power and oppression with racist ideas and beliefs. While Kendi argues that individuals can perpetuate both – enacting racist policies and/or holding racist beliefs – I would again argue that racism as a system of oppression is maintained through the power that whites hold over people of color, whether it is in an institutional role (e.g. president of a college, the CEO of a corporation, a U.S. senator, etc.) or as an individual (e.g. calling the police on black park-goers or birdwatchers, discriminating against a student or colleague of color, not patronizing a black-owned restaurant, etc.).

As Derman-Sparks and Brunson Phillips (1997) write, "racism [is] an institutionalized system of economic, political, social, and cultural relations that ensures that one racial group has and maintains power and privilege over all others in all aspects of life" (p. 2). In the example above, Snoop Dogg and the radio DJ may promote racist ideas through their music, but at the end of the day, he is not a racist because he does not possess the power to end or maintain racism as an oppressive system nor does he have the ability to end the privileges that white people enjoy due to their skin color. In fact, it should be pointed out that the real power lies with the media moguls that control the airwaves, the radio stations, and the record labels. Even more succinctly, Yosso (2006) defines racism in the following ways: "(1) a false belief in White supremacy that handicaps society, (2) a system that upholds Whites as superior to all other groups, and (3) the structural subordination of multiple racial and ethnic groups" (p. 5).

It is important for community college educators to understand these dynamics for several reasons. Most importantly, we need to understand how we fit into the power structure of racism. At the microlevel, we may ask how we negatively impact students of color in our classrooms? Do our assumptions about them affect how we grade their academic work? Do we feel threatened by students of color, particularly men? As faculty, we also wield institutional powers, from the department curriculum to institutional policies on academic and professional matters. At the macrolevel, we may ask ourselves how we perpetuate racism through the curriculum approval process, through course placement tests, through discipline hearings, and through other policies and procedures enacted through faculty governance committees, departments, and programs. Many of these curricular and pedagogical considerations will be covered later in the book. For strategies on enacting educational equity at the institutional level, see Sims, Taylor-Mendoza, Hotep, Wallace, and Conaway (2020).

c. Practicum: The Language of Equity

In this book, I attempt to bring together theory and practice in a way that gives you, the reader, tools that can be used in your classroom along with the theoretical origins and foundations for these tools. Throughout the book, you will find "Practicum" sections, which will highlight some of the tools and practices that you can integrate into your pedagogy and curriculum immediately. You can also find a list of these tools in Appendix A with short summaries and where they are located in the book. The first Practicum of the book deals with language and identity.

Two of the simplest steps that community college educators can take in creating a more equitable classroom is first, to understand what terms their students prefer for their group identities and, second, to learn how to say their students' names correctly. The latter is simple – just ask the students how to say their names correctly. Adopting ignorance and mispronouncing a student's name for an entire term is simply not acceptable. However, the former step is a little more complicated, as regional, generational, and political preferences may dictate how students identify with their communities. For example, the term Chicano was in vogue at the turn of the century, but many young students of Latin American descent often do not identify as such. Instead, young people of Latin American descent may prefer Latino or Latina or, more recently, Latinx (which rejects the gendering of their identity). Some students may still prefer Chicano, Chicana, or Chicanx while others may even go by Hispanic. It is the same for other communities of color – some students prefer African American while others prefer Black; some students prefer Indigenous over Native American; some students still identify as queer while others gravitate towards gay or lesbian. The point is that these terms are fluid and when we are in doubt, we should simply ask (and you should never tell a student how they should identify).

For this book, I have adopted some of the more recent group identifiers, and in some cases I may switch between them. Following Beverly Tatum's (1997/ 2017) lead, I use "people of color" to aggregate groups of people who are the targets of racism and white supremacy – people of African, Asian, and Latin American descent and indigenous people (note: even the term "Asian" is problematic considering that it is supposed to encompass people not only from East Asia, but also the people of the subcontinent of India, Southeast Asia, Central and Western Asia, and the Pacific Islands). When identifying specific groups of people of color, I use the following terms (which have been bulleted for easy reference):

- **Asian American**: I recognize the problems with this term; however, there is yet a term that is inclusive of the entire continent that recognizes the rich diversity of cultures.
- **Pacific Islander**: More and more studies are disaggregating this group from Asian American to highlight the inequities that exist for Pacific Islander students.
- I interchange **African American and Black**, usually depending on the research being cited. I also tend to prefer Black because it is, as Tatum (1997/ 2017) points out, "more inclusive than African American because there are Black people in the United States who are not African American – Afro-Caribbeans, for example – yet are targeted by racism and are identified

as Black" (p. 95). I have also learned this as an instructor in the Umoja Community, a learning community for students of the African diaspora, where I had not only African American students, but also Jamaican, Congolese, Nigerian, and a host of other African and Caribbean students. However, I also recognize that the Black-White dichotomy is steeped in the legacy of our American racial caste system wherein, as Sims (2018) writes, "whiteness [is] positioned as the thesis, and, Blackness, seemingly forever positioned as its antithesis" (p. 17). In other words, the concept of Blackness was constructed in opposition to the "norm" – whiteness – a legacy that was "overt, violent, and ubiquitous." Nonetheless, as an educator who has worked with African students and students of the African diaspora, Black seems most appropriate and inclusive.

- **Latinx**: As mentioned above, the term Latinx has many advantages. First, it rejects the more colonial terms, such as Hispanic, which, to many in this community, is considered a holdover from the Spanish colonization of the Americas. Second, many students identify more with Latinx than the increasingly dated term Chicano/a. Third, the root "Latin" is more inclusive of the rich diversity of North, Central, and South America – it includes everyone from those of Mexican descent all the way down to the residents of Cape Horn. Finally, the "x" rejects the gendering of the term, making it inclusive of men, women, and non-binary individuals.

- **Indigenous**: First things first, people of Native American heritage are not Indians. Indians are people who live in the subcontinent of India. Furthermore, while Native American is much more accurate than Indian, it can still be exclusive. Native American describes people who are indigenous to North, Central, and South America. However, it does exclude indigenous peoples of other continents (like the Aboriginals of Australia).

- **European American and white**: For me, this is the hardest to define. At the most fundamental level, whiteness has been constructed, as mentioned above, in opposition to blackness, which means a "white" identity is steeped in a history of racism, oppression, and violence. This is why there is a movement, albeit academic, to "eliminate whiteness" (Ignatiev & Garvey, 1996; Roediger, 1994). As a result, "European American" becomes a more relevant label (yet even this term excludes the people of Russia, the former Soviet countries, and certain regions of the Middle East who are labeled at "white" in America). Furthermore, as a writer, I must balance the clarity of my writing – constant use of European American can effectively stifle clarity – and reader expectations (not to mention, shying away from the label "white" implicitly means shying away from race and the violence that whiteness has inflicted, which is a focus of this book). The term "white," unfortunately, is the most common label that folks of European (and Russian, citizens of former Russian territories, and Jewish people) descent identify with. All this is to say that I want my readers to understand the complexity and baggage of whiteness; I will, however, use the terms interchangeably. Finally, I do not use the word "Caucasian" to refer to people of European descent; this term is very limiting, as it refers only to people who reside in the very small land mass between the Black and Caspian seas (in the Caucasus Mountains) and has a problematic history in anti-Black eugenics.

Furthermore, I would like to clarify some important terms that I have used in this introduction and that I will continue to use throughout this book:

- **Minoritized**: We often refer to people of color or other people who make up less than the majority of a particular subset of the population as "minorities." While mathematically correct at a national level, this term paints a distorted picture of a very different reality. Let us take African Americans as an example. At 12% of the total U.S. population, African Americans are very much in the minority. At my campus, they make up an even smaller percentage (3%). However, if one was to take a stroll through the campus of Howard University, one would notice that African Americans make up the vast majority of the student body. When I visit the dedicated space on my campus for the Umoja Community, Black students are in the majority (and when they aren't, students of color are in the majority). In other words, there are instances where African American students are in the minority, such as predominantly white institutions, and then there are instances where they are in the majority, such as traditionally Black churches and Historically Black Colleges and Universities. These students are forced into a minority status based on local demographics, traditions, discrimination, and systemic racism; they are "minoritized." As Harper (2015) writes, minoritized is preferable to minority because it "signif[ies] the social construction of underrepresentation and subordination in US social institutions, including colleges and universities" (p. 670). He continues:

Persons are not born into a minority status, nor are they minoritized in every social milieu (e.g., their families, racially homogenous friendship groups, or placed of religious worship). Instead, they are rendered minorities in particular situations and institutional environments that sustain an overrepresentation of Whiteness.

The term "minority" becomes even more problematic when referring to the Latinx community, which is the fastest-growing demographic in the country and already the largest ethno-racial group in many parts of the country (including the state of California and soon the state of Texas).

- **Hyper-marginalized**: Wacquant (2007), in his comparative sociological study of global urban areas, coined the term "hyper-ghettoes," which are characterized by their "extreme marginality" (p. 4). More specifically, Wacquant writes, "the American hyperghetto is an ethnically and socially *homogenous* universe characterized by low organizational density and weak penetration by the state in its social components and, by way of consequence, extreme levels of physical and social insecurity" (p. 5, emphasis in original). In other words, contemporary American hyper-ghettoes are intentional, or "the product of a novel *political* articulation of racial cleavage, class inequality and urban space in both dominant discourse and objective reality" (p. 47, emphasis in original). Hyper-ghettoes tend to be permanent, economically and politically contrived spaces wherein the inhabitants tend to be comprised overwhelmingly of a single (or very few) ethno-racial identity.

Moreover, the term "marginalized" has come into vogue recently in higher education, primarily to describe students of color who are relegated to the periphery of the academy through various mechanisms of discrimination. However, racial marginalization doesn't tell the whole story. More specifically, people of color, statistically, are more likely to live in impoverished neighborhoods, which adds an additional layer of complexity as they pursue higher education (Sims, 2018). Hyper-marginalization, then, is an offshoot of Wacquants "hyper-ghettoes," describing the intersectional obstacles students of color face due to poverty and its concomitant gaps in access to technology, quality housing, food, and healthcare. Said another way, hyper-marginalization describes the barriers students face as a result of their ethno-racial identity and as a result of their socio-economic realities. For example, the community college creates academic hyper-ghettoes when remedial courses are comprised predominantly of students of color, meaning that testing policies have intentionally segregated, or hyper-marginalized, students of color in courses that are separated (sometimes spatially) from mainstream course-work and are, in many respects, inescapable tracks characterized by the same types of fear and hopelessness as Wacquant's hyper-ghettoes.

- **Racialized**: As mentioned earlier, race has no scientific basis, yet race is very much real in a sociological sense. People in the United States (and beyond) have instead been "raced," or assigned a racial identity depending on the needs and climate of the dominant society. Just as one example, certain European ethnicities – like Italians, Poles, and the Irish – were not considered "white" until well into the 20th century. In other words, the assignment of race has always been one of power. As Magee (2019) notes, "Racism depends on the social construction of what sociologists have come to refer to as 'racialized' bodies, which is to say, the idea and prac-tice of people being assigned racial labels that, and we have been trained to understand, sit in a relative hierarchy of worth in relationship to other racial labels" (p. 13). In the end, the term "racialized" recognizes that race is not a biological fact, but is instead real in the sense that it is socially constructed and assigned.

d. Grassroots Equity and the Problem with National Initiatives

This book, in many ways, is a referendum on the overreliance on national and statewide initiatives that educational leaders and administrators believe will close "equity gaps." However, national initiatives are never going to be the cure all for a number of reasons, but chief amongst them is that every community college campus is different. They have different student and faculty demographics, mis-sions, programs, histories, and academic cultures. Too often, faculty and admin-istrators (in particular) get caught up in the latest educational fads, believing that the best way to respond to issues of equity and social justice is to "copy and paste" these frameworks. However, we seldom realize that these initiatives are simply providing recipes; Guided Pathways works really well for the community colleges included in Bailey's, Jaggar's, and Jenkins' study and acceleration of pre-transfer math and English has produced wonders at the Community College of Baltimore County, for instance. State and federal governments are spending billions of dollars to close educational opportunity gaps, yet this money rarely eliminates racialized educational inequities.

To look at one such initiative more closely, the "acceleration" movement has done little to improve success rates in English and math "remediation" across the board, and some states' mandates to eliminate pre-transfer English and math have been ill-conceived and overly optimistic. In my home state of California, for example, the legislature passed Assembly Bill 705 (Irwin, 2017), which essentially eliminated all pre-transfer coursework in English and mathematics, with the ultimate goal of increasing what advocates have dubbed "throughput." The bill was heavily lobbied for by myriad educational and special interest groups, including a number of California community colleges, the Campaign for College Opportunity, and the California Acceleration Project. Advocates for AB705 insisted that these laws were necessary for expanding access to college-level coursework and improving student progression through academic programs. Many advocates went as far as calling acceleration an "equity issue."

Unfortunately, these organizations and colleges have used students of color, in particular, as propaganda for acceleration while taking little to no steps to ensure that students of color would succeed under these new frameworks. While individual colleges may implement professional development training to ensure English and math classrooms that are free from discrimination and racism, national organizations and state legislatures have not provided such professional development, in the former, or mandated training, in the latter. In fact, the aforementioned law AB705 neither requires training for faculty in equity-minded curriculum and pedagogical development nor does it provide funding for the colleges to do so if they so elected to. In other words, the California legislature has put many students of color, who were predominantly placed into pre-transfer level courses and tended to have lower success rates than their white peers, in the same exact inequitable classrooms with same exact inequitable professors but called it a transfer-level class. In other words, we haven't changed anything about the class except the course number and its articulation to four-year universities. And if racism exists in our college's classrooms and curricula, as I will contend in this book, then laws and mandates like AB705 will not work to eradicate this, and any uptick in student success can only be attributed to the mathematical shell game that proponents are calling "throughput."

As Cornel West (1994) pointedly remarked, "Race matters." Yet national community colleges initiatives by and large fail to acknowledge this important maxim. In interview after interview, AB705's legislative sponsor, Jacqui Irwin, opted for what amounts to a colorblind approach to acceleration, failing to mention students of color, students with disabilities, and low-income students, all of whom make up the majority of "remedial" students. Not even in an op-ed co-authored with the Chancellor of the California Community Colleges, Eloy Ortiz Oakley, were hyper-marginalized students mentioned (Irwin & Ortiz Oakley, 2018). And in publications where minoritized students are mentioned, the nuances of these students' experiences are ignored. Take the joint Campaign for College Opportunity and California Acceleration Project report, "Getting There: Are California Community College Maximizing Student Completion of Transfer-Level Math and English?" (2019), which offers an update on the state's implementation of AB705. The report does acknowledge that "students of color have been disproportionately classified as 'remedial'" but that pre-transfer level courses "open the door to implicit bias" (p. 12). This sentiment is naïve at best for two reasons: first, it assumes that implicit bias can only exist in pre-transfer level coursework, and while the report fears racialized tracking into pre-transfer level courses, it ultimately fails to acknowledge that implicit bias is the product of people, not courses; second, implicit bias, as will be discussed in Chapter 2, is only the tip of the iceberg – we need to address the roles of racism and other forms of hatred and how they manifest both in policy and teaching.

Moreover, the Guided Pathways movement has suffered from the same "color-blind" implementation, wherein students of color and other minoritized students are used as justification yet are left out of important conversations around implementation. Bailey, Jaggars, and Jenkins' (2015) *Redesigning America's Community Colleges* is the seminal text in the guided pathways movement. In their book, the authors argue that the Guided Pathways framework "is for all colleges that serve economically disadvantaged students and that are committed to supporting the success not only of those students but of all students from all backgrounds" (p. viii). Indeed, throughout the book, Bailey et al. mention "disadvantaged" and "underrepresented" students numerous times. However, the only specific group of students explicitly noted in the book is economically disadvantaged students, which ignores the lived experiences of hyper-marginalized students, like poor students of color, as well as economically advantaged students of color who are still subjugated to racialized structures of inequity in the community college. Finally, the authors never really address the very real (and historical) practice of "tracking." Bailey et al. write of the Guided Pathway framework that "New students who are undecided about a major must choose one of a limited number of exploratory or 'meta-majors' that expose them to educational and career options within broad fields" (p. 22). Undoubtedly, students will be placed in a meta-major after consulting with an academic advisor or counselor, yet the book doesn't account for the implicit bias or outright prejudice of some of these staff and faculty members in placing – or tracking – the students into low-wage career paths.

To be clear, I am not saying that these initiatives are not needed or that our institutions were better without them. Developmental education has been fundamentally broken and our colleges' labyrinthine program and transfer requirements have been major obstacles for students, particularly students of color. Community colleges need to fundamentally restructure how they support students, including the elimination of pre-transfer-level coursework. However, it is my contention that if colleges can incorporate acceleration and guided pathways while acknowledging the hidden racialized consequences of these initiatives and implementing them using a framework that emphasizes educational equity and social justice, they can ensure that all students can achieve their educational goals. As a result, it is up to local colleges and faculty to create "grassroots" trainings, workshops, curriculum modifications, and other initiatives to implement what the country's political and think-tank leaders have failed to do.

In other words, community colleges must "disrupt the status quo" (Sims et al., 2020). Indeed, as open-access institutions that serve predominantly minoritized and hyper-marginalized students, we are obligated to do so. As Sims et al. (2020) note, our students "need us to ask paradigm-shifting questions and to propose, develop, and implement innovative disruptions to pathologized educational practices and policies predicated on white supremacy, anti-Blackness, deficit model thinking, homophobia, misogyny, etc." (p. 1). It is the goal of this book to give readers the tools to create this disruption in their spheres of influence, particularly the classroom.

e. Overview of this Book

One of the most important questions to address in this introduction is "how is this book different from other books that discuss race, equity, and social justice?" This is a fair question, and before delving into the answer, I'd like to first share some influential texts in the intersecting realm of education and social justice. In 2016, for example, Chris Emdin released his wildly popular and important *For White Folks Who Teach in the Hood: And the Rest if Y'all Too*. "Wildly popular" is really an understatement. Emdin, in many ways, changed how educational texts speak to their audiences. One needs only to hop on Twitter to see how this book impacted teachers, especially those who identify as white. Under the hashtag, #HipHopEd, teachers from around the country would share how the nuanced, accessible pedagogical strategies in the book changed the way they taught their minoritized students, creating an online community that was unprecedented. Emdin's book is a must-read for all critical educators who strive for social justice.

Emdin (2016) coined the pedagogical framework of "reality pedagogy," which is "an approach to teaching and learning that has a primary goal of meeting each student on his or her own cultural and emotional turf. It focuses on making the local experiences of the student visible and creating contexts where there is a role reversal of sorts that positions the student as the expert in his or her own teaching and learning, and the teacher as the learner" (p. 27). In other words, Emdin is encouraging educators to create a curriculum that not only highlights the experiences and cultures of their students, but to make them the basis of the entire course. Furthermore, Emdin's book provides practical methodologies for all educators, but particularly those who are white and unfamiliar with hip-hop culture (Emdin's framework, as mentioned above, is described as Hip Hop Ed). However, while *For White Folks who Teach in the Hood* is applicable to all educators of all levels, it is primarily written for K-12 teachers. As a result, this book will cover reality pedagogy, and its offshoot critical reality pedagogy, in more detail in Chapter 6 in the context of the community college.

Just as important to the literature on race, whiteness, and equity was Gary R. Howard's *We Can't Teach What We Don't Know: White Teachers, Multiracial Schools.* Originally released in 1999, Howard's book is in its third edition, which was released the same year as Emdin's book. Howard's (2016) book, like Emdin's, is primarily written for white K-12 educators, and it highlights the importance of multicultural teaching practices and pedagogy. Furthermore, Howard also highlights the importance of the student experience and expertise: "It is essential in this inner work of multicultural growth that we listen carefully to the perceptions others have of us, particularly students" (p. 6). *We Can't Teach What We Don't Know* emphasizes the personal transformation of white educators as a means of creating a truly inclusive, multicultural learning environment for all students, particularly students of color. Like Emdin, Howard's book is an important foundational text vis-à-vis K-12 pedagogy and curriculum, and I strive to fit Howard's framework into the context of the community college.

The fact is that there exists very little literature on race, equity, and social justice in community colleges, which is ironic considering most community colleges were originally created to serve as open-access institutions for those left behind by the universities. It is also extremely alarming considering community colleges serve the majority of minoritized and hyper-marginalized students in higher education. Two important exceptions are *Teaching Men of Color in the*

Community College by J. Luke Wood, Frank Harris III, and Khalid White (2015) and *Advancing Black Male Student Success from Pre-school through Ph.D.*, which is edited by Shaun R. Harper and J. Luke Wood (2016). In the case of the former, Wood et al. provide important pedagogical considerations and practices for supporting the personal and academic success of men of color. More specifically, this guidebook offers practical tips for all members of the community college faculty to build authentic relationships with male students of color as well as curricular and pedagogical best practices. Like Wood et al., this book strives to aid all faculty, particularly those of us who are labeled as white, in developing teaching and learning environments that are inclusive and affirming. However, as I will discuss later in this introduction, a great deal of *this* book is dedicated to what Magee (2019) calls the "inner work of racial justice," meaning that I will focus as much on the readers' privileges and racial identities as on curriculum and pedagogy. Furthermore, this book will emphasize the importance of developing a foundational understanding of educational equity and social justice, two terms that have recently come into vogue in the community college space yet are consistently misunderstood or "watered down."

In the latter book, Harper and Wood (2016) have compiled a series of essays that focus on the educational pipeline of Black males from pre-school to a terminal degree. Their goal is to disrupt the "social and educational hopelessness" of Black males and to "focus... on advancing their success through educational attainment" (p. xi). Because the book traces the entire educational pipeline of Black boys and men, it dedicates a single chapter to community colleges. In Chapter 5: "Black Male Collegians in Community Colleges," J. Luke Wood, Edward Bush, Terence Hicks, and Hassiem A. Kambui highlight the vast inequities that exist between Black male students and their white peers, and they challenge readers to shift their paradigm from one in which students have "*the right to fail*" to a "*right-to-succeed* philosophy" (pp. 78–79). This chapter emphasizes the importance of serving the needs of the whole student, including improving campus climate as well as the students' academic, societal, psychological, and environmental factors, and unlike the previous books, this chapter explores strategies for supporting Black male community colleges students outside the classroom, including in student services, faculty professional development, and hiring.

Ultimately, there are few books about social justice in community colleges written *by* community college educators. However, this is starting to change. Recently, Sims et al. (2020) published *Minding the Obligation Gap in Community Colleges and Beyond: Theory and Practice in Achieving Educational Equity*, which is intended for community college leaders, from the president to the faculty. This groundbreaking text offers readers practical strategies, along with their concomitant theories, to create equitable academic programs, to cultivate an equity-centered professional development program, to promote social justice through shared governance, and to reorient the college's executive teams to an agenda of educational equity. Like Sims et al. was a leader in providing community college *leaders* with a guidebook written by community college educators, this book strives to fill the gap in the literature vis-à-vis community college curriculum and pedagogy as experienced and written by a community college professor. In other words, what makes this book unique from those listed above is that I am "in the trenches," so to speak (though I do need to recognize my community college colleagues, Dr. Edward Bush and Dr. Khalid White). I am not observing from afar; I am in it.

The next logical question is "why am I qualified to write this book?" The fact is that I may not be. I am still fairly early in my career (I've been teaching for a decade), I don't have a PhD (in fact, my Master's isn't even in education; it's in English), and I don't share the lived and cultural experiences of the students whom I discuss in this book. However, I do have a few things going for me that I believe give me at least a distinct perspective on this topic and a modicum of authority. First, as I mentioned earlier in this introduction, my childhood has provided me with a very unique lens through which to see the issues of race, racism, and social justice in higher education. This certainly doesn't necessarily make me an expert on these subjects or qualified to speak to them, but the fact is that race and whiteness have not been entirely invisible to me. As the son of a mixed-race couple, I have been acutely aware of how my parents are perceived in public spaces, and I have been keenly aware of my own whiteness in spaces where I am the only person who is labeled as white. This is to say that I was forced to get comfortable in my own skin early in my life, which gave me a head start when beginning my career as an educator in a multicultural, multiracial community college. I have, by and large, been able to avoid experiencing the discomfort of discussing race and injustice with students and colleagues.

Second, I have spent this decade of my career working with minoritized students, most prominently in a learning community called the Umoja Community, a statewide organization in California that strives to create educational opportunities for and to empower students of the African diaspora. The Umoja Community was founded in 2008 by a handful of primarily Black community college educators, and as of this writing, the Umoja Community has programs in approximately sixty California community colleges, one Washington community college, and one California university. The Umoja program at my institution – College of San Mateo – was started in 2013 by a group of faculty (including me), staff, and administrators. From the outset, I was part of the design, proposal, and implementation phases, and I would co-coordinate with my colleague, Dr. Frederick Gaines, who taught the ethnic studies component of the program (which he teaches to this day). In addition to coordinating the program, I would teach the English course in the program for three years. When we launched the program with the first cohort in 2014, I would be starting my second year on the tenure-track, providing me with the opportunity to fine-tune my pedagogy and curriculum while simultaneously participating in statewide Umoja trainings and activities. It was the perfect storm of professional and personal growth, and it forced me to become comfortable as a white man in a new contingency – a classroom wherein every one of my students was a person of color.

With that being said, I am standing on the shoulders of giants, and I would be remiss if I didn't recognize the scholars, teachers, and researchers who have influenced my work, and hence, this book. Too often, white scholars and activists write and speak of their scholarship and activism with no real acknowledgment of those who came before them (sometimes, to the point where white scholars and activists start to become, ironically, privileged over their colleagues of color in academic spheres). For the most part, nothing that I share in this book is new. In fact, scholars and activists of color have been talking about educational equity and social justice for decades, centuries even, long before the term came into vogue in higher education. As a result, I would like to acknowledge and thank the colleagues and scholars who have inspired me and to thank them for enlightening me, supporting me in some cases, and transforming my teaching. This group includes those who I have read and listened to: Carter G. Woodson, Gloria Ladson-Billings, Sylvia Hurtado, Laura Rendon, Mike Rose, W.E.B. DuBois, J. Luke Wood, Chris Emdin, Cornel West, Jeremiah Sims, Shaun Harper, Frank Harris, and Tim Wise. And, of course, there have been countless colleagues, mentors, and teachers who have mentored me, pushed me, and even checked me: Frederick Gaines, James Carranza, Jennifer Taylor-Mendoza, Jeremiah Sims, Lasana Hotep, Tabitha Conaway, Henry Villareal, Krystal Duncan, Tom DeWit, and Jon Kitamura.

f. The Organization of this Book

At the most fundamental level, this book is meant to help community college educators who are committed to creating equitable, nurturing learning environments for all their students, particularly students of color, and who may not know where or how to start. As a result, this book is divided into two parts. Because the inequitable outcomes we see in higher education are not a consequence of our students' abilities or motivation, the first part focuses instead on the educator. In what I can attest to be a difficult journey, Part I asks readers to look inwards and to understand their biases, their privileges, and, yes, even their racist beliefs. However, while this journey may seem both daunting and hopeless, Part I will also look at how educators can build, for a lack of a better word, a mindfulness practice that allows them to work within an antiracist framework. I hope that my readers find that even though this journey is indeed uncomfortable, it is immensely liberating. Part II, then, focuses on the learning environment and how equity-minded, antiracist educators can create a learning space that values and affirms all students through the course curriculum and classroom practices.

In Chapter 2: Looking in the Mirror, I will ask you, my reader, to look inward. Since my primary audience for this book is European American community college educators, both men and women, I will challenge you to understand your positionally vis-à-vis your minoritized students, especially students of color. More specifically, this chapter will argue that European American educators – those who are labeled white – cannot engage in the social justice work necessary to transform America's community colleges until they understand how the legacy of white supremacy and the domination of people of color have created co-existing systems of privilege and domination that benefit us white folks to the detriment of people of color. In other words, we must understand how this system works, how we benefit from it, and how our privileges oppress people of color, including students. In this chapter, I will start with a critique of colorblindness in education (and society writ large) and how this paradigm has given us license to blind ourselves to the realities of people of color, which has led to a society in which whiteness does not exist and privilege becomes the consequences of merit, both of which I will describe and critique. It is my hope that this chapter will not only help readers understand terms like colorblind racism, white privilege, and white supremacy, but, more importantly, will provide a lens through which white educators can recognize and critique our own privilege and will provide the tools necessary to identify and deconstruct white supremacy in their lives and classrooms. This is the inner work necessary for tackling the more practical aspects of pedagogy and curriculum in Part II.

As mentioned above, this is a topic that is very personal to me, and for the sake of transparency, I will acknowledge that I am still undergoing this process of transformation. In reality, this is a process that will likely span our entire careers, if not lifetimes. As a result, Chapter 3: Antiracism for Community College Educators provides readers with a heuristic for continually recognizing what I call "white supremacy creep," the subtle and unconscious re-investment in white supremacy and privilege that is the consequence of a socio-political and media environment that is perpetually normalizing whiteness and painting people of color and other minoritized people as abnormal and inferior. Building on Magee (2019), this heuristic utilizes the iterative practice that I have termed antiracist reflective praxis (ARP). Furthermore, this chapter will provide practical strategies discussing race, racism, and white supremacy both in the classroom and within institutional settings.

Part II of the book will take the reader beyond the self and in its first chapter will look at the "other side of racism." Chapter 4: Stories from the Other Side of Racism will de-centralize the white educator and, instead, throw a spotlight on both the brilliance and struggles of our students of color. First, this chapter will build on the previous chapter's discussion of white supremacy by framing the community college as a microcosm of a larger inequitable society. As a result, I will provide readers with a crash-course in Critical Race Theory, a critical framework borne from Critical Legal Studies that allows practitioners to identify, critique, and dismantle institutionalized racism and other forms oppression, with special attention paid to those theories that expose the reproduction of white supremacy in community colleges. At the most fundamental level, the goal of this chapter is to provide readers with the theoretical and practical tools, including operationalizing the terms "equity" and "social justice," to uncover and deconstruct oppressive structures within their classrooms.

Furthermore, utilizing Critical Race Theory's storytelling methodology, this chapter will draw insights from both interviews conducted with African American students at College of San Mateo and from similar stories in the field, and this chapter will operationalize many of the challenges students of color encounter in the community college with particular attention paid to micro- and macroaggressions, stereotype threat, and institutionalized Eurocentrism. In other words, this chapter seeks to illuminate for readers the typical college experience for students of color. More importantly, this chapter will provide readers with counterstories to the dominant narratives of "achievement gaps" and "cultures of failure" by highlighting the incredible successes of the aforementioned students despite the racialized barriers they experience.

Chapter 5: Taking it Back to the Classroom: Equity and Pedagogy shifts the reader's attention from the larger institutional issues of equity to the more intimate space of the classroom. A fundamental argument of this book is that national and state-level initiatives and legislation will not eradicate the crises our students of color (and other minoritized students) are experiencing in higher education. We cannot spend our way out of this. This chapter will take it back to the classroom, where educators have the most freedom and opportunity to enact equitable practices. This chapter will define the various approaches to working with minoritized students and spotlight Critical Reality Pedagogy (Sims, 2018) as a framework that best meets the needs of a diverse classroom. Furthermore, drawing on the previous chapter's discussion of the "obligation gap," this chapter will delineate educator's responsibilities outside the classroom vis-à-vis student support services. This chapter will end with a discussion of how European American educators can best facilitate discussions around race, gender, socioeconomics, politics, etc. in a way that invites participation from all students, both students of color and white students, since this work cannot be done without bringing in European-American students and educating them on the lived experiences of their peers and even on their own privilege.

Finally, Chapter 6: The People's Curriculum will look specifically at curriculum development. Using CRT as a foundation, this chapter will critique curricular decisions as a means of reproducing European epistemologies and white supremacy, and it will describe how educators can proactively integrate nondominant epistemologies into their curriculum without tokenizing these writers and thinkers. This chapter will also discuss multicultural education in detail, with a particular goal of correcting any misconceptions and misuses of this theoretical and practical framework.

The conclusion of this book will critique the popular identifier "white ally." As the conclusion will argue, this term has been overutilized and exploited, resulting in what has come to be known as "performative allyship." As a result, the conclusion will reject this performance, which does little to eradicate racism and white supremacy, and argue for antiracist actions and radical compassion. Ultimately, words may be powerful, but it is only through action that we can begin to create antiracist, socially just classrooms and campuses.

g. The Power to Disrupt

Community colleges are unique institutions. In fact, the United States is one of the only countries in the world that has such institutions, and while they were originally meant to serve primarily low-income white males, their social justice missions have expanded boundlessly to include people from all walks of life with the promise of open access and opportunity. They have unique student bodies, unique professional cultures, and different standards of pedagogy. And because community colleges serve the majority of students who have traditionally been excluded from higher education, particularly low-income students and students of color, we have an immense opportunity to disrupt the status quo (Sims et al., 2020). In other words, we can truly start to dismantle all forms of oppression not only at our own institutions, but in our American society, writ large.

This project, however, will require a great deal of personal and professional development, compassion for others and the self, and collaborations with colleagues and students. More specifically, we have to understand and honor our students' lives and cultural capital, which requires us to acknowledge both the explicit and hidden manifestations of racism in our institutions. The two educators on my flight had a fairly keen sense of the former manifestations. When they saw overt racism from our political leaders, they could identify it. However, they seemed to reject that racism existed outside the internment camps at the border and the Muslim ban, which is problematic for community college educators in particular. It is worth noting that these two individuals were likely very effective educators for all their students, including their students of color. However, as I will discuss in more detail in Chapter 4, it is very difficult for any educator to fully serve their minoritized students when they don't understand, or even reject, their students' lived experiences and how this country's legacy of oppression, discrimination, and violence has shaped those experiences. We all have a lot of work to do in understanding and deconstructing our participation in these legacies.

To be clear, the journey outlined in this is not purely altruistic. The legacy of racism has taken its toll not only on its victims, but also on its victimizers, which is the root of so much of the discomfort that white people feel when discussing race, racism, and oppression. As Tatum (1999) observes, "The power of his emotions and of mine reminded me again of how the legacy of racism has damaged all of us and why we all must work to dismantle it" (p. xi).

Furthermore, this type of work is impossible to do alone. We need partners to help us grow and to call us out when we slip up. As Derman-Sparks and Brunson Phillips (1997) note, "None of us can do anti-racism education work in isolation. It is too complex" (p. 6). In this vein, my book is not a deep dive into the intricacies of race, racism, and white supremacy. It is, instead, meant to be an introduction to the work of educational equity and the ultimate goal of justice. It is a small contribution to a conversation that is decades, if not centuries, old and to the ever-evolving fields of critical race studies and antiracist education.

Finally, as an English professor, I would like to make a quick note about gender pronouns. I have adopted the increasingly popular convention that singular subjects (e.g. "a student") are described using the gender-neutral pronoun "they." For example, I might write something like "A student said X in class, and then they Y." Although this is grammatically incorrect, it is more inclusive than using the grammatically correct nomenclature "he/she" (and it is slightly less awkward).

h. Chapter 1 Synopsis and Questions to Consider

Synopsis

Community college students are becoming more and more diverse while faculty remain predominantly white, which obligates us white educators to do undergo personal and professional growth in order to better serve our minoritized students. One area where white folks need to grow is in our understanding of race and racism, the latter of which is both a system of privilege and a system of oppression that provide people who are racialized as white more opportunities and resources while depriving them from people of color. While community college educators have little power over racial injustice in America, we do have the power to transform our classrooms and colleges.

Questions to consider

Each chapter will conclude with a series of reflective questions that ask you, the reader, to both measure your understanding of the chapter's content and to draw connections between the content and your own personal and professional experiences. Please take a moment to consider these questions, as they will help prepare you for the next chapter and assist you in creating a strong foundation as you undergo this journey as an antiracist, justice-oriented educator.

1. What role has race played in your life, both personally and professionally? At what point in your life did you become aware of race and racism, including your own race?
2. I shared nationwide data on the demographics of community college faculty and students, but what do these demographics look like in your college? How does your college disaggregate your student demographics?
3. How would you define racism and white supremacy in your own words?

4. What types of student success initiatives has your college adopted and have they been effective in eradicating racialized barriers for students of color?

Keywords: race, racism, minoritized, hyper-marginalized, racialized, white supremacy

i. References

American Association of Community Colleges. (2019). *Community college enrollment crisis? Historical trends in community college enrollment.* Retrieved from https://www.aacc.nche.edu/wp-content/uploads/2019/08/Crisis-in-Enrollment-2019.pdf

Bailey, T.R., Smith Jaggars, S., & Jenkins, D. (2015). *Redesigning America's community colleges: A clearer path to student success.* Cambridge, MA: Harvard UP.

Bonilla-Silva, E. (2017). *Racism without racists: Color-blind racism and the persistence of racial inequality in America.* Lanham, MD: Rowman & Littlefield.

Campaign for College Opportunity and California Acceleration Project (2019). *Getting there: Are California Community Colleges maximizing student completion of transfer-level math and English?* Retrieved from https://accelerationproject.org/Portals/0/Documents/CAP%20Report%20v8.pdf

Chang, R.S. (1993). Toward an Asian American legal scholarship: critical race theory, post-structuralism, and narrative space. *California Law Review, 81,* 1241.

Coates, T. (2015). *Between the world and me.* New York: Spiegel & Grau.

College Board. (2016). *Trends in community colleges: Enrollment, prices, student debt, and completion.* Retrieved from https://research.collegeboard.org/pdf/trends-community-colleges-research-brief.pdf

Crenshaw, K. (1989). Demarginalizing the intersection of race and sex: A Black feminist critique of antidiscrimination doctrine, feminist theory and antiracist politics. *University of Chicago Legal Forum, 1*(8): 139–167.

Derman-Sparks, L. & Brunson Phillips, C. (1997). *Teaching/learning anti-racism.* New York: Teachers College Press.

Emdin, C. (2016). *For the white folks who teach in the hood... and the rest of y'all too.* Boston: Beacon.

Freedberg, L. (2019, September 23). Poverty levels in schools key determinant of achievement gaps, not racial or ethnic composition, study finds. *Edsource.* Retrieved from https://edsource.org/2019/poverty-levels-in-schools-key-determinant-of-achievement-gaps-not-racial-or-ethnic-composition-study-finds/617821

Harper, S.R., & Wood, J.L. (2016). *Advancing Black male student success from preschool through Ph.D.* Sterling, VA: Stylus.

hooks, b. (2015). *Ain't I a Woman: Black women and feminism.* New York: Routledge.

Howard, G.R. (2016). *We can't teach what we don't know: White teachers, multicultural schools* (3rd ed.). New York: Teachers College Press.

Ignatiev, N., & Garvey, J. (1996). *Race traitor.* New York: Routledge.

Irwin, J., & Ortiz Oakley, E. (2018). Trust students, not tests, to open pathway to community college success. *EdSource*. Retrieved from https://edsource.org/2018/trust-students-not-tests-to-open-pathway-to-community-college-success/596996

Kendi, I.X. (2016). *Stamped from the beginning: The definitive history of racist ideas in America*. New York: Nation.

Kozol, J. (1992). *Savage inequalities: Children in America's schools*. New York: Broadway.

Kraemer, J. (n.d.). *Statistic of the month: Comparing community college completion rates*. National Center on Education and the Economy. Retrieved from http://ncee.org/2013/05/statistic-of-the-month-comparing-community-college-completion-rates/

Leonardo, Z. (2009). *Race, whiteness, and education*. New York: Routledge.

Lorde, A. (1984). *Sister outsider: Essays and speeches*. New York: The Crossing Press.

Magee, R.V. (2019). *The inner work of racial justice: Healing ourselves and transforming our communities through mindfulness*. New York: TarcherPerigee.

McIntosh, P. (1989, July/August). White privilege: Unpacking the invisible knapsack. *Peace and Freedom Magazine*, 10–12. Retrieved from https://nationalseedproject.org/Key-SEED-Texts/white-privilege-unpacking-the-invisible-knapsack

Meckler, L. (2019, September 23). Achievement gaps in schools driven by poverty, study finds. *The Washington Post*. Retrieved from https://www.washingtonpost.com/local/education/achievement-gaps-in-schools-driven-by-poverty-study-finds/2019/09/22/59491778-dd73-11e9-b199-f638bf2c340f_story.html

National Center for Educational Statistics. (2008). *Community colleges: Special supplement to the condition of education 2008*. Retrieved from https://nces.ed.gov/pubs2008/2008033.pdf

National Center for Educational Statistics. (2016a). *Race/ethnicity of college faculty*. Retrieved from https://nces.ed.gov/fastfacts/display.asp?id=61

National Center for Educational Statistics. (2016b). *Status and trends in the education of racial and ethnic groups 2016*. Retrieved from https://nces.ed.gov/pubs2016/2016007.pdf

National Center for Educational Statistics. (2019). *The condition of education*. Retrieved from https://nces.ed.gov/pubs2019/2019144.pdf

National Student Clearinghouse. (2018). *Snapshot report: Persistence and retention-2018*. Retrieved from https://nscresearchcenter.org/wp-content/uploads/SnapshotReport33.pdf

Petersen, W. (1966, January 9). Success story, Japanese American style. *New York Times*, p. 180. Retrieved from https://timesmachine.nytimes.com/timesmachine/1966/01/09/issue.html

reardon, s.f., Weathers, E.S., Fahle, E.M., Jang, H., & Kalogrides, D. (2019). *Is separate still unequal? New evidence on school segregation and racial academic achievement gaps* (CEPA Working Paper No. 19-06). Stanford Center for Education Policy Analysis. Retrieved from http://cepa.stanford.edu/wp19-06

Roediger, D. (1994). *Towards the abolition of whiteness*. London: Verso.

Shapiro, D., Dundar, A., Huie, F., Wakhungu, P.K., Bhimdiwala, A., & Wilson, S.E. (2018). *Completing college: A national view of student completion rates - Fall 2012 cohort* (Signature Report No. 16). Herndon, VA: National Student Clearinghouse Research Center. Retrieved from https://nscresearchcenter.org/wp-content/uploads/SignatureReport16.pdf

Sims, J.J. (2018). *Revolutionary STEM education: Critical-reality pedagogy and social justice in STEM for black males*. New York: Peter Lang.

Sims, J.J., Taylor-Mendoza, J., Hotep, L.O., Wallace, J., & Conaway, T. (2020). *Minding the obligation gap in community colleges and beyond: Theory and practice in achieving educational equity.* New York: Peter Lang.

Staples, B. (1986). Black men and public space. *Harper's, 273*(1639), 1986.

Suzuki, B.H. (1977). Education and the socialization of Asian Americans: a revisionist analysis of the "model minority" thesis. *Amerasia, 4*(2): 23–51.

Tatum, B.D. (1997/2017). *Why are all the black kids sitting together in the cafeteria?: And other conversations about race.* New York: Basic Books.

Tatum, B.D. (1999). Introduction to the paperback edition (1999). In B.D. Tatum, *Why are all the black kids sitting together in the cafeteria?: And other conversations about race,* pp. ix–xii. New York: Basic.

West, C. (1994). *Race matters.* New York: Vintage.

Wood, J.L., Harris III, F., & White, K. (2016). *Teaching men of color in the community college.* San Diego, CA: Montezuma.

Yosso, T.J. (2006). *Critical race counterstories along the Chicana/Chicano educational pipeline.* New York: Routledge.

Part I: Looking Within

2

Looking in the Mirror

The 2014–15 academic year was my first teaching experience in the Umoja Community, an Afro-centric student success program based in California, which, as mentioned in the previous chapter, is comprised of dozens of community colleges from around the state (plus one in Washington). This learning community features curricula that are almost exclusively comprised of African and African American writers and thinkers, and while the courses and their topics are relatable primarily to the African and African American students, we, of course, had students from diverse racial and ethnic backgrounds. In Fall 2014, we had one European American student in the program; he was very active in the course discussions, he showed great respect and deference for the topics and his classmates, and he underwent a great deal of growth throughout the year. I believe this student got a great deal of value from the class, and because the Black students had "critical mass" – or the number to overcome any stigma pressure they may feel in otherwise predominantly white classrooms or spaces – they were able to discuss the topics freely and openly despite the presence of both a white professor and a white classmate (Steele, 2011).

In Fall 2014, I was also in my second year of tenure review, so all my classes, including my Umoja composition course, were observed by members of my committee. As those who have been through the tenure review process know, the early years are especially stressful, as one's curriculum and pedagogy are under close scrutiny, and one's career is determined by a handful of senior faculty. I should not have been surprised, but a class designed for and comprised of primarily Black students would become problematic during this evaluation. One member of the committee, in particular, had it out for Umoja and its students (and me?). After observing a class, it is customary to meet and discuss how the class went and any kudos or areas for improvement. During this one-on-one meeting in my office, this senior faculty member would express confusion (and a little indignation) over how I spent my class time. Perhaps this needs a little context.

In July of that year, Eric Garner had been killed by NYPD officer Daniel Pantaleo, and in less than a month, both John Crawford and Michael Brown would be murdered by police officers, the former in a Walmart and the latter while walking down the street. These murders would be followed by massive protests in Ferguson, Missouri, and, unsurprisingly, the Fall 2014 Umoja courses became places for the students to make sense of what was going on, to have honest dialogue about race and racism in America, and to simply grieve (and just as a reminder, Laquan McDonald would be killed by police in Chicago on October 20, 2014, and 12-year-old Tamir Rice was murdered in Cleveland on November 23, 2014). The Umoja Community organization has developed a research-based set of pedagogical and curricular techniques known as the *Umoja Practices*, one of which is called the Porch Talk. According to the Umoja Community, a Porch Talk, which is an allusion to the porches on many southern and Midwestern homes where neighbors would congregate to discuss current events, is "To say at all times, 'What is Really Going on Here', a learning environment should be open, respectful, playful; there should be argument, dissection, and revision" (*Umoja Practices*, 2017). The Porch Talk can be used to address concerns and topics inside and outside the classroom.

Needless to say, a classroom conversation about white supremacy, police brutality, and the Black Lives Matter movement did not follow the course outline for a reading and composition class very well. To force any kind of instruction, including informal writing, while the students were grappling with emotions like anger, fear, and anxiety would have been inauthentic and insensitive. Instead, I wanted the students to chat with each other about what they were feeling. And because the Umoja team suspected the students would want to have this Porch Talk, my colleague Dr. Frederick Gaines, the Umoja ethnic studies professor, was also present in class. This also happened to be the day that the evaluator noted above stopped in for her observation (in my department, observations are unannounced). And to the students' credit, they were willing to engage in this critical, emotional discussion with her in the room – they probably didn't know this woman held racist beliefs about them and their cultures (or they engaged in the conversation in spite of her).

After the observed class ends, it is customary for the evaluator to simply leave without much discussion or ceremony, usually because they have a class of their own in just a few minutes. So I left that class feeling anxious for the students but satisfied that I was able to facilitate such a great discussion. But when I would meet with my evaluator a week later, I was instead chastised for not using the class for course-related objectives. She was "confused" as to why I would spend almost an entire hour talking about police brutality and racism if it wasn't for the essay they were working on. She was "afraid that [she] didn't have anything to write about in [my] observation write-up." I tried to explain that the nature of this learning community necessitated such conversations from time to time, and I reassured her that the Porch Talk was rooted in academic research. We made some progress in this discussion until the kicker – she said:

"I feel sorry for the one white student."

What??!! I am ashamed to this day that I didn't push back on that comment. I was experiencing a mix of shock and fear. I was utterly flabbergasted that this woman – this *community college educator* – felt sorry for this student because he was the lone white kid in a room full of students of color. Why is that? Did she feel like he was uncomfortable because we were talking about white supremacy and racism? I don't think so – he was very much involved in the conversation that day. Was she projecting her own discomfort? Perhaps. Or was she concerned that this one white student wasn't getting the academic experience that she thought he'd get in a majority-white classroom space? (And did she ever feel sorry for the lone Black students in her classroom and those she observed?)

Unfortunately, it is a common belief that "academics" don't happen in majority-minoritized student spaces. Too many community college educators feel like their disciplines and academic rigor are being threatened when we encourage students to bring their experiences and identities into the classroom. And this is obviously what transpired that semester. My evaluator didn't see value in our discussion because it didn't explicitly address aspects of the essay or other course-related objectives, and as a result, she was worried that the one white student was being cheated of his education. Later that semester, when I met with my full committee, my evaluation, overall, was satisfactory. The one area of growth was my curriculum. According to the female colleague who observed the Umoja class, I had too many authors of color; she said I needed "more canonical authors – like Emily Dickinson." To her, it was ok to include authors of color but not at the expense of these white authors. In other words, I was officially sanctioned for being too inclusive in my curriculum and for not tokenizing the communities of color that mirrored the students in *all* my classes. And this was the will of my entire committee, which I thought was comprised of some pretty progressive, equity-minded colleagues. I have always wondered if they felt bullied into protecting the canon or if they truly believed my curriculum and pedagogy were too multicultural and inclusive. They have all retired at this point, so I may never know. (On a more positive note, I got a new dean the following semester who worked with the committee chair to revise the tenure evaluation recommendations.)

The point of this story is twofold. First, these types of professors are on hiring and tenure review committees all over the country, and while this experience was uncomfortable for me, it would likely have been unbearable for a professor of color. Imagine this for a second. If this was my experience in tenure review as a white male, what are our colleagues of color experiencing when they create multicultural courses and bring their lived experiences and cultures into the classroom? I think the answer is pretty clear. They, too, are being told to stick to the canon, except in their case, it becomes cultural violence, or as Kendi (2019) calls it, "cultural racism." And failure to comply is more likely to result in unsatisfactory marks, bad student evaluations, and, even, dismissal. As a tenured professor, I have seen all three happen to my colleagues of color. Second, professors like my evaluator are in classrooms with students of color and wreaking untold damage on the academic journeys and emotional well-being of their students. If she was comfortable enough expressing this type of racism to me and the rest of the tenure review committee, what was she willing to do and say to a student of color, over whom they have a greater deal of power?

The complicated part of this anecdote is that this professor didn't think she was racist. In fact, I heard her on several occasions praise President Barack Obama (during one conversation, however, she also told me to avoid Fire Island in New York because "that's where the gays hang out"). So how can a person be so dismissive, even repulsed, by African American history and culture but be an ardent supporter of the first African American president? I know the answer has many layers and it is not within the scope of this book, but people like her obviously have a mixture of cognitive dissonance (perhaps even denial), noxious Eurocentricity, and engrained cultural racism, and while this book isn't necessarily for someone like her, all of us European American educators have some degree of these attitudes. I believe the vast majority of educators would not identify as being racist, but we all have entrenched, often hidden, beliefs and attitudes that are, for all intents and purposes, racist. Whiteness is invisible, for both the cruel and the well-meaning.

This reality, as illustrated in the above anecdote, highlights how important it is for those of us who identify as white to understand the American racial order, to recognize their role in this social order, and to identify strategies for eliminating it. This process is even more important for educators. We wield a great deal of power over our students. It is not far-fetched to argue that as community college educators, in particular, we stand guard at the gateway to upward mobility for so many minoritized students. Indeed, the majority of African American, Latinx, and Native American college students attend a community college (Ma & Baum, 2016). And as mentioned in Chapter 1, I have written this book under the assumption that my readers are genuinely concerned for their minoritized students and that they are prepared to undergo the hard work of enacting educational equity in their classrooms and institutions. However, before we can even begin this important social justice work, we have to understand and critique our positionality vis-à-vis our minoritized students. More specifically, we need to first understand our identities as people who are labeled as white, how white supremacy has molded our worldviews, and how our identities, thoughts, and attitudes are intricately connected to the success and well-being of our students of color.

Unfortunately, the vast majority of white educators experience immense difficulty when discussing race and racism – some because they're not versed in race and racism and some because they prefer a colorblind approach to race. With respect to the former, race can be incredibly difficult to discuss, but as mentioned in the introduction, as the student demographics in higher education become more and more diverse, dialogue around race, racism, and privilege becomes more and more important. By and large, we get into this profession because we have a passion for sharing our discipline with our students. We are passionate about teaching (as opposed to the research-centric missions of our university colleagues), and we want our students to succeed. But as I also shared in the introduction to this book, there are racialized disparities in success, retention, and persistence rates in our colleges (in addition to disparities based on gender, sexual orientation, disability status, etc.), which necessitate this difficult conversation about whiteness, racism, and our country's racial hierarchy. I hope this book makes this journey a little easier.

As mentioned earlier, I am a European American heterosexual male – the epitome of privilege. However, my childhood is not typical of the average white guy. When I was eleven, my mother remarried, which is not unique in itself. However, what makes my childhood extraordinary was the fact that my mother married an African American man, and I spent much of my childhood, including the formative teenage years, living with and being raised by a Black man. As a result, I went on many family trips around the country visiting my African American family and many a weekend in South Phoenix, which traditionally had a large Black population, watching football and playing dominoes with family friends. Needless to say, I became aware of race, including my own, at a young age (though I wouldn't fully grasp its importance and power until well into my career).

Even with such childhood experiences, I still found it incredibly difficult to discuss race and racism early in my teaching career. In fact, I even found myself promoting a "post-racial" ideology in my courses, representing racism as an anomaly that existed only in certain fringe groups and in certain regions of the country. There was no way that a diverse, progressive place like San Francisco experienced widespread racism, right? This is even while I was teaching a curriculum as part of a three-section learning community that centered "identity" as its theme, one of which was race. I taught texts such as Brent Staples' seminal essay, "Black Men and Public Space," and August Wilson's iconic play *Fences*, and I missed so many important opportunities to discuss race and racism from a cultural and societal vantage point. Instead, racism was relegated to the periphery and prejudice to the unconscious bias of everyday people.

One may wonder how I could grow up in a household with an African American man, as a kid who was very well aware of the race of his new family as well as his own, and still be unable to recognize the racial hierarchy in the United States. I was after all a child of the Bill Clinton years and the "tough on crime" platform that defined his reelection campaign. I was only six when Rodney King was beaten by members of the LAPD, but I was a preteen when Hilary Clinton famously referred to African American boys as "super predators" with "no conscience, no empathy" and who needed to be "[brought] to heel," not to mention I was a youth who grew up with a healthy dose of *Cops*. In other words, I was a kid who was keenly aware of race, who came of age in a decade defined by race and racism, and who still couldn't recognize the social order of the country. There are a few reasons for this, but it ultimately comes down to a lack of dialogue around race and racism – in my household, in my school, and in society, writ large. The bottom line was I was never taught *how* to talk about race and racism; it was, to borrow from Three 6 Mafia, the "most known unknown." It was invisible even to a kid who knew something was there. This type of reality creates a paradox for European Americans – we must enter a dialogue about race (indeed, I am arguing that it is in fact a requirement for effective, critical community college educators), but we have no clue how to. As Malcolm X quipped, "we can't teach what we don't know" (Howard, 2006). To slightly revise this sentiment, we can't understand or teach what we don't (and oftentimes refuse to) see. And despite my childhood – which provided no guarantee that I could grapple with issues of race, anyhow – I was woefully ignorant of institutionalized racism and the problems with whiteness.

This chapter aims to make visible what to most of us is invisible – our white racial identities. Furthermore, I will briefly discuss how this white racial identity has been formed and evolved over the course of American history and, most importantly, how the maintenance of the white racial identity has had detrimental consequences for "nonwhite" people both historically and presently. This is an uncomfortable topic for so many of us who are labeled white, but for educators, in particular, it is imperative that we acknowledge our racial identity before pursuing the social justice work that has come to define the community college.

a. The Problem with Colorblindness

While many community college educators started to wake up to the reality of racism in America in the wake of the Black Lives Matter movement, particularly after the murder of George Floyd by police in 2020, too many of our colleagues still subscribe to a "colorblind" ideology. I'll be the first to admit that this was my preferred perspective early in my career. And while many of us may gravitate toward colorblindness for benign, perhaps even well-intentioned, reasons, as we will discuss in this section, it is extremely problematic. To be more specific, the rejection of race and "color" has ultimately led to a situation in which many white folks go as far as to reject the racialization of all people, claiming instead to be "colorblind." This is commonly stated as "we are all just human" or "I see no color." At first glance, color-blindness seems like a positive outlook at race relations; it claims to be race neutral and argues that the best way to rid this world of racism is to reject race altogether. It is a popular belief that "we are all human," so we shouldn't "pay attention" to race. However, colorblindness is, best case, willful ignorance, and, worst case, it is symbolic, even literal, violence against people of color.

In NBC's popular drama, *This is Us,* there is a poignant moment when Jack, the white patriarch of the family, is playing golf with his adopted African American son, Randall. Randall, who was entering the formative years of his childhood, had, for the very first time in his education, an African American teacher. Under the tutelage of his teacher, Randall started reading the likes of Ralph Ellison, Langston Hughes, and other prominent Black authors, igniting both a sense of wonder and pride in this missing piece of his identity, while also dealing with the isolation he felt as the only African American student on the debate team (and seemingly at the school). During a round of golf, which was inspired by Tiger Woods' incredibly successful entry into the PGA, Jack tried to relate to Randall's isolation by describing his own discomfort as a working-class Vietnam veteran thrust into the midst of his community's affluent residents. Unsurprisingly, Randall did not see the parallel, and when he pushed back, Jack said, "I don't look at you and see color. I see my son," to which Randall replied, "Then you don't see me."

This episode provides viewers, and I hope you, with two valuable lessons. First, we cannot separate the unique cultures that have evolved in parallel with racial formation, including those of the myriad African American, Latinx, Asian, and Indigenous communities around the country. This is particularly obvious when we look at the unique cultures that arose out of segregation, such as those in Harlem, Watts, and Oakland. We see similar phenomena happening with the Latinx communities of New York, Florida, and Los Angeles, and with the Asian American communities of San Francisco and New York. In other words, unique cultures have developed, in part, because members of these communities were forced to live in segregated spaces in their respective cities. Oppression under the regime of white supremacy was a major force in shaping these cultures. Second, there is no way that white folks can ever understand racial discrimination, no matter how difficult our lives have been due to poverty, sexism, or homophobia. The bottom line is that, as educators, it is irresponsible for us to strip our students of their identities and lived experiences because we would rather subscribe to "colorblindness" or to equate our own struggles with their experiences with racism, marginalization, and violence.

So to understand colorblindness, one must first understand its roots, and there are two primary origins that I will cover: the first is colorblindness as a response to both white and Black nationalism during the civil rights movements of the mid-20th century (Peller, 1990), and the second is this ideology's roots in Western humanism (Leonardo, 2009). Let's look at both in a little more detail.

First, during the civil rights movements of the 1950s and 60s, white Americans, as a whole, had to grapple with race and the country's racial hierarchy, and for many, this was the first time they had to do so. Many Americans saw the images of protestors being assaulted by police and other white folks on their television screens and in their newspapers. For many, racism was the product of race, and if this country was to eradicate racism, race must also be eliminated. This was inevitable considering the oft misinterpreted quote by Dr. Martin Luther King: "I have a dream that my four children will one day live in a nation where they will not be judged by the color of their skin, but by the content of their character." It soon became clear that any focus on race, or "race consciousness," was associated with two groups – white nationalists, like the KKK, and Black nationalists, like the Black Panthers. In other words, the new American common sense vis-à-vis race relations likened Black nationalism (and Black pride) to white nationalism and white supremacists like the KKK, neo-Nazis, and other hate groups (and white power). As Peller (1990) writes, "Along with the suppression of white racism that was the widely celebrated aim of civil rights reform, the dominant conception of racial justice was framed to require that black nationalists be equated with white supremacists, and that race consciousness on the part of either whites or blacks be marginalized as beyond the good sense of enlightened American culture" (p. 760). This new ideology resulted in what Peller calls the new "cultural center," which was characterized by "objectivity and neutrality" (p. 844).

Unfortunately, this justification for colorblindness has had some pernicious effects, the most significant being the "democratization" of racism. Any focus on race by anybody, regardless of racial identity, was now considered racist. As Crenshaw, Gotanda, Peller, and Thomas (1995) argue:

> the American cultural mainstream neatly linked the black left to the white racist right: according to this quickly coalesced consensus, because race consciousness characterized both white supremacists and black nationalists, it followed that both were racist. The resulting 'center' of cultural common sense thus rested on the exclusion of virtually the entire domain of progressive thinking about race within colored communities. (pp. xiv–xv)

Under this colorblind ideology, people of color could be called racist for any focus on race, no matter the context. An activist of color who described their experience with racial inequity was now considered racist because they were sowing seeds of racial division in a post-racial world. Furthermore, anyone describing racism by a white person or anyone who did anything to redress racial inequity was now considered a "reverse racist." As Kendi (2019) notes, "The most threatening racist movement is not the alt right's unlikely drive for a White ethnostate but the regular American's drive for a 'race-neutral' one. The construct of race neutrality actually feeds White nationalist victimhood by positing the notion that any policy protecting or advancing non-White Americans toward equity is 'reverse discrimination'" (p. 20). Ironically, this new common sense, which was supposed to alleviate racial stratification and oppression, instead perpetuated and compounded the racial hierarchy because it stifled many white folks' ability to dismantle racism (or gave them license to).

The second justification of colorblindness is the legacy of Western humanism, which puts the emphasis on our human identity rather than our racial identity. This usually manifests in phrases like "we're just human" or "I don't see race – just people." At face value, this seems like an honorable approach to interacting with others. However, as a product of Western philosophy,[1] humanism imagines a universal human experience, heritage, and worldview. However, this worldview is fundamentally European and white (Althusser, 2003; Leonardo, 2009). As a result, colorblindness has stemmed from this philosophical perspective, which tends to ignore the lived experiences of people of color. As Leonardo writes:

> Humanism's search for an originary, or genetic, human experience, is quickly betrayed when, upon deconstruction, human experience appears cultural or racial (usually Euro-centric or white) and not universal. So what initially appears as general becomes a front for the universalization of a particular racial experience, which is the lynchpin of humanist ideology. Transforming an event into something 'human' when it is racial in nature has been a staple of white humanism's inability to come to terms with people of color's concrete experience. (pp. 34–35)

In other words, simply seeing people as human dismisses the very real experiences of being raced as African American, Asian American, Latinx, or Indigenous and experiencing racism. Furthermore, humanism tends to erase the cultural identities of people of color and, instead, promotes a Eurocentric, "aracial" cultural heritage, and any deviation from this heritage is viewed with distrust, if not with outright hostility.

Similarly, hooks (1992) recalls experiences in which her white students find it hard to believe or understand the racialized experiences of their classmates of color. When students of color describe instances of racism, she notes that the white students' "rage erupts because they believe that all ways of looking that highlight difference subvert the liberal belief in a universal subjectivity (we are all just people) that they think will make racism disappear. They have an emotional investment in the myth of 'sameness'" (p. 167). Furthermore, hooks correlates this white despondency with a long, often violent, history of white control of the "black gaze," forcing people of color to "wear the mask" (p. 169). As a result, people of color, including students, "pretend to be comfortable in the face of whiteness." However, when one removes the mask and articulates serious concerns vis-a-vis racism and the racial hierarchy, we, white folks, tend to react uncomfortably because this experience does not fit nicely into the colorblind narrative we have constructed and perpetuated (Aleinikoff, 1991). Ultimately, we must look at colorblindness with much suspicion. On the surface, this ideology seems to have good intentions, but as noted above, it is instead another way for white folks to avoid discussing race (which is evident in the fact that you almost never hear a person of color arguing for a colorblind approach to human relations). And as Kendi (2019) argues, "Terminating racial categories is potentially the last, not the first, step in the antiracist struggle" (p. 54).

As I stated from the outset, I believe that the vast majority of community college educators care about the success of their students. In fact, I'd go as far as arguing that most community college educators strive to treat all their students equally. This was the point of the decades-long fight for civil rights, no? The assumption is if we treat all our students the same, all students have an equal opportunity to succeed; unfortunately, this simply has not been the case. The data just doesn't bear this out. As mentioned in the Chapter 1, there exist large outcome disparities between students of color and their European American and Asian American counterparts. But colorblindness prevents us from looking at this data critically because of its faulty assumption of equal opportunity. Let's take a closer look at this.

As we will see, the colorblind perspective starts to break down once we start to look at social, political, and educational disparities between whites and people of color. As Leonardo (2009) notes, colorblindness's "shortcoming comes from its failure to explain why a society looks *this way* and is organized with *these consequences*" (p. 34, emphasis in original). And this structure and these "consequences" are in plain sight via television, newspapers, and social media. Hardly a day passes without news of Black male being shot by the police, a passenger of color being dragged off an airplane, or new data that illustrates the wealth and health gaps between white folks and people of color. As such, colorblindness has morphed from a humanist attempt to bring people together (though it is reasonable to claim even this was never the case) in a way in which white folks can avoid talking about race altogether. This avoidance mechanism was best exemplified in an interaction between comedian Trevor Noah and conservative pundit

Tomi Lahren. In an interview on Noah's *The Daily Show,* Lahren responded to a critique of her beliefs about Black Lives Matter and Colin Kaepernick with the explanation, "I don't see color. I go after Hilary Clinton and she's as white as they come," after which Trevor Noah asked, "You don't see color? What do you do at a traffic light?" Noah would go on to comment that "I don't believe in that at all when people say that. There's nothing wrong with seeing color. It's how you treat color that's more important" (Noah, 2016).

While this exchange is momentarily comical, there is a deeper, more serious conclusion imbedded in Noah's rebuttal – colorblindness has become a way in which white folks are able to couch racism in race neutrality. And while Lahren is not an ideal representation of community college educators, who tend to lean much further to the left, the point remains. Though we tend to be more politically liberal, "colorblindness" dominates our institutions. However, if we look at educational data, "colorblindness" quickly breaks down when we try to explain it. I demonstrate this point in the following exercise, which I frequently ask my colleagues and readers to undergo. As mentioned in the introduction, nationwide community college student success data, when disaggregated by race, demonstrate that African American, Latinx, Pacific Islander, and Indigenous students have lower completion, persistence, graduation, and transfer rates than their European and Asian American counterparts. The question, like Leonardo's above, is why? In reality, there can only be four explanations, which I will describe and problematize in more detail.

The first "colorblind" explanation for the disparities mentioned above is that African American, Latinx, Pacific Islander, and Indigenous students are intellectually inferior to their European and Asian American counterparts. However, this explanation is so clearly racist in its origins that most educators would not consider it (at least, publicly). This is not to say that this view does not exist in academia. We only need to look as far as the book, *The Bell Curve,* or more recent comments by James Watson in which he argued that African Americans are genetically less intelligent.

The second possible "colorblind" explanation is that these students come from homes, neighborhoods, and schools that do not value education, especially higher education. However, it is very important that this point of view be called what it is: racist. The wholesale assumption that the entire cultures of these student groups are lacking is textbook racism, or what is called "cultural racism" (Jones, 1996; Kendi, 2019; Sue, 2003). Unfortunately, this belief is probably more pervasive than we would like to believe, often cloaked as diatribes against rap and hip-hop and the argument that men of color need to "pull up their pants" (no credible research has found a connection between hip-hop or clothing and educational success). So like the first explanation, we'll chalk this one up to racist beliefs.

The third "colorblind" explanation is more accurate but just as problematic (though in a very different way): that African American, Latinx, Pacific Islander, and Indigenous students are disproportionately impacted by financial obstacles, whether they be transportation issues, housing and food insecurity, the inability to pay for textbooks and materials, and so on. Indeed, this statement is true. As I will discuss later in this chapter, there exists significant "wealth and health" gaps that disproportionately impact students of color (Ladson-Billings, 2007). However, we need to step back and ask ourselves what this explanation really means. On the one hand, there are critical, equity-minded educators who help students overcome these obstacles (e.g., adopting free textbooks, connecting students to housing organizations, etc.). On the other hand, this explanation for educational disparities is used as a cop out for far too many educators who would rather not concern themselves with their students' struggles or who feel powerless in doing so. This often comes in the form of "those are issues that are out of our control." But we must overcome this nihilism and understand that we have an *obligation* to create initiatives and programs for counteracting these forces (Sims, Taylor-Mendoza, Hotep, Wallace, & Conaway, 2020). As a result, this explanation totally erases any race-based explanations for societal inequalities. Furthermore, blaming "outside" forces for educational inequities lets us off the hook for maintaining educational structures, policies, and procedures that maintain the racial hierarchy (e.g., placement tests, Eurocentric curricula, etc.).

The fourth explanation is that these student groups encounter institutional, identity-based barriers. Though I will not discuss institutional barriers (e.g., institutionalized racism) in great detail in this book (instead, see Sims et al., 2020), it is important to understand that our colleges are not set up in ways that are conducive for students of color and other minoritized students. At the very least, we must acknowledge that we have created obstacles and barriers for these students in everything from admissions and registration to curriculum and pedagogy. Though this explanation is the most progressive of the four, it is also possible to warp this viewpoint into a racist ideology in which one argues that colleges must simply help students navigate the existing racist structures, in essence taking race and racism out of the equation and putting the impetus on the student to "put on their mask" and morph themselves into the Eurocentric version of a college student that we project. Instead, we need to look inward, and we need to take the responsibility for radically transforming our institutions and our classrooms to meet our students' needs.

In essence, we cannot explain the above educational disparities without understanding that race and racism are contributing factors (as discussed in the introduction, class alone cannot account for these disparities). Unfortunately, a colorblind approach, which is far more prevalent in community colleges than many of us want to admit, forces us educators and institutional leaders to either "blame the victim" for their lack of educational achievement or to become apathetic to the socioeconomic barriers they encounter.

Ultimately, colorblindness, which perhaps has noble origins, has morphed into what Bonilla-Silva (2017) has termed "colorblind racism." This form of racism has allowed white folks to transition from racism that is based on biology to a form that is based on "cultural deficiency" (i.e., inequality exists because of the cultures of people of color). Bonilla-Silva writes:

> whites have developed powerful explanations – which have ultimately become justifications – for contemporary racial inequality that exculpate them from any responsibility for the status of people of color. These explanations emanate from a new racial ideology that I label *color-blind racism*. This ideology, which acquired cohesiveness and dominance in the late 1960s, explains contemporary racial inequality as the outcome of nonracial dynamics. (p. 2, emphasis in original)

It is from this ideology that many white folks promote the mythology of meritocracy, the belief that the system isn't rigged but that those who get ahead do so because of hard work and grit. This brings us to another tenet of colorblind racism – coded racist language. Instead of arguing that African Americans and Latinxes are "lazy," white folks can now shift the focus to other successful white folks (and people of color) and argue that they are simply "harder working" and "more motivated." Ultimately, they are making the same racist argument without using explicitly racist words and ideas.

So if colorblindness is extremely problematic – even covertly racist – what is the alternative? The answer is pretty clear – race consciousness. According to Peller (1990), race consciousness "is to recognize that racial cultures form a significant element of what goes into the construction of our social relations" (p. 847). At this point in the book, it should be clear that racism exists despite the fact that it does not biologically exist, and even though it is socially constructed, it has very real and material consequences and outcomes. Race consciousness requires us to recognize two important things:

1. That there is sometimes overlap between one's racial identity and one's cultural identity. For example, so many traditions and cultural values in the African American community were borne out of slavery and Jim Crow. To deny the existence of race is to deny these cultural practices, experiences, language, and artifacts (DeGruy, 2005/2017).

2. That everyone, including white folks, has a racial label, and with that label comes unique, racialized experiences. For people of color, as a whole, these racialized experiences often involve racial profiling, racial inequity, institutionalized discrimination, and other forms of oppression. For white folks, these racialized experiences are often marked by privilege, which usually comes at the expense of people of color (e.g., if we were to be shown a house for sale that a person of color was denied from seeing). Furthermore, in some cases, the racialized experiences of white folks are marked by racist actions – whether overt or covert – not to mention that the privilege of remaining silent and ignorant about race and racism upholds the racial hierarchy.

True race consciousness requires proficiency in understanding the complexity of race and racism, especially as it relates to the more widely known white privilege and the less understood white supremacy that undergird the racial hierarchy. What follows is an overview of these two paradigms with the disclaimer that this section is meant to be more of a primer than a comprehensive overview. I would encourage you to research these topics in more detail, starting with the sources I have cited.

b. Privilege and the Invisibility of Whiteness

Recently, a prominent comedian found himself at the center of a conversation about race and whiteness after posting a joke to his Twitter feed that seemed innocuous to most, but indicative of larger racial issues to others. It is the type of joke that we all have heard before, likely on multiple occasions; it starts roughly like this: "A guy walks into a bar and he is joined by a Black guy, a Mexican guy, and an Asian guy." After posting the joke, followers quickly inquired as to why the latter three men were raced while the first was not (and who was assumed to be white). To the comedian's credit, he took responsibility for the joke, admitted that he had not thought about the unnamed race of the first man, and he revised the joke to include the man's race.

This joke, and the subsequent dialogue it inspired, is demonstrative of one of the phenomena, and perils, of the American racial hierarchy – the invisibility of whiteness (Sue, 2016). White folks just do not see themselves, other whites, or the cultural norms of the United States as raced, a belief that has led many of us to claim that we are "just American." However, at the same time, people of color are almost always assigned a race, whether it be Black, African American, Latinx, Asian American, etc. "Nonwhite" people, no matter how hard they try, can never just be American. As Sims (2018) writes, "Whiteness is the default nationality" (p. 21).

This invisibility of whiteness has led to a society and American culture that have historically been based on white European (and heterosexual male) norms, traditions, and mores (Howard, 2006; Roediger, 2002; Sims, 2018), which are reinforced by our political and educational systems (Apple, 2000; Delpit, 2012; DuBois, 1965; Inoue, 2015). These norms include the way we dress, the way we speak, the food we eat, the music we listen to, and the list goes on. The basis for the norm is usually unknown, but in almost all cases, it is European in origin, and we tend to impose these norms on our students, which in some cases can be in contradiction to their own cultural norms and, in others, can be actual barriers to their academic success. A colleague of mine recently shared with me that several of his students were invited to an event that required them to dress in formal attire; however, these students didn't own formal attire nor could they afford it. Their solution was to buy the clothing, to keep the tags on, and to return the clothing later. From a socioeconomic standpoint, this is very problematic, especially in a community college. From a cultural standpoint, this is an example of how European norms become necessary "to play the game." I am sure none of the event organizers stopped to ask if this requirement for formal attire had economic consequences, and they surely didn't stop to ask whether the students of color would want to wear clothing that was more appropriate to their tastes and identity. This is the invisibility of both whiteness and European norms.

Furthermore, people who are labeled as White generally don't identify with their White racial identity nor can they recall when they realized they were socially constructed as such, as opposed to people of color who tend to remember childhood experiences of being raced – by their families, by strangers or acquaintances, or even by themselves (DiAngelo, 2018; Gallagher, 1996; hooks, 1992; Leonardo, 2009; Matias, 2016). As a result, children of color are forced to navigate an education system, and their families are forced to navigate a society, where they are constantly forced to check their identities at the door. Meanwhile, students of European descent are free to maintain their identity, their home cultures, and their histories without restraint, and as a result, anything that deviates from this standard is seen as abnormal and as an abomination. Race and racial identity for white folks are akin to water for fish. It is everywhere, yet it is unseen. As Aleinikoff (1991) states, "To be born white is to be free from confronting one's race on a daily, personal, interaction-by-interaction basis. Being white... means not having to think about it" (p. 1066). This gives children of European descent the mental, physical, and emotional freedom to self-actualize while hindering the mental, physical, and emotional development of students of color as they try to "assimilate." They are constantly forced to expend energy evaluating the myriad situations they may find themselves in – the classroom, the grocery store, their jobs, and all public spaces – and determining the most appropriate ways of acting and interacting so that they can avoid being punished, either formally or socially. This is a phenomenon known as "stereotype threat" (Steele, 2011).

All of the above has culminated in what is commonly labeled as "white privilege." In fact, when more progressive European Americans are pressed to discuss race, they will often default to an unwieldy discussion of white privilege and, sometimes, implicit bias – these are easiest to discuss (though certainly very hard for most whites). The term "white privilege," however, is often met with resistance from whites who see it as an affront to their hard work and accomplishments. It is not uncommon to hear the rebukes, "I was never handed anything" or "I worked hard to get to where I am. I'm not privileged." These rebuttals are misinformed by a class perception that relegates privilege only to those with means and wealth, such as kids with trust funds or Wall Street millionaires, but, ultimately, this resistance is misplaced. Many whites don't understand what this term actually means. So what is *white privilege*? Sue (2003) defines white privilege as

> the unearned advantages and benefits that accrue to White folks by virtue of a system normed on the experiences, values, and perceptions of their group. White privilege automatically confers dominance to one group, while subordinating groups of color in a descending relational hierarchy; it owes its existence to White supremacy; it is premised on the mistaken notion of individual meritocracy and deservedness (e.g., hard work and family values) rather than favoritism; it is deeply embedded in the structural, systemic, and culture workings of U.S. society; and it operates within an invisible veil of unspoken and protected secrecy. (p. 137)

In other words, the European norms described previously give us a great deal of cultural capital as we navigate public spaces, all because of our skin color. We are treated differently in stores because of the way we dress and speak and because there are no widespread stereotypes that white folks are thieves. We are treated differently by the police because white folks are not stereotyped as criminals and as dangerous. Our points of view are privileged in schools because our own ways of knowing and speaking are centered in the classroom. And the list goes on. Unbeknownst to most of us, we are able to navigate our society effortlessly because it is built upon European values and culture and because many of the people we interact with on a daily basis hold these same values.

To most people who are labeled white, these "unearned advantages and benefits" are largely invisible, what McIntosh (1989) calls the "invisible knapsack" of white privilege. She writes, "white privilege [is] an invisible package of unearned assets that I can count on cashing in each day, but about which [we are] 'meant' to remain oblivious. White privilege is like an invisible weightless knapsack of special provisions, maps, passports, codebooks, visas, clothes, tools and blank checks" (p. 1). Distinguishing her racial privilege from her economic (and "religious, ethnic status, or geographic location") privilege, she identified twenty-six advantages that she attributes to her skin color. For example, McIntosh explains that "If I should need to move, I can be pretty sure of renting or purchasing housing in an area which I can afford and in which I would want to live" and "I can be pretty sure that my neighbors in such a location will be neutral or pleasant to me" (p. 2). Furthermore, she notes that she can shop alone without being followed by security, she can speak and dress without them being attributed to race, and she can work and learn in spaces where those around her will look like her and where she feels like she belongs. These advantages – privileges – are so normal to us white folks that we scarcely recognize them.

Unfortunately, the invisibility of whiteness has created the myth of meritocracy in the United States wherein success and prosperity are simply and exclusively the results of hard work and perseverance. What Dalton (2016) refers to as the "curse of rugged individualism" has led, to the detriment of racially minoritized peoples, to the belief that those who have not reached educational and economic success are lacking in some way. Similarly, colorblind meritocracy has resulted in the arguments that identity-based remedies such as affirmative action have "lowered standards" and excluded whites from jobs and universities that they were otherwise entitled to (Kennedy, 1990). This is not to say that our accomplishments were not hard earned nor that they were handed to us; it simply means that we never had to encounter race-based obstacles to those accomplishments. The teachers who looked like us never made assumptions about our communities or our abilities; we were not stereotyped as lazy or unintelligent by potential employers; we felt like we belonged when we went to graduate school; lines of credit and student loans were made readily available to us when we needed to pay for graduate school and when we wanted to buy a house. Conversely, our privileges don't come without costs, and people of color are forced to navigate these same journeys but with those race-based obstacles. They are stereotyped and discriminated against in schools and jobs; they don't have a sense of belonging in graduate school or in the academy; and they aren't provided with the loans and credit needed to pay for college and their homes due to systemic racism in the banking system. So yes, we have worked hard to get where we are, but we are successful because our skin color protects us from widespread, systemic barriers.

Furthermore, since data indicate that people of color, immigrants, people with disabilities, and other historically marginalized and oppressed people disproportionately populate America's underclass, these beliefs in individualism and meritocracy have produced rather racist, ethnocentric, and ableist perspectives. One only needs to look as far as the widely popular 1994 book *The Bell Curve* by Richard J. Herrnstein and Charles Murray, which blames communities of color for the disparities in educational attainment, health, and wealth. This book is not worth a critical discussion, but the fact remains that it is common, not only in the mainstream media but also in academia, to explain away race-based disparities as pathologies in communities of color rather than prevalent racist structures. This creates a cognitive dissonance wherein white folks believe that success is only achieved by those who deserve it and worked hard for it, implying that those who do not are undeserving and lazy. Hence, this "curse" has perpetuated this cycle of racism.

As mentioned above, folks who are labeled as white do not have to worry about race-based obstacles and discrimination, and the existence of white privilege does not diminish the accomplishments of white folks who have worked hard in school, in their jobs, and in other aspects of their lives. It just means that we didn't encounter obstacles that were based solely on our racial identity. On the other hand, people of color have experienced race-based obstacles, both historically and in the present, what Ladson-Billings (2007) has dubbed the "health and wealth gaps." The racial inequities have been the topics of a plethora of important, ground-breaking books and articles. Given this fact, I do not want to dedicate too much of this chapter to describing the existence of racial inequity and institutionalized racism in America. But to name a few:

1. Economic discrimination
   - Sharecropping after the abolition of slavery created a new form of indentured slavery that kept families in poverty and debt for nearly a century after the Emancipation Proclamation.
   - People of color were excluded from unions, and when they were finally allowed to join, they were the "last in and first out," making them the most vulnerable to layoffs during economic downturns (they were "last in" because they were excluded for several decades).
   - People of color experience myriad forms of employment discrimination, such as hiring managers not calling applicants with non-European names not to mention outright racism during the interviews. In fact, statistically, a white man with no college degree *and* a criminal record is more likely to get a job than a Black man with no criminal record *and* a college degree! Finally, all this happens if the job is even advertised – many jobs are never announced but instead filled through informal networks that favor white folks, or what has been called "white affirmative action" (this term also describes the informal admission processes at many universities wherein the children of prominent alumni are admitted, or what are called "legacy" admissions).
2. Educational inequities:
   - Black vets and other vets of color were excluded from the GI Bill in the aftermath of World War II, limiting their access to both college degrees and low-rate home loans.
   - School funding in lower income, "urban," "majority-minority" school districts is severely lacking to the point of decrepit and unsafe classrooms and buildings (think Flint, MI), lack of books and other supplies, and a teaching staff of unqualified, uncredentialed, or brand-new teachers. This is in contrast to well-funded suburban schools comprised primarily of white students, who learn in fairly new or brand-new buildings, with the necessary books and supplies, and from highly qualified, seasoned teachers (Howard, 2014; Kozol, 1992; Milner, 2008).
   - Economic and housing discrimination has caused *de jure,* or informal, segregation, which has led to segregated schools, as illustrated in the previous bullet point. To be clear, the students' peers are not the problem – it is the underfunding of "majority-minority" schools (reardon, Weathers, Fahle, Jang, & Kalogrides, 2019).

- Families of color lack access to early childhood education programs, resulting in a preparation gap between children of color and white children in kindergarten (Johns, 2016).
- Students of color are disproportionately placed into special needs programs, based usually on nothing but disinterest in a curriculum that doesn't reflect their identities, cultures, epistemologies, or histories. It should be obvious that being tracked into special education diverts these students away from AP coursework and college tracks (Howard, 2014).
- Students of color are also suspended and expelled at much higher rates than their white peers – at all educational grades and levels – usually for loosely defined behavioral expectations that favor white students and punish Black students (CCEAL & SNAHEC, 2019; Wood, Harris, & Howard, 2018).
- Students of color are overwhelmingly tracked into career education courses and away from AP courses, which sets them up for lower wage technical and service careers rather than the higher paying professional careers that require college degrees.

3. Housing
   - Banks used "redlining" to deny home loans to Black and Brown families in the inner cities while simultaneously preventing them from finding housing in the suburbs (Loeb et al., 1996).
   - People of color were excluded from the New Deal Federal Housing mortgage program, which allowed European Americans to secure low-interest loans, fueling "white flight" to the suburbs and creating massive wealth for white families, wealth that still exists today.
   - People of color, particularly African Americans, were disproportionately given subprime loans leading up to the 2008 housing bubble – even when they qualified for the more desirable fixed-rate loans. The 2008 housing bubble would obliviate the wealth of Black and Brown families.
   - House hunters and renters of color have been historically and are currently not shown available houses and apartments by racist realtors and property managers, contributing to the wealth and health gaps mentioned above and denying students of color access to high-quality, well-funded suburban schools.

4. The U.S. Justice System
   - In the aftermath of slavery, Jim Crow laws not only segregated whites and Blacks, but they created minor criminal offenses, like vagrancy

infractions, that resulted in long prison sentences. These prisons would then contract the labor of their prisoners, who were overwhelming African American, to agricultural and public works projects, essentially creating a new form of slavery (Bennett, 1993).

- African Americans and other people of color are frequently given longer jail and prison sentences than European American offenders for the same or similar crimes, especially in the cases of drug use and possession. For example, crack cocaine would carry exponentially longer prison sentences than powder cocaine, the former being more common in communities of color and the latter being used more commonly by white users (Alexander, 2010; Loury, 2008).

- The disparities in drug enforcement and sentencing would lead to mass incarceration wherein prisoners of color would be severely overrepresented in the prison population (Alexander, 2010).

- The media frequently portrays suspects of color (and even victims of police brutality) as thugs and criminals while treating white suspects as innocent and deserving of empathy. Just consider the differences between Trayvon Martin, an innocent victim of vigilantism, and Brock Turner, the Stanford swimmer who raped an unconscious female student. In the media, more specifically, Trayvon Martin is frequently pictured in his hoodie while Brock Turner's senior year school photo is frequently used. Furthermore, recall the media's public evisceration of the Central Park Five, who were convicted but eventually exonerated.

- Similarly, the media (and the public) treats protestors of color (as well as white protestors who are speaking out for racial justice) as thugs, hooligans, and rioters while portraying armed white protestors, like those protesting the 2020 shelter in place order in Michigan, as patriotic. Furthermore, the police use riot gear, tanks, tear gas, and mass arrests on the former while barely making a presence in the latter. The January 6, 2021, insurrection against the United States legislature by predominantly white men who were egged on by Donald Trump is an exemplary example of how white supremacist policies impact policing.

- The use of force on peaceful protestors is exacerbated by the militarization of U.S. police departments. As part of a federal program, police departments are given military equipment, including tanks and grenade launchers, to quell these peaceful protests, which, again, are comprised primarily of protestors of color.

- African Americans and Latinxes are disproportionately impacted by racial profiling, "stop and frisk" policies, "see something, say something" campaigns, and recently, facial recognition technology. In other words, men of color, in particular, are subject to racial profiling by police, citizens, and technology.
- African Americans and other people of color make up the majority of police brutality incidents and murders, which social media and phone technology have brought to the forefront of the national conversations on race. Furthermore, Asian Americans were the targets of several race-based, vigilante attacks during the COVID-19 pandemic, a consequence of the federal government's racialization of the virus (e.g., President Trump's racist quip, "Kung flu").

5. Health care
   - Black patients are 22% less likely to receive pain medication than white patients due to centuries-old racist beliefs that African Americans can tolerate more pain (Sabin, 2020).
   - The infant mortality rate for Black babies is twice that for white babies, even when Black mothers seek prenatal care and white mothers do not (Daniels, 2008).
   - African Americans are more likely to have higher blood pressure, which researchers have linked to the trauma of racism (James, 1994; James et al., 1992).
   - Workers of color (and our students of color) were overrepresented within the ranks of frontline, essential workers during the COVID-19 pandemic, and many of them not only risked their lives to continue working for minimum wage, but many of them also lacked the health care necessary for covering COVID-19-related treatments.

This is a long, but not entirely comprehensive, list, and when each bullet point is taken in isolation, it is easy to downplay or ignore the impacts of racism on people of color. However, when taken as a whole, it is clear that African Americans and other people of color have been systematically and systemically oppressed in every facet of our society, leading to wide disparities in health, wealth, and education. It is hard to deny the impact of the above on African American, Latinx, Pacific Islander, Asian American, and Indigenous communities. Furthermore, the aforementioned information has several implications for the thesis of this book. First, as I have highlighted in this chapter, whiteness and its concomitant privileges maintain a certain level of invisibility, especially from those who benefit from it. However, even though white privilege remains in the shadows, its effects are exceedingly visible. In other words, we can see above that people who are labeled as white are better off economically and educationally and that they reap the benefits of whiteness in the U.S. education, justice, economic, and healthcare systems and that people of color are visibly and negatively impacted by these privileges.

Second, this information, when coupled with the problematic nature of colorblindness, uncovers the very real phenomenon of racism. Though race may not be real from a biological standpoint, it indeed manifests itself in our political, economic, and cultural institutions (Smedley & Smedley, 2005). As Franz Fanon (1952) writes, race is "epidermal," or as he described, it is only in the presence of whites that a Black man (or woman) must "experience his being for others... Ontology does not allow us to understand the being of the black man, since it ignores the lived experience. For not only must the black man be black; he must be black in relation to the white man" (p. 89, 90). As Fanon observes, the "white gaze" has the effect of destroying the "body schema" – or one's physiological self-awareness – of Black men and women and replacing it with what he calls the "epidermal racial schema" (p. 92). In this new epidermal racial schema, Black men and women are no longer self-aware but now see themselves through the white gaze, an observation that echoes DuBois's (1903/1944) "double consciousness." In this way, "race" is seen in terms of and in opposition to whiteness. Race exists because those in power needed it to exist in order to maintain social and economic control over Black and Brown bodies. Similarly, Sims (2018) argues, "Culture that is different from or perceived to be in opposition to whiteness is dismissed, denigrated, and sometimes destroyed" (p. 19). So while race may not be a biological fact, it has very real, existential consequences for people who are not labeled as white. As Coates remarked, "race is the child of racism, not the father" (p. 7).

Third, these disparities highlight how absurd claims of "reverse racism" are. As mentioned in the introduction, I subscribe to the definition of racism as a system of oppression wherein people of color and other minoritized people are deliberately relegated to second-class citizenry and are excluded from quality education, jobs, neighborhoods, and health care. The above realities bear this claim out. As such, any claim by a white person that they have been systematically discriminated against by a person of color (or another white person) is problematic. Indeed, white people can experience prejudice in certain situations (for example, as a patron of a Black-owned business or by an employer of color). However, these instances are so trivial in the grander scheme of the U.S. economy that white folks couldn't even begin to claim to be the victims of *institutional* racism. To see how illogical this claim can be and to illustrate the double standard of hiring practices, take the following scenario into account. Imagine that a college has a Black female president and that this president's executive level leadership is occupied by other women of color. Many people, especially whites, would look at this and argue that this president is showing favoritism to people who share her race and gender. Some might go as far as claiming reverse racism because so many (presumedly white and male) candidates were passed over for these high-level positions. In other words, this president would be accused of putting her own racial predilections over the well-being of the institution. However, where does such a claim come from? It is not hard to see that it is grounded in two beliefs: first, that these women of color are not deserving of their jobs over their white male counterparts; and second, that they are not competent in their jobs and that white men are more qualified and capable of being leaders. To see the double standard, imagine a college president who is a white male and who has an executive-level administration comprised of all white males (like many of the country's higher education administrations are). The same folks who would accuse the Black president of nepotism and reverse racism would likely see nothing wrong in this second scenario. In fact, it would likely be invisible to them, and if it was pointed out, they would probably argue that these White men were the best candidates or that "not enough people of color applied for these positions." Furthermore, if an applicant of color claimed that they were the victims of racism and discrimination during the application and interview process, they'd likely be accused of hyperbole and exaggeration.

Fourth, these inequities demonstrate the necessity of identity-based programs and solutions, including affirmative action and hiring quotas. Whites tend to hire or admit other whites into their companies and schools, and if this trend continues, not only will the economic gaps continue to grow, but our economy will continue to miss out on the contributions of all its workers and intellectuals.

Finally, these data, especially those economic in nature, make it clear that community colleges have an important role in disrupting the status quo (Sims et al., 2020). Due to historical educational disparities, people of color are relegated to menial, unskilled labor with no hope of escape, especially for those living in poverty. However, community colleges provide that opportunity for economic mobility because they can offer a path to higher skilled jobs and educational attainment. But this mission relies heavily on our ability to create educational opportunities that are equitable for every student that steps on our campus, which means that we will have to reevaluate and restructure how we offer our curricula and how we function as institutions.

The colorblind ideology has ultimately led to the belief that we live in a post-racial, or race-neutral, society (Flagg, 1993; Roediger, 2002; Wise, 2010). Unfortunately, this widespread belief (among whites, that is) has created a situation wherein any attempt to redress racial inequity is met with accusations of "reverse racism" or of "pulling the race card." Undoubtedly, these responses are the consequences of a presumed white innocence where the true "victims" are the white people who must "lose" in order to make amends for racial injustice. Ross (1990a, 1990b) terms this phenomenon the "rhetoric of innocence." More specifically, Ross (1990a) analyzes the rhetoric of innocence in Supreme Court decisions vis-a-vis affirmative action, noting that judges who have ruled in opposition to affirmative action have done so on the basis that this civil rights era initiative has negative impacts on white applicants and that affirmative action does not mitigate actual instances of racial discrimination. As Ross writes, the rhetoric of innocence "question[s] the 'actual victim' status of the black beneficiary of the affirmative action plan... 'Victim' status thereby is recognized only for those who have been subjected to particular and proven racial discrimination with regard to the job or other interest at stake" (p. 301). As such, the rhetoric of innocence disregards societal and institutional racism, and the admission of an African American college applicant over a white applicant, instead, victimizes the latter, leading to an instance of "reverse racism," especially since the rhetoric of white innocence absolves all white people of past racial injustices.

This white innocence has also led to racist abuse (Kendi, 2019) that is often explained away by acculturation and subconscious biases. In fact, white folks tend to be more comfortable speaking about this form of prejudice – or what is most commonly known as "implicit bias" – (though admittedly, even this group is likely very small) because the "unconscious" part lets us off the hook. The logic goes that if we are simply products of our society and that these beliefs are not known to us, then we can't be racist. We need to problematize this belief because, no matter what we tell ourselves, bias and microaggressions have very real and tangible consequences for the people at whom they are directed. Let's look at this a bit more.

Staats, Capatosto, Wright, and Contractor (2015) define implicit bias as beliefs that "operate outside of our conscious awareness. Thus, it is possible that [our] thoughts and actions are being influenced by implicit associations beyond [our] recognition" (p. 5). Indeed, implicit biases may be subconscious, but that doesn't exonerate us for their consequences. We know that we all have biases;

as a result, we should be actively working to identify and to deconstruct them. And while implicit biases are by definition subconscious, they manifest in very concerning ways and they have negative consequences for the groups we are biased against. Dovidio, Gaertner, Kawakami, and Hodson (2002) describe these consequences: "four contemporary prejudices held by Whites toward Blacks in the United States... contribute to the divergence of perceptions and interracial distrust in the United States: (a) contemporary racism among Whites is subtle, (b) these racial biases are often unintentional and unconscious, (c) these biases influence the perceptions that Whites and Blacks have of these same behaviors or events, and (d) these racial biases have different consequences on the outcomes for Blacks and Whites" (p. 89). These biases, ultimately, not only lead to distrust, confusion, and miscommunication, as Dovidio et al. acknowledge, but they can and do often lead to trauma. The simple truth is that implicit biases can be mitigated (Staats et al., 2015). Community college educators committed to the success of their minoritized students, particularly students of color, must engage in the work of attenuating, if not outright eliminating, these beliefs (see Chapter 3 for such a reflective process).

Colorblindness and implicit biases are in direct contrast to a perspective that I argue community college educators must adopt – race consciousness. However, this perspective, as mentioned earlier in this book, has a tumultuous history dating back to the civil rights movement, wherein white liberals (and some African American leaders) equated Black nationalists and white supremacists on the basis of their racial consciousness (Peller, 1990). According to Peller, "Whites who took race as central to their self-identity thereby expressed a commitment to racial supremacy, whereas whites who opposed racism understood that opposition to require transcendence of racial identity in favor of integration and colorblindness... [whites liberals] never developed either a consciousness or a political practice that comprehended racial identity and power as centrally formative factors in American social relations" (p. 761). In other words, whites who are conscious of race are generally believed to be white supremacists, not to mention that race consciousness runs counter to the popular belief among whites that ignoring race and racism will end their existence and importance.

However, this silence has obviously not eradicated racism in our country. As mentioned earlier, the data bear this out. In fact, the belief that colorblindness has worked over the last several decades and that this current stance of race neutrality will eventually eliminate these race-based inequities is farcical. As Aleinikoff (1991) so bluntly put it, we "are not currently a colorblind society, and... race has a deep social significance that continues to disadvantage blacks and other

Americans of color" (p. 1062). It is important to understand where "race neutral-ity" and "colorblindness" come from: we white folks! As Peller (1990) writes, the "colorblind" center "had a distinctly white, upper-middle class and Protestant fla-vor... Instead of comprehending racial justice in terms of the relations of distinct, historically-defined communities, the embrace of integrationism has signified the broad cultural attempt not to think in terms of race at all" (pp. 844, 845). This highlights one of the fundamental problems with colorblindness – it has been proposed and fought for almost exclusively by the very people who benefit from silence on racism and the maintenance of a racial hierarchy. Think about it; how often do you hear people of color arguing for colorblindness?

Instead, I believe that we – white educators – need to adopt *race consciousness*, a perspective in which we account for race in how we see ourselves, how we see our students, how we offer our curricula, and how we interact with students of color. Race consciousness also means being conscious of and celebrating our students' other intersectional identities – gender, sexual orientation, religious affiliation, immigration status, etc. (Crenshaw, 1989). It means honoring the communities of color around the nation so that they may flourish. And, as educators, it means helping our students of color discover their full potential, which means providing an academy that reflects and centers their communities' histories, epistemolo-gies, struggles, and triumphs. Just as importantly, race consciousness allows us white educators to undertake the difficult work of understanding our part in the creation of a racial hierarchy, how we benefit from that hierarchy, and how it is built upon a foundation of white supremacy, the new elephant in the room. As Aleinikoff (1991) argues, such a race-conscious approach to our lives and pro-fessions can "undermin[e] and shift... deep cultural assumptions and ultimately, perhaps, mak[e] progress in overcoming racism" (p. 1081). With that, let us now delve into the origins and preservation of White supremacy.

c. The Foundations of White Supremacy

For most white folks, the term "white supremacy" is a callback to the Civil Rights era and is a reference to skinheads, neo-Nazis, and Klan members, past and pres-ent. In other words, we often mistakenly tie white supremacy to white *suprema-cists,* itself a product of the misconception that only certain individuals perpetuate racism (Peller, 1990). However, a white supremacist, sociopolitical framework undergirds our legal, educational, professional, and other institutions. It is the foundation for the dual systems of racism – advantage and oppression. Said another way, white supremacy is a set of beliefs, values, rules, and structures that propagate the conviction that Western European culture and traditions are superior to non-European cultures, and it is the historically insidious belief that white minds, bodies, and mere existence are more valuable than Black, Indigenous, and other "nonwhite" minds, bodies, and existence. White supremacy is an engrained set of beliefs and values – not people (the people we traditionally think of as white supremacists – skinheads, neo-Nazis, fascists, the alt-right, etc. – are more accurately described as white nationalists).

With this in mind, it is important to understand that what we term "white privilege" is actually a pillar of white supremacy. The two do not coexist as equal and separate ideologies, nor can one exist without the other. White privilege is a consequence of white supremacy. But what is white supremacy, exactly? And where did it come from? Why has an ideology like white supremacy been so powerful in shaping our society (indeed, the world)?

To understand white supremacy, one needs to first start with capitalism and, perhaps unsurprisingly, with the trans-Atlantic slave trade. In describing the history of racism, historian Ibram X. Kendi (2019) traces the nexus of capitalism and racism to Spain's foray into the African slave trade in the 15th century by Prince Henry the Navigator. According to Kendi, Prince Henry's:

> racist policy of slave trading came first – a cunning invention for the practical purpose of bypassing Muslim traders. After nearly two decades of slave trading, King Alfonso asked [advisor] Gomes de Zurara to defend the lucrative commerce in human lives, which he did through the construction of a Black race, an invented group upon which he hung racist ideas. This cause and effect – a racist power creates racist policies out of raw self-interest; the racist policies necessitate racist ideas to justify them – lingers over the life of racism. (p. 43)

In other words, in order to justify the kidnapping and commodification of Black bodies, Prince Henry and pseudo-scholar de Zurara would engage in the first of what Coates (2015) terms "race-craft" (p. 56); they would create artificial labels in order to support their economic, *capitalistic* enterprise.

In the centuries that would follow, religion, science, and sociology would all contribute to the maintenance of white supremacy and anti-Blackness, all in the name of economic development (Bennett, 1993; DuBois, 1965; Kendi, 2016; Robinson, 1983/2000). Slave traders and slaveholders would use Christianity as justification for "owning" other humans, supposedly in an attempt to save the souls of the "savage" Africans, not to mention the oft-cited "curse of Ham,"[2] which was used to justify the dehumanization and enslavement of Africans and

African Americans. The natural sciences would be used to construct the belief that Black and Brown peoples were genetically inferior, even subhuman, as a way to rationalize the sins of chattel slavery and forced sterilization (and more recently to justify the under-education of Black and Brown students as attempted by the racist 1994 book *The Bell Curve: Intelligence and Class Structure in American Life*). In tandem, the social sciences would be wielded to place the blame for social inequities, like the health and wealth gaps, on communities of color themselves, blaming their cultures and lifestyles, not systemic racism, for their marginalization. All of this was in the name of money and power. As Kendi (2016) highlights, "Their own racist ideas usually did *not* dictate the decisions of the most powerful Americans when they instituted, defended, and tolerated discriminatory policies that affected millions of Black lives over the course of American history. Racially discriminatory policies have usually sprung from economic, political, and cultural self-interests" (p. 9).

In order to describe this phenomenon, Cedric J. Robinson (1983/2000) would coin the term "racial capitalism." In Robinson's essential reading, *Black Marxism,* he argues that capitalism and racism evolved jointly: "The development, organization, and expansion of capitalist society pursued essentially racial directions, so too did social ideology. As a material force, then, it could be expected that racialism would inevitably permeate the social structures emergent from capitalism. I have used the term 'racial capitalism' to refer to this development and to the subsequent structure as a historical agency" (p. 2). In his comprehensive history of European capitalism, Robinson traces the roots of modern capitalism to feudal Europe and its use of indentured labor in transitioning from a land-based agrarian society to an urban, commerce-based economy. While Eastern European and Mediterranean ethnic groups and British ethnic minorities like the Irish would comprise the majority of the servant class, European nationalism and Enlightenment philosophy would require a new labor source – Africans and Indigenous peoples. Nonetheless, as Robinson argues, the aforementioned European ethnic minorities were "racialized" in order to justify their servitude. In this way, African chattel slavery would not happen in a vacuum, but it would be an extension – albeit far more violent, massive, and with longer lasting consequences, especially in America – of feudal European indentured servitude. As Robinson notes, "The institution of American slave labor could not be effectively conceptualized as a thing in and of itself. Rather, it was a particular historical development for world capitalism that expropriated the labor of African workers as primitive accumulation. American slavery was a *subsystem* of world capitalism... Slavery, then, was not a historical aberration, it was not a 'mistake' in an otherwise bourgeois democratic age. It was, and its imprints continued to be, *systemic*" (p. 200, emphasis in original). In other words, this system has been codified into the very soul of capitalism.

While American chattel slavery was officially abolished with the 13th amendment, our capitalistic economic system would maintain its racialized foundation. The exploitation of workers of color persists while the vast wealth of the elite continues to grow. In other words, the system continues to be rigged against people of color. As Sims et al. (2020) note, "in the perverse capitalistic system that operates here in the United States, capitalism is anything but a neutral system where there is equitable access to wealth building opportunities... White supremacy is, first and foremost, a political orientation that works in the interest of accruing, centralizing, and hoarding both money and power" (p. 7, 8). Even during the 2020 SARS-CoV-2 (more commonly known as COVID-19) pandemic, the wealthiest Americans continued to accumulate wealth at a shocking pace. In mid-July 2020, and four months into a pandemic that had decimated the economy, it was reported, for example, that Amazon founder Jeff Bezos had grown his wealth by $13 billion (Kelly, 2020). On that same day, the United States had recorded over 60,000 new cases, the majority of which affected people of color (Oppel, Gebeloff, Lai, Wright, & Smith, 2020). Sims et al. continue, "In racialized capitalism, capital is accrued by extracting surplus value from the mind, bodies, and spirits of poor, ethno-racially minoritized peoples. This is true of immigrant populations that traverse dangerous material and political terrain in order to achieve their American Dream. This is true of Black and Brown peoples that are used as frontline fodder for the military industrial complex. This is also true of the Black and Brown peoples that are entrenched in the prison industrial complex. This is also true of Black and Brown women and children that are ensnared in human trafficking" (p. 8). And more recently, economic disparities have been highlighted by the 2020 pandemic, in which so-called "essential workers" – grocery workers, delivery drivers, and other low-wage service employees – were "frontline fodder" to a deadly virus while droves of middle-income and higher income workers "sheltered in place." And it is, of course, worth noting that the majority of these "essential," or what Dr. Abdul El-Sayed calls a euphemism for "expendable," workers were Black and Brown peoples (Pfeiffer & Favreau, 2020). Presciently, Sims et al. conclude, "Because poor people do not own the modes of production, historically, they only have their corporeal bodies as a mode of production."

Ultimately, white supremacy serves the capitalistic interests of the dominant group, and these interests have been codified in law and policy and perpetuated by the mainstream media and popular culture. During World War I, the U.S. Army commissioned a recruitment poster by artist Harry R. Hopps, which portrayed a gorilla kidnapping a nearly nude white woman with the message "Destroy this Mad Brute: Enlist" (Hopps, 1918). While the imagery associated with the gorilla seemed to allude more to the country's German enemies, the racial undertones of the monkey were undeniable. Just over a decade later, Hopps' enlistment poster would inspire the movie poster for the 1933 production of *King Kong*, which again would portray the gorilla kidnapping a distressed, semi-nude white woman – Ann. Regardless of their intended messages, both implicit and explicit, the poster's racialized undertones would be laid bare in 2008's *Vogue* cover depicting LeBron James and Gisele Bundchen. In the photo, James bears the same facial expression, stance, and props (except a basketball instead of a club and shoes that mimic the gorilla's feet) as the gorilla in the poster (Shea, 2008). They are eerily similar, so much so that it is hard to believe it was accidental. Nonetheless, African Americans have been depicted as savage, uncivilized, unintelligent, and lazy in mainstream and popular media from the minstrel shows of the early 20th century to more modern forms, including shows like *Cops* and the news media's representations of criminal suspects (Bogle, 2001).

At its most foundational level, White supremacy is about "white racial domination" (Leonardo, 2009, p. 75). As Leonardo argues, this type of domination has an institutional bent that dispels the argument that racism is simply about individual bad actors: "Domination is a relation of power that subjects enter into and is forged in the historical process. It does not form out of random acts of hatred, although these are condemnable, but rather out of a patterned and enduring treatment of social groups" (p. 77). And as Magee (2019) highlights, "white supremacy [is] the dominant culture's deep-seated belief that white is above black in the hierarchy of all things" (p. 14). Moreover, as mentioned above, this entire system has evolved to remain invisible to those who benefit most from it. In a "colorblind" society that values meritocracy, it is difficult for us white folks to comprehend that race- and other identity-based barriers have been created in order to marginalize and oppress non-dominant groups. Leonardo (2009) describes this never-ending cycle of domination: "set up a system that benefits the group, mystify the system, remove the agents of actions from discourse, and when interrogated about it, stifle the discussion with inane comments about the 'reality' of the charges being made" (p. 88). In other words, the colorblind discourse in our country has obscured the reality that people of color are actively and intentionally thwarted in their life pursuits, and when this reality is brought to our attention, we will deny it, falling back on the discourse of meritocracy and its embedded racist belief that something is wrong with people and communities of color if they can't realize professional and economic success.

While it may be easy writing this history off as benefitting only the top 1% of wage earners, the wealth accrued through racialized capitalism encompasses far more than the elite's monetary wealth but extends to all people who have been labeled as white. As W.E.B. DuBois (1940/2007) famously observed, whites enjoy "public and psychological wages," and whiteness has "income-bearing value" (pp. 48, 65). Building on DuBois, Harris (1993) argues, "The origins of property rights in the United States are rooted in racial domination" (p. 1716). In her seminal work, "Whiteness as Property," Harris looks at the historical and parallel evolution of white supremacy and property ownership and how these two phenomena would eventually fuse into one ideology – whiteness as property. More specifically, the very acts of owning African slaves and the theft of Indigenous lands were an amalgamation of white racial domination and the "ownership" of "property." As Harris writes:

> it was the *interaction* between conceptions of race and property that played a critical role in establishing and maintaining racial and economic subordination... The hyper-exploitation of Black labor was accomplished by treating Black people themselves as objects of property. Race and property were thus conflated by establishing a form of property contingent on race – only Blacks were subjugated as slaves and treated as property. Similarly, the conquest, removal, and extermination of Native American life and culture were ratified by conferring and acknowledging the property rights of whites in Native American land. Only white possession and occupation of land was validated and therefore privileged as a basis for property rights. These distinct forms of exploitation each contributed in varying ways to the construction of whiteness as property. (p. 1716, emphasis in original)

In the decades following slavery and even the Civil Rights Acts, Harris found that the U.S. government, and specifically the U.S. Supreme Court, continually upheld the legal protection of whiteness, even noting that legally, the white racial identity meets the standards of property. Historically, privilege has been legally attached to the white racial identity while "non-whites" have been excluded from those same privileges. Centuries ago, property ownership, voting, and even *existing* as a human being required one to possess a white racial identity. In the last several decades, those who are labeled as white have benefitted from almost exclusive access to higher education, mortgages in sought-after communities, and even the quality health care necessary to maintain one's body property (Lipsitz, 2006). Harris (1993) argues that the possession, or ownership, of white skin provides privileges and access to tangible economic mobility, or what Roediger (1991/2007) calls the "wages of whiteness." "Non-whites," on the other hand, have been excluded from higher education, housing (e.g., redlining), and quality health care, meaning that they are, as a whole, unable to tap the wealth provided by such privileges.

Extreme entitlement to this property and wages has resulted in what Lipsitz (2006) has termed the "possessive investment in whiteness." As Lipsitz bluntly writes, "Whiteness has a cash value" (p. vii). He continues:

> I use the adjective *possessive* to stress the relationship between whiteness and asset accumulation in our society, to connect attitudes to interests, to demonstrate that white supremacy is usually less a matter of direct, referential, and snarling contempt and more a system for protecting the privileges of whites by denying communities of color opportunities for asset accumulation and upward mobility. (p. viii, emphasis in original)

Said another way, this investment in whiteness is an either/or proposition; the privileges and material wealth are either possessed by whites or they are possessed by people of color. And centuries of exclusive access to these privileges and wealth have resulted in a sense of entitlement and the questionable belief that any gain for communities of color is a loss for whites (McGhee, 2021).

To demonstrate, I'd like to highlight student phenom Michael Brown, a Houston, Texas, high school student who applied to and was accepted to every university he applied to, including Stanford and four Ivy League universities. Brown smashed the average GPA for admission to each college with his astronomical 4.68 GPA and was offered full-ride scholarships to each university (Talarico, 2018). Objectively, this is an amazing feat, and one that should be celebrated. However, the conservative news media saw this accomplishment quite differently and relied primarily on dog whistle reporting to disparage Brown, an African American teen, for "taking spots" from other students, presumably the white students who generally make up the incoming freshmen classes of these universities. One Fox News anchor, in particular, called Michael Brown "obnoxious" for "taking a spot from someone who worked really hard" and that because of him, "19 kids come off the waitlist" (Think Tank, 2018). These types of comments feed the trope that the successes of Black and Brown people are in conflict with the successes of white people and that the latter are indeed losing something tangible to the former. In this case, college admissions to prestigious universities are a form of property that has historically been possessed by white applicants and families, and when this property is perceived to be threatened, there is often a white backlash (not to mention that it is quite common for high school students of all races to apply to a wide range of universities).

This is further underscored by the nation's move away from affirmative action. At the heart of anti-affirmative action positions is the belief that proportionate representation in higher education and public sector employment gives economic gain to people of color while simultaneously denying whites these spots. In other words, whites, as a group, feel entitled to admissions to the university or employment at the agency of their choice. This entitlement was abundantly clear in the Supreme Court case *Fisher v. University of Texas*, in which a white Texas resident, Abigail Fisher, claimed that she was unfairly denied admission to the University of Texas, Austin (UTA) because of her race. However, court documents would show that Fisher was uniquely *un*qualified for admission to UTA. Her GPA and test scores were above average but not excellent (she didn't graduate in the top 10% of her class, which guarantees admission), and as many observers have noted, many applicants of color with *better* grades and test scores were denied admission to UTA (Hannah-Jones, 2016). Ultimately, Fisher felt entitled to admission to the University of Texas because she "work[ed] hard for it." For Fisher, it did not matter that many applicants of color worked harder and were admitted, nor that many of them were also denied admission even though they were more qualified. The only thing that mattered was that she did not receive what she felt entitled to.

These examples illustrate the inextricable link between white supremacy and white privilege. One cannot exist without the other. As Leonardo (2009) argues, "white supremacy makes white privilege possible" (p. 75). Leonardo, in a similar style to McIntosh, lists the several ways in which white supremacy has molded this country's racialized caste system, has created and sustained its incredible wealth, and had maintained the subordination of women, people of color, and immigrants (pp. 85–88). Similarly, Yosso (2006) defines white privilege "as a system of advantage resulting from a legacy of racism and benefitting individuals and groups based on the notions of whiteness" (p. 5). But it's important to realize that white supremacy has not only provided the conditions for whites to gain advantages and wealth, but it has also resulted in a loss for people of color. For example, when applicants of color are systematically rejected admissions to elite universities (whether it's a consequence of underfunded schools, little to no access to private tutoring or test prep, or a lack of legacy admissions, or what Katznelson (2005) terms white affirmative action), they lose out on the high-quality education and its concomitant economic mobility as a result of their white counterparts' privilege and gain. And the white applicants' widespread access to adequately funded K-12 schools, their ability to afford tutors and test prep, and their parents' alumni status at these elite universities are all the intentional effects of white supremacy and racialized capitalism. So even if at the moment that the admissions staff grants admissions to the white applicants while denying admission to applicants of color may not be steeped in explicit racism and bias, the system was set up so that the white applicants succeed without any racialized barriers as a default. This is how white privilege exists as a by-product of white supremacy.

Understandably, this reality creates mixed feelings for white people new to such concepts, including discomfort, guilt, and even anger. Matias (2016) found, for example, that white folks – in her case, white students in a teacher training program – often feel "singled out" when conversations of racism and white supremacy arose: "white emotionality is expressed in guilt, defensiveness, and anger. Interpretively, this is revealed in [their] word usage of 'being singled out' or 'blamed' when merely learning about whiteness" (p. 34). Grounded in the scholarship of emotionality and sociology, Matias demonstrates that human emotion is "both innate *and* social" and that because racism and white supremacist ideologies are endemic in American society, they ultimately inform our emotionality vis-à-vis race and whiteness (p. 5). Unfortunately, Matias has found that these emotions often manifest as anger, ignorance, and guilt.

Similarly, DiAngelo (2018) would term this confluence of emotions "white fragility." As DiAngelo describes:

> We consider a challenge to our racial worldviews as a challenge to our very identities as good, moral people. Thus, we perceive any attempt to connect us to the system of racism as an unsettling and unfair moral offense. The smallest amount of racial stress is intolerable – the mere suggestion that being white has meaning often triggers a range of defensive responses. These include emotions such as anger, fear, and guilt and behaviors such as argumentation, silence, and withdrawal from the stress-inducing situation. These responses work to reinstate white equilibrium as they repel the challenge, return our racial comfort, and maintain our dominance within the racial hierarchy. I conceptualize this process as *white fragility*. Though white fragility is triggered by discomfort and anxiety, it is born of superiority and entitlement. White fragility is not weakness per se. In fact, it is a powerful means of white racial control and the protection of white advantage. (p. 2, emphasis in original)

In other words, many white folks respond to uncomfortable discussions about racism with a sort of defensiveness that usually ends the discussion altogether. DiAngelo's point about "entitlement" makes complete sense here – we feel entitled to *possess* an environment free of racial animus and discomfort, and when someone, usually a person of color but also sometimes fellow whites, disrupts that comfort, we use our racial power in response. And when we're in the company of other whites, we usually enjoy the comfort of accomplices in reestablishing the racial order.

At the most fundamental level, this fragility is a consequence of shifting the gaze from people of color to us. We are used to discussing race and racism in the context of people of color or, in our spheres, students of color. Many of us are more comfortable with discussing race and racism as a problem that occurs in communities of color and fringe white communities instead of looking in the mirror and critiquing our own culpability in racism. When hooks (1992) turns the mirror on white privilege and supremacy in her classrooms, students oftentimes react angrily:

> In these classrooms, there have been heated debates among students when white students respond with disbelief, shock, and rage, as they listen to black students talk about whiteness, when they are compelled to hear observations, stereotypes, etc., that are offered as 'data' gleaned from close scrutiny and study... Often their rage erupts because they believe that all ways of looking that highlight difference subvert the liberal belief in a universal subjectivity (we are all just people) that they think will make racism disappear. They have a deep emotional investment in the myth of 'sameness,' even as their actions reflect the primacy of whiteness as a sign of informing who they are and how they think. Many of them are shocked that black people think critically about whiteness because racist thinking perpetuates the fantasy that the Other who is subjugated, who is subhuman, lacks the ability to comprehend, to understand, to see the working of the powerful. Even though the majority of these students politically consider themselves liberals, who are anti-racist, they too unwittingly invest in the sense of whiteness as mystery. (pp. 339–340)

Our responses to these types of discussions come from a decades-, if not centuries-, long desire to be seen as racially sensitive and politically "liberal" or progressive while simultaneously denying the existence of white privilege and our complacency in the racial hierarchy. It is easier to be "antiracist" when the racists are abstractions that exist in the margins of this country.

Unfortunately, this is just a form of denial. Most of us white folks might not be the stereotypical racist who dons swastikas and flies the confederate flag, but unless we are actively working to dismantle racism in our spheres of influence, we are actively, or at best tacitly, maintaining the racial injustices mentioned in the previous pages. As Kendi (2019) attests, "Denial is the heartbeat of racism, beating across ideologies, races, and nations. It is beating within us... How often do we become reflexively defensive when someone calls something we've done or said racist? How many of us would agree with this statement: 'Racist' isn't a descriptive word. It's a pejorative word. It is the equivalent of saying 'I don't like you'" (p. 9). Kendi is getting at an important and widespread belief – that the word "racist" is associated with white nationalists, neo-Nazis, the KKK, and other fringe groups. Most white folks don't believe that racism – and therefore, racists – is widespread. We need to deconstruct the association between racism/racists and white nationalism and instead take the broader view that racism/racists happen anytime someone of European descent (i.e., someone who is labeled as white) actively or tacitly upholds systemic and systematic racial oppression, marginalization, and violence. As Kendi (2019) argues, there is no such thing as "not racist"; you can only be racist or antiracist.

This change in perspective won't happen overnight, and as a result, we need to become comfortable with being uncomfortable. First and foremost, we need to accept that there exists a racial caste system in this country and that we white folks benefit in many ways from that caste system, whether we can see it or not. And while we may not have built this system, we have certainly been its beneficiaries and its keepers. We need to start taking responsibility, even if that means wrestling with feelings of guilt and shame; otherwise, we are engaging in what King (1991) calls dysconscious racism, or the "uncritical habit of mind (including perceptions, attitudes, assumptions, and beliefs) that justifies inequity and exploitation by accepting the existing order of things as given... Dysconscious racism is a form of racism that tacitly accepts dominant White norms and privileges. It is not the *absence* of consciousness (that is, not unconsciousness) but an *impaired* consciousness or distorted way of thinking about race as compared to, for example, critical consciousness" (p. 135, emphasis in original). As King has observed, when white people feel uncertainty about race, racial domination, and white supremacy, we tend to fall into feelings of guilt and that we "often express such feelings of guilt and hostility suggests [we] accept certain unexamined assumptions, unasked questions, and unquestioned cultural myths regarding both the social order and their place in it" (p. 136). However, we must accept and even embrace these feelings of discomfort because they allow us to do the important work of racial justice, both on ourselves and in the spaces around us. In fact, as Leonardo (2009) argues, these intense feelings are actually a prerequisite for whites working for social justice: "As long as whites ultimately feel a sense of comfort with racial analysis, they will not sympathize with the pain and discomfort they have unleashed on racial minorities for centuries" (pp. 89–90). Racism – and its concomitant violence and trauma – is uncomfortable, and it is time that those of us who are labeled as White remove the blinders and start to work for social justice. Our very well-being as an American society is at stake, and I hope this chapter – and this book – will help you take the first step in fighting for our common humanity.

W.E.B. DuBois (1965) makes this final point better than I ever can, so I'd like to conclude this chapter with a lengthy, yet important, excerpt from his book *The World and Africa*:

> Here in America we must learn to be proud of the things of which we are ashamed, and ashamed of things of which we are proud. America should be proud of the fact that she is a nation with increasing democracy composed of the most unlikely peoples and groups on earth; that out of criminals, paupers, and slaves she has built this land of promise. We should be ashamed that despite this known historical fact, we are trying to build up class and race differences and refusing to carry out the democratic methods which we profess... If we refuse to do this; if we stubbornly cling to our race prejudices, what of the future of this civilization? The continuity of a social group, the continuity of a civilization is at best doubtful and precarious... The broader the basis of a culture, the wider and freer its conception, the better chance it has for the survival of its best elements. This is the basic hope of world democracy. No culture whose greatest effort must go to suppress some of the strongest contributions of mankind can have left in itself strength for survival... Peace and tolerance is the only path to eternal progress" (pp. 258–259).

d. Chapter 2 Synopsis and Questions to Consider

Synopsis

It is important that community college educators understand race, racism, and white supremacy as well as their own racial identity and privileges. However, most of us white folks have never been taught how to see or speak about race and racism, and as a result, we often feel discomfort, guilt, and even denial when issues of racism and white supremacy emerge. This chapter argues that we need to embrace this discomfort because it is the only way to engage in the self-reflection necessary for social justice work. Lastly, our collective ability to take on our own privileges and racist beliefs has major implications for our common humanity and the strength of our democracy. We can't have a truly pluralist society when we white folks cling to our privileges and comfort.

Questions to Consider

1. Why is it important for white educators to understand this country's racialized hierarchy and history?
2. Why is colorblindness problematic? Why is race consciousness a better approach?
3. How comfortable are you discussing race, racism, and white supremacy? Why is that? Can you think of an example where a discussion of this sort went well? What about when it went poorly?
4. What did you learn about the legacy of injustice and inequity in this country? In the education system?
5. How are "white privilege" and "white supremacy" interconnected?
6. Why do *you* believe that critical racial self-reflection is important?
7. Do you believe racism is a threat to higher education and our society and democracy, writ large? Why or why not?

Keywords: white privilege, colorblindness, white supremacy, race consciousness, racialized capitalism, dysconscious racism, white fragility

e. Notes

1. It is important to acknowledge here that humanism, as a philosophy, has earlier, non-Western roots and to challenge the privilege we place on this particular iteration.
2. The "Curse of Ham," which is a bit misleading, is drawn from Genesis 9, where Noah curses his grandson Canaan for the "transgressions" of Canaan's father – and Noah's son – Ham (who gazed upon Noah's naked body). Noah decrees that Canaan and his ancestors will be "servants of servants" to their "brethren." This passage was often translated by slaveowners as "slave of slaves." Nonetheless, no evidence exists – in the Bible or otherwise – that Canaan and his ancestors were African or even Black (the Canaans settled in an area including modern Israel, Palestine, Jordan, and Lebanon).

f. References

Aleinikoff, T.A. (1991). A case for race-consciousness. *Columbia Law Review, 91*(5), 1060–1125.

Alexander, M. (2010). *The new Jim Crow: Mass incarceration in the age of colorblindness.* New York: New Press.

Althusser, A. (2003). *The humanist controversy and other writings.* F. Matheron (Ed.) and G.M. Goshgarian (trans.). London: Verso.

Apple, M.W. (2000). *Official knowledge: Democratic education in a conservative age* (2nd ed.). New York: Routledge.

Bennett, L. (1993). *Before the Mayflower: A history of Black America.* New York: Penguin.

Bogle, D. (2007). *Toms, coons, mulattoes, mammies, & bucks: An interpretive history of Blacks in American films.* New York: Continuum.

Bonilla-Silva, E. (2017). *Racism without racists: Color-blind racism and the persistence of racial inequality in America* (5th ed.). Lanham, MD: Rowman & Littlefield.

CCEAL & SNAHEC. (2019). *From boarding schools to suspension boards: Suspensions and expulsions of Native American students in California public schools.* Retrieved from https://cceal.org/wp-content/uploads/2019/09/Suspension-Boards-Final.pdf

Coates, T. (2015). *Between the world and me.* New York: Spiegel & Grau.

Crenshaw, K. (1989). Demarginalizing the intersection of race and sex: A Black feminist critique of antidiscrimination doctrine, feminist theory, and antiracist politics. *University of Chicago Law Review, 1*(8), 139–167.

Crenshaw, K., Gotanda, N., Peller, G., & Thomas, K. (1995). *Critical race theory: The key writings that formed the movement.* New York: New Press.

Dalton, H. (2016). Failing to see. In P.S. Rothernberg (Ed.), *White privilege: Essential readings on the other side of racism.* New York: Worth Publishers.

Daniels, J. (2008, July 6). Racism as the root cause of infant mortality. *Racism Review.* http://www.racismreview.com/blog/2008/07/06/racism-as-the-root-cause-of-infant-mortality/

DeGruy, J. (2005/2017). *Post traumatic slave syndrome.* Joy DeGruy Publications.

Delpit, L. (2012). *Multiplication is for White people: Raising expectations for other people's children.* New York: New Press.

DiAngelo, R. (2018). *White fragility: Why it's so hard for White people to talk about racism.* Boston: Beacon Press.

Dovidio, J.F., Gaertner, S.L., Kawakami, K., & Hodson, G. (2002). Why can't we just get along? Interpersonal biases and interracial distrust. *Cultural Diversity and Ethnic Minority Psychology, 8*(2), 88–102.

DuBois, W.E.B. (1903/1994). *The souls of Black folk.* New York: Dover.

DuBois, W.E.B. (1940/2007). *Dusk of dawn.* H.L. Gates (Ed.). New York: Oxford UP.

DuBois, W.E.B. (1965). *The world and Africa.* New York: International Publishers.

Fanon, F. (2008). *Black skin, white masks.* R. Philcox (Trans.). New York: Grove Press. (Original work published 1952).

Flagg, B.J. (1993). "Was blind, but now I see": White race consciousness and the requirement of discriminatory intent. *Michigan Law Review, 91*(5), 953–1017.

Gallagher, C.A. (1996). White racial formation: Into the twenty-first century. In R. Delgado & J. Stefancic (Eds.), *Critical White studies: Looking behind the mirror* (pp. 6–11). Philadelphia: Temple University Press.

Hannah-Jones, Nikole. (2016, June 23). What Abigail Fisher's affirmative action case was really about. *ProPublica.* Retrieved from https://www.propublica.org/article/a-colorblind-constitution-what-abigail-fishers-affirmative-action-case-is-r

Harris, C.I. (1993). Whiteness as property. *Harvard Law Review, 106*(8), 1707–1791.

hooks, b. (1992). *Black looks: Race and representation.* Boston: South End Press.

Hopps, H.R. (1918). Destroy this mad brute Enlist – U.S. Army [poster]. *Library of Congress.* Retrieved from https://www.loc.gov/pictures/item/2010652057/

Howard, G.R. (2006). *We can't teach what we don't know: White teachers, multiracial schools* (2nd ed.). New York: Teachers College Press.

Howard, T.C. (2014). *Black male(d): Peril and promise in the education of African American males.* New York: Teachers College Press.

Inoue, A.B. (2015). *Antiracist writing assessment ecologies: Teaching and assessing writing for a socially just future.* Anderson, SC: Parlor Press.

James, S.A. (1994). John Henryism and the health of African-Americans. *Culture, Medicine, and Psychiatry, 18*(2), 163–182.

James, S.A., Keenan, N.L., Strogatz, D.S., Browning, S.R., & Garrett, J.M. (1992). Socioeconomic status, John Henryism, and blood pressure in black adults: The Pitt County study. *American Journal of Epidemiology, 135*(1), 59–67.

Johns, D.J. (2016). Expanding high-quality early care and education for Black boys. In S.R. Harper & J.L. Wood (Eds.), *Advancing Black male student success from preschool through Ph.D.* (pp. 1–19). Sterling, VA: Stylus.

Jones, J.M. (1996). *Prejudice and racism* (2nd ed.). New York: McGraw-Hill.

Katznelson, I. (2005). *When affirmative action was white: An untold history of racial inequality in twentieth-century America.* New York: Norton.

Kelly, J. (2020, July 22). The rich are getting richer during the pandemic. *Forbes.* Retrieved from https://www.forbes.com/sites/jackkelly/2020/07/22/the-rich-are-getting-richer-during-the-pandemic/#4c6e132e5c7e

Kendi, I.X. (2016). *Stamped from the beginning: The definitive history of racist ideas in America.* New York: Nation.

Kendi, I.X. (2019). *How to be an antiracist.* New York: One World.

Kennedy, D. (1990). A cultural pluralist case for affirmative action in legal academic. *Duke Law Review, 1990*(4), 705–757.

King, J.E. (1991). Dysconscious racism: Ideology, identity, and the miseducation of teachers. *The Journal of Negro Education, 60*(2), 133–146.

Kozol, J. (1991). *Savage inequalities: Children in America's schools.* New York: Broadway.

Ladson-Billings, G. (2007). Pushing past the achievement gap: An essay on the language of deficit. *The Journal of Negro Education, 76*(3), 316–323.

Leonardo, Z. (2009). *Race, whiteness, and education.* New York: Routledge.

Lipsitz, G. (2006). *The possessive investment in whiteness: How white people profit from identity politics.* Philadelphia: Temple UP.

Loeb, P., Cohen, W., Johnson, C., Shapiro, J.P., Glastris, K, Sherrid, P., & Wright, A. (1996). The new redlining: It's different from the old, but minorities are still shortchanged. In M. Hudson (Ed.), *Merchants of misery: How corporate America profits from poverty* (pp. 18–27). Monroe, ME: Common Courage Press.

Loury, G.C. (2008). *Race, incarceration, and American values.* Cambridge, MA: MIT Press.

Ma, J., & Baum, S. (2016, April). "Trends in community colleges: Enrollment, process, student debt, and completion." *College Board Research Brief.* Retrieved from https://research.colle geboard.org/pdf/trends-community-colleges-research-brief.pdf

Magee, R.V. (2019). *The inner work of racial justice: Healing ourselves and transforming our communities through mindfulness.* New York: TarcherPerigree.

Matias, C.E. (2016). *Feeling white: Whiteness, emotionality, and education.* Rotterdam: Sense.

McGhee, H. (2021). *The sum of us: What racism costs everyone and how we can prosper together.* New York: Penguin Random House.

McIntosh, P. (1989, July/August). White privilege: Unpacking the invisible knapsack. *Peace and Freedom Magazine,* 10–12. Retrieved from https://nationalseedproject.org/Key-SEED-Texts/white-privilege-unpacking-the-invisible-knapsack

Milner, H.R. (2008). Disrupting deficit notions of difference: Counter-narratives of teachers and community in urban education. *Teaching and Teacher Education, 24*(6), 1573–1598.

Noah, T. (2016, December 1). *Tomi Lahren - Giving a voice to conservative America on "Tomi": The Daily Show* [Video file]. Retrieved from https://www.youtube.com/watch?v=F2xv4fba65U

Oppel, Jr. R.A., Gebeloff, R. Lai, K.K.R., Wright, W., & Smith, M. (2020, July 5). The fullest look yet at the racial inequity of coronavirus. *The New York Times.* Retrieved from https://www.nytimes.com/interactive/2020/07/05/us/coronavirus-latinos-african-americans-cdc-data.html

Peller, G. (1990). Race consciousness. *Duke Law Review, 1990(4),* 758–847.

Pfeiffer, D., & Favreau, J. (Hosts). (2020, July 16). Parscale finds something new. In *Pod Save America.* Crooked Media. Retrieved from https://crooked.com/podcast/parscale-finds-something-new/

reardon, s.f., Weathers, E.S., Fahle, E.M., Jang, H., & Kalogrides, D. (2019). *Is separate still unequal? New evidence on school segregation and racial academic achievement gaps* (CEPA Working Paper No. 19-06). Stanford Center for Education Policy Analysis. Retrieved from http://cepa.stanford.edu/wp19-06

Robinson, C.J. (1983/2000). *Black Marxism: The making of the Black radical* tradition (2nd ed.). Chapel Hill: University of North Carolina Press.

Roediger, D.R. (1991/2007). *The wages of whiteness: Race and the making of the American working class.* London: Verso.

Roediger, D.R. (2002). *Colored White: Transcending the racial past.* Berkeley: University of California Press.

Ross, T. (1990a). Innocence and affirmative action. *Vanderbilt Law Review, 43,* 297–316.

Ross, T. (1990b). The rhetorical tapestry of race: White innocence and Black abstraction. *William and Mary Law Review, 32,* 1–40.

Sabin, J.A. (2020, January 6). *How we fail black patients in pain*. American Association of Medical Colleges. Retrieved from https://www.aamc.org/news-insights/how-we-fail-black-patients-pain

Shea, D. (2008, April 5). Uncovered: Possible inspiration for controversial LeBron James Vogue cover. *Huffington Post*. Retrieved from https://www.huffpost.com/entry/uncovered-possible-inspir_n_93944

Sims, J.J. (2018). *Revolutionary STEM education: Critical-reality pedagogy and social justice in STEM for Black males*. New York: Peter Lang. Kindle.

Sims, J.J., Taylor-Mendoza, J., Hotep, L., Wallace, J., & Conaway, T. (2020). *Minding the obligation gap in community colleges: Theory and practice in achieving educational equity*. New York: Peter Lang.

Smedley, A., & Smedley, B.D. (2005). Race as biology is fiction, racism as a social problem is real: Anthropological and historical perspectives on the social construction of race. *American Psychologist, 60*(1), 16–26.

Staats, C., Capatosto, K., Wright, R.A., & Contractor, D. (2015). *State of the science: Implicit bias review 2015*. Columbus, OH: Kirwan Institute for the Study of Race and Ethnicity. Retrieved from http://kirwaninstitute.osu.edu/wp-content/uploads/2015/05/2015-kirwan-implicit-bias.pdf

Steele, C.M. (2011). *Whistling Vivaldi: How stereotypes affect us and what we can do*. New York: Norton.

Sue, D.W. (2003). *Overcoming our racism: The journey to liberation*. San Francisco: Jossey-Bass.

Sue, D.W. (2016). The invisible Whiteness of being: Whiteness, White supremacy, White privilege and racism. In P.S. Rothernberg (Ed.), *White privilege: Essential readings on the other side of racism*. New York: Worth Publishers.

Talarico, L. (2018, April 5). Teen offered full ride to 20 universities, including four Ivy League Schools. *USA Today*. Retrieved from https://www.usatoday.com/story/news/nation-now/2018/04/05/teen-offered-full-ride-20-universities-including-four-ivy-league-schools/490924002/

Think Tank. (2018, April 12). *Local Fox anchors criticize Black student for being too smart* [video]. YouTube. Retrieved from https://www.youtube.com/watch?v=ZAg7bILCUxE

Umoja Practices. (2017). Umoja community. Retrieved June 27, 2020, from https://umojacommunity.org/umoja-practices

Wise, T. (2010). *Colorblind: The rise of post-racial politics and the retreat from racial equity*. San Francisco: City Lights.

Wood, J.L., Harris III, F., & Howard, T.C. (2018). *Get out! Black male suspensions in California public schools*. San Diego, CA: Community College Equity Assessment Lab and the UCLA Black Male Institute. Retrieved from https://cceal.org/wp-content/uploads/2018/06/GET-OUT-Black-Male-Suspensions-in-California-Public-Schools.pdf

Yosso, T.J. (2006). *Critical race counterstories along the Chicana/Chicano educational pipeline*. New York: Routledge.

3

Antiracism for Community College Educators

"In a racist society, it is not enough to be non-racist - we must be antiracist."

- Angela Davis

Soon after starting my tenure-track position at College of San Mateo, I was walking from my office to my classroom when I passed an elderly man who was clearly a professor at the college. He was wearing a brown vested suit with a pocket watch, and on his tie was a Confederate tiepin. Needless to say, I was flabbergasted. I thought, "this was the San Francisco Bay Area, isn't it?" I had a hard time believing there was a confederate flag within a 100-mile radius of my campus (which was clearly a ludicrous assumption). I'd later find out from a colleague that the man was a history professor and that this colleague and that professor had engaged in too many academic conversations about this tiepin to count. Even as an early professional who hadn't quite delved into critical pedagogy and critical race studies, I knew this accessory was problematic to say the least. It loudly said so much about the professor – at worst, he was an overt racist and white supremacist, of the stock that we usually attribute to the Ku Klux Klan or the Trump Administration. But at best, he was absolutely delusional about the symbolism of this flag for students of color and had absolutely no regard for the students for whom this symbol represented hatred, bigotry, and violence. In the middle, there is quite a bit of disdain, complacency, and ignorance. The fact is that there is no winning on this scale. The professor who is overtly racist is as much a problem as the professor who is blind to the violence they inflict.

However, this anecdote is not truly about my colleague, who has thankfully retired at this point. It is really about me. This story says as much about me as it does him. You see, I knew that wearing a Confederate flag in a place of higher learning, or in any place of learning (or any place, period), was an issue, and I knew that this symbol had real consequences for the college's students. Yet I did nothing. And I may be able to let myself off the hook since I was a brand-new member of the faculty, a newbie in his first year of tenure review, but even if this was an acceptable excuse (it isn't), it doesn't account for the fact that I would see this colleague several times over the course of my time on the tenure track, most of the time in the presence of my tenured colleagues whom I could call on for support. All of this is to say that simply being aware of white supremacy and of one's own prejudices just isn't enough. We could be the most "woke" white person that higher education has ever seen, yet if we just keep it all inside and to ourselves, if we are just observers, we will never promote the social justice that our colleges and our society so badly need. Early in my career, I was too afraid to speak out against such a clearly racist symbol and, as a result, hundreds more students were forced into a classroom with a man who was an existential threat to them (and simply because they needed one of the college's impacted history courses to transfer to a university). At that moment, I was complacent in overt racism instead of an antiracist who worked to eliminate that type of symbolic violence.

As professionals in some of the most diverse institutions of higher education in the world, we have a choice about what kind of educators we want to be. At this point, I hope I have convinced you that racial hierarchies exist in higher education, including your own, that this hierarchy is a microcosm of the larger society, and that this hierarchy is not an accident. It is the intentional consequence of centuries of white supremacy and the subjugation and oppression of people of color (in addition to women, immigrants, religious minorities, and members of the LGBTQ community, among others). It really comes down to three choices: 1) we can promote this system as an overt racist and bigot; 2) we can choose to ignore it as a "colorblind" racist or so-called "non-racist," both of which perpetuate and maintain this racial hierarchy; or 3) we can actively take steps to deconstruct and ultimately destroy this system as an antiracist. There are no other options.

At this point, it is fair to ask why being a non-racist is so problematic. It is obvious that overt racism and bigotry are repulsive, but isn't non-racism the opposite of racism? Doesn't non-racism eliminate racism? There are several problems with this approach, however, the first of which is that non-racism, or its more popular construction, "colorblindness," attempts to erase race altogether. And while race is a social construct and has no basis in biology, it still very much exists in very tangible ways – both in the cultures that have evolved as part of these racial categories and in the racial hierarchy and inequities that exist in our society (as discussed in Ch. Two). Let's tackle each of these in more detail.

We live in a country stratified by race and where so-called "equal opportunities" have not resulted in equal outcomes. Our educational, political, social, health, and other institutions have contributed to a racial hierarchy whose foundation is supported by racism, bigotry, and White supremacy. It may seem logical to simply reject racism in favor of colorblindness, but we have already covered how this ideology is not an adequate solution because it not only denies people of color their unique identities and cultures, but it also rejects any race-conscious explanation of the racial hierarchy of this country and the racialized outcomes of our institutions. Colorblindness, or non-racism, is also problematic because it ignores the racialized outcomes of our society, most of which are the products of these very beliefs. Think about it, if we believe that the majority of white Americans are not racist, how do the inequities described in Chapter 2 exist? The racists and bigots of the Ku Klux Klan, the Nazi Party, and other white supremacist groups do not wield enough power and influence to create such glaring inequities in so many different socio-political institutions. Instead, it is the covert racism of "colorblind" people, those who do not believe themselves to be racist but who have for centuries supported racist policies (Kendi, 2019). This has resulted in a society where there is "racism without racists" (Bonilla-Silva, 2017).

Consequently, antiracism becomes the only viable option for educators who are committed to closing the opportunity gaps in our institutions. As Bonilla-Silva writes, "I urge a personal and political movement away from claiming to be 'non racist' to becoming 'antiracist.' Being an antiracist begins with understanding the institutional nature of racial matters and accepting that all actors in a racialized society are affected *materially* (receive benefits or disadvantages) and *ideologically* by the racial structure" (p. 15, emphasis in original). Being antiracist educators requires us to understand the racialized society we live in, to identify ways in which its concomitant racial stratification materializes in higher education, and to commit ourselves to deconstructing and destroying racialized barriers and discrimination in our spheres of influence.

This chapter will build on the existing antiracism literature and frame it within a community college context. More specifically, I will describe what it means to be an antiracist community college educator, both cognitively and in our practices. Unfortunately, we can't sit through training or read a book on antiracism and expect that we will permanently embody the values of social justice. Unlearning the quotidian racism and white supremacy of our society and its institutions not only takes time but constant reflection. As such, this chapter will highlight a heuristic for continually recognizing what can be called "white supremacy creep," the subtle and unconscious *re*-investment in white supremacy and privilege that is the consequence of a socio-political and media environment that is perpetually normalizing whiteness and painting people of color and other minoritized people as abnormal or inferior. This heuristic utilizes the iterative practice that I have termed *antiracist reflective praxis*. No matter what we do, we can never be "not racist"; however, I hope the practices in this chapter will help us begin to continually identify, critique, and deconstruct our own racist beliefs and actions.

a. What is Antiracism?

Before delving into the practice of antiracism, it is important to review this book's definitions of racism and colorblindness and to put antiracism into a historical context. First, as discussed in the introduction, I have adopted the frameworks described by Tatum (1997), which posits that racism is a system of privilege, and Leonardo (2009), which positions racism as a system of oppression. Said another way, racism is comprised of policies, structures, and both de facto and de jure discrimination that oppress people of color while simultaneously providing white people with privileges and power. As such, any idea, action, or inaction by white folks that supports this system of privilege and oppression is inherently racist. Consequently, "colorblindness," or what Bonilla-Silva calls "colorblind racism," is inherently racist because it maintains this system. Educators who adopt this so-called "colorblindness" not only maintain the racialized hierarchy of our colleges, but we deprive our students of color of an important aspect of their identities, engaging in what Kendi (2019) calls "cultural racism."

Cultural racism is one of the most common forms of racism I encounter from my colleagues on a day-to-day basis, and it is often used as a way to "blame the victim." It is argued by these educators that if only our students of color would reject the "pathologies" and the "culture of failure" of their neighborhoods or families that the so-called "achievement gaps" wouldn't exist. This is highly problematic, and it is ignorant at best. It promotes the racist ideas that we all, in theory, are trying to work against. So what does this look like? It might help to start with a definition of racist ideas as described by Kendi (2019): "A racist idea is any idea that suggests one racial group is inferior or superior to another racist group in any way. Racist ideas argue that inferiorities and superiorities of racial groups explain racial inequities in society" (p. 20). Cultural racism, then, is the belief that the cultural artifacts, symbols, and practices of our students of color are inferior and are the cause of any disparities in college success rates. This can include, but is not limited to: judging a student's clothing, including disparaging thoughts about sagging pants or revealing clothing; beliefs that some ethnic foods are superior to others; assumptions based on a student's native language or judgments based on their mastery of "standard" English; beliefs that a student's music is inferior to Western European and more "American" genres, most notably comparisons between rap, hip-hop, and alternative rock to classical or classic rock; and judging an individual's actions or inactions as demonstrative of the entire group (e.g. believing that African Americans as a whole are lazy because one African American student doesn't turn in homework). This type of racism is rooted in the dominant culture's push to assimilate non-dominant groups. As Kendi writes, "Assimilationist ideas are racist ideas. Assimilationists can position any racial group as the superior standard that another racial group should be measuring themselves against, the benchmark they should be trying to reach. Assimilationists typically position White people as the superior standard" (p. 29). We can also find ourselves promoting racist ideologies when judging a student's family, including the neighborhood they live in, their state or country of origin, their educational background, their mastery of "standard" English, and their cultural practices. In other words, we are promoting racism any time we compare minoritized cultural practices and artifacts to a Western European standard and then deem those practices and artifacts as inferior.

Because colorblindness and non-racism are inherently racist – they are complicit in the racist structures of their colleges and society, writ large – the only option for educators who work with diverse student bodies is antiracism. As Kendi writes, "The opposite of 'racist' isn't 'not racist.' It is 'antiracist'... One endorses either the idea of a racial hierarchy as a racist, or racial equality as an antiracist. One either believes problems are rooted in groups of people, as a racist, or locates the roots of problems in power and policies, as an antiracist. One either allows racial inequalities to persevere, as a racist, or confronts racial inequalities, as an antiracist. There is no in-between safe space of 'not racist.' The claim of 'not racist' neutrality is a mask for racism" (p. 9). So what does anti-racism look like in practice?

1. Antiracists believe in the equality of all racial groups and their cultural artifacts, symbols, and belief systems (e.g. music, clothing, language, values, food, etc.) (Derman-Sparks & Brunson Phillips, 1997; Kendi, 2016, 2019).

2. Antiracists reject the Eurocentric standards of beauty, language, art, literature, and forms of culture and appearance (Derman-Sparks & Brunson Phillips, 1997; Kendi, 2019).

3. Antiracists are continually identifying and critiquing their own privileges, biases, and racist beliefs (Pollock, 2008; Thompson, 2008).

4. Antiracists reject the belief that race is biological and, instead, acknowledge that race is real only insofar as it has social consequences for those at "the bottom of the well" (Bell, 1992; Derman-Sparks & Brunson Phillips, 1997; Kendi, 2016, 2019).

5. Antiracists believe that institutions, including laws and policies, create inequity – not the people who are victimized by these inequitable institutions (Kendi, 2016, 2019).

6. Antiracists fight for equitable resource allocation and speak out against policies and laws that take away or eliminate resources from communities of color while simultaneously over-resourcing spaces that are predominantly white (McGhee, 2021; Kendi, 2019).

7. Antiracists do not racialize habits, decisions, or behaviors nor do they attribute habits, behaviors, and decisions to a student's culture. As Kendi (2019) writes, "To be an antiracist is to recognize there is no such thing as racial behavior. To be an antiracist is to recognize there is no such thing as Black behavior, let alone irresponsible Black behavior" (p. 95).

8. Antiracists take action to counteract and eliminate racialized inequities caused by traditions, laws, policies, and unspoken rules (Derman-Sparks & Brunson Phillips, 1997; Pollock, 2008).

b. A Call for Antiracist Educators

I want to take this opportunity to make a call for my community college colleagues to adopt a professional philosophy of antiracism. Heck, I'd like to also invite my university colleagues, those in business and tech (especially tech), and the myriad professionals in medicine, law, and science to do so also. Antiracism is for everyone. Nevertheless, we need to also proceed with caution. The term antiracism has recently come into vogue in education, thanks in large part to

Mica Pollack's 2008 anthology *Everyday Antiracism* and, of course, Ibram X. Kendi's (2019) *How to be an Antiracist.* These are important texts, and if you haven't read them, I would encourage you to do so. However, I want to reemphasize that, as I will discuss later in this chapter, *we need to proceed with caution.* I have met innumerable educators who have read texts like these and are suddenly the messiahs of antiracism who, in one breath, can expound the virtues of social justice and equity while simultaneously disparaging students and lamenting the "achievement gap." Instead, I encourage my readers to approach antiracism with *humility* – this is a lifelong journey that we're going to mess up several times, and edicts of antiracism are hollow without living the struggle to eradicate racism in one's sphere of influence.

Too often, white educators pick up the flag of antiracism and social justice while maintaining their places of power and without understanding what it means to really engage in this struggle. These are individuals who I like to label as "white saviors." Originating with Rudyard Kipling's "White Man's Burden," the term "white saviorism" ranges from white folks who travel to third-world countries, particularly Africa, to "help out," to white couples who adopt "unfortunate" children from said third-world countries, to the rampant TV and Hollywood depictions of white saviors such as Louanne Johnson in *Dangerous Minds*, the white family in *The Blindside* and the founders of the *Kony 2012* con. White saviorism has ballooned so much that writer Teju Cole (2012) has coined the term "The White-Savior Industrial Complex," wherein white folks, at best, enter spaces of color to "help out" but are unable (or unwilling) to see the larger sources of poverty, hunger, and other inequities, or what he calls the "serious problems of governance, of infrastructure, of democracy, and of law and order" (par. 14). In other words, it isn't good enough to go into these spaces and simply feed the hungry, shelter the homeless, and treat the sick; we must also deconstruct the forces that have caused the hunger, the displacement, and the diseases and mental trauma. However, too many whites go into these spaces for purely selfish reasons. As Cole argues, Africa, for instance, "is a liberated space in which the usual rules do not apply: a nobody from America or Europe can go to Africa and become a godlike savior or, at the very least, have his or her emotional needs satisfied" (par. 12).

So what does white saviorism look like in higher education, especially community colleges? Simply put, it is any white professor, administrator, or staff member who strives to "help" students of color without understanding the students' lived experiences and without working to dismantle the institutional barriers that act as obstacles. I see this in my colleagues all over California's community college system (and if I'm honest, I was one of these professors early in my career). Recently, my state's community college system has rightly challenged colleges to find ways to support students of color, but too often, this "support" is simply a course or learning community. The thought is that if the educators can shower the students with love and support for a semester or year, it will be enough to propel them through the rest of their time at the college. Unfortunately, these educators rarely take on the role of an activist or agent of change. As I mentioned earlier, the so-called "achievement gaps" do not exist because there is something wrong with the students; they exist because there is something wrong with the system, and if we simply create a few courses to support a handful of students of color, we are doing exactly what Cole warns us against – we are feeding the hungry without understanding what structures led to that hunger while simultaneously patting ourselves on our backs because a few more dozen students of color succeeded in our programs.

Hence, one of the most important attributes of an antiracist educator is the ability to take action against policies, procedures, and other institutional frameworks that perpetuate a racial hierarchy. We need to be able to create learning communities and students support services for students of color AND we need to be challenging our colleagues and administrators who maintain this system of oppression. In other words, antiracist educators must be unapologetically and vocally anti-bigotry, anti-discrimination, anti-sexist, anti-homophobic, anti-transantagonist, anti-Islamophobic, and antiracist, among many, many other forms of justice-oriented thinking. An antiracist (n.), in addition to being *antiracist* (adj.), must also fight against the oppression and discrimination of all minoritized peoples, especially within one's sphere of influence.

Furthermore, antiracist educators can also learn much from the equity-mindedness movement that has gained traction in recent years, especially as described by Estela Bensimon and the Center for Urban Education (CUE). According to CUE, equity-mindedness "refers to the perspective or mode of thinking exhibited by practitioners who call attention to patterns of inequity in student outcomes. These practitioners are willing to take personal and institutional responsibility for the success of their students and critically reassess their own practices. It also requires that practitioners are race-conscious and aware of the social and historical context of exclusionary practices in American Higher Education" ("Equity Mindedness," n.d.). Furthermore, Malcolm-Piqueux and Bensimon (2017) argue that equity-minded educators must be "(1) race conscious, (2) institutionally focused, (3) evidence based, (4) systematically aware, and (5) action oriented" (p. 6). In other words, equity-minded individuals must merge knowledge of inequity with a desire to do something about it. In this same vein, antiracism requires us to become proficient in the nuances of race, racism, and white supremacy, to critique our own complacency in maintaining the racial hierarchy, and to dismantle these oppressive systems through actions in our spheres of influence.

In a nutshell, what does it mean to be an antiracist community college educator? I'd like to offer some suggestions with the caveat that this list is likely incomplete. Indeed, I would challenge readers to delve into the literature, some of which I have included in this book, and come up with their own characteristics. But for me, this is what it means to be an anti-racist educator:

1. An antiracist educator must have the desire and ability to consistently and fully critique one's racial, economic, gender, and other privileges and one's power over those from minoritized groups. This means that they understand the origins and history of this privilege and power, how it is maintained, and how this privilege and power has been created at the expense of others.

2. Similarly, an antiracist educator must admit that they have racist beliefs and thoughts and that they commit racist actions. We live in a society saturated in racist imagery, misinformation, and ideologies, and we are acculturated to believe that whiteness and Western ideals are normal while others are abnormal and inferior. This is to say that us white folks have grown up believing in racist ideas, which means we are bound to reproduce them, both consciously and unconsciously. Yes, antiracist educators can have a "racist bone" in their bodies.

3. However, an antiracist educator is always striving to identify these racist ideas, beliefs, and actions, to deconstruct them, and to make amends where necessary and possible. The antiracist reflective praxis described in the next section is meant to facilitate this type of critical reflection.

4. Antiracist educators are publicly, and proudly, antiracist. In other words, they call out racism when they see it, they speak truth to racist power, and they educate those around them. This can be as easy as identifying racialized hierarchies in the institution and as difficult as calling out a colleague for a racist remark.

5. Antiracist educators *take action* to deconstruct and eliminate barriers that disproportionately impact students of color, including racist policies, racist procedures, racist symbols, racist budgets, etc.

6. Antiracist educators strive for an equitable, inclusive, socially just campus environment, which includes advocating for equitable funding for programs and spaces that predominately serve students of color, creating practices that diversify the professoriate and other campus personnel, constructing a curriculum that celebrates the cultures and epistemologies of all students (not just those of European descent), and working with colleagues and student groups to create public spaces, like lobbies and dining rooms or building and parking lot names, that reflect the demographics of the campus.

Ultimately, antiracism is a way of living, not just a set of classroom practices. An anti-racist educator doesn't save the antiracism for the campus. It is not a button that you turn off when you leave the campus parking lot and one you turn back on when you get to campus the next day. I'll be the first to acknowledge that all professionals working on racial justice need to have a healthy self-care routine (more on this in the book's conclusion), but if we simply relegate our antiracist practices to the classroom or campus, we will never actually reach the level of self-realization necessary to authentically connect with our students of color or to effectively destroy racialized barriers at our campuses. In other words, we can't allow ourselves to have racist ideas or thoughts while driving through our neighborhoods or strolling down our main streets and expect that we will be suddenly antiracist when we get to campus. It does not work like that. We need to be constantly critiquing and analyzing our ideas and beliefs about people of color and how our actions perpetuate the privilege and power of racism and white supremacy. This is why I have developed what I call antiracist reflective praxis, which I will cover in the next section.

c. Practicum: Antiracist Reflective Praxis – Reflection and Metacognition

As mentioned in the introduction, the contents of this book are very personal to me. I have grown up thinking about race in America, and even though I was fortunate to get this early "education," I am still very much undergoing a process of transformation and understanding, in part because our society's understanding of race and racism is constantly changing and in part because racism is ever-evolving. I am constantly checking my beliefs, assumptions, and absorption of racist ideas. As Kendi (2019) notes, "being an antiracist requires persistent self-awareness, constant self-criticism, and regular self-examination" (p. 23). Consequently, if even those who have been studying race and privilege for decades – whether formally or informally – must constantly engage in this "self-examination," educators who are new to the nuances of race, racism, white supremacy, and antiracism must be even more vigilant. For the vast majority of us, this is an examination that will likely be career-long.

So how do we engage in such a reflective practice? Is it as simple as identifying racist thoughts and biases? Is awareness enough? I would argue that awareness alone is not enough, and simple awareness can be problematic in so many ways. One of the major fads in higher education (and in corporate America) is the use of "unconscious bias" training for employees. In these trainings, participants learn what bias is, where it comes from, and how it plays out in hiring decisions, in interactions with students, colleagues, or customers, and in evaluations of subordinates or peers. Furthermore, these trainings tend to overemphasize the role of the media and our surroundings in inculcating these biases. They usually try to quell the fears of participants with the motto "everyone is biased!"

Yet very few trainings actually teach participants how to deconstruct these biases and how to operationalize an anti-biased approach in interactions and tasks like hiring. In my home state, for example, the Chancellor's Office of the California Community Colleges (CCCCO) has invested quite heavily in unconscious bias training for the 116 state community colleges with the hope that these trainings will increase diversity in the faculty, staff, and administration of the system. Unfortunately, according to the latest statistics, these trainings have done little to diversify the state's professoriate. In Fall 2013, which is a couple of years prior to the implementation of mandatory unconscious bias training throughout the system, 64% of all tenured and tenure-track faculty were white as compared with 5.83% who were African American, 0.88% who were Indigenous, 8.87% who were Asian American, 13.88% who were Latinx, 0.57% who were Pacific Islander, 0.85% who were multi-ethnic, and 4.80% who were unknown (n=16,954). In Fall 2019, years after these unconscious bias trainings became mandatory throughout the system, 58.17% of all tenured and tenure-track faculty were white, while 5.85% were African American, 0.60% were Indigenous, 10.74% were Asian American, 17.28% were Latinx, 0.40% were Pacific Islander, 1.62% who were multi-ethnic, and 5.36% who were unknown (n=12,752). While these numbers imply progress, it has been slow-going, and it certainly has not come close to mirroring the system's student population (as of Fall 2019, 22.86% were white, 4.42% were African American, 0.31% were Indigenous, 9.81% were Asian American, 2.07% were Filipino, 3.03% were multi-ethnic, 0.31% were

Pacific Islander, 7.26% were unknown, and 49.93% were Latinx). Furthermore, this unconscious bias training is only renewed every three years, which means the vast majority of the people making important hiring decisions are sitting through training for a couple of hours every three years, and unfortunately, there is only a hope and a prayer that they put the training into practice in the intervening time.

Instead, we must go beyond recognizing our racist beliefs and biases and start to deconstruct them in an iterative process that forces us to continually reflect on these beliefs and our values. I call this process "antiracist reflective praxis" (ARP). It is a process that I have developed over several years as a way to continually check my own racist beliefs and privilege on a consistent basis and to *actively* address them. In many ways, antiracist reflective praxis is a mindfulness practice, which I know carries a bit of baggage in educational settings. To be clear, when mindfulness became more prominent in educational scholarship, I was one of the first people to roll my eyes. I still believe using mindfulness in the classroom is a little too "new age." However, this antiracist iterative process requires a deep level of awareness and reflection, which means there is much to gain by being mindful, or if you prefer, metacognitive.

The antiracist reflective praxis is composed of four steps. While from the surface they may seem easy, I can assure you that they require a great deal of reflection, humility, and even discomfort. But as Leonardo (2009) writes, "antiracism is historically self-reflective" (p. 122). In brief, the four steps of antiracist reflective praxis are:

1. **Acknowledgment:** antiracist educators must be able to identify thoughts, beliefs, and actions that are racist, which requires a great deal of knowledge and understanding of race, racism, and white supremacy. This also requires antiracist educators to be continually curious and mindful and to learn how racism and white supremacy are evolving over time. At the end of the day, this first step is taking responsibility for our thoughts and actions.

2. **Understanding:** once we have identified the racist belief, thought, or action, we need to figure out where it originated from. We may ask ourselves, "why do I believe in [fill in the blank]?" or "Why did I think it was ok to say or act in that way?" These racist beliefs and actions will never go away if we don't understand where they came from.

3. **Deconstruction:** once we identify their source(s), we can understand that while it may be impossible to eliminate racist beliefs and thoughts entirely, we can attenuate them. The less power we give these thoughts

and beliefs and the more cognizant we are of their presence, the easier it is to eliminate them from our subconscious. Furthermore, deconstruction requires us to reflect and learn about why these beliefs and thoughts are patently false.

4. **Action:** I can't say this enough but antiracism requires action, even when working on what Magee (2019) calls the "inner work of racial justice." In this practice, we may need to apologize and make amends with those who we injure and traumatize with our actions. If we had a racist thought or we hold a racist belief, we need to commit ourselves to always being aware of such thoughts and to continually deconstructing them. And, of course, we need to be committed to calling out others for the same beliefs, thoughts, and actions.

As Derman-Sparks and Brunson Phillips argue, antiracism is "the beginning of a new approach to thinking, feeling, and acting. Anti-racist consciousness and behavior means having the self-awareness, knowledge, and skills – as well as the confidence, patience, and persistence – to challenge, interrupt, modify, erode, and eliminate any and all manifestations of racism within one's own sphere of influence. It requires vision and will, an analysis of racism's complexities and changing forms, and an understanding of how it affects people socially and psychologically" (p. 3). With that in mind, let's dive into each of the above steps in more detail.

Step 1: Identification and Acknowledgment of Racist Beliefs and Actions

As mentioned previously, race consciousness is the foundation of antiracism, and this reflective practice is no different. There is simply no room for "colorblindness" or "non-racism." As discussed throughout the book, these stances perpetuate the status quo – a racial caste system built on white supremacy – and this is simply not acceptable to a critical, antiracist educator. But what does it mean to be "race conscious"? What does this look like in practice? Before answering these questions, it is best to first look back at the Civil Rights Movement for a historical perspective on race consciousness in American society.

American race relations can be thought of as a long, labyrinthine path wherein we have collectively failed to take the road that would lead to equity and social justice. These often come in the form of major governmental decisions – Plessy v. Ferguson, the "Great" Compromise, the Dred Scott Decision, and many more. Even our reactions to seemingly progressive and landmark decisions, such as Brown v. The Topeka Board of Education and the Civil Rights Acts, have proven to lead us astray. During the civil rights movements of the 1960s and 70s, we came to an important crossroads vis-a-vis race relations. The Black rights movements (from the Southern Christian Leadership Conference to the Black Panthers to the Nation of Islam), the Chicano rights movement (including the activism of the United Farmworkers), the Asian American Political Alliance, and the American Indian Movement all advocated for a society that was race-conscious. In other words, the leaders of these movements challenged Americans to engage intentionally and deliberately with the question of race and racism in America. At that moment, we came to a split in the path: one in which we continued to discuss the intersections of race, white supremacy, and systemic oppression in the pursuit of racial justice; the other in which we tell ourselves that the Civil Rights Acts and similar Supreme Court decisions were enough to eradicate racial inequities and that we could now move on from the race consciousness of the 60s and 70s toward a "post-racial" America.

But in the wake of these civil rights movements, many Americans mistakenly believed that "race conscious" individuals belonged to two groups of people: the first were white supremacists who used race consciousness in order to label whites as superior to people of color; and the second were people, mostly people of color but certainly many white academics, who were supposedly perpetuating racism by talking about racism. In the latter half of the 20th century, many Americans subscribed to the colorblind philosophy that is the precise opposite of race consciousness (Bonilla-Silva, 2017; Peller, 1990). However, these "colorblind" individuals were asking the wrong questions. We believed, at least publicly, that even the slightest mention of race and racism was enough to make people think racist thoughts and act in racist ways, as if the mere mention of racism was a powerful curse from a Harry Potter novel. But in reality, we were living a lie and a contradiction. In the first instance, we mistakenly believed that discussing race caused racism when in fact we simply just did not want to talk about it. Remember, racialized outcomes exist without an utterance of race or racism because our society's institutions and structures have been built on a foundation of white supremacist beliefs. In the second instance, we had deluded ourselves into thinking that because we refused to talk about race, we were magically "not racist." We can call it the "wizarding world" of colorblindness. Yet the reality is that even people who do not talk about race and racism can be racist – we will still choose predominantly white neighborhoods over more diverse neighborhoods, we will still discourage our children from dating people of color, and we will still clutch our purses or other valuables when they see a man of color walking toward us. Racism cannot be wished away, and in all reality, as Derrick Bell argues, racism is permanent. In other words, we can never simply stop thinking racist thoughts and doing racist things simply by ignoring race.

But we cannot let this discourage us. I firmly believe that institutionalized racism can be identified and eradicated, and it certainly can be in our classrooms. As community college educators, we can eliminate racist policies and curricula from our institutions quite easily – if we are up to the task. I will discuss this in much more detail in Part II of this book. However, it is much more difficult to eradicate our own personal biases and racism (which undergird structural racism), but again I am hopeful, and this is one of the reasons why I have developed this heuristic. With a little metacognition and reflection, we develop a feedback loop that allows us to identify our racist thoughts and actions to prevent similar thoughts and actions in the future or at least a mindfulness of them. But in order to do any of this, we must turn back on this road to colorblindness. We must go back to the civil rights movements of the mid-20th century and heed the calls of their leaders to become race-conscious and to engage in an honest, and difficult, conversation about race. This is the only way we can move forward.

Mindfulness in Antiracism

Let me start by sharing that I am not one of those educators who espouses incorporating mindfulness and meditation in the classroom. In fact, the first time I read of such a practice in an academic journal, I think I sprained my eyes rolling them. Furthermore, I am not an avid meditator in my personal life – I meditate every once in a while, and it's honestly probably been a couple of years since I last sat down and actually went through the practice. I say this because I want it to be clear that I am not promoting this as a classroom practice and that I am not suggesting that you become a yogi or mindfulness guru as part of this journey, nor that you need to be. I am neither of these. However, I think there are some useful strategies that we can borrow from mindfulness practices in order to identify and acknowledge racist beliefs or behaviors. This is particularly necessary in an age where our attention spans are becoming more and more sporadic at the same time that our worlds are becoming more and more complex.

Rhonda V. Magee (2019) has pioneered the use of mindfulness in responding to racism in her book *The Inner Work of Racial Justice: Healing Ourselves and Transforming our Communities through Mindfulness.* In her book, Magee describes unique meditation and mindfulness practices that educators can incorporate into their personal and professional lives with the ultimate goals of bringing communities together through compassion and healing the wounds of racial injustice. Magee's book, in other words, provides readers with an in-depth introduction to mindfulness and meditation practices, and she encourages these practices as ways to identify and deconstruct white supremacy and racism. If this type of practice resonates with you, I highly recommend Magee's book – it is genuine, honest, and nourishing. Even if you are uninterested in such an intense meditation practice, the book is an important contribution to antiracist scholarship. Furthermore, I think there are several mindfulness practices that can be useful in your antiracist practice.

But, first, what is mindfulness? This is a term that is commonly used to describe a variety of spiritual and secular practices, and as mentioned above, it has come into popularity in educational circles in recent years, yet it is still fairly nebulous and misunderstood. Jon Kabat-Zinn (2017) defines mindfulness as "awareness that arises through paying attention, on purpose, in the present moment, non-judgmentally... in the service of self-understanding and wisdom" (par. 2). According to Gil Fronsdal (2006), mindfulness, as translated from seminal Buddhist texts, means "knowing the mind; training the mind; and freeing the mind" (par. 1). And, of course, Magee (2019) defines mindfulness as the act of "paying attention to life as it unfolds, grounded in body and breath, and allowing that awareness to settle the mind, increase presence and consciousness of interconnectedness with others" (p. 2). In essence, mindfulness is simply being aware of one's thoughts, actions, and surroundings in the present moment.

So why is mindfulness so important to antiracism, especially for white educators? Simply put, after we have accepted that we do indeed harbor racist beliefs and we do indeed act in racist ways, we must be able to identify the moments in which they materialize. It does no good to simply acknowledge that one has racist beliefs – we have to know when this happens so we can take action to deconstruct these beliefs. This is essentially what is missing from the unconscious bias training that has become so popular. Too often, white educators may think or act in racist ways without, as Magee (2019) puts it, "thinking twice about it" (p. 13). This is because we have been socialized to think and act in these ways. But how do we know if we have a racist belief or committed a racist action? What are we looking for? This isn't as challenging as we may first believe, and it really comes down to two steps. First, we need to have a fundamental understanding of white supremacy and racism, and their origins, machinations, and manifestations. Reading this book, especially Chapters 1 and 2, is a good start for reaching this understanding, but I highly recommend that you look at many of the sources I have cited in this book in order to deepen your understanding. Second, you need to develop a mindfulness routine that is sustainable and effective. In other words, if you are like me and you aren't an avid meditator or mindfulness champion, you need to develop a practice that meets your own unique needs and values. Nevertheless, I believe it is nearly impossible for a white educator to effectively practice antiracism without some form of mindfulness (and to be clear, I am not talking about "hitting the cushion," or sitting down, eyes closed, and meditating). You need to be able to recognize your racist beliefs and actions and the situations in which they may manifest (the following sections will cover what you do after you recognize them).

As mentioned above, I am not interested in persuading you to develop a mindfulness practice in the traditional sense (though, again, if you are, Magee's book is an excellent resource). Instead, I'd like to borrow the most pertinent aspects of her antiracist mindfulness practices for the heuristic that I have termed "antiracist reflective praxis." Magee's most salient practice is what she calls "the Pause," which she describes as "an aspect of the *practice* of mindfulness meditation that can lead you to the *experience* of body-based mindfulness. What is mindfulness? It is simply paying attention, on purpose, with the attitude of friendly, open, nonjudgmental curiosity, and a willingness to accept... what arises" (p. 17, emphasis in original). In other words, when we are aware of a racist thought or action through the course of our day, we need to take a moment to look at it critically in a nonjudgmental way, which is a hallmark of traditional meditation. This is not to say that we do not take responsibility for these thoughts or actions, as there needs to be a certain level of discomfort in order to avoid them in the future. Furthermore, in instances of behavioral racism, we need to understand that our actions have traumatizing effects on the victims of our actions. But wallowing in this guilt and discomfort is also unproductive, and it compels us to reject this practice altogether. As such, we need to be aware of the discomfort, but we also need to affirm ourselves – the very act of pausing and being mindful of these thoughts and actions is something that the vast majority of white folks refuse to do. This reflective practice, while born from an ignorant place, is a positive step toward deconstructing our racist beliefs and ideas.

So what does this "pause" look like in practice? The answer is that it depends on the context, and it will be different in a classroom while teaching than when walking down the street. But at the most fundamental level, it means being present. As Magee (2019) suggests, "To practice The Pause, you simply stop what you are doing and intentionally bring your awareness to the experience of the present moment" (p. 17). If the time allows, you can be present in this moment for several minutes, and you'll be able to not only understand the origin of the racist thought, belief, or action, but you'll be able to also deconstruct it and take appropriate action. In other words, in an ideal situation, you'll be able to run through the entire praxis. But what if you're in a classroom teaching? Can you afford the time to go through this entire recursive practice? Maybe not at first. Early in this journey, it may not be possible to reflect deeply on your thought or action, and in the case of the latter, there is an important learning moment available to you. If you say or do something insensitive or downright ignorant, acknowledge your mistake publicly, and if the students are willing, engage in a dialogue about what happened (Chapter 5 will discuss how to talk about race and other sensitive issues). No matter what, take a moment after class to reflect on the thought/action, the moment it happened, and the dialogue with students, if applicable. And ask yourself a simple question: "who was impacted by my words, action, or pedagogy and were they affected in a negative way?" Afterward, process it using the steps outlined in this chapter. Furthermore, you will find that the more experience you have with this type of mindfulness practice, the more efficiently and effectively you'll be able to catch yourself and respond. As Magee notes, "Mindfulness is essential to developing the capacity to *respond*, rather than simply *react* as if on autopilot, to what we experience" (p. 17, emphasis in original).

Before moving on to understanding the origins of our racist thoughts and actions, I'd like to briefly share some thoughts on how mindfulness can help educators process the uncomfortable feelings that come from this type of practice – anger, guilt, anxiety, and hopelessness. One of the core tenets of mindfulness is investigation. Prominent Buddhist teacher Tara Brach (n.d.), for example, describes this investigation as "calling on your natural interest – the desire to know the truth – and directing a more focused attention to your present experience" (par. 8). In writing about Brach's RAIN practice, Magee (2019) further explains, "It is through our gentle, compassionate, and courageous investigations that we learn and grow in self-awareness, empathy, and wisdom. We move in close and look underneath the hood" (p. 104). This journey will, at times, uncover some uncomfortable realities, and it will force us to confront some of our own ignorance, missteps, and, yes, racism, all of which will create complex and uncomfortable feelings that need to be investigated. If we say something in class that we later realize was problematic, we may feel embarrassment or regret. If we are in a workshop or discussion with colleagues about race and racism, and a colleague of color calls out our racism, we may feel angry. But we need to step back for a moment and understand where these feelings are coming from, particularly in the latter case. What possible reason do we have for becoming angry when called out for an utterance that was problematic?

In a recent example in my own teaching, I was lecturing on the origins of the English language in my survey of British literature course. During the Norman Invasion, Old English, a Germanic-based language system, was infused with French, a Latin-based language system, which resulted in the pre-cursors of modern English. At some point during the lecture, the class was discussing languages and how they evolve, and I made a very ignorant – and academically untrue – statement that all languages are derived from Germanic and Latin (I know, I know... that was dumb). As soon as it left my mouth, I knew I had made a false statement, and before I could acknowledge the mistake, one of my students called me out on it: "That's not true!" My immediate reaction was embarrassment; I was probably turning red. I was embarrassed because I said something that was factually incorrect and culturally insensitive (I had erased the language contributions of more than half the world), and I was feeling really insecure since I was still a fairly young professor, as the imposter syndrome creeped in. But I stepped back, and instead of saying something that would add insult to injury or simply ignoring it, I publicly acknowledged my mistake, apologized to the class, and went on to correct myself, briefly describing the languages of Asian, African, Indigenous, and Middle Eastern cultures. This type of mindfulness may have been uncomfortable and slightly affected my enjoyment of the class, but it is important. My students did not deserve to be discomforted or erased by my ignorant remarks, and our students, colleagues, friends, and acquaintances of color don't deserve to be microaggressed, erased, or marginalized by our comments and actions.

One of the most common feelings that white educators feel as they undergo this process of racial literacy is guilt, a feeling that has even been given its own term – white guilt. However, in many ways, mindfulness allows us to take the guilt out of the equation. In traditional mindfulness practice, for example, when meditators find their thoughts drifting from their breathing (or other focus), they avoid judgment and instead bring the focus back to their meditation. Similarly, an effective mindfulness practice requires practitioners to simply notice the drifting. For instance, if a person is trying to be more mindful of their eating habits and dietary choices, they do not simply languish in self-pity and guilt when they succumb to temptation and eat a cupcake. Instead, this person reflects on triggers, the circumstances, and of course, their larger goals.

There is much to learn from this practice in acknowledging our racist attitudes and actions. Instead of guilt or defeat, mindfulness allows to step back from judging ourselves and identify the roots of these assumptions and actions. To be clear, I am not promoting a practice that lets us off the hook for racism; racist actions and discrimination negatively impact the recipient, causing anything from loss of opportunity to trauma. Nonetheless, as Magee (2019) suggests, "Try not to judge your feelings and sensations. Be as specific as you can about what you notice. Most important: as much as possible, be kind to yourself" (p. 18). Magee is kinder than I have the intention or right to be. White educators, like us, who have racist beliefs and commit racist actions shouldn't overindulge in self-compassion, at least not at first. It wouldn't be a bad thing if we sat in the guilt of our actions and attitudes, if only for a moment. But guilt can also have negative consequences for the projects of antiracism and social justice if it consumes us. As DeAngelo (2018) points out, "guilt functions as an excuse for inaction" (p. 135). Said another way, there needs to be a certain amount of discomfort and guilt. We must feel pain in order to stop this vicious cycle; otherwise, it becomes a relentless feedback loop of self-compassion to oneself and violence against others.

Step 2: Understand where this Belief/Action Came From

Too often, I have spoken to colleagues and students who will imply (or say out loud) something racist or intolerant, immediately recognize that their utterance was problematic, but then wonder why it was. In one instance, I had a colleague blame rap and hip hop for the student outcome disparities at our college. She said something along the lines of "if these students didn't listen to that rap music, they might have higher aspirations for themselves." This is how racism operates in our educational systems and American society, at large – coded language that implies that our students' cultural artifacts are pathological and that these "pathologies" are the foundation for the educational, health, and wealth gaps in our country. One need not dig too deep to understand who this colleague was referring to with "these students" – students of color. And unfortunately, when educational, health, and wealth gaps are brought up in conversation, rap and hip hop are often blamed even though the history of these musical genres is rich in a history of celebrating the African American community and culture and of resisting social injustice. Inevitably, these colleagues, including the one mentioned above, will insist that they are advocates for students of color.

With that being said, my colleague did acknowledge that she was likely being ignorant: "I know that sounds bad, and I am sure I am overgeneralizing." This is an incredible statement. My first thought in this situation was, "why are you saying it if you know you are wrong?" But then I realized that this colleague was looking for answers. She had successfully completed the first step of antiracist reflective praxis – acknowledging (kind of) the racist foundation of her statement. This colleague was now looking for where it came from – in this case, mainstream media's and America's general disdain for rap and their ignorance of the genre's roots. This colleague's admission opened up a conversation that helped her better understand her racist belief, and this became an important step in eradicating that type of cultural racism.

Similarly, I have had students express very problematic beliefs about authors of color. Most recently in one of my rhetoric courses, I assigned Te-Nehisi Coates' 2017 *Atlantic* article, "The First White President," in which Coates draws on the country's history of white supremacy and oppression of African Americans as a way to understand how white voters were able to support a candidate who was so obviously, and by his own admissions, racist and sexist, and who used overtly racist rhetoric to garner political support. One student wrote in his essay that Coates was "bias" because he is a "black man in America." Obviously, this student hadn't thought broadly about the implications or origins of such a statement, so when we met to chat about his essay, we had the opportunity to discuss it. I started by asking him if he believed that women could not critique a man for saying something misogynistic or for maintaining a sexist policy or practice, to which the student responded, "of course not." We then engaged in a discussion about why, then, a black man could not call out racism. However, this simply isn't enough. I needed to also ask the student to reflect on why he *believed* that a black man can't call out a white man's racism, no matter how small that belief might seem to be. We weren't able to pinpoint any particular racist beliefs, but we were able to interrogate it and discuss how it is the consequence of a society that has acculturated him to believe in the infallibility of white leaders and the "unfounded complaints" of people of color. Was this conversation enough? Probably not. But this speaks to the importance of continual reflection and introspection. We can't understand, and eventually deconstruct, these beliefs if we are not pausing to recognize them.

Ultimately, awareness and acknowledgment simply aren't enough, and an apology without some type of deep reflection and amends is not sincere. We cannot utter or think something that is racist and simply say sorry; it does not mend the wounds it created, and it does nothing to prevent such things from happening again. However, this type of reflection is meaningless unless we understand the origins of our racist beliefs. If you've made this far in the book, you know where almost all your racist beliefs came from – your family and friends, your teachers, books and movies you've read and seen, and, of course, the news media. We have been socialized from childhood to believe that people of color are inferior to whites, and we have been socialized to be entitled to the privileges of white skin (DiAngelo, 2018; Fleming 2019; Matias, 2016). As Derman-Sparks and Brunson

Phillips (1997) explain, "In a racist society an ideology of racism – a system of beliefs, attitudes, and symbols constructed and legitimized by those with political and cultural power – socializes each succeeding generation" (p. 2).

So what does this step – understanding – in the praxis look like? It is fairly simple: once we have acknowledged that we had a racist thought or we committed a racist action, we need to ask ourselves "where did that come from?" In the case of my colleague above, she needed to uncover the origins of her belief that rap music is having an adverse effect on her minoritized students' success. After just a few moments of reflection, she realized that this belief is rooted in a type of ethnocentrism that privileges predominantly "white" forms of music, like classic rock or country, and an ignorance of rap's historical roots and its ability to uplift the marginalized, all of which is the consequence of our society's privileging of Eurocentric art forms. It is also very possible that you might not know the origins of the racist thought or action. That is ok! You are an academic, which means you likely have the capacity for doing a little research. But as a general suggestion, after reading this book, I suggest you start reading books that discuss the history of racism in America regularly.

Finally, it is important to understand that racism has always evolved and morphed as society and racial attitudes have changed. During American chattel slavery, for instance, a number of justifications were used to enslave Africans and to continue slavery in the Americas, from religious justifications (e.g. "the curse of Ham") to the Enlightenment's "scientific" explanations of African "inferiority." More recently, racism in America shifted from the overt racism and discrimination of Jim Crow, Indigenous land theft, and Asian exclusion laws to more covert forms of racism, such as harsher sentencing for crack cocaine, voter ID laws, and redlining. In other words, we have shifted from a society that was very transparent in its disdain for people of color to one in which our bigotry has gone "underground," resulting in what Bonilla-Silva (2017) calls "colorblind racism." Furthermore, racism isn't distributed equally. It is quite contextual. Overt racism about African Americans today is considered taboo, but racist remarks about people of Arabic descent, especially those who are Muslim, are fairly commonplace, including among those who consider themselves progressive. This is one reason why this journey is lifelong. The racism and hatred that we see in our society today (like those targeted at Muslims and immigrants of color) may not be the same types that we see in two decades. Educators tend to have careers that are 20-40 years long, so we need to be vigilant to racism's ever-evolving face.

Ultimately, "understanding" means that we take a moment to interrogate why we think and act the way we do vis-a-vis minoritized students. And because we may not know that our utterances are problematic, we need to be open to criticism from others without taking it personally and quickly jumping to feeling like we are being called racists. Instead, we need to choose to engage with the people, whether they are a person of color or white, who "call us out." They are taking a big social risk in speaking out, and we should see that as a sign that they haven't given up on us. And if we can understand how our society acculturates us to have racist thoughts and beliefs, and we can understand their origins, we will develop a great deal of power to eradicate them.

Step 3: Deconstruct the Racist Ideas

Racist ideas (and actions) are the result of a lifetime of socialization and acculturation, and they are perpetuated by a cycle of misconceptions, falsehoods, and sometimes outright hatred. However, if you are reading this book and you've made it this far, I will assume that you do not harbor hateful feelings toward the students you serve. But as discussed so far in this book, even white educators who dedicate their careers and lives to the mission of the community college can still hold unconscious and conscious biases and racist beliefs. This is the consequence of growing up in a society that privileges whiteness and marginalizes people of color and other minoritized groups. So the real question becomes how do we combat this socialization? If racist ideas and beliefs are manifested by a lack of knowledge, how do critical, antiracist educators fill those knowledge gaps? While there is no simple solution, and even comprehensive solutions might take many years to implement, I'd like to offer some strategies, which at the basic level, start with the acquisition of knowledge, or what is called cultural competency. While we will look at Critical Race Theory (CRT) in more detail in Chapter 5, this discussion requires that we delve into one important component in this chapter – storytelling and counterstorytelling,

However, before delving into storytelling, I think it is important to revisit one of Kendi's (2019) tenets of antiracism – the belief that individuals are not representatives of the group. As Kendi argues, "To be an antiracist is to think nothing is behaviorally wrong or right – inferior or superior – with any of the racial groups. Whenever the antiracist sees individuals behaving positively or negatively, the antiracist sees exactly that: individuals behaving positively or negatively, not representatives of whole races. To be antiracist is to deracialize behavior, to remove the tattooed stereotype from every racialized body" (p. 105). In other words, as antiracist educators, we need to start understanding the behaviors of individual students as their behavior alone and not some kind of indicator for the whole racialized group. To be clear, this is *not* colorblindness. We do not get to use this perspective as an excuse to reject race altogether and to see the students as "just people" (for a refresher on why, revisit the introduction to this chapter). Let's explore what this looks like in practice? Let's say that you are collecting an essay and one of your Latinx students doesn't have theirs or you are grading some exams and one of your African American students fails, what types of assumptions would you make? If you are honest with yourself, you're going to, if only for a moment, assume that it's because of their race. You will, if you are honest, connect the former student's behavior with the stereotype that people of Latin American descent do not value education, and you will, if you are honest, assume that the latter student's exam grade is associated with the stereotype that Black students as a group lack intellect. If you are denying these preemptive thoughts, I encourage you to pay more attention to your mind next time you are in a similar situation. And when you have these thoughts, simply take notice, and remind yourself that they are absolutely false and the result of racial socialization.

Similarly, we need to reject the stereotypes associated with our students' appearances and cultural artifacts. For example, what thoughts and beliefs come up when you see a student sagging, or listening to rap, or driving a lowrider. Are you saying to yourself "of course that students would wear/listen to/drive that"? If so, you are practicing cultural racism (Kendi, 2019). And like above, it is important that these types of appearances and cultural artifacts are not representative of the entire racial group, and they do not indicate any type of inferiority or superiority, not to mention there is nothing inherently wrong with sagging, rap, and lowriders. In other words, we should celebrate our cultural differences and firmly deny that these differences have any bearing on students' abilities or intellect or that there exist cultural deficits. Furthermore, when you see a male of color, especially in an isolated place, do you automatically picture a mugger or someone who is violent? This whole practice is based on our ability to be absolutely honest with ourselves, and if we are honest, we will admit that we do feel a certain amount of fear in these situations. We have been trained our entire lives to think like this.

This is what this book's heuristic is meant to help you deconstruct, however. We need to first, notice the racist thought/belief/action, second, understand the historical, social, and political origins of this racist thought/belief/action, and third, deconstruct it. And in order to deconstruct these beliefs, we need to first continually remind ourselves that the behavior, appearance, or artifact that we are responding to is simply not true for this individual (in the case of the mistaken mugger) or for the racialized group (in the case of the missing essay and failed exam). Deconstruction is the ability to look inward and to reject the racist socialization we have come into.

Moreover, counterstories can become a powerful tool for deconstructing racist thoughts, beliefs, and/or actions because they help us realize that these beliefs are fundamentally flawed. But this requires a fairly broad schema vis-à-vis the realities of race relations in the U.S. and the true beauty and brilliance of our students of color. Perhaps more importantly, we must reject the mentality of exceptionalism – the idea that the students who disprove the stereotypes are simply one-offs or exceptional in some way (i.e. believing that the star black student in your class is not representative of the black community as a whole and that they are an exception to the rule). However, in order to build this schema, we need to normalize Black and Brown excellence, and we need to see every minoritized student that walks into our spheres of influence as budding intellectuals that have a great deal of cultural capital (Yosso, 2005). Seeking out these counterstories – or those examples that disprove the dominant beliefs about students of color and other marginalized students – is the most effective way to do so.

While I will dive into talking about race in much more detail in Chapter 5, especially as it relates to the classroom, I think there are a few tenets that are worth mentioning, as they will help inform this discussion of counterstories. First, as I mentioned earlier, traditionally marginalized people have zero obligation to educate you on their culture, race, neighborhood, etc., nor do they have an obligation to share their academic, professional, and other achievements with you. In other words, no one is obliged to "be your counterstory." In fact, once you develop this mindfulness practice, you will start noticing that these counterstories are actually the norm. Black and Brown brilliance has been right in front of us all this time. Second, this can be an uncomfortable process. As a result, as you progress through this journey, you're going to hear some uncomfortable truths about white supremacy and the lived realities of people of color. You're going to hear people group whites into one large group that is racially insensitive, fragile, and close-minded. But it is ok! You do not need to be flustered or angry when a person of color says something negative (and likely truthful) about white folks. You don't need to feel uncomfortable or guilty. You just need to accept their reality as truth, and you need to remind yourself that you are on a journey to become an antiracist educator. As someone who has undergone this process, I can attest that it becomes easier and easier to not only engage in these tough discussions but also to see the brilliance of our students that many see as the exception to the norm.

Delgado (1989) explains the importance of storytelling as both a means of oppression and as a means of resistance for what he calls the "in-groups" and "out-groups," respectively. In the case of the former, the in-group, or the dominant group, "creates its own stories... The stories of narratives told by the in-group remind it of its identity in relation to outgroups, and provide it with a form of shared reality in which its own superior position is seen as natural" (p. 2412). In other words, dominant groups use stories as a means of expressing its superiority, maintaining power, and perpetuating narratives of inferiority and "abnormality." Consequently, *counter*narratives become an important tool for marginalized groups both as a means of opposition and as a means of intragroup solidarity. As Delgado argues, "stories create their own bonds, represent cohesion, shared understandings, and meanings... Stories are the oldest, most primordial meeting ground in human experience" (pp. 2412, 2438).

For our purposes, counternarratives have two very important purposes, the first of which is to uncover the lived experiences of the "out-groups" and their day-to-day experiences with oppression and marginalization. In other words, these narratives shed light on the repercussions of racism and white supremacy. At the most fundamental level, counternarratives help us understand how our power and privilege marginalizes, excludes, and even violates historically marginalized students: "They can show that what we believe is ridiculous, self-serving, or cruel. They can show us the way out of the trap of unjustified exclusion. They can help us understand when it is time to reallocate power. They are the other half – the destructive half – of the creative dialectic" (p. 2415). In more concrete terms, these types of counterstories help marginalized people, like many of our students, express and narrate their experiences with racism, sexism, homophobia, and other forms of hatred. And while these narratives have immense benefits for the "out-groups," their power is often limited in changing the dominant narrative, especially for members of the "in-group" who are resistant to their messages (e.g. "colorblind" people who reject narratives of race and racism). As a result, it is up to us to seek these narratives out and bring them into our schema and value system. As critical educators, we need to understand how our privilege and power impact marginalized students.

Similarly, counternarratives have the capacity to challenge our misconceptions and presumptions about marginalized groups, and in the context of this reflective practice, they help us deconstruct the dominant narratives that trigger these misconceptions and assumptions. As Delgado states, counternarratives are "competing versions that can be used to challenge a stock story and prepare the way for a new one" (p. 2416). This function of the counternarrative is very exciting because it opens us up to our minoritized students' brilliance, their accomplishments, and their creativity while simultaneously disabusing us of our preconceived notions about them: "Hearing stories invites hearers to participate, challenging their assumptions, jarring their complacency, lifting their spirits, lowering their defenses" (p. 2440). These stories, as a result, become tremendously important to this larger antiracist practice because they help counteract our racist beliefs and thoughts. Once we have acknowledged these racist beliefs and understood their origins, we can easily remind ourselves that these beliefs simply are not true because there is overwhelming evidence to the contrary all around us. But as mentioned above, we need to be active consumers of these counternarratives since they are not widely disseminated amongst the dominant groups.

Similarly, Solórzano and Yosso (2002) describe five elements of critical race theory and methodology that are relevant to education and to storytelling in particular: 1) the intersections between race and other forms of oppression; 2) the challenge to hegemonic power, knowledge, and discourse; 3) a social justice orientation; 4) the importance of "experiential knowledge"; and 5) a framework that pulls from many disciplines, or what they term as "the transdisciplinary perspective" (pp. 132–134). Most of these tenets will be covered in more detail in Part II, but for our purpose's here, I'd like to focus on number four – experiential knowledge. In a critique of dominant ideology and research paradigms, critical race practitioners, like Solórzano and Yosso, not only give weight to qualitative research methodologies, but they "recognize that the experiential knowledge of people of color is legitimate, appropriate, and critical to understanding, analyzing, and teaching about racial subordination" and they "draw explicitly on the lived experiences people of color by including such methods as storytelling, family histories, biographies, scenarios, parables, *cuentos, testimonios,* chronicles, and narratives" (p. 133). In other words, a critical race methodology rejects the privileging of quantitative data collection and the dominant centrality of white, European narratives.

In giving equal authority to these types of qualitative data, critical race theorists and practitioners give us two very powerful tools. First, they allow us to go beyond the raw numbers that we community college educators are constantly bombarded with. Institutional researchers and state agencies are constantly presenting data that demonstrate that our students of color (and other minoritized students) are not realizing the same outcomes as their peers who benefit from hegemony (think African American and Latinx students versus their white and Asian classmates), yet these raw numbers and percentages can never tell us the whole story. They can never tell us why these students are struggling, which often leads to false assumptions and overgeneralizations about our students (such as those I shared in Chapter 2). Second, these stories give us important evidence of our false beliefs about students of color and other minoritized students. As Solórzano and Yosso (2002) write, "Standard, majoritarian methodology relies on stock stereotypes that covertly and overtly link people of color, women of color, and poverty with 'bad'... Whether explicitly or implicitly, social science theoretical models explaining educational inequality support majoritarian stories" (p. 136). Too often, I hear these "majoritarian stories" in leadership, committee, and departmental settings. My colleagues might ask why the college's or department's African American, Latinx, female, low-income, or other-abled students are "achieving" at lower rates than peers who come from dominant groups. Unfortunately, too many are too eager to settle on the explanations that range from transportation, housing, or food insecurity to cultural deficiencies or under-preparedness. This is not to say that transportation, housing, and food insecurity aren't obstacles for our students; the problem is that these explanations are the end all be all, and they tend to give us a pass from scrutinizing our role in these data.

Instead, we need to practice two important strategies: first, we need to recognize that our students of color experience daily instances of racism, stereotyping, and microaggressions in order to move beyond the simplistic explanations named above; second, we need to deconstruct our assumptions about our students by tapping into the counterstories that disprove the "majoritarian" or "ingroup" narratives. And we need to go beyond token activities, such as attending a campus event on equity or a Black History Month celebration. We need to de-socialize ourselves, and we can't simply rely on one-off events to do so. We need to be intentional in choosing the spaces we intend to occupy (with permission, of course), and if we want to see black excellence, for example, we need to be around Black students! Nonetheless, there is a substantial number of books, articles, and literature that can educate us.

Admittedly, I had the privilege of learning to deconstruct my racist beliefs and ideas early in my life. As mentioned in the Introduction, I was raised by Black man, I spent much of my free time in predominantly Black neighborhoods, and I grew up with an extended family of Black people (though these types of experiences don't guarantee understanding). This is why I know that this type of deconstruction works. Ultimately, there is no substitute to learning about people who have different racial identities than to actually be in the same social spaces.

At the same time, we need to make sure we navigate these spaces with permission, humility, and critical reflection (like I have described in this chapter).

For instance, Magee (2019) describes a type of storytelling technique called the ColorInsight strategy, in which educators using her mindfulness practice share and seek out others' stories of racism. It is an interpersonal communication strategy that uses "engagement with individuals from diverse groups" (p. 24). More specifically, the strategy emphasizes the need for people of different backgrounds to engage in the form of kinship where the speaker, who comes from a marginalized group, is able to share their "Race Story" with a person from a different background, presumably someone who identifies as white. Magee argues that this relationship "starts the process of healing for the speaker" while for the listener, "it serves to soften and encourage [them] to respond by sharing his or her own stories" (p. 25). Ultimately, Magee notes that this is "a process that ultimately leads to healing in the broader community… strengthen[ing] the inner justice advocate in us as well."

At the surface, this may seem like an acceptable approach to creating cross-racial conversations, and if storytelling is such an important component of both critical race methodology and social justice work, practitioners will need to find these "race stories" somewhere. However, the ColorInsight can be problematic for most educators for two reasons: first, it is not the responsibility of people of color to help us better understand race and racism (DiAngelo, 2018; Fleming, 2018). In other words, we cannot simply enter Black and Brown spaces and ask for these types of narratives, nor can we approach colleagues or students looking for help with our racial ignorance and education. Second, even if this were socially acceptable, it doesn't help us respond to the myriad racist thoughts and actions at the moment. In other words, if we find ourselves in a space occupied by people of color, and we find ourselves thinking stereotypically or even prejudicially, what do we do? The simple answer is that we utilize the antiracist reflective praxis described in this chapter.

Step 4: Antiracist Action

Unfortunately, as mentioned previously, a "not racist" approach is simply not an effective way to eradicate racism within our spheres of influence; it is simply a way for us to feel better about ourselves while the people of color around us continue to suffer from acts of racism. "Not racist," in other words, maintains the status quo – racialized hierarchies in our institutions and the maintenance of white supremacy. To think about this more concretely, imagine that you had the ability to instantaneously stop your own racist beliefs – you no longer microaggressed your students, you didn't stereotype students of color, you stopped believing in their supposed cultural "deficiencies," and you now understood the role of white supremacy in your belief system, your discipline, and your pedagogy. Imagine that you were able to instantaneously transform your classroom into a space where students felt identity-safe and where they felt represented and empowered. That would make you feel, as our students would say, "woke."

However, what happens when your students walk outside your classroom? Will they feel the same level of safety and empowerment? Sadly, they won't. They will still encounter racism from other educators, from racist institutional policies at the college and beyond, and a political and media environment that pathologizing their families, cultures, and neighborhoods. Yes, your classroom may become a beacon of hope and energy for them, but it simply won't be enough (not to mention that in this scenario, you become the perfect critical educator, which none of us can ever become). In this way, simply challenging one's own racism, being "not racist," still maintains racism, which as Kendi (2019) argues is simply another form of racism: "A racist is someone who is supporting a racist policy by their actions or *inaction* or expressing a racist idea" (p. 22, emphasis added). Consequently, the final step of this antiracist reflective process is *action*.

As previously mentioned, even when our students feel identity-safe in our classroom and office spaces, this is no guarantee that the students will not experience racism and microaggressions outside of these spaces. In fact, it is pretty evident that they will. And one reason for this is that not all our colleagues have undergone the same transformations as we have. They may be willingly or unwillingly ignorant to the existence of their racist beliefs and the racist policies of the institution. As Tatum (1997) reminds us:

> There is always someone who hasn't noticed the stereotypical images of people of color in the media, who hasn't observed the housing discrimination in their community, who hasn't read the newspaper articles about documented racial bias in lending practices among well-known banks, who isn't aware of the racial tracking pattern at the local school, who hasn't seen the reports of rising incidents of racially motivated hate crimes in America – in short, someone who hasn't been paying attention to the issues. (p. 83)

The major takeaway from this observation is that most white folks *haven't been paying attention*. But does this give them a pass? Maybe... Maybe not. The more important question, however, pertains to our culpability in this ignorance. As antiracist educators, if we are keenly aware of the racialized hierarchy and its concomitant inequities, should we be held responsible for the ignorance of our peers, our neighbors, and our colleagues? I would argue yes, which is why I believe this final step is so important. We need to take responsibility for the inequities in our institutions, which means we need to find opportunities to educate our white colleagues (and students).

So what do we do in the face of this ignorance? First, we need to understand where our white colleagues and students are coming from. In fact, they are coming from the same place as we are – socialization inside a culture that normalizes whiteness and pathologizes people of color. This socialization is the result of the media, our friends and families, our educations, our geographic area, who we regularly interact with, what we read, and many, many other factors. Our beliefs are contextual, so we need to educate our peers with empathy and compassion. As a result, when we are in a setting in which a colleague or student says or does something insensitive or racist, we need to call them on it, which will depend on how well we know them and on the context of the situation. Public humiliation is usually ineffective, so we should approach them privately to explain why their utterance or action was racially insensitive. Similarly, when others do critique your colleague publicly, it is also not your place to intervene, especially if it is a colleague of color speaking up to denounce this racism. These types of interventions against a colleague of color on behalf of a white colleague acts to perpetuate racism and promote "white solidarity" (DiAngelo, 2018, p. 125).

On a larger scale, we also need to enact institutional changes that eliminate policies, procedures, curricula, and pedagogies that negatively impact students of color. This topic will be discussed further in Part II and is outlined extensively in Sims, Taylor-Mendoza, Hotep, Wallace, and Conaway (2020). Nonetheless, it is worth emphasizing here that as a final step in this process, we have a responsibility to enact changes in our spheres of influence, from our classrooms, to our departments, to our entire college.

***

Finally, I'd like to wrap this section up by clarifying that this antiracist reflective praxis is *not* a way to explain away racism, prejudice, and stereotyping. This reflective process is not an excuse for racism, and it does not pardon the violence caused by white supremacy and racial ignorance. Racism does far too much harm to our students to be excused. But this growth is also an important part of the journey. As Derman-Sparks and Brunson Phillips (1997) note, "Anti-racism education is not an end in itself but rather the beginning of a new approach to thinking, feeling, and acting" (p. 3). Furthermore, Magee (2019) implores us to embrace this type of recursive reflection for an even more critical reason: "By experiencing new ways of looking at race, we can grow in our capacity to be with one another in ways that promote healing and make real our *common humanity* and radical interconnectedness. And this will set us on the path toward acting with others for justice – in solidarity with those suffering the most – with humility, kindness, and the capacity to keep growing and rowing on" (p. 8, emphasis mine). Antiracist work is just that – work. But, ultimately, it has incredible benefits for our mental well-being and for the well-being of our fellow humans.

d. Keep on Keepin' on

To be blunt, antiracism is hard. And I don't mean that it is difficult to be "nice" to people. Indeed, the entire foundation of colorblindness is simply being nice. Rather, I mean that it is difficult to constantly monitor our thoughts and actions, and when necessary, to actually make an effort to change our beliefs and values. This is particularly true when we consider that societal forces are constantly working against us and are ceaselessly normalizing whiteness and white supremacy and othering people of color, women, immigrants, religious minorities, and other minoritized groups. It is no secret that us white folks who engage in this type of critical reflection can easily go back to a life of what Flagg (1993) describes as a state of blindness. White folks have the privilege of returning to a reality wherein we can avoid issues of race and racism and wherein we can always feel like we belong. It is easy to fall into a state of what Flynn (2018) calls "white fatigue," the experiences of white individuals who understand that racism is wrong yet misunderstand it as a belief system held by individual racists. The "fatigue" is triggered when these individuals learn that racism goes beyond individual attitudes and actions to an entire system of advantage and oppression and when the scope of this revelation becomes overwhelming. However, while this work may feel overwhelming, it is important to increase what DiAngelo (2018) calls our racial stamina in order to avoid the temptation of taking – for those of you who have seen *The Matrix* – the proverbial "blue pill." It would be immoral and inhuman to return to a state of ignorance and blindness.

So with such an easily accessible escape pod at our disposal, why should white, antiracist educators continue to do this work, especially in the face of discomfort, guilt, active resistance from others, and a generally adverse reaction to issues of race in our institutions and society? The simple answer is that it is the morally right thing to do. If you have made it this far in the book, you should understand that the racial hierarchies that exist in our colleges are not an indication of our students' abilities, intellect, motivation, and wherewithal. At this point, you know something is going on and that these inequitable outcomes are the consequence of institutionalized white supremacy. At this point, can we simply turn our backs on our students because this work is mentally (and sometimes physically) challenging? I don't think we can. It is just too selfish, too cynical, and too inhumane. It would be a betrayal that subverts our human desire for compassion.

Likewise, it has become abundantly clear that our country's legacy of racism and oppression has fundamentally deprived us collectively of our humanity (Freire, 1970/1993; McGhee, 2021). We simply cannot turn a blind eye to the suffering of our students without losing that humanity. We simply cannot call ourselves good people while simultaneously ignoring what is happening to minoritized students in our classrooms and colleges. So to invert this argument, this antiracist project becomes a means of finding our own individual humanity and working toward our collective humanity in the name of social justice (Kendi, 2016). Many of us got into teaching at a community college because we had a strong desire to help others and because we believe in the institution's promise of access to higher education and upward mobility.

I realize that this type of intrinsic motivation is not a primary driver for those educators that are more extrinsically motivated through their identities as effective pedagogues and by their colleagues' and administrators' opinions of them as members of the academic community. If this is the case, an antiracist, social justice-driven pedagogy is still appropriate. It is my belief that the knowledge and practices described so far in this book can help community college educators substantially improve the overall retention and success rates of their classes. Furthermore, the pedagogical and curricular practices that I describe in Part II have been proven to increase the success and retention of students, particularly students of color. So even though social justice is generally a noble and altruistic journey and goal, there is still room for those who are more motivated by data and the perceptions of others.

Finally, antiracism for educators is a means of self-preservation. It is an unfortunate fact that community colleges (indeed all public education) have become a means for scoring political points for our elected officials. Too often, policymakers and politicians are willing to dabble in not only educational policy but in pedagogy and curriculum, thereby undermining the expertise of the professoriate. One needs not look further than California's Assembly Bills 705 1705, which eliminated all developmental education in the state's community colleges, or Illinois' General Senate Bill 2527, which prohibited community college faculty from limiting the number of dual enrollment sections offered in the state's high schools. Unfortunately, these bills and others like them were either written and passed without faculty consultation or against the wishes of faculty leadership, and they are often justified by our systems' low success, retention, and graduation rates. An antiracist approach to higher education, then, becomes a way to reduce the meddling politicians and their "justifications" for doing so.

e. Chapter 3 Synopsis and Questions to Consider

Synopsis

Becoming an antiracist educator (and person) is a lifelong commitment that requires daily reflection, understanding, and action. This is an uncomfortable process, but it is necessary if we are going to reclaim our humanity. As a result, we need to be comfortable with being in uncomfortable situations and discussions, and we must be mindful when thinking and talking about race. The "antiracist reflective praxis" can help us develop this mindfulness. In this heuristic, we can identify and dismantle our racist beliefs by acknowledging their existence, understanding where these beliefs come from, disproving and dismantling them, and taking action to eliminate them from our lives and our spheres of influence. Ultimately, we need to muster the racial courage and fortitude to accept that we have been the beneficiaries of institutional white supremacy and that our denial and unwillingness to engage in conversations about race, racism, and white supremacy continue to maintain the status quo. We must start to engage in these conversations and in the fight for social justice.

Questions to Consider

1. How would you define antiracism in your own words? What does an antiracist educator believe and do? What do they *not* believe or do?
2. Why is it important to reflect on one's privilege and racist beliefs? How does this reflection help us become antiracist?
3. Why is it important to be "race conscious"? What are the fundamental flaws in colorblindness?
4. What is mindfulness? How can a mindfulness practice help us to think and act in more antiracist ways?

5. How do we begin to understand where our racist beliefs and actions come from? How do we become more "culturally competent"?
6. How might you deconstruct your racist beliefs and actions?
7. How will you promote the projects of antiracism and social justice in your spheres of influence?

Keywords: antiracism, antiracist reflective praxis, colorblind, race conscious, mindfulness

f. References

Bell, D. (1992). *Faces at the bottom of the well: The permanence of racism.* New York: Basic Books.

Bonilla-Silva, E. (2017). *Racism without racists: Color-blind racism and the persistence of racial inequality in America* (5th ed.). Lanham, MD: Rowman & Littlefield.

Brach, T. (n.d.). *Working with difficulties: the blessings of RAIN.* Retrieved from https://www.tarabr ach.com/articles-interviews/rain-workingwithdifficulties/

Cole, T. (2012). The White-savior industrial complex. *The Atlantic.* Retrieved from https://www.theatlantic.com/international/archive/2012/03/the-white-savior-industrial-complex/254843/

Delgado, R. (1989). Storytelling for oppositionists and others: A plea for narrative. *Michigan Law Review, 87*(8), 2411–2441.

Derman-Sparks, L., & Brunson Phillips, C. (1997). *Teaching/learning anti-racism.* New York: Teachers College Press.

DiAngelo, R.J. (2018). *White fragility: Why it's so hard for white people to talk about racism.* Boston: Beacon Press.

"Equity Mindedness." (n.d.). Center for Urban Education. Retrieved from https://cue.usc.edu/about/equity/equity-mindedness/

Flagg, B.J. (1993). "Was blind but now I see": White race consciousness and the requirement of discriminatory intent. *Michigan Law Review, 91*(5), pp. 953–1017.

Fleming, C.M. (2018). *How to be less stupid about race.* Boston: Beacon.

Flynn, J.E. (2018). *White fatigue: Rethinking resistance for social justice.* New York: Peter Lang.

Freire, P. (1970/1993). *Pedagogy of the oppressed.* M. Bergman Ramos (Trans.). New York: Continuum. (Original work published 1970).

Fronsdal, G. (2006). *Mindfulness meditation as a Buddhist practice.* Insight Meditation Center. Retrieved from https://www.insightmeditationcenter.org/books-articles/mindfulness-meditation-as-a-buddhist-practice/

Kabat-Zinn, J. (2017). *Defining mindfulness.* Mindful.org. Retrieved from https://www.mindful.org/jon-kabat-zinn-defining-mindfulness/

Kendi, I.X. (2016). *Stamped from the beginning: The definitive history of racist ideas in America.* New York: Nation.

Kendi, I.X. (2019). *How to be an antiracist.* New York: One World.

Leonardo, Z. (2009). *Race, Whiteness, and education.* New York: Routledge.

Magee, R.V. (2019). *The inner work of racial justice: Healing ourselves and transforming our communities through mindfulness.* New York: TarcherPerigee.

Malcolm-Piqueux, L., & Bensimon, E.M. (2017). Taking equity-minded action to close equity gaps. *Peer Review, 19*(2), 5–8.

Matias, C.E. (2016). *Feeling white: Whiteness, emotionality, and education.* Rotterdam: Sense.

McGhee, H. (2021). *The sum of us: What racism costs everyone and how we can prosper together.* New. York: Penguin Random House.

Peller, G. (1990). Race consciousness. *Duke Law Review, 1990*(4), 758–847.

Pollock, M. (2008). *Everyday racism: Getting real about race.* New York: New Press.

Sims, J.J., Taylor-Mendoza, J., Hotep, L., Wallace, J., & Conaway, T. (forthcoming). *Minding the obligation gap in community colleges: Theory and practice in achieving educational equity.* New York: Peter Lang.

Solórzano, D.G. & Yosso, T.J. (2002). Critical race methodology: Counter-storytelling as an analytical framework for education research. *Qualitative Review, 8*(1), pp. 23–44.

Tatum, B. (1997). *Why are all the black kids sitting together in the cafeteria?: And other conversations about race.* New York: Basic Books.

Thompson, A. (2008). Resisting the "lone hero" stance. In M. Pollock (Ed.), *Everyday anti-racism: Getting real about race in school* (pp. 328–333). New York: New Press.

Yosso, T.J. (2005). Whose culture has capital? A critical race theory discussion of community cultural wealth. *Race Ethnicity and Education, 8*(1), 69–91.

Part II: Looking Beyond the Self

4

Stories from the Other Side of Racism

I was acutely aware of the power of storytelling in my first year as academic senate president for my college. Several of my equity-minded colleagues and I were trying to jumpstart an ongoing conversation about race, educational equity, and social justice at the college, particularly amongst the faculty. Many of our colleagues still lacked even an elementary understanding of these topics and issues, so some of our earliest discussions focused on coming to a shared definition of educational equity and social justice. This shared definition and vision would eventually be incorporated into a document that would help guide the body's work on identifying and eliminating identity-based institutional barriers for minoritized students, particularly students of color. Ultimately, this document would serve as the foundation for the senate's new business related to promoting equity-minded policies and procedures. These initiatives included overhauling program review and developing a syllabus statement that directed students to the Office of Equity if they felt discriminated against.

While the dialogue, which spanned several meetings, went into many expected and sometimes unusual directions, one particular conversation was especially memorable. While senate proponents of an institutional commitment to equity were rationalizing its need, one senator interjected, asking "Is all this necessary? Are students actually discriminated against in classrooms? I mean, do students really experience racism on campus?" For many in the room, it was a fair question, as evidenced by their head nods. Luckily, I had many allies in the room in addition to an outstanding student body president (at my college, the student body president sits on the academic senate in an advisory role). That year's student body president was an African American male, and before anyone on the senate could respond, he made a slight chuckle and simply replied, "yes" before sharing the narrative of his day-to-day interactions with classmates and professors. He explained that he would, on a daily basis, experience racist abuse (e.g. microaggressions), meaning that his professors and classmates would covertly and overtly disparage his racial identity. He was told that it was "surprising" that he did so well on his math tests, that he was very "articulate" in class, and in one extreme case, told he would not pass the class because "students like him" struggled in the course. On top of that, he would, on numerous occasions, hear non-black students use the n-word or downplay the racism experienced described by him and by the course readings. This was not a rare occurrence; it happened on a near-daily basis.

After this student spoke, several other senators were able to corroborate and validate his experiences as the questioning senator sat quietly. To his credit, he listened intently to what the others shared, and he never publicly questioned their validity. I am not sure that this individual ever changed his perspective about the experiences of students of color at our college, but the whole discussion demonstrated the power of storytelling. It was incredible, and potentially groundbreaking for my colleagues, to hear a high-performing, black male student describe instances of blatant and coded racism. In other words, it was shocking for many of my colleagues that a student who had nearly a 4.0 GPA, a college leader, and a member of several campus clubs and organizations experienced such prejudice on campus.

In that vein, this chapter is meant to reveal the myriad experiences of our students of color. Unfortunately, their experiences are invisible to us, especially since so many of them are unwilling or afraid to confront their professors and campus staff on instances of racism. In too many community colleges (and universities), there exists a culture of fear wherein minoritized students are frequently the victims of discrimination – both implicit and explicit – and they are too afraid to speak up, sometimes for fear of retaliation, sometimes because feelings of shame, and sometimes as an act of rebellion in which they are driven to prove the aggressor wrong. Whatever the reason, this culture of fear leaves educators ignorant to the harm they and their colleagues are causing, oftentimes unintentionally. In that regard, this chapter is broken down into several sections meant to help you better understand the underbelly of discrimination, particularly racism, in America's community college system. This chapter starts with a literature review that describes systemic racism, or those structures wherein racism is both engrained and perpetuated institution-wide, of the education system, with an emphasis on higher education, and introduces not only the scholarship of critical race theory, but also how it has helped scholars uncover this racism. It is my hope that you will learn more about these scholars and their works so you too can undercover racism and other forms of oppression at your institution. In fact, after a brief overview of critical race theory, we will hone in on how CRT has been uniquely applied to the field of education. The second part of this chapter will highlight one of the primary methodologies of CRT in education – storytelling and counterstorytelling. After providing an overview of the dominant discourse, or what Solórzano and Yosso call the "majoritarian narratives," about students of color in higher education.

a. An Introduction to Critical Race Theory

On September 4, 2020, President Trump directed the White House Office of Management and Budget to ban cultural sensitivity and implicit bias trainings because, according to OMB Director Russell Vought (2020), these trainings promoted "divisive, anti-American propaganda" (p. 1). More specifically, the memorandum attacked trainings that covered white privilege and institutional racism, and Vought directed his departments to "begin to identify all contracts or other agency spending related to any training on 'critical race theory,' 'white privilege,' or any other training or propaganda effort that teaches or suggests either (1) that United States is an inherently racist or evil country or (2) that any race or ethnicity is inherently racist or evil." Furthermore, President Donald Trump issued an executive order on September 22, 2020, creating a ban on these types of trainings throughout the entire federal government and its contractors. As a result of these two documents, Critical Race Theory (CRT) was thrust into the political spotlight despite its rather niche existence in academia, and it was erroneously argued by many on the political right that CRT was being used in both schools (it's not) and implicit bias trainings (maybe some of the tenets, but not the framework) to indoctrinate the country's citizens and to depict the country as "inherently racist or evil." This political upheaval has been so powerful that it has outlasted Trump's presidency and permeated even the smallest of elections, such as those for school boards and city councils. In fact, during the 2021 Virginia gubernatorial race, an interview with a voter went viral after he cited critical race theory as the most important issue in the election but was unable to describe in even the vaguest way what CRT actually was, noting, "I'm not going to get into the specifics of it because I don't understand it that much" (The Good Liars, 2021). The video, created by the comedy group The Good Liars, was watched over 3 million times in the lead-up to election day. Thus, it is important to start this chapter with a more accurate and complete description of CRT.

CRT came to prominence in many leading law schools during the 1980s in response to the shift away from traditional civil rights litigation in the nation's courts and law schools (Peller, 1990). As Yosso (2006) writes, CRT "originated... with a group of scholars seeking to examine and challenge race and racism in the United States legal system and society" (p. 6). Though this movement was initiated in legal studies, it has permeated a number of other academic disciplines, including history, ethnic studies, women's studies, and educational research, to name a few. As Crenshaw, Gotanda, Peller, and Thomas (1995) write, CRT "can provide a useful theoretical vocabulary for the practice of progressive racial politics in contemporary America" (p. xxvii). At the most basic level, CRT is a framework or lens through which researchers, theorists, and practitioners can identify, critique, and dismantle structures that perpetuate racism and intersectional forms of oppression. Crenshaw et al. (1995) note that CRT is:

> unified by two common interests... The first is to understand how a regime of white supremacy and its subordination of people of color have been created and maintained in America, and, in particular, to examine the relationship between that social structure and professed ideals such as 'the rule of law' and 'equal protection.' The second is a desire not merely to understand the vexed bond between law and racial power but to *change* it. (p. xiii, emphasis in original)

According to Crenshaw et al., CRT scholars, or "crits," "share an ethical commitment to human liberation" (p. xiii).

Depending on the scholar, the tenets of CRT can vary, but there are few consistent themes, including: 1. The permanence of racism; 2. Challenge to the status quo; 3. A Commitment to Social Justice; 4. Race-consciousness; 5. Intersectionality; 6. The "interest convergence" principle; 7. Structural determinism; and 8. Interdisciplinary perspectives. What follows is an overview of these tenets.

Permanence of Racism

In 1992, CRT founding scholar Derrick Bell wrote the seminal book *Faces at the Bottom of the Well: The Permanence of Racism*, which among other things, concretized the discipline's focus on institutional racism over the racist actions and beliefs of individuals. In this book, Bell (1992) provides a framework for "continuing the struggle for racial justice, a struggle we must continue even if... racism is an integral, permanent, and indestructible component of this society" (p. ix). Delgado and Stefancic (2013) expanded on this point by noting that "CRT begins with a number of basic insights. One is that racism is normal, not aberrant, in American society. Because it is an ingrained feature of our landscape, racism looks ordinary and natural to persons in the culture" (p. 2). And to be clear, "normal" does not mean natural, but instead, they point to the ubiquity of race and racism in everyday life and in our institutions.

However, while Bell's assertions may seem nihilistic, there is much more nuance to the "permanence of racism" than is evident on the surface. First, Bell, for example, does not argue that the fight for racial justice should be given up in the face of entrenched institutional racism. Instead, he urges defiance in the face of oppression. In recollecting the tales of heroes and heroines who "face even death without flinching," he writes, "while no one escapes death, those who conquer their dread of it are freed to live more fully. In similar fashion, African Americans must confront and conquer the otherwise deadening reality of our permanent subordinate status. Only in this way can we prevent ourselves from being dragged down by society's racial hostility" (p. 12). In other words, antiracism and the fight for racial justice are, at the very least, a form of liberation for those who suffer racial oppression and marginalization. Second, critical race theory, as praxis, focuses on institutions and racist structures, not on individual acts of racism. As such, Bell is pointing to the permanence of racism in our society as constructed, and thus, he is implicitly challenging us to deconstruct and rebuild more just institutions, which for us means a system of higher education that empowers and nurtures minoritized students (see Sims, Taylor-Mendoza, Hotep, Wallace, & Conaway, 2020).

As you will see later in this book, equity is not the end goal because equity simply maintains the existing structures. As Isabel Wilkerson argues in her book *Caste*, "America is an old house. We can never declare the work over. Wind, flood, drought, and human upheavals batter a structure that is already fighting whatever flaws were left unattended in the original foundation" (p. 15). One of the flaws that Wilkerson speaks to is racism, and to extend Wilkerson's metaphor a bit further, a broken foundation takes a great deal of money and labor to fix. Sometimes, it even requires the entire structure to be deconstructed and rebuilt. Equity is a temporary fix, but racial justice requires a whole new foundation, and while college educators have little power to fix the larger flaws in our American foundation, we do have control over our classrooms and even our institutions. The work of social justice, like building a new foundation, takes a lot of energy and work, but if we are unwilling to engage in that work, then, indeed, racism will continue to remain a permanent flaw in higher education.

Challenge to Dominant Ideologies

Because race and racism are embedded in American society and its institutions, racial ideologies and hierarchies become not only invisible but part of the "common sense." Thus, one of CRT's primary goals is to challenge these ideologies and their concomitant structures, which are, as Bell (1992) argues, bolstered by "media-nurtured public opinion" (p. 5). More specifically, crits challenge the dominant ideologies of colorblindness, equal opportunity, and merit because they stifle critiques and discussions of racial inequities and injustices. As Yosso (2006) writes, "Critical race scholars argue that traditional claims of race neutrality and objectivity act as a camouflage for the self-interest, power, and privilege of dominant groups in U.S. society" (p. 7). In other words, these dominant ideologies maintain the racial status quo. Moreover, crits problematize the legal system's overreliance on civil rights legislation as the cure-all for institutionalized racism, in part because of the law's "painstakingly slow process of arguing legal precedence to gain citizen rights for people of color" and in part because legal interventions like affirmative action have primarily benefitted white women (Ladson-Billings, 2009, p. 22). Furthermore, many of the gains of the civil rights movement have been undone as state and federal governments and the U.S. Supreme Court have passed laws or made rulings barring affirmative action in university admissions and in hiring (e.g. Prop. 209 in California) and have passed laws making voting more difficult for voters of color (e.g. the 2021 Georgia voting law).

The dominant ideologies of colorblindness, objectivity, and merit and the weakening of civil rights laws have also impacted academia, where they maintain and exasperate a racialized educational system wherein white and high-income students continue to benefit from higher education and students of color and low-income students continue to be excluded. As a result, crits expose institutionalized racism in higher education and seek to eradicate it. As Martinez (2020) explains, "Concerning educational and institutional injustice, CRT's [challenge to dominant ideologies] questions arguments against policies like affirmative action and interrogates admissions and hiring practices that claim neutrality in their selection of candidates, while justifying a passing over of people of color on the 'colorblind' basis of merit and 'fit'" (p. 11). Ultimately, this tenet compels educators to understand the dominant ideologies of race and to expose and dismantle the structures that are undergirded by these ideologies, including our classrooms' role in disseminating these ideologies and upholding these structures.

A Commitment to Social Justice

In line with critical theorists like Antonio Gramsci, Louis Althusser, and Paulo Freire, CRT is undergirded by the notion of "praxis," or the use of theory and scholarship to inform reflection and action. CRT is not simply about theorizing race and racism or simply identifying racialized structures and hierarchies; CRT is about dismantling these structures and hierarchies and advocating for a more socially just world. Speaking more specifically to CRT in education, Yosso (2006) writes, "CRT is dedicated to advancing a social justice agenda in schools and society. Acknowledging schools as political places and teaching as a political act, CRT views education as a tool to eliminate all forms of subordination and empower oppressed groups – to transform society" (p. 7).

Race-consciousness

As mentioned in Chapter 2, Peller (1990) and Crenshaw et al. (1995) trace the roots of modern colorblind ideology to the mistaken belief that Black nationalism is akin to white supremacist organizations like the KKK and neo-Nazis. "Race consciousness" became associated with extremism (though history would teach us that Black nationalism was anything but extreme), and as Peller notes, "The commitment to a race-conscious perspective by many critical race theorists is dramatic because explicit race consciousness has been considered taboo" (p. 759). Furthermore, as Peller notes, "black nationalists asserted a positive and liberating role for race consciousness, as a source of community, culture, and solidarity to build upon rather than transcend. They developed a thoroughgoing critique of integrationism as either inevitably, or at the very least historically, linked to assimilation" (p. 761). This final point is worth highlighting. Centuries of enslavement, violence, and oppression, like Jim Crow and mass incarceration, have resulted in a unique African American culture. Black nationalism celebrates this culture, so a critique of black nationalism is a push for rejecting African American culture in favor of the dominant European culture. This type of "colorblind" assimilationism has led to the marginalization and "alienation" of people of color. Race consciousness, then, is the opposite of colorblindness, or what

Peller calls "integrationism" (p. 759). And as we already discussed in Chapters 1 and 2, colorblindness rests on a faulty foundation and is problematic in how we treat race.

For this reason, as was previously noted, colorblindness is extremely problematic since it maintains the racial hierarchy under the faulty conviction in merit. As Crenshaw et al. (1995) note, liberal "ambivalence toward race-consciousness is best understood as a symptom of liberalism's continued investment in meritocratic ideology and its unacknowledged resistance to reaching any deep understanding of the myriad ways racism continues to limit the realization of goals such as equal opportunity... Our critiques of racial power reveal how certain conceptions of merit function not as a neutral basis for distributing resources and opportunity, but rather as a repository of hidden, race-specific preferences for those who have the power to determine the meaning and consequences of 'merit'" (p. xxix). However, as Peller argues, this recent shift back to race consciousness gives educators an opportunity to create more equitable and inclusive learning environments: "The reemergence of race consciousness among scholars of color should be an occasion for liberal and progressive whites to reevaluate our position concerning the racial compromise that mainstream visions of racial justice embody" (p. 762). Peller, in other words, calls for white folks to conceptualize "a liberating rather than repressive meaning of race consciousness." If community colleges are to enact a framework that strives for educational equity, we must first allow ourselves to see color and honor our students' racial identities.

Intersectionality

One of the most important contributions to the scholarship of Critical Race Theory is Kimberlé Crenshaw's contributions around the intersections of racial and gender oppression. Crenshaw (1989) critiques the historical focus on *either* race *or* gender in what she calls a "single axis framework," which, as she notes in her seminal article "Demarginalizing the Intersection of Race and Sex," excludes the unique experiences of Black women. She notes that most have a "tendency to treat race and gender as mutually exclusive categories of experience and analysis" (p. 139). Unsurprisingly, this approach to social justice work can inhibit the important work of liberation:

> This focus on the most privileged group members marginalizes those who are multiply-burdened and obscures claims that cannot be understood as resulting from discrete sources of discrimination... I argue that Black women are sometimes excluded from feminist theory and antiracist policy discourse because both

are predicated on a discrete set of experiences that often does not accurately reflect the interaction of race and gender. (p. 140)

In other words, Black men and Black women experience racism in very different ways simply because Black women must experience a form of racism that has historical, and very tangible, roots in sexism. And while Crenshaw's initial publications on intersectionality focused on Black women, her framework of intersectionality has been used for any group that is "multiply-burdened" (e.g. lesbians, gay Black men, transgender people of color, women of color, Muslim women, etc.). In focusing on Black women, Crenshaw highlights the need for embracing an intersectional lens: "sex and race doctrine are defined respectively by white women's and Black men's experiences. Under this view, Black women are protected only to the extent that their experiences coincide with those of either of the two groups" (p. 143). However, it is important to acknowledge that the experiences of Black women differ from white women and Black men precisely because they are *both* women and Black (Davis, 1981/1983; Lorde, 1984/2007). It is a completely different lived experience and Black women experience a unique form of oppression, or what Crenshaw calls "compound discrimination" (p. 148). To "embrace intersectionality" is to honor that.

I should also note that this is a very simplistic explanation of intersectionality, but I think it is useful as an entree into this critical framework. I suggest reading Crenshaw's original article 1989 article, "Demarginalizing the Intersection of Race and Sex," as well as her 1991 follow-up, "Mapping the Margins: Intersectionality, Identity Politics, and Violence against Women of Color." For a detailed analysis of how intersectionality has been appropriated and misinterpreted, see Carastathis (2016).

The Interest Convergence Principle

At the most fundamental level, the interest-convergence principle, which was theorized by Critical Race and legal scholar Derrick Bell, describes a phenomenon in which racial progress happens only when the interests of the dominant group (e.g. whites) are aligned with the interest of the minoritized group (e.g. Blacks). As Bell (1980) notes, most white people will acknowledge that "blacks are citizens and are entitled to constitutional protection against racial discrimination, but few are willing to recognize that racial segregation is much more than a series of quaint customs that can be remedied effectively without altering the status of whites" (p. 522). In other words, we may support equal protection and equal opportunity but not if that equality interferes with the privileges, comfort, and "property" we believe we are entitled to (see Chapter 2). Bell, here, is asking us to recognize that racism and white supremacy are embedded in our systems and that equality, or as we will discuss later in this chapter, equity, will require systemic changes that will make us white folks uncomfortable. And because we white folks only support equality insofar as it does not disturb our privileges and power, Bell argues that any racial progress for Black folks and other people of color relies on a shared interest:

> The interest of blacks in achieving racial equality will be accommodated only when it converges with the interests of whites. However, the fourteenth amendment, standing alone, will not authorize a judicial remedy providing effective racial equality for blacks where the remedy sought threatens the superior societal status of middle and upper class whites... Racial remedies may instead be the outward manifestations of unspoken and perhaps subconscious judicial conclusions that the remedies, if granted, will secure, advance, or at least not harm societal interests deemed important by middle and upper class whites. (p. 523)

In his case study, Bell (1980) scrutinizes the *Brown v. Board of Education* decision, which outlawed *de jure* segregation in public schools. American lore would have us believe that this Supreme Court decision and Congress's Civil Rights Acts are long overdue acknowledgments that Black and Brown citizens deserved equal protection and opportunity under the law. Our American mythology would have us believe that these progressive policies were enacted because of our country's moral compass. However, as Bell would argue, *Brown v. Board of Education* "helped to provide immediate credibility to America's struggle with Communist countries to win the hearts and minds of emerging third world peoples" (p. 524). In other words, communist countries, particularly the Soviet Union, were denouncing democracy and using the clashes between civil rights protesters and government agents, such as the police, as propaganda. Bell would also argue that many political leaders saw "state-sponsored segregation" as a barrier in the South's transition from a "rural, plantation society" to "industrialization in the South." Finally, once the interests of whites and people of color diverge, institutions return to the status quo. This is seen most prominently in the re-segregation of public schools, the elimination of affirmative action, and the weakening of voting and other civil rights oversight.

Structural Determinism

Structural determinism describes how policies and structures constantly and endlessly reproduce themselves in cycles that perpetuate racism and maintain the white supremacist status quo. In studying the corpus of civil rights legal scholarship, Delgado (1984), in a foundational text on structural determinism, found that the entire body of literature was dominated by just a small handful of white men who almost exclusively cited one another, creating an insular, self-sustaining system of scholarship that privileged European American perspectives. Delgado named this phenomenon "imperial scholarship." At the most fundamental level, Delgado argues that this type of "scholarly tradition" is problematic because it creates a paternalistic system in which white men are speaking and fighting on behalf of people of color. As Delgado highlights, this creates a disconnect between the ideologies of the civil rights lawyers and scholars and those they represent. As Delgado writes, imperial scholarship "causes bluntings, skewings, and omissions in the literature dealing with race, racism, and American law" (p. 573). Similarly, Delgado and Stefancic (1989) identified an analogous cycle within the three primary case law databases in what they call the "Triple Helix Dilemma." In analyzing the Library of Congress subject heading system, the *Index to Legal Periodicals*, and the West Digest System, Delgado and Stefancic find that these systems "function like DNA; they enable the current system to replicate itself endlessly, easily, and painlessly. Their categories mirror precedent and existing law; they both facilitate traditional legal though and constrain novel approaches to the law" (p. 208). More specifically, the three systems are intricately linked, as a change to one is replicated in the other two, and most changes to these three systems are proposed and approved by internal editors and librarians (the exception is the Library of Congress, where member libraries can propose changes, but these decisions are ultimately made by its editorial team). As Delgado and Stefancic note, this has resulted in a body of knowledge that is self-contained and resistant to innovative approaches to the law, such as those associated with critical legal studies and critical race theory. This triple helix dilemma, then, becomes an important example of how Eurocentric knowledge and whiteness are centered and structurally pre-determined.

Storytelling

In his important contribution to the body of CRT literature, "Storytelling for Oppositionists and Others: A Plea for Narrative," Delgado (1989) highlights the subjective nature of dominant viewpoints vis-à-vis race and the experiences of people of color, and he describes the dueling realities of those in power, with their "majoritarian stories," and those who are marginalized, with their "countersto-ries." After describing the increasing importance of storytelling in the academy, Delgado operationalizes the two forms of storytelling embedded in the legal dis-course and society, at large. The first, majoritarian stories, are "stories or narratives told by the ingroup [which] remind it of its identity in relation to outgroups, and provide it with a form of shared reality in which its own superior position is seen as natural" (p. 2412). These majoritarian stories often erase the effects of white supremacy, and they misrepresent or misconstrue the lived realities of people of color. On the other hand, Delgado writes, "The stories of outgroups aim to sub-vert that ingroup reality... [They] challenge the received wisdom... They can open new windows into reality, showing us that there are possibilities for life other than the ones we live. They enrich imagination and teach that by combining elements from the story and current reality, we may construct a new world richer than either alone. Counterstories can quicken and engage conscience" (pp. 2413, 2414–2415). Counterstories, then, bring to light the effects of racism and white supremacy, and they give a platform for the outgroup – or marginalized groups – to share their suffering in the face of oppression and their triumphs despite it.

To illustrate these dueling forms of storytelling, Delgado simply shares a story of an African American legal scholar who is denied a faculty position at a prominent law school. In a conversation between one of the law school's profes-sors and a student member of the appointments committee, the latter presses the professor on why he and his colleagues did not hire the African American candi-date who the students endorsed. Delgado (1989) uses what he calls a "stock story," which includes composite characters whose experiences reflect those of real peo-ple and groups. In other words, they are "fictionalized" characters that embody the reality and real-world experiences as seen in primary data and as uncovered in existing scholarship. The professor and the student are composite characters, and in their discussion, the former cites the department's justifications for not hiring the African American candidate:

> We didn't think he wanted to teach for the right reasons. He was vague and diffuse about his research interests. All he could say was that he wanted to write about equality and civil rights, but so far as we could tell, he had nothing new to say about those areas. What's more, we had some problems with his teaching interests. He wanted to teach peripheral courses, in areas where we already have enough people. And we had a sense that he wouldn't be really rigorous in those

areas either... Henry [the candidate] wasn't on the law review at school... and has never written a line in a legal journal" (p. 2419).

The meeting was ended by the professor to the dissatisfaction of the student, who expressed a need for courses in "employment discrimination and civil rights." As Delgado notes, the professor in this story "justifies the world as it is. It emphasizes the school's benevolent motivation ("look how hard we are trying") and good faith. It stresses stability and the avoidance of risks. It measures the black candidate through the prism of preexisting, well-agreed-upon criteria of conventional scholarship and teaching. Given those standards, it purports to be scrupulously meritocratic and fair; Henry would have been hired had he measured up" (p. 2422). But as Delgado emphasizes, this process was designed by white men based on the qualifications, beliefs, and values of those same white men (e.g. writing for a law review), and nobody questions this design and its reproduction of the existing professoriate.

On the other hand, the candidate – John Henry – sees the entire interview process differently. In a conversation with a friend, Henry recounts, "I gave a colloquium, and that's where it began. A good half of the faculty looked bored or puzzled and asked no questions. A quarter jumped down my throat after I had spoken maybe ten minutes, wanting to know if I would advocate the same approach if the plaintiff were white and the defendant black... During the small-group interviews, many of them didn't even show up... Several asked what my grade point average was in law school – fifteen years ago, can you believe it! – and whether I was on the law review" (pp. 2423, 2424). In fact, as Henry points out, the interviewers had his resume, which would have informed them that Henry had, in fact, declined an offer to join the law review in favor of working for a prison law program. Henry was given the impression that the law school was looking for a token Black legal scholar who would "keep the students in line" (p. 2423). Amongst other conclusions, Delgado notes that these stories show "how different 'neutrality' can feel from the perspective of an outsider" and how the college's so-called colorblind processes ultimately give white candidates an advantage (p. 2425). These stories demonstrate Delgado's larger point that the same exact objective reality can have two very different stories, and in racialized power dynamics, these stories can either maintain the status quo or seek to resist it.

Interdisciplinary Perspectives

Contrary to what we see in the news cycle and hear from political pundits, critical race theory remains almost exclusively within the halls of academia, particularly in America's law schools. As mentioned earlier, CRT originated in legal studies in the 1980s, partly in response to Harvard's failure to replace prominent law professor Derrick Bell – the only Black member of the Harvard law school faculty – and partly as a result of the Critical Legal Studies National Conference in 1989, which centered "race and silence" (Crenshaw et al., 1995, p. xix). To demonstrate CRT's origins in legal studies, Crenshaw et al. (1995) write that CRT had two primary goals: "to understand how a regime of white supremacy and its subordination of people of color have been created and maintained in America, and in particular, to examine the relationship between that social structure and professed ideals such as 'the rule of law' and 'equal protection.' The second is a desire not merely to understand the vexed bond between law and racial power but to *change* it" (p. xiii).

While Critical Race Theory was born out of critical legal studies with many of its founding scholars coming from the legal field, it has grown to inform the work of a variety of disciplines, including education, ethnic studies, composition, sociology, and history, all of which have adopted the fundamental belief, as Ladson-Billings (2006) writes, "that no one discipline could fully reveal the complexities of human experience and thus amalgamations were deemed necessary" (p. vii). In other words, in order to identify and eradicate structural racism in our institutions and society, writ large, we need an *interdisciplinary* approach that borrows from various disciplines and utilizes the two tenets above (and indeed all the tenets mentioned in this chapter). In demonstrating this interdisciplinary perspective, Ladson-Billings (2009) highlights the overlap between legal studies and education in critiquing educational policy and structures: "Since education in the USA is not outlined explicitly in the nation's constitution, it is one of the social functions relegated to individual states. Consequently, states generate legislation and enact laws designed to proscribe the contours of education" (p. 28). Said another way, critical educators cannot understand how racism works within the education system without understanding how race is fundamental to the laws that govern education, especially in K-12 where so much of the curricula is mandated by state and federal laws. And while college educators enjoy a great deal of academic freedom, our institutions are still informed by not only the law but also by the social reality outside our campuses (note: it is also important to investigate how academic freedom perpetuates racist ideologies and Western European social norms).

b. Critical Race Theory in Education

Since this book is focused on social justice in community colleges, it is important to briefly expand on CRT's role in educational theory, research, and practice. As mentioned previously, at its most fundamental level, CRT is a theoretical framework that can help scholars identify structures of racial oppression within a given institution or discipline, dismantle them, and replace them with those of liberation. More specifically, Solórzano and Yosso (2002) describe CRT's role in education:

> critical race theory advances a strategy to foreground and account for the role of race and racism in education and works toward the elimination of racism as part of a larger goal of opposing or eliminating other forms of subordination based on gender, class, sexual orientation, language, and national origin... critical race theory in education is a framework or set of basic insights, perspectives, methods, and pedagogy that seeks to identify, analyze, and transform those structural and cultural aspects of education that maintain subordinate and dominant racial positions in and out of the classroom. (p. 25)

They further describe the following five tenets of critical race theory and methodology in education:

- "The intercentricity of race and racism with other forms of subordination": race is central to educational research, theory, and praxis, yet it is acknowledged that race is intricately linked, or "intersects," with other forms of oppression, including sexism, classism, homophobia, ethnocentrism and xenophobia, and others (p. 25).
- "The challenge to dominant ideology": critical race theory in education rejects the façade of objectivity and the pervasiveness of "deficit-informed research" in educational institutions (p. 26).
- "The commitment to social justice": social justice is at the heart critical race theory and its methodologies in education, and it strives to not only eliminate racism and other forms of oppression but also to "emancipate and empower" traditionally marginalized peoples.
- "The centrality of experiential knowledge": critical race theory in education recognizes that stories and storytelling, including "family histories, biographies, scenarios, parables, *ceuntos, testimonios,* chronicles, and narratives," are valuable in understanding race, racism, and other forms of oppression.

Furthermore, Ladson-Billings (2009) argues that "CRT can be a powerful explanatory tool for such sustained inequity that people of color experience" in education, highlighting "curriculum, instruction, assessment, school funding, and desegregation" (p. 28). In other words, critical race theory provides a sort of lens through which we can scrutinize, reflect on, and transform our colleges, or "for illuminating our thinking about school inequity" (p. 33). In her urgent call for CRT in education, Ladson-Billings continues, "If we are serious about solving these problems in schools and classrooms, we have to be serious about intense study and careful rethinking of race and education. Adopting and adapting CRT as a framework for educational equity means we will have to expose racism in education *and* propose radical solutions for addressing it" (p. 33, emphasis in original). It is my hope that this book provides a springboard for my readers in their "intense study and careful rethinking of race and education." But to be clear, this book is not the end all, be all. It is a starting point, and readers should continue to explore the primary scholarship on critical race theory (many pivotal works are cited in this book). With that in mind, the remainder of this chapter will explore these themes in the community college.

c. White Supremacy in Community Colleges

Many European American educators have heard the term "institutionalized racism" or "systemic racism," but few understand what this really means, and even fewer understand the role of white supremacy in creating these systems of oppression. As mentioned in Chapter 2, white privilege and implicit bias often mask the root causes for the inequities that exist in community colleges and other educational institutions – white supremacy. As educators, we need to stop dancing around the racist history of our country and the racial hierarchy that has been created. Even though we are not the architects of this system of oppression, we are beneficiaries, and simply naming what causes this oppression can be powerful in and of itself. As Rothenberg (2016) asserts, "The first step toward dismantling the system of privilege that operates in this society is to name it" (p. 5).

But in order to truly "name it," we need to understand what we are bringing into the light. As Flagg (1993) notes, institutional racism is "the maintenance of institutions that systematically advantage whites" (p. 959). As mentioned earlier, racism is both a system that privileges whiteness, but it is also a system that dominates people of color, so institutional racism in community colleges, for instance, means that our colleges have been intentionally designed to promote the success of our white students while, at the same time, marginalizing students of color. Sims et al. (2020) observe that the institution of the community college, or as they were more commonly known in the early 20th century, junior college, was meant to further the eugenics agenda of prominent leaders of higher education. Sims et al. note:

> Six of the junior college framers were active eugenicists. Eugenics was more than a movement or theory. In the guise of objective science, eugenics informed beliefs, practices, policies, theories, and doctrines related to the improvement of the human condition by promoting the reproduction of 'superior' genetic traits (European American males), while discouraging and preventing reproduction of other 'inferior' genetic traits (ethno-racial minority groups and white females from impoverished backgrounds). Since the university presidents envisioned a system that nurtured the so-called superior race, it is no coincidence or surprise that the junior college system was conceived to maintain social and class in equality and necessarily white supremacy. (pp. 41–42)

While the mission of many community colleges has changed drastically in the last century, we must still contend with our legacies of white supremacy, whether it is encoded in the institutions' structures, in the curriculum, or in the classroom pedagogies. As Derman-Sparks and Brunson Phillips (1997) write, "Institutional racism includes the mission, policies, organizational structures, and behaviors built into all institutional systems and services" (p. 10). To demonstrate, Derman-Sparks and Brunson Phillips contend, "practices such as IQ testing, tracking, a lack of understanding about differences in learning styles, curriculum materials centered on Euro-American culture, and ineffective bilingual education all create unequal educational opportunity and foster outcomes that maintain the status quo of institutional racism" (p. 11).

d. The Dominant Narrative about Students of Color

Institutional racism is perpetuated, in part, by flawed and insidious assumptions about students of color, which are the product of centuries of bad science, perverse sociology, and treacherous media portrayals (Cokley, 2003; Harper, 2009; Yosso, 2006). In other words, our understandings and assumptions about the students of color who set foot on our campuses and in our classrooms are ultimately based on a dominant narrative that informs how we interact and educate our students. These dominant narratives, or majoritarian stories, as Delgado described them, are the consequence of decades of acculturation promoted by our families and friends, our country's politicians, and the media (which in the 21st century must also include social media). As Yosso (2006) writes:

> Majoritarian storytelling is a method of recounting the experiences and perspectives of those with racial and social privilege. Traditionally, mainstream storytelling through mass media and academia rely on 'stock' stereotypes if and when they discuss issues of race... Majoritarian narratives tend to silence or dismiss people who offer evidence contradicting these racially unbalanced portrayals. (p. 9)

In other words, white educators are not only vulnerable to the media's misrepresentations of students of color, but we also perpetuate them. We use a curriculum that centers whiteness and the achievements of Europeans and European Americans, and in our research, we often pathologize the students and communities of color we serve (Harper, 2015). And the perverse element that maintains this cycle is our unwillingness to see academia and our society through a lens different from the one we have created. In other words, we reject race-consciousness and then commit violence on those who challenge our worldviews. As a result, the dominant narrative about intelligent, successful students of color is that they are "exceptional" and that the rest were admitted because of affirmative action (in the case of universities). These are absurd assumptions that have been engrained in the American psyche through mass media, including social media, community prejudice, and even our own academies. Yosso concludes, "Majoritarian narratives, in other words, essentialize, tokenize, and stereotype based on generalizations" (p. 13) So what are these dominant narratives that have such a profound effect on us and our institutions?

In general, our students of color are seen by their white professors and other campus employees as "underprepared," from homes and communities uncommitted to education, and, in some cases, as intellectually deficient. For example, Yosso (2006) describes the dominant narrative for Latinx students:

> Majoritarian stories along the Chicana/o educational pipeline often feature Chicana/o parents who supposedly do not care about educating their children, or Latina/o and Black students who ostensibly receive 'racial preferences' in college admissions. The majoritarian story asserts: if Chicana/o students perform poorly in school, then their parents probably do not 'value' education enough to inculcate academic excellence in their children. (p. 9)

Similarly, if Latinx students do well in school, they are perceived as the exception rather than the rule. Similarly, Harper (2009) found that African American students not only contended with stereotypes about their homes and neighborhoods, but also in their intellectual capacities, a clear consequence of the centuries-long fight to justify slavery and Jim Crow. Harper writes, "Blacks, especially Black men, continue to be caricatured as second- and third-rate citizens through the media, the preponderance of deficit-oriented discourse regarding our lives, and the inequitable distribution of resources, justice, and opportunity... their experiences are often overshadowed by the master narrative that amplifies Black male underachievement, disengagement, and attrition" (p. 698, 708).

The deficit language about Black students, indeed all students of color, has, as Sims et al. (2020) argue, "fetishized" the so-called "achievement gap." With the above master narrative in mind, we need to question the language we use vis-à-vis students of color. Unfortunately, the term "achievement gap" has become so pervasive that is has become common sensical. However, if we pause for a moment, the semantics of achievement become extremely problematic, as the "achievement gap" implies that the students are lacking in something that inhibits their success. This makes sense when we break down the phrase. Specifically, when we use the word "achievement," who are we referring to? Who achieves? The answer is our students, so when we say that there is an "achievement gap" between African American and Latinx students and their white peers, we are arguing that the former has failed to achieve. It becomes their problem and their fault. Said another way, their failures become innate, and I'd be remiss not to point out that this is indeed racism. As Kendi (2019) notes, "There is an even more sinister implication in achievement-gap talk – that disparities in academic achievement accurately reflect disparities in intelligence among racial group" (p. 101). The language of achievement is long overdue for scrutiny and criticism, starting with this problematic term "achievement gap." Indeed, it is time to retire this term altogether. No educator truly concerned with equity and social justice can promulgate a term that implicitly argues that students of color are inferior to their white peers. As such, no educator truly concerned with equity and social justice should continue to use such a term in their dialogue or writing. As Pollack (2008) urges, we must use "precision" in speaking about equity and inequity (p. 26).

Similarly, equity-minded educators need to rethink other deficit-minded ideologies, including our use of the terms "unprepared for college" or "underprepared." We need to step back and ask ourselves what we really mean by such statements – unprepared for what? College? Says who? Who determined what "prepared for college" means? Was it a diverse body of academics who represented different ethnoracial identities, sexualities, socio-economic statuses, and genders? I think we know what the answer is. The belief that a student is "unprepared for college" is, if we are honest with ourselves, a form of cultural racism (Kendi, 2019). We label students as unprepared and then relegate them to remedial coursework or track them into career education (and away from transfer and high-salary professional careers). This is the inevitable result of how the system was designed; community colleges were founded over a century ago on the belief that white men, particularly those who came from the lower economic ranks, needed a pipeline into the states' university systems. These community colleges were never intended for students of color or women, and we still see the vestiges of this history today, even in colleges that have been founded in the last few decades. White supremacy, as I have mentioned in the previous two chapters, is engrained in our system of higher education. In fact, as previously mentioned, Sims et al. (2020) argue that the founding of the entire junior college system was, as mentioned above, an early experiment in eugenics.

To demonstrate this phenomenon, I like to share a story about the community college I teach at – College of San Mateo (CSM), which is located almost exactly halfway between San Francisco and San Jose, California. Founded in 1922, CSM is nearly 100 years old and one of the oldest community colleges in California (and in the country). After CSM moved from downtown San Mateo in the mid-20th century to a perch just west that overlooks the entire San Francisco Bay Area, it gained a reputation of excellence, as graduates would transfer to top-tier universities and go on to be leaders in their fields. It was eventually nicknamed "Harvard on the Hill." When I ask my students if they knew this, they always answer that they had no idea. Not one student had ever heard of this nickname. As I share this story with them, I ask them why this name fell out of usage, and we always land on the changing demographics and perceptions of community colleges. In other words, when community colleges served a predominantly white, university-bound student body, they enjoyed a bit of prestige. However, as the civil rights movements gained traction, especially in school desegregation, and the student body diversified in the latter half of the century, we started to see "Harvard on the Hill" replaced with "remediation," "unprepared," and "basic skills." The language of excellence was replaced with the language of deficit, and it is no coincidence that this shift happened as the colleges diversified.

Ultimately, terms like "achievement gap" and "unprepared for college" contribute to a master narrative, one informed by higher education's eugenic mission, that students of color and other minoritized students do not belong, not because we don't want them but because they are lacking in ability, intellect, culture, and resources. In other words, we are engaging in what Solórzano and Yosso (2002) call "deficit storytelling," which is the byproduct of "deficit-informed research that silences and distorts epistemologies of people of color" (p. 26). Solórzano and Yosso point to the 1994 text *The Bell Curve* by Richard J. Hernstein and Charles Murray as the so-called "objective" science that perpetuates the belief that students of color are biologically inferior to their white peers. This is a belief that was more recently espoused by geneticist James Watson, one of the three discoverers of DNA, in 2007 and then again in 2019. As Amy Harmon (2019) reported, Watson had argued, of Africans, that "all our social policies are based on the fact that their intelligence is the same as ours, whereas all the testing says, not really... people who have to deal with black employees find [intellectual equality] not true" (par. 3). These two instances point to a larger problem with how the natural and social sciences, particularly educational research, contribute to the centuries-old master narrative that people of color are inferior to those of Western European descent.

Furthermore, these quack studies, and those like them, are further bolstered by the widespread belief that we live in a post-racial, colorblind America. As Yosso (2006) writes in her book *Critical Race Counterstories along the Chicana/Chicano Educational Pipeline*, "A majoritarian story implicitly begins from the assumption that all students enjoy access to the same educational opportunities and conditions from elementary through postsecondary school. From this premise, and utilizing seemingly neutral and objective formulae, the majoritarian story faults Chicana/o students and community cultural traditions for unequal schooling outcomes" (p. 4). In other words, if we buy into a colorblind perspective, racism no longer exists systematically in institutions like colleges and universities, so the institution couldn't be the reason why students of color, by and large, are not succeeding and persisting at the same rates of their white classmates. If educators assume that every student that steps foot on campus or in the classroom is treated equally and fairly – since we supposedly live in a colorblind society – then any differences in racialized outcomes are attributed to some deficiency in the students, as Hernstein, Murray, Watson, and hordes of other researchers contend. But as I discussed in length in Chapters 2 and 3, this simply isn't the case.

As a result, we need to be more progressive in how we frame student achievement, and in recent years, scholars have proposed terms that shift the focus from the students to the institutions. Carter and Welner (2013), for example, shift the conversation from one of achievement to one of opportunity. They write:

The "opportunity gap" frame... shifts our attention from outcomes to inputs – to the deficiencies in the foundational components of societies, schools, and communities that produce significant differences in educational – and ultimately socioeconomic – outcomes. Thinking in terms of "achievement gaps" emphasizes the symptoms; thinking about unequal opportunity highlights the causes. (pp. 2–3)

Furthermore, Kendi (2019) argues, "The lack of resources leads directly to diminished opportunities for learning. In other words, the racial problem is the opportunity gap, as antiracist informers call it, not the achievement gap" (p. 103). Many community colleges, in recognition of inequitable opportunities, respond with various student success and retention programs, like learning communities, dedicated counseling, assistance with housing, and other types of economic and academic supports. My own college, for instance, has at least a dozen programs for minoritized and traditionally marginalized students.

However, we too often operate under the belief that "if we build it, they will come." Moreover, these student success and retention programs can let instructors and campus leaders "off the hook" for student equity because it becomes too easy to say that particular services are the responsibility of certain programs. But equity-minded educators take a more proactive approach wherein we take the responsibility for ensuring that each of our students has the resources they need to succeed in our classrooms and other spaces. This is what Sims et al. (2020) call the "obligation gap." As they write, "the obligation gap calls out the institution, not the student, to be the prime agent of change. This gap necessitates acts of genuine care and calls for a civic consciousness, predicated on justice, with the intention to inspire epistemological disruption and reconstruction of educational structures" (p. 36). The obligation gap framework, then, compels educators to take responsibility for their students' success, both in the classroom and at the institutional level. It is not enough to simply create programs, but it is about intentionally funding them and ensuring that every student that needs them uses them. And semantically, this term has the most solemn implications. Both "achievement" and "opportunity" speak to what the students either possess or lack. Obligation, conversely, speaks to the institution's and its educators' investment in their students' success.

e. Counterstories of Struggle and Campus Climate

One of the primary assertions in this book is that white community college educators need to understand and to take seriously the lived realities of students in our classrooms and on our campuses while recognizing that our own actions and beliefs often perpetuate a culture of power built upon Eurocentrism and white supremacy (Delpit, 1988). Understanding the "campus climate" of one's own institution is an important step in recognizing these lived realities and how they impact the emotional and academic well-being of our students. As Hurtado (1992) argues, "we need a better understanding of what constitutes a racially tense interpersonal environment before considering how these climates are related to student development" (p. 540). The following sections, then, strive to accomplish this goal in a broader sense by including scholarship and literature that lay bare these "racially tense interpersonal environments." In this section, I will discuss the many racialized experiences of students of color – such as microaggressions – as well as the race-based obstacles – like stereotype threat – that students must navigate on a daily basis. However, it is irresponsible to represent our students as hopeless victims because the fact is that many of our students of color are flourishing despite these barriers. As a result, in the next section, I would like to present the counter-narratives that challenge the assumptions that our students of color, particularly our African American students, are defined by our student success data.

Solórzano, Ceja, and Yosso (2000), for example, found a college's campus climate can be profoundly impacted by microaggressions, which they define as "subtle insults (verbal, nonverbal, and/or visual) directed toward people of color, often automatically or unconsciously" (p. 60). More specifically, they discovered through their interviews with several students that microaggressions can have a profoundly negative impact on campus climate and student success. Some of the microaggressions described by the students in Solórzano et al.'s study included:

- Feeling "invisible" in class and being ignored by faculty and classmates
- Seeing "their experiences as African Americans...omitted, distorted, and stereotyped in their course curriculum" (p. 65)
- Feeling like their professors have "low expectations of them, even in the face of contradictory evidence," including accusations of cheating (p. 66)
- Being ostracized and isolated in peer and study groups, such as when they are not included in the discussion or when they are called on last (if at all)

- While not as relevant to community colleges, being directly or indirectly accused of being admitted to the university as part of affirmative action (p. 67)
- Being racially profiled by campus police

Ultimately, the students in the study had to contend with two equally challenging realities: if they struggled with assignments or they acted or spoke in a way that their white professors and classmates found stereotypical, the students felt like they were confirming their suspicions about Black students as a whole; on the contrary, if they excelled in class or on assignments, they were seen as special and the exception to the rule. Solórzano et al. found that racial microaggressions led to a "negative racial climate and African American students' struggles with feelings of self-doubt and frustration as well as isolation. This means that the African American students on the campuses studied must strive to maintain good academic standing while negotiating the conflicts arising from disparaging perceptions of them and their group of origin. Additionally, they must navigate through a myriad of pejorative racial stereotypes that fuel the creation and perpetuation of racial microaggressions" (p. 69). As the students shared, these stressors made them "despondent" and "made them feel that they could not perform well academically." It is important to note that the participants in the study were students at elite universities and who were themselves vanguard students. In other words, the consequences of racial microaggressions were severe enough to affect the academic performance of some of higher education's most brilliant students, and these microaggressions would often act as cues that reminded affected students of the negative stereotypes associated with their identities. As Harper (2015) found, "stereotypes were most often conveyed through racial microaggressions" (pp. 657–658).

This phenomenon has been labeled by Steele and Aronson (1995) as "stereotype threat." Simply put, stereotype threat is "being at risk of confirming, as self-characteristic, a negative stereotype about one's group" (p. 797). In other words, any student who is negatively stereotyped academically, including African Americans in academic settings and women in the sciences, will feel acute pressure to do well academically for *fear* of confirming these negative stereotypes in the eyes of their professors and peers (Steele, 1997; Steele & Aronson, 1995). They fear "that other people will see them that way" (Steele & Aronson, 1995, p. 797). However, stereotype threat is not an equal opportunity malady; it happens primarily under very specific circumstances. First, the student in question must feel stigmatized and isolated in the academic environment, meaning that they must be in the minority, or lack what is termed "critical mass," "the point at which there are enough minorities in a setting, like school or a workplace, that individual minorities no longer feel uncomfortable there because they are minorities... they no longer feel stereotype threat" (Steele, 2010, p. 135). Furthermore, stereotype threat is most severe for the "vanguard" students (Fries-Britt & Turner, 2002; Steele, 1997, 2010; Taylor & Soto Antony, 2000). In other words, the students most susceptible to stereotype threat are some of the highest performing students, and as Steele and Aronson originally discovered, stereotype threat was primarily experienced in evaluations in which the students were pushed to the limits of their abilities, such as in high-level courses or other advanced academic circumstances.

It is important to understand that stereotype threat has nothing to do with ability. The fact that it most acutely impacts high-performing students who care immensely about their academic success bears this out (Steele, 2010). It is simply the fear of confirming the stereotype, but this fear is so intense and so real that stereotype threat has very tangible consequences for students (Cabrera, Nora, Terenzini, Pascarella, & Hagedorn, 1999; D'Augelli & Hershberger, 1993). For example, Solórzano et al. (2000) confirmed in their study that high-performing Black students are negatively impacted academically by stereotype threat, including "drop[ping] a class, changing their major and even leaving the university to attend school elsewhere" (p. 69).

Because the consequences of racial microaggressions are so severe and high-stakes, Kendi (2019) prefers to describe them for what they are: "racist abuse" (p. 47). And while a negative campus climate can have profound effects on the college's vanguard, as demonstrated above, microaggressions affect all minoritized students and can have the same deleterious impacts for them regardless of academic standing, ability, or potential. As Kendi (2019) writes, "I do not use 'microaggression' anymore. I detest the postracial platform that supported its sudden popularity. I detest its component parts – 'micro' and 'aggression.' A persistent daily low hum of racist abuse is not minor. I use the term 'abuse' because aggression is not as exacting a term. Abuse accurately describes the action and its effects on people: distress, anger, worry, depression, anxiety, pain, fatigue, and suicide" (p. 47). Unfortunately, microaggressions and their close relative, unconscious bias, are explained away as the unlucky consequences of acculturation. In other words, it becomes too easy to argue that we are simply the by-products of a society and media that aim to inculcate anti-Blackness and other forms of hatred and biases. But if we're honest, this is just a cop-out. Ultimately, we are responsible for our own thoughts and actions, and it is incumbent upon white educators to undergo the process of reflection and self-critique described in Chapter 3, so that we may be cognizant of our unconscious biases and so that we may be aware of when we microaggress our minoritized students and colleagues. We need to see these phenomena for what they are – racism – and we need to be proactive in eliminating them from our worldviews and subconscious.

Much like Kendi, Harper (2009) is blunt in his assessment of microaggressions against Black men, in particular, and for Harper, the term microaggression is just a softer term for overt racism. In order to highlight the true roots of microaggressions, Harper has coined the term "niggering" to both accurately describe the racism inherent in microaggressions and to remind us of the particularly troubling history of racism and white supremacy that still oppresses students of color, particularly Black men. As Harper writes, "a Black male student could be 'niggered' in various ways (e.g. being told that he is unlikely to accomplish much in life; that he is no good, just like the rest of them; and that being successful in school is an anomaly for people like him)" (p. 698). Harper's participants identified the following examples of "niggering" in their day-to-day interactions:

- "What sport do you play?"
- "You got weed?"
- "You wrote this?"
- "Hello, [other Black guy in class]"
- "You from the hood?"

Ultimately, Harper found that "the most pervasive stereotype confronting participants... was the presumption that they were student-athletes... achievers elsewhere also described how they were constantly asked which sport they play. Some had grown accustomed to being congratulated repeatedly on Mondays if the football or basketball team beat its weekend opponent" (pp. 658–659, 660). These microaggressions – or racist abuse – all alienate the students who experience them; they tell the victim of this racist abuse that they simply do not belong. Even in the case of being mistaken as an athlete, there are implications for the students' sense of belonging. When an educator mistakes a student of color, especially a male of color, for an athlete, that educator is suggesting that students of color only belong in college if they have athletic abilities. They are being told that their minds do not matter. For academically-identified students, this can create feelings of alienation from the institution, but for students who do not have a strong academic-identity, this can alienate them from higher education altogether. Nevertheless, the consequences are unacceptable.

Additionally, minoritized students must contend with a variety of macroaggressions, including racism, sexism, and other forms of overt hatred and discrimination. D'Augelli and Hershberger (1993) found, for example, that Black college students, "borne the brunt of racist remarks and most assumed that African Americans would be mistreated on campus. Many had experienced verbal insults themselves or knew of others being mistreated" (p. 77). Similarly, Feagin, Vera, and Imani (1996) found that students of color consistently experienced racism from their white classmates. Furthermore, minoritized students experience these microaggressions from not only their peers but also from their professors and college staff (D'Augelli & Hershberger, 1993; Feagin et al., 1996; Fries-Britt & Turner, 2001).

Cumulatively, this racial abuse and stereotype threat results in a psychological dilemma called "racial battle fatigue." Smith, Allen, and Danley (2007) define racial battle fatigue as "the physiological and psychological strain exacted on racially marginalized groups and the amount of energy lost dedicated to coping with racial microaggressions and racism" (p. 555). Utilizing an interdisciplinary approach, Smith, Allen, and Danley found that students who experience racial battle fatigue – whether from micro- or macroaggressions – experience health consequences from headaches to ulcers, psychological trauma, including anxiety, loss of sleep, and hyper-vigilance, and emotions like anger, withdrawal, and resentment (pp. 552, 556; Smith, Hung, & Franklin, 2011). Unsurprisingly, students who experience racial battle fatigue are more likely to see a drop in their grades and/or drop out of college. Similarly, Smedley, Myers, and Harrell (1993) identified what they termed "minority status stresses," which "confer an additional burden of stress and would be associated with an increased risk for negative outcomes beyond that which is attributable to the stresses of being a student at a highly competitive academic institution" (pp. 445–446). In other words, minoritized students, especially students of color, must cope not only cope with the stressors experienced by all college students but also with the additional burdens mentioned earlier – micro- and macroaggressions, stereotype threat, stigmatization, and isolation. This creates an educational experience where all students, regardless of race, have a limited mental and emotional load, but minoritized students are forced to expend much of this mental and emotional capacity on identity-based stressors.

f. The Importance of Counterstories: Challenging the Dominant Narrative

While it is important to understand the challenges that our students of color are experiencing in our colleges, it is equally important to simultaneously avoid defining our students by these struggles. Despite the obstacles mentioned in the previous section, many our students of color are thriving. In other words, while almost all of our students of color experience racism, stereotype threat, and/or racial battle fatigue, they are not hopeless. Indeed, many of our students of color are extremely successful *despite* our best attempts to construct obstacles and barriers. Additionally, our students of color, especially our African American, Latinx, and Pacific Islander students, are contending with a dominant – or as Delgado (1989) would call it, majoritarian – narrative that they do not belong in the academy, and if they do, it is because they are athletes. This dominant narrative is exasperated in community colleges, which have open-door policies that grant all students admission regardless of their GPA or past academic record. In other words, our community college students of color may not have to deal with the enigma of affirmative action like their university counterparts, but they are, instead, forced to confront the deficit-thinking and low expectations of their professors and classmates.

As a result, this section strives to disabuse readers of this deficit-orientation and low expectations by presenting the reality, or the counter-narrative to the majoritarian stories of students of color of our colleges: that we have a great deal of brilliant, motivated, striving students of color all around us. My hope is to change the narrative from those that see students of color as academic imposters or hopeless victims to one in which we see our students of color as smart, highly motivated students with dreams and goals who also face a great deal of identity-based violence and barriers. Sometimes these barriers are insurmountable, but often, our students persist. But first, it is essential that we first look at counterstorytelling in a little more detail. As mentioned before, counter-stories first entered the academic conversation with Richard Delgado's (1989) influential article, "Storytelling for Oppositionists and Others: A Plea for Narrative." In this article, he not only operationalizes majoritarian, or ingroup, narratives – those incomplete and warped stories told by those in power in order to oppress the "other" – but he also calls for the use of counterstories to challenge dominant common sense. He writes that counterstories "aim to subvert that ingroup reality" and "can open new windows into reality, showing us that there are possibilities for life other than the ones we live. They enrich imagination and teach that by combining elements from the story and current reality, we may construct a new world richer than either alone" (pp. 2413, 2414–2415).

Solórzano and Yosso (2002) posed a framework for counterstorytelling in academia, which can help educators to see the lived experiences of their students. For Solórzano and Yosso, critical race methodologies, specifically counterstorytelling, can counteract the dominant, or majoritarian, narratives that our students are "unprepared," come from a "culture of poverty," and other misrepresentations that our Black and Brown students are hopeless victims in need of our "saviorism." Unfortunately, these misrepresentations have been enshrined in the educational literature and are bolstered by the façade of objectivity, or what Wacquant (2008) calls "semi-scholarly approximations of conventional research" (p. 1). In fact, as Harper (2009) has criticized, "conventional research" has "the almost exclusive fascination with problems encountered by this population" (p. 699). Similarly, Solórzano and Yosso argue counterstorytelling "exposes deficit-informed research and methods that silence and distort the experiences of people of color and instead focuses on their racialized, gendered, and classed experiences as sources of strength" (p. 26). In other words, counterstories act as a counterweight to the dominant narratives about students of color, and instead, treat the students as whole people who have unique funds of knowledge, a great deal of cultural capital, and the same motivation and brilliance as any other student in our colleges (Gonzalez, Moll, & Amanti, 2005; Moll, Amanti, Neff, & Gonzalez, 1992). Ultimately, Solórzano and Yosso describe four functions for counterstorytelling: "a) They can build community among those at the margins of society by putting a human and familiar face to educational theory and practice, b) they can challenge the perceived wisdom of those at society's center by providing a context to understand and transform established belief systems, c) they can open new windows into the reality of those at the margins of society by showing possibilities beyond the ones they live and demonstrating that they are not alone in their position, and d) they can teach others that by combining elements from both the story and the current reality, one can construct another world that is richer than either the story or the reality alone" (p. 36).

Moreover, counter-stories can begin to shift the focus from student achievement (e.g. the "achievement gap") to our collective responsibility for creating equitable and just community colleges (e.g. the obligation gap). Yosso (2006) writes that a counterstory "begins with an understanding that inadequate educational conditions limit equal access and opportunities" (p. 4). She further argues that counterstories make visible the disparities in educational funding, teacher preparation, and college-prep curricula, noting, "Instead of blaming [students of color] or community cultural traditions, a counterstory addresses the structures, practices, and discourses that facilitate high dropout (pushout) rates." While Yosso is specifically referring here to the K-12 educational pipeline, counterstories can help community college educators understand the realities of their students of color both inside and outside the college in a way that traditional data-collection techniques cannot. Let's take, for example, student classroom surveys. Student evaluations often include a question along the lines of "On a scale of 1–5, the instructor respects all students regardless of race, ethnicity, gender, etc." If one or two Black students in a particular class feel regularly microaggressed, their experience is reduced to a blip on the professor's student evaluation, and their lived experiences on the campus become invisible across different courses. In other words, traditional data measures can often mask a negative racial climate. On the other hand, counterstories, which are a form of qualitative data-collection, can better illustrate the experiences of students of color both in the classroom and across the college, which resists the popular majoritarian story that racism isn't embedded in the fabric of the college. As Yosso writes, "Recognizing these stories and knowledges as valid and valuable data, counterstorytellers challenge majoritarian stories that omit and distort the histories and realities of oppressed communities. Drawing also on academic research, social science and humanities literature, and judicial records, counterstories question racially stereotypical portrayals implicit in majoritarian stories" (p.10).

However, counterstories also celebrate the widespread achievement of students of color despite the obstacles and barriers constructed by community colleges and their educators. Harper's (2009) phenomenological study of over 200 high-achieving Black men at dozens of colleges and universities, most of which were Predominantly White Institutions (PWIs), is one such project that strives to celebrate the successes of students of color, particularly Black men, despite the negative racial climate of their universities. Harper's study found that these high-achieving Black male students were not immune to the racism that many believe has been reserved for struggling students of color. Despite their high GPAs, their involvement in campus activities, like student government, and other traditional measures of success, these students were still seen in light of the stereotypes of Black men – they were consistently asked if they played sports, they were consistently praised for how "articulate" they were, and sometimes even told that they surprised their professors with their intelligence. But, most importantly, Harper found that the Black men in his study all had one thing in common: they rejected, oftentimes publicly, the dominant narrative of Black men in higher education.

They simply refused to be stereotyped, discriminated against, and denigrated. One participant in Harper's study "refused to be treated as [a stereotype]. Thus, he immediately became involved in the Student Government Association and the Residence Hall Council during his freshman year. It was through these student organizations that he deliberately went about presenting a more positive view of Black men" (p. 706). Other men in the study "foster[ed] relationships with White administrators," started publications, and became active in organizations like the Black Student Union, all of which were partly done to disprove negative perceptions of students of color. Some of the students would even take the riskier approach of challenging their professors' and classmates' racism; one student "recalled an instance when a White faculty member was offensively shocked by a thoughtful contribution he made to a class discussion" (p. 707). Many students would bluntly ask their professors and classmates "why [they] were so visibly astonished." These "acts of resistance" became psychologically necessary to avoid "the psychological burden of wondering if the professor [or classmates] was so surprised because he didn't expect a Black man to have anything smart to contribute."

Similarly, Harper (2015) found that many students of color actually use instances of racism as motivation to get more involved in campus leadership, especially where they could work on racial justice. In fact, many of the Black men in Harper's study found that while they were often microaggressed by their professors, students of color who were not campus leaders were often targeted more frequently and overtly. One student noted, "I guess you could say they are selectively racist, and I benefit from this ignorant selectivity while other students of color suffer" (p. 664). Because of this dynamic, many of the students in Harper's study felt compelled to use their voices and positions on campus to fight racism on campus. As Harper observed, "As they began to garner reputations for themselves as student leaders outside the classroom, the achievers became more conscious of their self-representation and voices in the classroom. That is, they emerged as leaders in their classes and were more empowered to speak up on behalf of other Blacks when troublesome race-based stereotypes arose in class discussion" (p. 664). As mentioned at the beginning of this chapter, I have witnessed the power of this voice firsthand in academic senate meetings. While the academic senate at my college was striving to take a leadership role in promoting a culture of educational equity and social justice amongst the faculty, there were detractors. These professors believed in the majoritarian narrative of a colorblind, post-racial America wherein racism was relegated to extremist, white nationalist groups. When the one senator asked whether microaggressions happened, it was our student body president, a high-achieving Black male, who told his story about dealing with racial abuse on a daily basis. He fundamentally changed the tenor of the meeting, and while I don't think he changed that senator's perspective, he made a profound impact on many others in the academic senate, enough to move the conversation forward and in a new direction.

But where there exists racism, we can often find its intersections with class, and it is important to note that our student body president was "safe" for so many of my colleagues. He was what we might call "preppy"; he frequently wore khaki shorts and polos, he had a closely cropped hairdo, and he would wear a nice suit to campus events. He came from a middle-class family, and he learned how to navigate the college, both on his own intuition and likely with help from his parents, both of whom were professionals. Harper observed a similar phenomenon in his study:

> The achievers perceived their White instructors to be racist toward other Black students but not as much toward them. This is an interesting finding, because it appears that erroneous assumptions White faculty members make about *certain* Black students subside once they see those students in high-profile leadership roles, have meaningful interactions with them outside of class, and observe their intellectual aptitude in venues other than the classroom. Thus, it seems essential to create opportunities for meaningful engagement between White faculty and Black male students. (p. 667, emphasis in original)

In other words, our class biases as professionals have allowed us to express racist beliefs about some students of color while subjecting others, like our leaders of color, to forms of racist abuse like microaggressions. More specifically, we see the struggling Black student in our class who fits into our stereotypical worldview of Black students and write him off as a product of a "neighborhood that doesn't care about education" (i.e. cultural racism). And then we see the Black student leader who fits into our Eurocentric worldview (read: khakis and polos), and while we don't assume they are from a "bad neighborhood," we measure them up against our racist beliefs about Black students, which results in microaggressions like "you are so articulate." All of this is to say that the work of anti-racism requires us to understand our racist beliefs and our class biases and how these two belief systems intersect (not to mention the intersections with gender bias, homophobia and transphobia, and other forms of prejudice and biases). It is worth a reminder that our ignorance leads to maladies like stereotype threat and racial battle fatigue. Many students have figured out how to cope with such ignorance and racist abuse, using them as motivation to become socially conscious student leaders. But as open access institutions, many of our students haven't developed coping mechanisms specific to environments like community colleges, so our ignorance and racist actions will often lead to more serious consequences like poor grades, spotty attendance, and even dropping out. Neither of these situations is acceptable.

g. Educational Equity

This section will coalesce the two preceding chapters into a discussion of how community college instructors can best meet the needs of their diverse students given the structural barriers present in higher education. It will start by drawing a distinction between educational equity and its ubiquitous counterparts equality and diversity. This chapter will also ask readers to look beyond simply providing access and opportunity with a discussion of our collective obligation to achieving social justice.

Now that we've looked at the identity-based obstacles that our minoritized students are experiencing in our colleges, we can turn to the focus of this book – educational equity and social justice. But before delving into these concepts, it is important to differentiate equity and equality, a distinction I am often asked about by colleagues. Many of us have seen the popular illustration where three children are trying to watch a baseball game from the outfield: in one slide, the tallest child is able to easily peer over the fence while the shorter children are unable to watch the game, which is ostensibly a photo depicting equality because each child has the same resources (e.g. the ground); in the second slide, all three children are able to watch the game because the two shorter children now have boxes to stand on, enabling them to see over the fence. The second slide is meant to illustrate equity. While the picture is too simplistic and does not concretely depict equality and equity in educational practice, it is a good starting point because, at its very root, equity is about giving resources and support to those who need it (e.g. the boys in the picture needing the boxes to see the game).

Earlier in this chapter (and in Chapter 2), we discussed equality in the context of colorblindness, which can be used in two types of arguments. First, a colorblind perspective argues that the United States is in a postracial era wherein racism is no longer mainstream but is instead relegated to the fringes of our country. In this instance, since racism no longer exists, no racial group needs special access to resources and support. The second argument is the egalitarian belief that all people are equal and should be treated equally. At its very core, this colorblind perspective insists that racism will end when we stop seeing races, which means that no racial group should get "special privileges." As a result, all students should get equal access to academic resources and support because it would be unfair to give one racial group extra support and resources when all people are equal. I will not discuss why these perspectives are problematic since both this chapter and Chapter 2 already deconstruct them and highlight their deficiencies. But as Sims et al. (2020) note, "our educational system features a problematic one size fits all approach" (p. 7). Similarly, educators often conflate educational equity with diversity, as if numbers alone can remedy prejudice and racism. Admittedly, more diverse classrooms and student bodies can alleviate maladies like stereotype threat (Steele, 2010). However, all of the barriers and inequities discussed throughout this book can and do exist in colleges and universities that have extraordinarily diverse student bodies. In other words, a Black female student can step foot onto her campus, see lots of students from different ethnoracial groups and still be microaggressed by her professor, feel isolated in her classes, and deal with psychological trauma like racial battle fatigue.

So what does educational equity mean in the context of a community college? In the illustration mentioned previously, equity is shown to be the targeted distribution of resources in a way that promotes equal outcomes. The two shorter children are given boxes so they can see the game while the tall child is not given anything because he can already see it. As a result, all three children can see the game. But this illustration is misleading in an educational context because it implies that we can just throw money at inequities and racialized academic hierarchies. Unfortunately, this has been the approach to educational inequities, and it has not proven to be effective. Educational equity requires a fundamental shift in how we operate as colleges and how we offer our courses. It is about providing students with the learning environment they need to thrive and excel while simultaneously providing the necessary resources to succeed (e.g. free or reduced-cost textbooks, necessary technology like computers and software, etc.). Sims (2018) writes that educational equity "is intentional work toward the creation of positive, nutritive educational spaces that actively combat structural and institutionalized inequity so that all students are empowered, encouraged, and equipped to succeed academically precisely because they have been afforded rigorous and rich educational opportunities that allow them [to] work toward the realization of their full academic and human potential" (p. 12). This requires community college educators to undergo substantial professional development in how they teach their classes and in what curriculum they offer. This requires colleges to reimagine their spaces, their budgets, and their institutional practices.

Educational equity requires us to change the student experience at our colleges so that every student feels "empowered, encouraged, and equipped to succeed academically."

h. Practicum: Social Justice and Disrupting the Status Quo

Ultimately, this whole movement is not about educational equity but about social justice. If equity is giving the short children in that well-known illustration boxes to stand on, social justice is tearing down the entire fence. Educational equity is simply a band-aid. Social justice is the change in behavior and structures that prevents the wound in the first place. Educational equity is a response to racialized academic hierarchies, and social justice is the elimination of all components of that hierarchy, including the ideologies that undergird it (read: white supremacy, sexism, transphobia, etc.). Ultimately, social justice is the end goal. For example, Sims et al. (2020) write that social justice is "work that identifies, interrogates, and seeks to redress social injustices that serve the interests of white supremacy, anti-Blackness, and settler colonialism" (p. 14). Magee (2019) equates social justice to a form of "radical compassion" where social justice is "love in action for the alleviation of suffering" and the "Alleviat[tion of] the socially constructed, unevenly distributed suffering of all marginalized people" (pp. 6, 20–21). In other words, educators fighting for social justice must not only be committed to dismantling institutional barriers and identity-based hierarchies as promoted by Sims et al., but they must also feel genuine compassion for their students and the cause.

To that end, I think it is important to understand the term *compassion* and how it relates to its cousins, *sympathy* and *empathy*. The *Oxford English Dictionary (OED)* defines "compassion" as "The feeling or emotion, when a person is moved by the suffering of distress of another, and by the desire to relieve it." It is important to notice the final words – "desire to relieve it" – because this is what distinguishes compassion from other emotions like sympathy and empathy. Not to belabor the point, but the *OED* defines sympathy as "The quality or state of being affected by the condition of another with a feeling similar or corresponding to that of the other." In other words, if your friend or loved one is sad, feeling sympathy for them simply means that you also feel sad. Empathy takes this a little further. Again, the *OED* defines empathy as "The ability to understand and appreciate another person's feelings." This emotional response goes beyond simply feeling the same emotions as another, and it is when we are able to understand why they are feeling as they do. We sometimes call this "putting ourself into another's shoes." In a conversation with former gang members, Father Gregory Boyle recalls a discussion on these very definitions. Perhaps their words, as recounted by Boyle (2010) are more powerful than a dictionary's:

> "Well, sympathy," one begins, "is when your homie's mom dies and you go up to him and say, '*Spensa* – sorry to hear 'bout your moms.'"
>
> Just as quickly, there is a volunteer to define empathy.
>
> "Yeah, well, empathy is when your homie's mom dies and you say, '*Spensa*, 'bout your moms. *Sabes qué*, my moms died six months ago. I feel ya, dog.'"
> (p. 62)

When Boyle pushes the students to define compassion, they take a while, but eventually one says, "Compassion – that's sumthin' altogether different... That's what Jesus did. I mean, Compassion... IS... God." For less religious readers, Boyle goes on to write that "Compassion is not a relationship between the healer and the wounded. It's a covenant between equals... Compassion is always, at its most authentic, about a shift from the cramped world of self-preoccupation into a more expansive place of fellowship, of true kinship" (p. 77).

These words are very important for community college educators who wish to fight for social justice. We know that our students of color are constantly battling racism, racist abuse like microaggressions, racial battle fatigue, and a host of other forms of violence. We know this causes a great deal of stress, anxiety, fear, loneliness, anger, and sadness. We have a decision to make. Do we simply feel sympathy? When a student trusts us enough to share their sadness because they were microaggressed, do we simply mirror that emotion? Do we feel empathy? Do we try to imagine ourselves in their shoes? Or do we feel compassion and commit ourselves to rectifying the situation? To be clear, social justice requires the *action* as implied by the *OED* definition and by the feelings of kinship encouraged by Boyle. Sympathy and empathy are fine emotions to have when a student shares their experience with racism, but it simply is not enough. Our sympathy and empathy do *not* change the reality of that student and the other students' realities. This is why we collectively shake our heads when politicians "send their prayers" to the victims of school shootings. Only action can change these circumstances, and action is required when feeling compassion. Thus, social justice requires a great deal of compassion.

This compassion compels us to the work of social justice: to be disruptive in order to eliminate the injustices experienced by our minoritized students. Sims et al. (2020) posit that community colleges function as a sort of "disruptive technology." They write:

> in technology, disruption is good... a disruptive technology significantly alters the way businesses or entire industries operate. It often forces companies to change the way they approach their business... community colleges hold the potential to function as a kind of disruptive technology... Disruptive technologies make disruptive innovation possible. They provide space for innovation that disrupts rigid, cyclical practices. *Justice*-centered disruptive community college policies, practices, and pedagogies... not only make disruptive innovation possible – it makes it imminent. (pp. 2,3)

Community colleges have the opportunity to disrupt higher education, writ large, because we are open-access institutions that the majority of college students of color attend at some point in their lives. Imagine the ripple-effects if community colleges committed themselves to social justice, and they – we – fundamentally altered our way of educating *all* our students and not just those who looked and thought like us? How powerful would that be?

As mentioned in the Introduction, this book's focus is primarily on the classroom and is meant primarily for teaching faculty. This does not mean that staff, administrators, and non-instructional faculty cannot get something of value from this book. On the contrary, the first few chapters, in particular, are meant for anyone who works with community college students of color. However, the next two chapters will hone in on two areas that uniquely impact teaching faculty: pedagogy, or *how* we teach, and curriculum, or *what* we teach. I know it has been a long journey from this book's first pages to this moment, but I absolutely believe that our pedagogies and curricula – our classrooms – cannot change until us white community college educators first look in the mirror and work on what Magee (2019) calls the "inner work of racial justice."

i. Chapter 4 Synopsis and Questions for Consideration

Synopsis

Critical Race Theory, especially storytelling and counterstorytelling, can help community college educators better understand the racialized experiences of students of color. Research indicates that community college students of color experience negative academic climates and hostile learning environments due to the prevalence of microaggressions from professors and classmates, stereotype threat, and racial battle fatigue. While many students of color cope with this academic trauma, others do not, and this negative racial climate can lead to lower grades, poor attendance, and/or dropping out of classes or college entirely. After engaging in the "inner work of racial justice," white community college educators must disrupt this cycle by utilizing the tenets of educational equity, which is itself a pathway to the more important goal of social justice.

Questions to Consider

1. How can critical race theory and its tenets help us better understand racial oppression in the community college?
2. Why do minoritized students experience negative campus and classroom climates?
3. What are microaggressions, and how do they create a negative climate for students of color? How do microaggressions create stereotype threat?
4. What is stereotype threat, and how can community college educators alleviate its causes?
5. How do the intersections of race, class, sexual orientation, and gender identity culminate in unique racist abuse? In other words, what type of racist abuse might a middle-class Black student experience as opposed to a poorer Black student?
6. What is the difference between equity and equality? What about equity and social justice?
7. Why is compassion so important in our social justice work?

Keywords: interest convergence principle, race consciousness, intersectionality, structural determinism, counterstories, stereotype threat, microaggressions, racial battle fatigue, educational equity, social justice

j. References

Bell, D.A. (1980). Brown v. Board of Education and interest-convergence dilemma. *Harvard Law Review, 93*(3), 518–533.

Bell, D.A. (1992). *Faces at the bottom of the well: The permanence of racism.* New York: Basic Books.

Boyle, G. (2010). *Tattoos on the heart: The power of boundless compassion.* New York: Free Press.

Cabrera, A.F., Nora, A., Terenzini, P.T., Pascarella, E., & Hagedorn, L.S. (1999). Campus racial climate and the adjustment of students to college: A comparison between white students and African-American students. *The Journal of Higher Education, 70*(2), 134–160.

Carastathis, A. (2016). *Intersectionality: Origins, contestations, horizons.* Lincoln: University of Nebraska Press.

Carter, P.L., & Welner, K.G. (2013). Achievement gaps arise from opportunity gaps. In P.L. Carter & K.G. Welner (Eds.), *Closing the opportunity gap: What American must do to give every child an even chance* (pp. 1–10). Oxford, UK: Oxford UP.

Cohen, A.M., & Outcalt, C.L. (2001). *A profile of the community college professoriate: A report submitted to the small research grants program of the Spencer foundation.* Retrieved from https://eric.ed.gov/?id=ED454930

Cokley, K.O. (2003). What do we know about the motivation of African American students?: Challenging the "anti-intellectual" myth. *Harvard Educational Review, 73*(4), 524–558.

Crenshaw, K. (1989). Demarginalizing the intersection of race and sex: A Black feminist critique of antidiscrimination doctrine, feminist theory, and antiracist politics. *University of Chicago Law Review, 1*(8), 139–167.

Crenshaw, K. (1991). Mapping the margins: Intersectionality, identity politics, and violence against women of color. *Stanford Law Review, 43*(6), 1241–1299.

Crenshaw, K., Gotanda, N., Peller, G., & Thomas, K. (1995). *Critical race theory: The key writings that formed the movement.* New York: New Press.

Davis, A.Y. (1981/1983). *Women, race, & class.* New York: Vintage.

D'Augelli, A.R., & Hershberger, S.L. (1993). African American undergraduates on a predominantly white campus: Academic factors, social networks, and campus climate. *The Journal of Negro Education, 62*(1), 67–81.

Delgado, R. (1984). The imperial scholar: Reflections on a review of civil rights literature. *University of Pennsylvania Law Review, 132*(3), 561–578.

Delgado, R. (1989). Storytelling for oppositionists and others: A plea for narrative. *Michigan Law Review, 87*(8), 2411–2441.

Delgado, R., & Stefancic, J. (1989). Why do we tell the same stories?: Law reform, critical librarianship, and the triple helix dilemma. *Stanford Law Review, 42*(1), 207–225.

Delgado, R., & Stefancic, J. (Eds.). (2013). *Critical race theory: The cutting edge.* Philadelphia: Temple UP.

Delpit, L. (1988). The silenced dialogue: Power and pedagogy in educating other people's children. *Harvard Educational Review, 58*(3), 280–298.

Derman-Sparks, L., & Brunson Phillips, C. (1997). *Teaching/learning anti-racism.* New York: Teachers College Press.

Feagin, J.R., Vera, H., & Imani, N. (1996). *The agony of education: Black students at white colleges and universities.* New York: Routledge.

Flagg, B.J. (1993). "'Was blind, but now I see': White race consciousness and the requirement of discriminatory intent. *Michigan Law Review, 91*(5), 953–1017.

Fries-Britt, S.L., & Turner, B. (2001). Facing stereotypes: A case study of Black students on a White campus. *Journal of College Student Development, 42*(5), 420–429.

Fries-Britt, S.L., & Turner, B. (2002). Uneven stories: Successful Black collegians at a Black and a White campus. *The Review of Higher Education, 25*(3), 315–330.

Gonzalez, N., Moll, L.C., & Amanti, C. (Eds.). (2005). *Funds of knowledge: Theorizing practices in households, communities, and classrooms.* New York: Routledge.

The Good Liars. (2021, November 1). *This guy says Critical Race Theory is the most important issue in the Virginia Election. He also says he has no idea what Critical Race Theory is* [video attached] [Tweet]. Twitter. https://twitter.com/TheGoodLiars/status/1455243036795998212

Harmon, A. (2019, January 1). James Watson had a chance to salvage his reputation on race. He made things worse. *The New York Times.* Retrieved from https://www.nytimes.com/2019/01/01/science/watson-dna-genetics-race.html

Harper, S.R. (2009). Niggers no more: a critical race counternarrative on Black male student achievement at predominantly White colleges and universities. *International Journal of Qualitative Studies in Education, 22*(6), 697–712.

Harper, S.R. (2015). Black male college achievers and resistant responses to racist stereotypes at predominantly white colleges and universities. *Harvard Educational Review, 85*(4), 646–674.

Hurtado, S. (1992). The campus racial climate: Contexts of conflict. *The Journal of Higher Education, 65*(5), 539–569.

Kendi, I.X. (2019). *How to be an antiracist.* New York: One World.

Ladson-Billings, G. (2006). Foreword. In A.D. Dixson & C.K. Rousseau (Eds.), *Critical race theory in education: All God's children got a song* (pp. v–xiii). New York: Routledge.

Ladson-Billings, G. (2009). Just what is critical race theory and what's it doing in a *nice* field like education? In E. Taylor, D. Gillborn, & G. Ladson-Billings (Eds.), *Foundations of critical race theory in education* (pp. 17–36). New York: Routledge.

Lorde, A. (1984/2007). *Sister outsider: Essays and speeches.* Berkeley: Crossing Press.

Martinez, A.Y. (2020). *Counterstory: The rhetoric and writing of critical race theory.* Champaign, IL: Conference on College Composition and Communication of the National Council of Teachers of English.

Moll, L.C., Amanti, C., Neff, D., & Gonzalez, N. (1992). Funds of knowledge for teaching: Using a qualitative approach to connect homes and classrooms. *Theory into Practice, 31*(2), 132–141.

Oxford English Dictionary. (1989a). Compassion. In *oed.com.* Retrieved October 7, 2020, from https://www-oed-com.ezproxy.collegeofsanmateo.edu/view/Entry/37475?rskey=krHZbY&result=1#eid

Oxford English Dictionary. (1989b). Empathy. In *oed.com.* Retrieved October 7, 2020, from https://www-oed-com.ezproxy.collegeofsanmateo.edu/view/Entry/61284?redirectedFrom=empathy#eid

Oxford English Dictionary. (1989c). Sympathy. In *oed.com*. Retrieved October 7, 2020, from https://www-oed-com.ezproxy.collegeofsanmateo.edu/view/Entry/196271?rskcy-WVs Ld7&result=1#eid

Peller, G. (1990). Race consciousness. *Duke Law Journal, 4*, 758–847.

Pollack, M. (2008). *Everyday antiracism: Getting real about race in school*. New York: Norton.

Rothenberg, P.S. (2016). Introduction. In P.S. Rothenberg (Ed.), *White privilege: Essential readings on the other side of racism* (5th ed., pp. 1–5). New York: Worth.

Sims, J.J. (2018). *Revolutionary STEM education: Critical-reality pedagogy & social justice in STEM for Black males*. New York: Peter Lang.

Sims, J.J., Taylor-Mendoza, J., Hotep, L.O., Wallace, J., & Conaway, T. (2020). *Minding the obligation gap in community colleges and beyond: Theory and practice in achieving educational equity*. New York: Peter Lang.

Smedley, B.D., Myers, H.F., & Harrell, S.P. (1993). Minority-status stresses and the college adjustment of ethnic minority freshmen. *The Journal of Higher Education, 64*(4), 434–452.

Smith, W.A., Allen, W.R., & Danley, L.L. (2007). "Assume the position... you fit the description": Psychosocial experiences and racial battle fatigue among African American male college students. *American Behavioral Scientist, 51*(4), 551–578.

Smith, W.A., Hung, M., & Franklin, J.D. (2011). Racial battle fatigue and the miseducation of Black men: Racial microaggressions, societal problems, and environmental stress. *The Journal of Negro Education, 80*(1), 63–82.

Solórzano, D.G., Ceja, M., & Yosso, T. (2000). Critical race theory, racial microaggressions, and campus racial climate: The experiences of African American college students. *The Journal of Negro Education, 69*(1/2), 60–73.

Solórzano, D.G., & Yosso, T.J. (2002). Critical race methodology: Counter-storytelling as an analytical framework for education research. *Qualitative Inquiry, 8*(1), 23–44.

Steele, C.M. (1997). A threat in the air: How stereotypes shape intellectual identity and performance. *American Psychologist, 52*(6), 613–629.

Steele, C.M. (2010). *Whistling Vivaldi: How stereotypes affect us and what we can do*. New York: W.W. Norton & Company.

Steele, C.M., & Aronson, J. (1995). Stereotype threat and the intellectual test performance of African Americans. *Journal of Personality and Social Psychology, 69*(5), 797–811.

Taylor, E., & Soto Antony, J. (2000). Stereotype threat reduction and wise schooling: Towards the successful socialization of African American doctoral students in education. *The Journal of Negro Education, 69*(3), 184–198.

Townsend, B.K., & Twombly, S.B. (2007). Community college faculty: Overlooked and undervalued. *ASHE Higher Education Report, 32*(6), 105–125.

Twombly, S.B. (2004). Looking for signs of community college arts and sciences faculty professionalization in searches: An alternative approach to a vexing question. *Community College Review, 32*(1), 21–39.

Vought, R. (2020, September 4). *Memorandum for the Heads of Executive Departments and Agencies*. Executive Office of the President, Office of Management and Budget. https://www.whitehouse.gov/wp-content/uploads/2020/09/M-20-34.pdf

Wacquant, L. (2008). *Urban outcasts: A comparative sociology of advanced marginality.* Cambridge, U.K.: Polity.

Wilkerson, I. (2020). *Caste: The origins of our discontents.* New York: Random House.

Yosso, T.J. (2006). *Critical race counterstories along the Chicana/Chicano educational pipeline.* New York: Routledge.

5

Taking it Back to the Classroom: Equity and Pedagogy

A fundamental argument of this book is that national and state-level initiatives and legislation will not eradicate the crises our minoritized students are experiencing in higher education. We cannot spend or regulate our way out of this. Instead of looking outside our colleges to these large initiatives, we need to look within our colleges and classrooms. This is not to say that we should not be seeking experts in the fields of educational equity, antiracist pedagogies, and other professional development opportunities that promote equity and justice in teaching and learning. However, too often, large-scale initiatives follow a "one-size-fits-all" model that allows too little flexibility, and worst yet, most of these initiatives claim to help *all students*, implying a colorblind approach to student success. To be clear, there is nothing wrong with initiatives that are meant to support all students; the problem is that these colorblind initiatives are modeled after the teaching and learning of the dominant group – white, middle-class students. Unfortunately, as I mentioned in Chapter 1, too few of these national initiatives fail to take race into account (or to take it seriously), which means that the racialized structures and hierarchies will remain after implementation. Instead, I argue for a grassroots social justice movement where community college educators take ownership over making their own colleges and classrooms equitable and socially just.

As such, this chapter will take it back to the classroom, where educators have the most freedom and opportunity to enact equitable practices. More specifically, this chapter will look at pedagogy, or *how* we teach, and at the classroom environment we create and maintain. This chapter will first define the various critical pedagogical approaches to working with minoritized students and spotlight critical reality pedagogy (Sims, 2018) as a framework that best meets the needs of a diverse classroom. Furthermore, drawing on the previous chapter's discussion of the "obligation gap," this chapter will delineate educator's responsibilities outside the classroom vis-à-vis student support services and how we integrate student support into our classrooms. Finally, this chapter will end with a discussion of specific tools European American educators can use to create equitable, justice-centered classrooms, from how we talk about topics like race to our course policies.

a. Critical Pedagogy

The father of critical pedagogy is undoubtedly Paulo Freire, the Brazilian educator and educational philosopher who worked with poor, rural farmers and residents. Freire is most known for his literacy work with poor Brazilian farmers, which would eventually lead to his expulsion from his home country and years of exile. Freire's body of work is so robust and so deep that it is impossible to do it justice in this chapter. However, it is important to describe some of Freire's basic tenets in order to understand more recent pedagogical practices like *reality pedagogy* and *critical reality pedagogy*. I hope the reader can forgive me for trying to provide a short overview of such an extensive body of educational theory and practice.

The Banking Model and Problem-Posing

In Freire's (1970/1993) seminal text, *Pedagogy of the Oppressed*, he delineates the pedagogical approaches of the oppressor from the pedagogical approaches of the critical educator. In the former, he describes this oppressive educational framework as the "banking concept of education." In this approach to teaching, the teacher – or the supposed bearer of knowledge – "deposits" said knowledge into the students – or those who supposedly lack knowledge. Freire writes, "Education thus becomes an act of depositing, in which the students are the depositories and the teacher is the depositor. Instead of communicating, the teacher issues communiqués and makes deposits which the students patiently receive, memorize, and repeat. This is the 'banking' concept of education, in which the scope of action allowed to the students extends only as far as receiving, filing, and storing the deposits" (p. 72). In this type of classroom, the teacher usually stands in the front of the room and long-windedly explains some topic while the students quietly take notes, which they will need because they will be tested on how well they memorized this information. We have all experienced this type of classroom, and many of us would confirm that this "authoritarian tradition of lecturing," as Freire's student Donaldo Macedo (2000) calls it, simply does not work for most students (p. 19).

Freire rails against this form of pedagogy for one primary reason – it diminishes the students' abilities to think critically about the world, which works to ensure that those in the power – the oppressors – stay there. Ultimately, this diminishment objectifies the students because it takes away the one thing that makes them human – the capacity to think critically and independently and the ability to transform their realities. Those who subscribe to the "banking concept of education" believe that the society we inhabit is fixed and that the majoritarian stories of the in-group are common sense, which means that the students – the oppressed – have no need, no capacity, for critical thinking. As Freire writes, "The more students work at storing the deposits entrusted to them, the less they develop the critical consciousness which would result from their intervention in the world as transformers of that world" (p. 73). Ultimately, the banking method "turn[s] women and men into automatons – the very negation of their ontological vocation to be more fully human" (p. 74). This type of miseducation is akin to what Sims et al. (2020) call "racialized capitalism."

The antithesis to the banking model of education is "problem-posing," which manifests when instructors invite students to cocreate knowledge and to use that knowledge to transform the world. As Freire (1970/1993) writes, educators "must abandon the educational goal of deposit-making and replace it with the posing of problems of human beings in their relations with the world. 'Problem-posing' education, responding to the essence of consciousness – *intentionally* – rejects communiqués and embodies communication" (p. 79, emphasis in original). In other words, critical educators do not see themselves as the sole source of knowledge and critical thought in a classroom, but they recognize that their students have knowledge and experiences to contribute to the learning space. Furthermore, course content is not treated as objective, apolitical knowledge that can be transferred and assessed but as subjective, political knowledge that can be leveraged for the purposes of oppression or liberation. An educator that uses problem-posing invests in the latter – liberation – and presents information as concrete problems that must be worked through collaboratively. The outcomes of these dialogues must be cocreated. For example, while Freire was working with the Brazilian peasants who lived in extreme poverty, he recalls, "I must intervene in teaching the peasants that their hunger is socially constructed and work with them to help identify those responsible for this social construction, which is, in my view, a crime against humanity" (Freire & Macedo, 1995, p. 391).

Problem-posing can only be accomplished through authentic and critical dialogue between educator and students. In this form of critical pedagogy, the educator presents the world as ever-evolving and "in the process of transformation" rather than "as a static reality" (Freire, 1970/1993, p. 83). When problem-posing, knowledge becomes cocreated by teachers and students, allowing the students to teach and the teacher to learn. As Freire writes, "Through dialogue, the teacher-of-the-students and the students-of-the-teacher cease to exist and a new term emerges: teacher-student with student-teachers. The teacher is no longer merely the-one-who-teaches, but one who is himself taught in dialogue with the students, who in turn while being taught also teach. They become jointly responsible for a process in which all grow" (p. 80). For example, a critical educator may bring up an issue or topic in class – let's say about a global pandemic that has turned the world completely upside down. In a classroom where the banking model is utilized, the educator would simply lecture about the pandemic, how it relates to the discipline, and offer their thoughts on its impact on the world. In a classroom that uses problem-posing, the critical educator does not tell the students what to think about the pandemic and its connection to the discipline, but instead asks them to enter into a dialogue where the students are able to use their expertise and schema to cocreate knowledge about the pandemic. As Freire describes, "The students – no longer docile listeners – are now critical co-investigators in dialogue with the teacher. The teacher presents the material to the students for their consideration, and re-considers her earlier considerations as the students express their own. The role of the problem-posing educator is to create... problem-posing education involves a constant unveiling of reality... [and] strives for the *emergence* of consciousness and *critical intervention* in reality" (p. 81, emphasis in original). This is why Freire and Macedo (1995) call "dialogue... an epistemological relationship" (p. 379).

Praxis

This type of critical pedagogy results in what Freire (1970/1993) calls "praxis," which he defines as "*reflection* and *action* directed at the structures to be transformed" (p. 126, emphasis in original). In a critical classroom, this means that the knowledge that has been cocreated by educators and students is used to promote change; for the oppressed, this means striving for social justice. As Freire writes, "Liberation is praxis: the action and reflection of men and women upon their world in order to transform it" (p. 79). Praxis is the required outcome of truly critical dialogue, itself a by-product of effective problem-posing. As the Freire Institute (2020) attests, "It is not enough for people to come together in dialogue in order to gain knowledge of their social reality. They must act together upon their environment in order [to] critically reflect upon their reality and so transform it through further action and critical reflection" (par. 2). If, in the scenario noted before, the students had come to realize that they were underserved by the college as a result of the COVID-19 pandemic, praxis could only happen if they advocated for changes with the college administration. And to be clear, critical pedagogy – including problem-posing, dialogue, and praxis – can happen in any classroom, from the humanities to the sciences. Students simply need to be empowered as co-creators of knowledge and as agents of change. In a math classroom, for example, this could be using mathematical principles and formulas to better understand the world and to use these principles to promote change. It is our decision as community college educators whether we want to subscribe to the banking model and lecture at the students or whether we want to adopt a critical approach to education that brings our students into the dialogue in our disciplines and equips them to use this new knowledge to promote change. As Macedo (2000) notes, critical pedagogy "go[es] beyond the classroom boundaries and effect[s] significant change in society" (p. 17).

Critical pedagogy is also required if we are to promote educational equity and social justice inside and outside the classroom. Achieving social justice means equipping our students with critical thinking skills that empower them to conceptualize their world and to transform it, and not to do so is detrimental to our students' growth and self-fulfillment. We have a choice as to which classroom we want to create. As Shaull (1993) writes, "There is no such thing as a *neutral* educational process. Education either functions as an instrument that is used to facilitate the integration of the younger generation into the logic of the present system and bring about conformity to it, *or* it becomes 'the practice of freedom', the means by which men and women deal critically and creatively with reality and discover how to participate in the transformation of their world" (p. 34, emphasis in original).

Freire's problem-posing pedagogical strategy is student centered in that its primary goal is to empower the students to think critically about their world and to become change agents who seek to alter it. However, the professional growth of the "teacher-student" is tantamount to this framework, especially as it relates to evaluating the effectiveness of our classroom practices. In other words, classroom research as professional inquiry is an important tenet of the community college professoriate, which distinguishes community college faculty from our university peers. Our primary emphasis is on teaching, and consequently, our primary form of research – and praxis – is in how to create more critical classroom spaces. Freirean praxis can help us refocus and reprioritize our overarching goal of evaluating the effectiveness of our classroom to an iterative practice of reflecting on our classroom practices using a justice lens and on adjusting our pedagogical practices in order to create a more equitable and just classroom (read: action). Said another way, we can use Freire's critical framework as a way to scrutinize how equitable our teaching practices are and then to use this information to make important changes.

Moreover, if we are striving to create more equitable classrooms for our students of color, the tenets of critical race theory (CRT) can provide a strong foundation. Traditionally, CRT has been utilized as an academic lens used in the scholarship of many disciplines – including legal studies, women's studies, ethnic studies, and others – and it has been a pivotal theoretical and methodological framework in educational research, which has been dominated by the university in their pursuit of new knowledge. The use of CRT in community colleges is still fairly novel, but community college educators should not be reticent to understand and utilize a critical race framework in their pedagogies just because it seems more relevant to the universities. In fact, I would argue that this is a misconception for two reasons. First, critical race scholarship was borne out of the need to understand and eradicate oppressive, racist structures in the American legal field. As mentioned above, this framework has expanded to a variety of fields, including the educational field. Furthermore, a fundamental component of CRT, despite the word "theory" in its name, is action. Crits, as CRT scholars are called, do not seek to merely identify and understand systemic and institutionalized racism – they are driven to dismantle it. There is no better place to identify, study, and dismantle institutionalized racism than in the community college, where, as previously stated, the majority of students are students of color and the majority of African American and Latinx students enter higher education. If CRT belongs in the educational field, it belongs nowhere more than in the community college.

Second, we need to critique the myth that educational research only happens in the university. It is indeed true that the majority of research *publications* are written by university researchers. It is not necessarily true that only university researchers engage in the scholarship of teaching and learning and that only university researchers are creating new knowledge and practices in higher education. In fact, it is this misconception that has created so much contention between university and community college faculty that some members of the former do not see the latter as a distinct academic profession, a bias that is itself based on the history of higher education as being comprised predominantly of research institutions in pursuit of new knowledge (Cohen & Outcalt, 2001; Outcalt, 2002; Townsend & Twombly, 2007; Twombly, 2004). In other words, since universities, at least the R1 institutions, have historically focused primarily on conducting research and on publishing and disseminating their findings, many academics have argued that community colleges can't be true institutions of higher education because our focus is on teaching (the origins of community colleges in the K-12 system doesn't help either). However, Palmer (1992) argues that community college faculty do indeed constitute a distinct academic profession because of, not in spite of, our focus on teaching. Palmer offers "four frames of reference... [through] which [community college] faculty professionalization can be conceptualized" (p. 30). Among these frames – which includes the obligation to "imbue their teaching with the insights gained from active scholarship" – is "the classroom research frame of reference":

> The teaching emphasis of the community college leads naturally to a focus on the fourth scholarly process, the scholarship of teaching, and to a consideration of the faculty role in systematically analyzing the classroom as a learning environment... Under the classroom research frame of reference, then, faculty professionalism is anchored in a process of teaching that has its roots... in the traditions of action research. (pp. 30, 33, 34)

In other words, effective educators are constantly assessing the effectiveness of their curriculum and pedagogies and using both quantitative and qualitative data about how their students learn. I argue that community college educators need to reject the belief that they are not engaging in research because they "just teach" and that they should instead think of themselves as community college educational researcher-practitioners.

This new identity as a researcher-practitioner is necessary for the work of educational equity and social justice. The data covered in Chapter 1 make it clear that, by and large, our system is not serving students of color and other minoritized students, in large part because of institutionalized inequities but also as a result of our overreliance on the banking model of education. If we are to create classrooms that are more equitable and just, we need to eradicate oppressive structures in our pedagogies and curricula, and we need to reject the banking model of education in favor of one steeped in critical pedagogy. Both of these changes require both praxis (reflection and action) and the type of educational research described by Palmer. In other words, we need to be active in the scholarship of both critical pedagogy and our disciplines, and we need to continually measure and assess the effectiveness of our teaching and curriculum. Furthermore, CRT provides a proven lens through which to examine and critique our classrooms. Indeed, praxis and classroom research as a professional inquiry are the distinguishing characteristics of community college faculty from our university peers.

b. Culturally (Fill In the Blank) Pedagogy: Navigating Educational Theory and Research

As you begin to overhaul your pedagogy and curriculum in order to promote educational equity, you may start to see a plethora of pedagogical and equity-minded frameworks, from culturally relevant pedagogy to reality pedagogy. In my experience, there is no "one-size-fits-all" teaching and learning framework that critical educators must use exclusively. In fact, I believe an effective educator draws from various frameworks in order to create a classroom space that best serves its unique students. As a result, I tend to incorporate elements from all the frameworks that follow, which, in some form or another, draw on the theories and praxis of Freire's critical pedagogy. Please note that this list is not exhaustive, and I encourage readers to learn more about these teaching and learning frameworks, especially from the educators who originally developed them.

Culturally Relevant Pedagogy

One of the oldest equity-minded frameworks in educational theory is Ladson-Billings' writings about "culturally relevant pedagogy" (CRP). In line with the tenets of critical pedagogy, Ladson-Billings (1995) argues that teachers must move away from the deficit-minded framework of "student fit," which dominated the socio-linguistic field in the late 20th century and into one in which students are encouraged to transform their worlds. Previously, scholarship, especially in the fields of language arts and reading, had emphasized the students' home cultures in the curriculum in order "to 'fit' students constructed as 'other' by virtue of their race/ethnicity, language, or social class into a hierarchical structure" (p. 467). In other words, students' home cultures were temporarily used as a bridge into the academic space, but as soon as the students were accustomed to the language and expectations of the academic culture, the bridges were eliminated. Consequently, Ladson-Billings writes, "A next step for positing effective pedagogical practice is a theoretical model that not only addresses student achievement but also helps students to accept and affirm their cultural identity while developing critical perspectives that challenge inequities that schools (and other institutions perpetuate). I term this pedagogy, *culturally relevant pedagogy*" (p. 469, emphasis in original). Ladson-Billings' conceptualization of a culturally relevant pedagogy would have three hallmarks: "produce students who can achieve academically, produce students who demonstrate cultural competence, and develop students who can both understand and critique the existing social order" (p. 474). In her study of elementary school teachers who were particularly successful in educating African American children, Ladson-Billings found that the teachers were especially competent in allowing the students to bring their home cultures into the academic space and in treating the students, with their cultural capital, as knowledge creators. In this way, CRP is undergirded by Freire's problem-posing pedagogical practice.

The assumption of the students' inherent brilliance is a pivotal aspect of the entire framework because it breaks down home/school cultural binaries and creates high expectations for the entire classroom community (p. 479). CRP practitioners, in other words, reject the deficit thinking of "achievement gap" agitprop. Ladson-Billings (1995) writes, "The culturally relevant teachers encouraged a community of learners rather than competitive, individual achievement. By demanding a higher level of academic success for the entire class, individual success did not suffer. However, rather than lifting up individuals (and, perhaps, contributing to feelings of peer alienation), the teachers made it clear that they were working with smart classes" (p. 480). This is in line with the findings of Cohen, Steele, and Ross (1999), who found that when mentors couple critical feedback with remarks that they have high standards and that they believe the student can meet those standards, the students, especially students of color, were actually more motivated and successful and felt stereotype threat less acutely. They call these educators "wise" because they "assure the students that they will not be judged stereotypically – that their abilities and 'belonging' are assumed rather that doubted... The educators in these programs all refute negative stereotypes by conveying a clear faith in each student's intellectual potential. But they do not impart this message by assigning easier work to ensure student success or by offering heavy doses of unstinting praise – all too common tactics of well-meaning but unwise teachers" (p. 1303). In other words, and seemingly paradoxically, difficult coursework coupled with high expectations actually inspires and motivates students. For students of color, this was "like water on parched land" (Steele, 2010, p. 163). More specifically, Cohen et al. write, "minority students... are challenged with high performance standards – standards that *presume* their motivation and ability to succeed. The educators often go an important step further by explicitly assuring students of their capacity to meet those standards through greater effort" (p. 1303, emphasis in original).

Steele (2010) calls this phenomenon the "Tom Ostrom Strategy" after his graduate school faculty adviser, who Steele notes "had no knowledge of stereotype threat, or much knowledge of African American experience, for that matter" (p. 161). So how did this older, white professor not only create an identity safe learning environment (one where minoritized students are not at risk of stereotype threat) but also motivate his students to improve in the face of critical feedback and high expectations? As Steele explains, the Tom Ostrom Strategy of high expectations and genuine belief in the students' capabilities "resolved [the students'] interpretive quandary. It told them they weren't being seen in terms of the bad stereotype about their group's intellectual standards, since the feedback giver used high intellectual standards and believed they could meet them. They could feel less jeopardy. The motivation they had always had was released" (p. 163). Recall that stereotype threat is a psychological phenomenon in which the subject – in this case, a student – is afraid of confirming a negative stereotype about their group. This often leads to mental overload – or what is called "racing mind" – and feelings of isolation because they don't want others to see their struggles. Educators who use the Tom Ostrom Strategy alleviate this fear because their students aren't afraid that their struggles will confirm those bad stereotypes. They are comfortable struggling because they know that their teacher believes in their capabilities and unrelentingly holds them to those capabilities with high standards and expectations. This is exactly what the teachers in Ladson-Billings' study were doing.

Moreover, as Ladson-Billings (1995) notes, many students of color, particularly African American students, sometimes have to choose between academic success and their cultures, as they can be seen as "acting white" by peers for being academically successful. Often, this leads to social isolation and emotional trauma, which ultimately impacts their academics. As such, "culturally relevant pedagogy must provide a way for students to maintain their cultural integrity while succeeding academically" (p. 476). As Sims (2018) noted, students of color are often forced to "check their culture at the door" (p. 129; see also Paris, 2012). However, educators who adopt a culturally relevant pedagogy invite students to be true to themselves in the academic space, which alleviates some of the identity struggles experienced by minoritized students. As Ladson-Billings observes in her study, "Because these African-American students were permitted, indeed encouraged, to be themselves in dress, language style, and interaction styles while achieving in school, the other students, who regarded them highly... were able to see academic engagement as 'cool'" (p. 476). In other words, when critical educators allow students to be true to themselves in the classroom and to bring their cultures and identities into the curricula, it not only engages them in the curricula, but it also helps them feel comfortable doing so (and, as an added bonus, inspires other students).

Finally, in line with the critical framework promoted by Freire, CRP promotes praxis in the pursuit of social justice. Ladson-Billings terms this type of praxis as "cultural critique": "Not only must teachers encourage academic success and cultural competence, they must help students to recognize, understand, and critique current social inequities" (p. 476). As such, CRP is not simply including the cultural artifacts of the students' cultures (more on this in Chapter 6), but it instead takes on a form of problem-posing in which the professor and students co-identify social injustice in their community and, using the tools of the discipline, cocreate the solution. In Ladson-Billings' study, the teachers she observed worked with students on proposals that were meant to improve their community, one of which was even presented to the city's council.

Critical Reality Pedagogy

Culturally relevant pedagogy and its offshoots (e.g., culturally responsive pedagogy, culturally sustaining pedagogy, etc.) have emphasized the role of the classroom in affirming students' languages and cultures and empowering them to be agents of change. This is the heart of critical pedagogy. As Macedo (2000) notes, Freire's "radical pedagogical proposals... go beyond the classroom boundaries and effect significant changes in the society as well" (17). Recently, however, a new pedagogical paradigm has gained traction – reality pedagogy. Popularized by Chris Emdin's seminal 2016 book, *For White Folks who Teach in the Hood... and the Rest of Y'all Too: Reality Pedagogy and Urban Education,* reality pedagogy builds on Ladson-Billings' scholarship on culturally relevant pedagogy; however, for Emdin, CRP doesn't go far enough. As Emdin writes, "This approach to teaching advocates for a consideration of the culture of the students in determining the ways in which they are taught. Unfortunately, this approach cannot be implemented unless teachers broaden their scope beyond traditional classroom teaching" (p. 10). In other words, CRP, as Emdin infers, is a teacher-centric framework wherein the teacher determines the best practices for integrating the cultures of the students into the curriculum.

Instead, Emdin advocates for a pedagogical framework in the Freirean tradition in which students co-construct the classroom space and epistemologies. This approach is reminiscent of Freire's teacher-student and student-teacher classroom and learning roles that frame the teachers, not only as content experts but also as learners who see their students as experts and meaning makers. As Emdin writes:

> Reality pedagogy is an approach to teaching and learning that has a primary goal of meeting each student on his or her own cultural and emotional turf. It focuses on making the local experiences of the student visible and creating contexts where there is a role reversal of sorts that positions the student as the expert in his or her own teaching and learning, and the teacher as the learner. It posits that while the teacher is the person charged with delivering the content, the student is the person who shapes how best to teach that content. Together, the teacher and students co-construct the classroom space. (p. 27)

In this way, the teachers are no longer the primary decision-makers on how the students' cultures will be reflected in the curriculum. Taking into consideration their own learning styles, expertise, and cultures, the students now have a voice in how they are taught. The teacher may have the content, but only the students know how they can best learn that content.

Furthermore, Emdin challenges monolithic cultural programming that is often the consequence of CRP, though this certainly was not Ladson-Billing's intent. In fact, as Ladson-Billings and Tate (1995) observe, teachers' attempts at bringing the students' cultures into their classrooms can often fall flat: "Current practical demonstrations of multicultural education in schools often reduce it to trivial examples and artifacts of cultures such as eating ethnic food, singing songs or dancing, reading folktales, and other less than scholarly pursuits of the fundamentally different conceptions of knowledge or quests for social justice" (p. 61). These types of trite exercises are exactly what Ladson-Billings was trying to avoid in her initial scholarship on CRP, as evidenced in its third tenet of "develop[ing] students who can both understand and critique the existing social order" (p. 474). In order to avoid this pitfall, Emdin encourages educators to reject monolithic understandings and cultural programming:

> Instead of seeing the students as equal to their cultural identity, a reality pedagogue sees students as individuals who are influenced by their cultural identity. This means that the teacher does not see his or her classroom as a group of African

American, Latino, or poor students and therefore does not make assumptions about their interests based on those preconceptions. Instead, the teacher begins from an understanding of the students as unique individuals and then develops approaches to teaching and learning that work for those individuals. (pp. 27–28)

Emdin encourages educators to tailor their pedagogies to the students in their classrooms, and many of his teaching practices for doing so are derived from a framework called Hip Hop Education. These techniques include practices like cogenerative dialogues – or the co-creation of knowledge – and what he calls "Pentecostal Pedagogy," a classroom practice that includes elements of the Black church, such as call-and-response. While many of Emdin's pedagogical techniques may seem to be tailored only for African American students, it is important to recognize that these techniques are simply derived from Emdin's school community. In other words, cogenerative dialogues and call-and-response are effective techniques for any classroom, regardless of demographics.

Nevertheless, reality pedagogy seems to have a unidirectional focus in which the cultural and social practices and artifacts of the students are brought into the classroom in order to make it a more engaging, inclusive space. But critical educators, especially in the Freirean tradition, strive for a pedagogical framework that not only creates a more engaging learning atmosphere but also one that compels the students to see themselves as change agents who are obligated to transform their communities. This is the goal of a framework called "critical reality pedagogy," which was coined by Jeremiah J. Sims (2018) in his book *Revolutionary STEM Education: Critical-reality Pedagogy and Social Justice in STEM for Black Males*. Sims differentiates reality pedagogy from critical-reality pedagogy in the following way:

> while both critical and reality pedagogy emphasize student voice and student empowerment, the primary goal of critical-reality pedagogy extends beyond creating comfortable safe-spaces and equipping students with critical analytical tools. A critical-reality pedagogical approach is chiefly concerned with action. Reality pedagogy, which I must point out is intrinsically critical, is concerned with action; however, the action consists of creating opportunities for students to thrive in their classroom spaces by co-creating knowledge, by positioning them as co-teachers and by inviting aspects of their variegated cultures into their learning spaces... while creating opportunities for students to co-create knowledge in a classroom/educative space is indispensable to efficacious, equitable pedagogy, students must also be empowered, encouraged, and equipped to take their classroom learning out of the classroom and apply it to issues that are important to them.

Students, then, are encouraged and empowered to develop critical analytical thinking so they can use their knowledge to shift the socio-political constraints that oppresses them. (p. 9)

Critical-reality pedagogy, then, is an omnidirectional framework, which not only encourages students to cocreate the classroom space and to become co-teachers in the pursuit of knowledge, but it also obliges the students to take their tools and knowledge into their communities in order to exact change. As Sims notes, "criticality is not achieved until transformative, socially just action takes place" (p. 10).

So what does this look like in practice? While the next chapter will delve into the curricular implications a little more, it is worth noting some pedagogical shifts informed by critical-reality pedagogy. Informed by Emdin's reality pedagogy, the first shift should be to the classroom climate in which students can feel "identity safe" (Steele, 2010). This certainly includes increasingly popular teaching practices like introductions that include one's pronouns, making the effort to learn the correct pronunciation of students' names, or learning the appropriate terms for different groups of students (e.g., adopting Latinx over Hispanic and learning a student's preference of African American over Black) (just as a sidenote – don't tell everyone how "woke" you are because you do these very basic, fundamental practices). However, creating an identity-safe classroom happens in the margins. It is what you do between those introductions with pronouns and that discussion about a course topic or reading. Do you stand at the lectern for the entire class or do you interact more intimately with the students? When you sit next to a student, do you lean in when chatting with them or do you lean back in a standoffish way? Is your body language open or closed? When a student shares a personal story or reflection about race, gender, or class, do you validate them or do you change the subject (or, worse, tell them they misinterpreted that experience)? In other words, we need to interact with our students in a way that expresses *our* curiosity for *their* knowledge, *our* respect for *their* experiences and realities, and *our* humbleness in the face of topics that we are still learning about and, in many cases, can never understand (no matter how many times we get pulled over by the police, we white folks will *never* know what it feels like to inhabit a Black body in those situations, so we shouldn't act like we do or can). Ultimately, we can have the most amazing and inclusive curriculum, but if we don't teach it correctly, our students won't learn, and the first step in teaching it correctly (after doing the "inner work of racial justice") is respecting our students, admiring their intellect and talents, and becoming a teacher-student. And they need to know that you like them and respect them because as educator Rita Pierson (2013) said, "kids don't learn from people they don't like." And there is no better way to turn students off than to act like you don't want to be around them and to act like you are better than them because you are "the discipline expert."

Second, we need to reconsider our courses' content so that they match the demographics and interests of our students. Many community colleges are now so-called "majority-minority" institutions, meaning that most of the students are African American, Asian American, Latinx, and Pacific Islander, and as mentioned in Chapter 1, most African American and Latinx students start their higher education journeys in community colleges. It is absurd if our courses continue to reflect the knowledge, values, and beliefs of Western European men (and their descendants in America and beyond). For instance, if you teach philosophy, your course can't focus exclusively on the scholarship and theories of the Greeks, Romans, British, and French philosophers. A truly introductory philosophy course must include Asian, Indigenous, and African philosophies as well, and they can't simply be "add-ons" or what I like to term "a la carte equity." Non-European epistemologies and bodies of work must be central. In my discipline, for example, I simply can't teach a literature survey course that only includes white authors. Even in my area of expertise – British literature – there are enough contributions from people of color, including those from India, Africa, and the Caribbean, to create a course that is inclusive of all my students, not just those descended from the British Isles. And in the tradition of critical pedagogy, I need to provide space for the students to cocreate the knowledge about the content. I can't just lecture on the authors and texts I have chosen for my literature class, but I need to instead allow students to make their own conclusions and connections. I often find my students making astute arguments about our readings and topics that I hadn't even considered, which is less likely to happen if I just stand at the front of the room and tell them what to think. Similarly, my courses need to compel students to transform their communities and our society, writ large. Not only do the critical thinking skills developed while reading literature translate to the real world, but I make it clear that the American literary canon tends to marginalize voices of color and that through literature and art, students can actually start to tear down those walls.

c. Practicum: Facilitating Sensitive Classroom Conversations

In a critical classroom that is inclusive of its diverse students and that allows its students to co-construct the teaching and learning environment, topics of race, racism, prejudice, anti-Blackness, and other sensitive topics are bound to arise (in fact, it is a guarantee). But many white educators shy away from such topics because they don't want to "say the wrong thing" or they are simply uncomfortable with such topics themselves. This isn't surprising – white educators are not taught how to talk about race, and for many of us, issues of racism and whiteness were just not in our orbit until recently (if at all). But we cannot be, as Beverly Tatum (1997/2017) argues, a "color-*silent* society" (p. 24, emphasis in original). We can never disrupt the legacies of racism and white supremacy if we simply ignore them. As a result, critical educators are not only ready for such conversations, but they welcome and even encourage them. This section will provide some best practices on how to talk about race and for facilitating such conversations.

Let's be honest – talking about race is hard and it is uncomfortable, so first and foremost, critical, justice-minded educators must embrace this discomfort. Admittedly, much of this discomfort comes from our lack of knowledge about race and racism. White people are "raced" just like any other group of people, yet we are never forced to see our own race because whiteness is normalized and is the foundation of our government, our schools, and other institutions. Unfortunately, this has debilitated us. As a result, we can only become comfortable with talking about race once we have developed the schema necessary to engage in critical discussions about it. And, of course, even then, we need to actually engage in the actual dialogues consistently in order to alleviate the discomfort. I hope that this book helps you take the first steps to developing this knowledge base, and as mentioned previously, I encourage you to refer to the lists of references after each chapter for important works written by some of the best minds in their fields. Ultimately, we should heed Magee's (2019) advice: "we need to be able to sit with these feelings and experience that discomfort in order to learn and grow together. So a big part of racial justice work is becoming more comfortable with being uncomfortable" (Magee, p. 28). Or as two of my students recently contended in a class discussion about race and dialogue:

- "We are all, in some way, comfortable in the position that we are in now, but it is not until we step out of our comfort zone and attempt to step into someone else's reality that we can learn how to truly listen and understand them when they tell us about their experiences or reality."

- "The topic of racism and injustices will never be comfortable for those who do not speak about it nor experience it."

Reading these quotes, one would assume they were written by great philosophers or prominent social justice advocates. But they were uttered by two community college students, which reinforces the fact that we have so much to learn from our student-teachers.

Furthermore, engaging in these dialogues about race and racism can be difficult, especially if there are no other white folks in our lives willing to have those conversations. At this point, it is worth a reminder that it would be inappropriate to recruit people of color to educate us on race and racism. Our colleagues and friends of color have no obligation to correct our ignorance or to help us navigate the muddied racial waters created by our forbearers and maintained by us and our peers. Remember, scholars and writers of color have been publishing books and essays for centuries to help us understand race, racism, whiteness, white supremacy, and antiracism. We must look to these resources and to each other as we build our racial schema and develop our capacities and comfort in discussing race. Similarly, it is tantamount that we push ourselves to learn about *institutional* racism and to reject the notion that racism is simply an ideology that exists within and between individuals. To not do so will invariably lead to either a false feeling of accomplishment (e.g., if no one around me is racist, then it must be gone) or a feeling of defeat (e.g., no matter how hard I work at this, those around me just don't get it and continue to have racist beliefs). The latter leads to what Flynn (2018) calls "white fatigue": "a temporary state in which individuals who are understanding of the moral imperative of antiracism disengage from or assume they no longer need to continue learning about how racism functions due to a simplistic understanding of racism as primarily an individual's problem" (p. 31). Said another way, the problematic belief that racism is an individual phenomenon could result in resistance to conversations about racism as an institutional one. Antiracist educators work on both the minds and the structures in their spheres of influence. In other words, we talk about antiracism with our students and colleagues while simultaneously dismantling racialized and racist structures in our colleges.

Unsurprisingly, the work of antiracism, educational equity, and social justice requires a great deal of commitment and motivation. Unfortunately, our inability to talk about race has inevitably led to the decision to just stay quiet and hope that it goes away, the equivalent of my infant son covering his face when he doesn't want any more dinner – it'll just disappear if he waits long enough. This approach, for many of us, has made it mentally impossible for building up any type of stamina to engage in these discussions, which becomes a foundational cause of color blindness. And when we do decide to engage in discussions of race and racism, many of us often demand a "safe space" for doing so where any insensitive or downright hurtful comments are protected. Indeed, this type of "safe space" is usually a default setting for our conversations about race, which happen in meetings, seminars, colloquia, and workshops that are usually dominated by other white educators. This critical mass then becomes a safety net for us because we are infrequently "called out" for our ignorance, and if we are, the rest of the group is ready to defend us. DiAngelo (2018) unabashedly rejects these types of safe spaces, especially for educators and professionals. As she writes, "White fragility is... evidenced in the need for so many white progressives to 'build trust' before they can explore racism in workshops, supports groups, or other educational forums" (p. 126). DiAngelo goes on to recount the various "guidelines" that are demanded by white folks in these spaces, including "don't judge," "don't make assumptions," "assume good intentions," "speak your truth," and "respect," all of which, as DiAngelo contends, work to "coddle white fragility" (p. 127). As a consequence of these guidelines, white folks feel empowered to say and act without filters and without consequences; if a colleague in these spaces "breaks" the rules and questions an assumption or belief, they are usually reprimanded by the group while the original perpetrator is comforted. In fact, DiAngelo goes as far as to call these situations "white women's tears," a phenomenon in which white folks break down after microaggressing a participant of color only to elicit sympathy from others while the victim of the microaggression is isolated and marginalized. Ultimately, white educators who are antiracist and justice oriented must enter these spaces without any preconditions, and when we err, we must take responsibility for it, apologize, and rectify our beliefs and actions (see Chapter 2).

DiAngelo's critiques of white fragility in professional spaces are warranted, but I argue that we must approach these discussions much differently when engaging with students about race, racism, and other forms of oppression. Classrooms need a different set of norms that do create safety for all students – we cannot alienate any students, including the white students. We'd be derelict in our duty to make a classroom so uncomfortable for a student that they drop the course. This simply flies in the face of our higher education mission. Instead, we need to be creative with how we construct these spaces and how we facilitate these conversations.

I contend that we need to create "safe discourse spaces" where students can express their ideas and lived experiences in a non-judgmental space without fearing reprisal from classmates or the instructor. To provide a little context, the safe space movement originated in the LGBTQIA community and their desire to find spaces where they could escape repression and find a supportive community (usually of other members of the LGBTQIA community). As Kenney (2001) writes, these spaces were originally gay communities and concomitant local spaces, such as gay bars. When safe spaces made their way to university campuses as a way for LGBTQIA students to escape homophobic and transantagonistic rhetoric, conservatives and liberals alike were unrelenting with their criticism. Members of the right, for example, trumpeted the horn of "free speech" while the left, including higher education faculty and administration, argued for "academic freedom." Unfortunately, these arguments are nothing more than thinly veiled justifications for homophobic rhetoric and the infliction of pain and trauma. Indeed, college safe spaces came out of the preservation of both free speech and academic freedom, as safe spaces are generally spaces on campus that are away from the classroom. And while the debate around safe spaces is beyond the scope of this book, it is important to address the role of classrooms as safe spaces vis-à-vis antiracist pedagogy. Part of our responsibilities as antiracist educators is the creation of a classroom environment where students of color (and other minoritized students) do not fear being microaggressed or abused. Furthermore, classrooms are unpredictable public spaces, especially classrooms that are high energy and engaging, and there is always a risk that a student (or one of us!) will say or do something offensive or insensitive. What matters, however, is how we react when this happens.

This is why I argue for the creation of "safe discourse spaces" rather than safe spaces in the traditional sense. The campus safe space movement provides marginalized students with an environment in which they can surround themselves with others of the same identity and in which they can recuperate from trauma inside and outside the campus. A classroom is by nature a heterogeneous space, and it would be a form of malpractice if we were to avoid sensitive topics in our curricula just to avoid conflict or debate. In fact, I would argue that we'd be doing our students a disservice by avoiding conversations of race, sexuality, gender, immigration, and other sensitive topics, and we'd be setting all of our students up for failure if they left our colleges for a real world where these topics are the fodder of workplaces, interpersonal relationships, and the 24-hour news cycle. Instead, we need to competently facilitate critical discussions of these topics and do so in a way where any issues that do arise are dealt with quickly and communally. Hence, a safe discourse space is a classroom environment where students are invited into critical, sensitive discussions on issues of race, sexuality, gender, class, and others, where these discussions are scaffolded by the instructor, and where students can feel both safe to express their ideas but are also accountable to the class when they "slip up." Classrooms are not safe spaces in the traditional sense, but they must be safe for critical discourse on topics of real import.

This type of space does not happen by accident, and as mentioned above, the discourse is highly scaffolded by the instructor. One important technique for creating a safe discourse space is an early activity (as in the first or second day of class) where the students are asked to create a set of "classroom norms." Schoenbach, Greenleaf, and Murphy (2012) write that classroom norms "are a set of agreements you and your students make so that everyone can invest in learning... [where students] feel safe and supported to share not only what they are confident about but also what confuses them" (p. 64). Schoenbach et al. are primarily concerned with creating a classroom space where quiet and reticent students are coaxed into the public learning and meaning making of the classroom. Creating classroom norms is a collaborative activity where instructors ask students to reflect on the following prompts, as prescribed by Schoenbach et al.:

- What makes you feel comfortable in the classroom?
- Uncomfortable?
- What are some things the teacher can do to support your learning?
- Not do?
- What would get in the way of your learning? (p. 64)

After the students have brainstormed individually, the teacher then facilitates a classroom discussion or has students write their answers on the board. From the students' answers, the class can derive a set of norms, or guidelines, that will dictate the behavior of the students and teacher and regulate the dynamics of the class discussions. And as the authors write, these classroom norms should be revisited and even revised throughout the semester.

I have adapted Schoenbach et al.'s activity slightly to fit a classroom wherein topics of race, gender, sexuality, and class are the bedrock of the course. On the second day of class, I ask students to think and write about the following prompt:

> How would you feel most comfortable approaching topics like racism, racial inequity, and other injustices? How do we as a class discuss these topics in an

insightful and productive way? You may draw on examples from previous classes where these types of conversations were positive or negative.

After the students have individually brainstormed, I break them into small groups where they can vet their ideas with their new classmates, and as a group, the students then come up with 2–3 "rules" that are derived from the students' free-writes. Once the groups have created their guidelines, I will facilitate a discussion where I will ask follow-up or clarification questions, challenge or expand on their ideas, and help articulate the guideline they would like to contribute to our safe discourse space. As the students are sharing, I will write the norms down either on a projected Word document or directly into our learning management system. It is always a great pleasure to hear what the students come up with, and I almost never have to fill in any gaps (though I often do help them wordsmith). To highlight our students' brilliance, here are the classroom norms from one of my Fall 2020 courses:

1. Ask for permission to respond to someone's opinion.
2. Debates and dialogue are inevitable and are necessary for the learning process.
3. Don't make any personal attacks – be respectful.
4. Respect everyone's right to express themselves/let others speak their truth.
5. When a conversation gets heated, one person should be speaking at a time.
6. Be open-minded/be ok with being wrong.
7. Be curious – don't be afraid to ask questions.
8. Try to understand where folks are coming from in discussions.
9. Do not invalidate others' emotions.
10. Do not police the conversation (don't interrupt and "tone police").
11. Show that you are listening through your body language and facial expressions.
12. Don't take constructive criticism as a personal attack.
13. Embrace discomfort – be ok with being uncomfortable.
14. Engage in self-reflection before and after discussions.

We revisit these classroom norms frequently during the semester, especially when I know a charged or sensitive discussion is coming up. And we add and revise as needed, which is why this list is so long!

The fundamental goal of norming and creating safe discourse spaces is to instill empathy and compassion in the students. One of the classroom norms that comes up almost every semester in every class is the belief that every student in the classroom comes from a different community or culture and that everyone has been conditioned to believe many untruths about people who come from different communities than them. A white student may make assumptions about their classmates of color based on this acculturation at the same time that their classmates may be making their own assumptions. The truth is that our families, friends, communities, social media feeds, and news networks have been shaping our beliefs about other people our entire lives. I remember growing up in the 90s when *Cops* was one of the most popular shows on television and when the O.J. Simpson trial was dominating the news cycles. As I look back, it was clear that the media was feeding us an unfettered stream of anti-Black ideologies. Unfortunately, this has not changed much, and while we college-educated professionals should be held to a higher understanding of these forces, our students are still learning about them, and the heartening part is that they know it. Our students know that they are being tricked, but they have yet to really pinpoint the broader implications of how they've been acculturated.

A critical classroom is meant to expose our society's untruths and misrepresentations about race, racism, white supremacy, and other forms of hatred, and as justice-oriented educators, we are responsible for backfilling these realizations with empathy and compassion. This is what Freire and Macedo (1995) were alluding to in their discussion about dialogue: "dialogue characterizes an epistemological relationship. Thus, in this sense, dialogue is a way of knowing and should never be viewed as a mere tactic to involve students in a particular task" (p. 379). Our students have a great deal of knowledge and experiences to bring to the classroom, and I have found that while our students know something is amiss and they can clearly describe their experiences with racism and racial violence, they sometimes lack the language to describe the larger forces that are at work. Together, students-as-teachers and teachers-as-students can start to uncover the hidden and invisible forces of white supremacy, anti-Blackness, and other forms of hatred in the institution and the broader community and to undertake the project of social justice and transformation.

d. Practicum: You're Not a Therapist...but You Are a Navigator

At the heart of educational equity is the goal of both providing traditionally marginalized students with the support and resources they need to meet their full potential and to eliminate any identity-based barriers that exist in our colleges. Too often, however, I hear white educators argue that this type of assistance is the responsibility of student support professionals, like academic and mental health counselors, financial aid specialists, and other colleagues whose jobs focus on providing academic and personal support outside the teaching and learning of the classroom. I have often heard colleagues say, "I am a professor – not a therapist!" This is indeed true. And our colleges do have professionals who have expertise in student support and who have dedicated their careers to helping students persevere through various barriers and obstacles. The fault in the aforementioned white educators' logic is that it is *only* the responsibility of student services professionals to support students outside the classroom. Community college faculty have just as much responsibility for the academic and personal support of our students. It just looks different. No, we are not supposed to be therapists or counselors (except for those of us who are academic advisors), but as representatives of the college, we do have a responsibility to know the services provided by the institution and to help our students utilize them. As I like to say, we are navigators, which means that we have an obligation to help direct the students to the professionals who can best serve them.

e. Practicum: The Syllabus and Course Policies

The course syllabus is your first impression to your students, and it has the capability of empowering and motivating students or creating dread and overwhelm. In sum, it can contribute to a positive or negative classroom climate. Certainly, our syllabi are sometimes governed by outside standards and policies – for example, we may need to include the student learning outcomes, Title IX procedures, and information for students with disabilities. But this required language is often just a small part of our whole syllabus, and we will find that we have a great deal of autonomy in the tone of the document, the types of grading, and homework policies we use, among others. This section will provide some strategies for creating a more student-centered, equity-driven syllabus.

Like our calendars or budgets, our syllabi are an expression of our priorities, but instead of illuminating our personal values, they express our academic and professional values (though there is certainly an argument that our syllabi express personal values, as well). So when we have a syllabus that is chock full of policies and penalties, we are telling our students that above all else, we value rules and their adherence to them. For example, a typical syllabus might be organized something like this:

1. Course and instructor information
2. Course description
3. Prerequisites
4. Student learning outcomes
5. Books and materials
6. Grading policies (including test or essay information)
7. Homework policies
8. Attendance policies
9. Cellphone and computer policies
10. Plagiarism and academic honesty policies
11. Legally mandated policies, like those around accommodations for disabilities and sexual harassment policies (e.g., Title IX)
12. Important dates and deadlines or a course calendar

For many students, including my college-aged self, syllabi organized in this way and with this information can be extremely daunting and can turn students off to the course and to college itself. This is particularly true for students with disabilities, students who have had traumatizing educational experiences in the past, veterans, and older returning students. Furthermore, minoritized students who feel isolated in class can feel further marginalized by such a strict focus on policies and punishments.

Equity-minded educators should open themselves to the possibility of a different kind of syllabus, one in which students can feel welcomed, supported, and empowered. Our syllabi are our first impressions, and we should be using them to invite our students into the academic community – not maintain feelings of imposter syndrome. Consequently, a syllabus that is "student forward" is much more welcoming for our students. While many of the policies are necessary in a college syllabus, I suggest rethinking their order (plus some student-centered additions). Here is one such example that I have utilized (see Appendix B for a syllabus example):

1. Overview of the course, which expresses your excitement for the material and describes the journey that you will be taking with your students
2. Course information (e.g., days, times, section, room, etc.)
3. Contact information
4. Brief narrative that includes your excitement to work with the students and what you will be working on with them (i.e., student-centered course description)
5. Learning outcomes (this is often mandated by accreditors, but have some fun and make them interesting for your students)
6. How will you get your students to these outcomes?
7. Office hours and conferencing
8. Communication outside class (e.g., email, LMS direct messages, etc.)
9. A list of the college's students support services, including the following:
   a. Resources for students with disabilities
   b. Resources for low-income students
   c. Communities or programs for minoritized students (e.g., affinity groups, first-generation students, immigrants, working adults, parents, etc.)
   d. Discipline-specific resources (e.g., writing centers, math centers, computer labs, etc.)
   e. On-campus contacts for help with housing, transportation, health services, food pantries, clothes pantries, etc.
10. Your commitment to a safe learning environment
    a. A statement that affirms your commitment to educational equity and social justice
    b. Regulations governing discrimination and harassment (such as Title IX regulations for sexual harassment)
11. A section that describes how the students get to the end of this journey successfully
    a. Grading policies
    b. Homework policies
    c. Participation and attendance
    d. Information on essays, test, project, or other major assessments
    e. Revision or retake policies
    f. Cellphones
    g. Plagiarism and academic honesty

Notice that this type of syllabus starts with the students and the academic journey everyone will be taking together, and a student reading this type of syllabus might feel like a member of academic community rather than a vessel for simply taking in knowledge. In other words, the syllabus should let the students know that they are a contributor to the co-creation of knowledge in this classroom (think: Freire's problem-posing pedagogy) and not an unthinking receptacle meant for absorbing predetermined information from the "sage on the stage" (think: banking method of teaching). Only after the student learns about the professor, their commitment to their students, and what the class will be like does the syllabus cover the rules and the penalties for not adhering to those policies. A student with this type of syllabus would know that students and their academic and personal well-being were front and center.

Furthermore, the language we use in our syllabi can also have a dramatic impact on how our students perceive us and our courses. From the terms we use to identify students to the way we describe achievement and standards, our language has the power to create a welcoming classroom or one that reproduces the inequities and hostility of our society at large. As a result, Sadat Ahadi and Guerrero (2020) call on community college educators to "decolonize the syllabus." They write, "A decolonized syllabus infuses anti-racism and equity at the forefront. Student learning outcomes, the course outline of record, textbooks, and any ancillary materials should all address anti-racism rhetoric. Faculty need to reflect, rethink, and reconstruct course syllabi so that they support BIPOC [Black, Indigenous, and other People of Color] engagement, validation, and sense of belonging in education. The design, content, and tone of the course syllabus will either engage or disengage students" (p. 43). In addition to the organizational revisions mentioned above, syllabi should make it evident that the instructor cares about student success and that they are willing to support students in order to achieve high expectations and standards (e.g., the "Tom Ostrom Strategy"). And firm deadlines are acceptable, but student-centered, equity-minded educators also realize that community college students experience a greater variety and degree of obstacles than their university counterparts, including poverty, housing and food insecurity, underemployment or unemployment, and issues with transportation. As such, an equity-minded syllabus will provide firm deadlines, but it will also acknowledge that emergencies and barriers come up and that the key is open communication. Students are more likely to share these emergencies with an instructor who has an "open door policy" and whom they are comfortable reaching out to in these instances. An educator who is aloof, unavailable, and insensitive to the unique needs of many community college students will always be caught off guard when a student has an emergency and when that student falls behind and eventually disappears (if they notice). This type of behavior only acts to reproduce the inequities in student success and completion that we have witnessed for last several decades.

Equity-minded educators can also consider moving some, if not all, of their assessments from quantitative tasks (e.g., tests and quizzes) to qualitative tasks, like essays, projects, and creative arts. Most educators accept that students have different learning styles and there is now a wealth of scholarship on test anxiety (Hembree, 1988; Kahan, 2008; Rasor & Rasor, 1998). So why do we, knowing this, continue to administer high-stakes, multiple-choice exams and quizzes? Luckily, these types of tests have been more closely scrutinized by community college educators in the midst of the SARS-CoV-2 (i.e., COVID-19) global pandemic, as concerns around logistics and privacy came to light. As a result, many educators shifted to more qualitative assessments that ask students to use their knowledge in unique and critical ways and that force them to make connections between different topics and even different disciplines. These include research papers and other essays, posterboards and wikis, visual arts, and group projects. The irony is that these types of qualitative assessments actually require a greater deal of critical thinking and higher academic standards, and they also happen to be the form of assessment that students are most adept at, as it allows them to use skills and knowledge that they have developed inside and outside the classroom.

Certainly, we can't just create a justice-centered syllabus and then teach the class the ways we have always done so. We need to walk the walk, and our student-centered, justice-informed *actions* start on the first day of class with community building exercises that let the students get to know each other and their professor, and these activities must be interspersed throughout the semester. Popular activities include "two truths and lie," bingo, scavenger hunts, jeopardy, and "speed dating." Moreover, instructors have unique responsibilities for creating and fostering community. As Sadat Ahadi and Guerrero (2020) write, "Introductions at the start of each course, recalling students' names correctly, and knowing students' gender pronouns are impactful practices. Being sensitive to the needs of students and demonstrating unconditional positive regard will build a strong community in a course" (p. 44). It always surprises me when my colleagues do not know their students' names weeks or even months into the term (sometimes they never do). Not knowing a student's name in some situations can be extremely awkward, but it is also the most effective way to dehumanize that student (in addition to mispronouncing their name). It is fairly obvious that when we know students' names and recognize them as people, we are more likely to feel an obligation to their success.

Finally, there are actions that we take before the term even begins that can either foster a strong, equity-centered classroom community or foster a classroom community characterized by anxiety, disengagement, and even hostility, one of which is the books we choose to adopt for our courses. Many students will have a first impression of a course based solely on what they see at the bookstore (or on its website) before they even step foot in our classrooms, so it is worth reflecting on how we choose our course materials. For some students, the act of buying school supplies and books is exciting, an annual tradition that marks the beginning of the school year. However, for others, this experience is fraught with anxiety, insecurity, and stress. Let us investigate why.

First, textbook costs are unquestionably a barrier to many of our students, as community colleges serve a greater proportion of low-income students than four-year universities and colleges. For many of these students, the price of course materials and textbooks can have unintended consequences – delaying pricier courses for later, the accumulation of debt, changing to a less expensive major, or even leaving college altogether. This is especially disheartening when we consider how excited many of our students are to start college. It is tragic to imagine the student who wants to major in biology because they want to work with animals suddenly rethinking that dream because they can't afford the hundreds of dollars of materials each semester. Even if they manage, suddenly the students' excitement has been replaced by anxiety and fear. As a result, we should be looking for ways of cutting these costs as much as possible. One such solution is to use open access resources, like free or reduced-cost textbooks, which are written by discipline experts and peer reviewed. We may also consider writing our own course reader, which bookstores can make available to students for a nominal fee (or you can post for free on your LMS). Are we able to completely eliminate the high costs of course materials? Probably not. But we can chip away at them little by little in the pursuit of expanding access to higher education.

Second, we need to consider the representation in our course materials. Are our resources authored exclusively by white men (or women)? Do our course materials privilege European ideologies and epistemologies? Do our book selections mirror the students that attend our colleges and enroll in our classes? This topic will be covered in more detail in the next chapter, but it is worth considering these choices. We may instead ask ourselves if there are resources written by authors and experts of color or whether our resources highlight injustices and disparities in the discipline instead of omitting them or treating them as unchangeable facts of life. The key here is to choose texts that not only provide students with the knowledge of the discipline but that also compel the students to enter into the process of problem-posing. Do your texts invite students to enter into a dialogue about their experiences and realities? Do your resources highlight injustices and also empower the students to promote transformation in their communities (and even the discipline)? In other words, do our course materials support the project of critical pedagogy in your classroom?

f. Conclusion

As higher educational professionals, we have the power – or as I would argue, the obligation – to truly transform our classrooms into spaces where the students' cultures and identities are celebrated, where we engage in critical conversations about oppression and marginalization in our disciplines inside and outside the academy, and where we can strive for social justice. We must, as Macedo (2000) urged, be "committed to imagine a world... that is less ugly, more beautiful, less discriminatory, more democratic, less dehumanizing, and more humane" (p. 25). This starts in our classrooms – in both *how* we teach and *what* we teach. Now that we've discussed the former, the next chapter will cover the latter – our curriculum.

g. Chapter 5 Synopsis and Questions to Consider

Synopsis

To truly engage our students in our disciplines and the benefits of a liberal arts education, we must shift from the "banking model of education," or a lecture-based pedagogy, to what Freire calls a "problem-posing" education, which encourages students to become co-creators in the pursuit of knowledge. Scholars like Chris Emdin and Jeremiah J. Sims have taken this further, utilizing reality pedagogy and critical reality pedagogy, respectively, which encourage educators to incorporate the cultural interests and artifacts of the students into the classroom and to create a classroom wherein students feel empowered and obligated to transform their communities. Furthermore, a critical reality classroom requires us to rethink how we engage with our students and how we create a classroom that is welcoming, nurturing, and rigorous. Transforming our classrooms starts with how we engage our students on the first day and beyond, how we facilitate sensitive, critical conversations, and how we assess our students, among other considerations.

Questions to Consider

1. How does the critical pedagogy proposed by Freire differ from traditional teaching, or what he calls "the banking model" of education? Why is *praxis* an important component of critical pedagogy?
2. What does it mean to be a researcher-practitioner? Why is it important for community college educators to approach their classrooms "in the traditions of action research"? (Palmer, 1992).
3. What are the differences between critical pedagogy, reality pedagogy, and critical reality pedagogy? Where do they overlap?
4. How can you create a classroom environment that is welcoming and nurturing while simultaneously rigorous?
5. What is a "safe discourse space" and how can you create one in your classroom?
6. How are your syllabi organized and what are their tones? How can you revise your syllabi in a way that welcomes your students into the class and that makes it clear they are a valuable member of the classroom community?
7. In what ways do students create first impressions of us and our classes? How can we ensure that these first impressions are positive?

Keywords: critical pedagogy, problem-posing, banking model, praxis, culturally relevant pedagogy, reality pedagogy, critical reality pedagogy, safe discourse spaces

h. References

Cohen, A.M., & Outcalt, C.L. (2001). *A profile of the community college professoriate: A report submitted to the small research grants program of the Spencer Foundation*. Retrieved from https://eric.ed.gov/?id=ED454930

Cohen, G.L., Steele, C.M., & Ross, L.D. (1999). The mentor's dilemma: Providing critical feedback across the racial divide. *Personality & Social Psychology Bulletin, 25*(10), 1302–1318.

DiAngelo, R. (2018). *White fragility: Why it's so hard for White people to talk about racism*. Boston: Beacon Press.

Flynn, J.E. (2018). *White fatigue: Rethinking resistance to social justice*. New York: Peter Lang.

Freire Institute. (2020). *Concepts used by Paulo Freire*. Retrieved from https://www.freire.org/concepts-used-by-paulo-freire/

Freire, P. (1993). *Pedagogy of the oppressed*. M. Bergman Ramos (Trans.). New York: Continuum. (Original work published 1970).

Freire, P., & Macedo, D. (1995). A dialogue: Culture, language, and race. *Harvard Educational Review, 65*(3), 377–402.

Hembree, R. (1988). Correlates, causes, effects and treatment of test anxiety. *Review of Educational Research, 58*(1), 47–77.

Kahan, L.M. (2008). *The correlation of test anxiety and academic performance of community college students* (Doctoral dissertation). Capella University.

Kenney, M.R. (2001). *Mapping gay L.A.: The intersection of place and politics*. Philadelphia, PA: Temple UP.

Ladson-Billings, G. (1995). Toward a theory of culturally relevant pedagogy. *American Educational Research Journal, 32*(3), 465–491.

Ladson-Billings, G., & Tate, W.F. (1995). Toward a critical race theory of education. *Teachers College Record, 97*(1), 47–68.

Macedo, D. (2000). Introduction. In P. Freire (Ed.), *Pedagogy of the oppressed* (pp. 11–27). New York: Continuum.

Magee, R.V. (2019). *The inner work of racial justice: Healing ourselves and transforming our communities through mindfulness*. New York: TarcherPerigee.

Outcalt, C.L. (2002). Toward a professionalized community college professoriate. In C.L. Outcalt (Ed.), *Community college faculty: Characteristics, practices, and challenges* (pp. 109–115). New Directions for Community Colleges, no. 188. San Francisco, CA: Jossey-Bass.

Palmer, J. (1992). Faculty professionalization reconsidered. In K. Kroll (Ed.), *Maintaining faculty excellence* (pp. 29–38). New Directions for Community Colleges, no. 79. San Francisco, CA: Jossey-Bass.

Paris, D. (2012). Culturally sustaining pedagogy: A needed change in stance, terminology, and practice. *Educational Researcher, 41*(3), 93–97.

Pierson, R. (2013, May). *Every kid needs a champion* [video]. TED. Retrieved from https://www.ted.com/talks/rita_pierson_every_kid_needs_a_champion?language=en

Rasor, L.T., & Rasor, R.A. (1998). *Test anxiety and study behavior of community college students in relation to ethnicity, gender, and age*. Retrieved from https://eric.ed.gov/?id=ED415942

Sadat Ahadi, H., & Guerrero, L.A. (2020, November). Decolonizing your syllabus: An anti-racist guide for your college. *Rostrum*. Retrieved from https://www.asccc.org/content/decolonizing-your-syllabus-anti-racist-guide-your-college

Schoenbach, R., Greenleaf, C., & Murphy, L. (2012). *Reading for understanding: How reading apprenticeship improves disciplinary learning in secondary and college classrooms*. San Francisco, CA: Jossey-Bass.

Shaull, R. (1993). Foreword. In P. Freire (Ed.), *Pedagogy of the Oppressed* (pp. 29–34). New York: Continuum.

Sims, J.J. (2018). *Revolutionary STEM education: Critical-reality pedagogy and social justice in STEM for black males*. New York: Peter Lang.

Sims, J.J., Taylor-Mendoza, J., Hotep, L.O., Wallace, J., & Conaway, T. (2020). *Minding the obligation gap in community colleges and beyond: Theory and practice in achieving educational equity.* New York: Peter Lang.

Steele, C.M. (2010). *Whistling Vivaldi: How stereotypes affect us and what we can do.* New York: W.W. Norton & Company.

Tatum, B.D. (1997/2017). *Why are all the Black kids sitting together in the cafeteria?: And other conversations about race.* New York: Basic.

Townsend, B.K., & Twombly, S.B. (2007). Community college faculty: Overlooked and under-valued. *ASHE Higher Education Report, 32*(6), 105–125.

Twombly, S.B. (2004). Looking for signs of community college arts and sciences faculty profes-sionalization in searches: An alternative approach to a vexing question. *Community College Review, 32*(1), 21–39.

6

The People's Curriculum

When I ask colleagues where they learned how to teach and why they teach the way they do, the most common response I get is "I teach how I was taught." Most of us did not take classes on teaching and learning while in graduate school, so our models for effective teaching tend to be the professors and teachers that we learned most effectively from, and we utilize their techniques and methods in our own classrooms, assuming that if they were effective for our classmates and ourselves, they must be effective for our students. This is an important insight for two reasons. First, it presumes that all students learn the same way and that curriculum is "one size fits all"; however, as mentioned in the previous chapter, students learn in different ways, and their interest in our curriculum and discipline is going to vary, especially depending on how we represent and present it. Second, this insight speaks to the cyclical nature of pedagogy, curriculum, and, consequently, ideology and knowledge. In other words, we *reproduce* the knowledge and curriculum that we were taught in graduate school, so, in many ways, the representation and inclusivity of our curriculum can be dependent on how representative and inclusive our graduate school courses were. If we went through graduate school only learning about the "dead white men" that contributed to our disciplines, it follows that we are going to teach our students about those same dead white men – unless this cycle is disrupted, that is.

Critical pedagogy is not possible without substantive changes to the course curriculum, from the learning outcomes to course content. In other words, to be clear, it is not possible to maintain a Eurocentric curriculum, which, as we have discussed earlier in the book, upholds white supremacy and European norms and knowledge, while also being an equity- and justice-focused educator. Indeed, one of the very premises of critical pedagogy is to make the curriculum more relevant to the lives and experiences of the students and to create a learning environment in which the students can question the privileging of whiteness, masculinity, heteronormativity, and other forms of hegemony. A critical pedagogy must be paired with a critical curriculum. Using CRT as a foundation, this chapter will critique curricular decisions as a means of reproducing European epistemologies and white supremacy, and it will describe how educators can proactively integrate non-Western European epistemologies into their curriculum without tokenizing these writers and thinkers. Furthermore, this book is almost exclusively focused singularly on the classroom and how individual educators can engage in what Magee (2019) calls "the inner work of racial justice" and how they can transform their teaching and curricula in order to promote educational equity and social justice. With that being said, the institutional curricular approval process and the college curriculum committee are important spaces for disrupting Eurocentricity and the perpetuation of white supremacist ideologies, which I have written about elsewhere (see Sims, Taylor-Mendoza, Hotep, Wallace, & Conaway, 2020).

a. "Official Knowledge": Structural Determinism and the Perpetuation of White Supremacy

The college curriculum is, with very few exceptions, the domain of dead and living white men of Western European descent. I think if we really take a moment to reflect on our own college educations and we take a moment to look at our own curricula and that of our colleagues, we'll admit this is true, whether it is the Greco-Roman and European thinkers that provide the basis for our philosophy courses, or the European and American scientists that are recognized as pioneers in the natural and physical sciences, or even my own discipline of literature and its emphasis on writers like Shakespeare and Whitman. If we blasted our college curriculum into space and it was intercepted by an intelligent life-form millions of light-years away, they would assume that the Earth was inhabited only by white folks and that our cultures and civilizations only existed in Europe, and maybe the United States (in fact, many right-wing hacks, like Dinesh D'Souza, actually do believe this).

However, if we think about it, this also isn't surprising. America's first colonial colleges and universities were founded to train students in professions like medicine, theology, and the law, and they had few permanent faculty and only archaic undergraduate liberal studies programs (Gerber, 2014). It wasn't until after American independence that American universities started to morph into their current form, which was based in large part on the German universities. As Gerber writes:

> No American institution in the antebellum years was comparable in quality or reputation to the modern universities that were being created in Germany in the late eighteenth and early nineteenth centuries. The modern German university, with its new emphasis on academic specialization, original research, the seminar method of instruction, and freedom of inquiry for professors enjoying high status as professionals would eventually become a model for institutions of higher learning in the United States and elsewhere in the world. (loc. 416)

In other words, the American universities were shifting from their practical missions of preparing wealthy men for professional jobs to the pursuit of new knowledge and research. The "transient" faculty of the colonial colleges would give way to permanent faculty who were experts in their disciplines. This history of American higher education is fascinating, and it exemplifies why our colleges and universities – including community colleges – are steeped in European knowledge, thought, values, and structures – they are modeled after European universities.

As a result, any threat to this Eurocentric paradigm is challenged and, if not altogether quashed, then marginalized in the academy. The ethnic studies movement and the development of critical race theories are clear examples of the academy's hostility to disciplines and ideologies that don't center Western Europe and whiteness. In the case of the former, ethnic studies departments – if they even exist on a campus – are usually on the margins of the institution, and they are often charged with providing the only curricula on campus that center the voices, experiences, and knowledge of people of color and that critique the perverse consequences of white supremacy. In the case of the latter, critical race theory has not only been marginalized in the academy, but it more recently has come under fire by conservatives as being "un-American propaganda." Take also the backlash from conservatives in California when Professor J. Luke Wood offered a graduate course in education entitled "Black Minds Matter." One critic of the class complained, "Now we want to give them taxpayer dollars to train educators on how to indoctrinate our children?" Another critic believed, "We should be spending public funds on courses that will actually prepare the next generation for meaningful jobs instead of teaching them how to be victims" (Warth, 2017). To be clear, Wood's course was simply meant to help future teachers understand the challenges that Black children face in the education system and to help them remedy race-based barriers for these children.

This backlash stems from a perceived threat to what Apple (1979/2019) has termed the "official knowledge" of our educational systems. The previously mentioned pundits and critics believe that any deviation from the existing and traditional school and college curriculum is agitprop because the "official" curriculum is supposedly objective and true to reality. However, it is important to understand that curriculum is not neutral and that what we teach and how we teach it are political acts, whether we recognize that or not. Each day we are in our classrooms, we are presenting a version of reality that is informed by certain social norms, values, and ideologies while simultaneously excluding others. The curriculum is not objective. As Apple (1979/2019) argues, the claim that curriculum and education are neutral:

> ignores the fact that the knowledge that gets into schools is already a choice from a much larger universe of possible social knowledge and principles. It is a form of cultural capital that comes from somewhere, that often reflects the perspectives and beliefs of powerful segments of our social collectivity. In its very production and dissemination as a public and economic commodity – as books, films, materials and so forth – it is repeatedly filtered through ideological and economic commitments. Social and economic values, hence, are already embedded in the design of the institutions we work in, in the 'formal corpus of school knowledge' we preserve in our curricula, in our modes of teaching, and in our principles, standards, and forms of evaluation. (p. 8)

Indeed, this curriculum is very intentional. In the K-12 system, this "hidden curriculum," as Apple calls it, is formalized through a series of laws (e.g., No Child Left Behind and Common Core) and assessments (such as state assessments – which start as early as elementary school – and state graduation requirements). Functionally, these laws, assessments, and graduation requirements, which are themselves the products of politicians with agendas, undergird an inequitable education system – both in K-12 and in higher education – that rewards schools in wealthy neighborhoods with more funding from property taxes (thus, better facilities and technology and more qualified teachers), which often lead to higher test scores, the result of which is higher funding. Meanwhile, students in low-income schools are learning a curriculum that they cannot identify with and that pathologizes their neighborhoods and communities in subpar facilities, with outdated technology, and often with unqualified teachers. The consequence is less funding from the state for schools already lacking adequate property tax funding.

This entire system is predicated on a curriculum that imbues ideologies that privilege the middle-class and Eurocentric norms and values. Historically, the curriculum and Eurocentric ideologies have always been about power and forcing majoritarian norms and values on immigrants and people of color. This has resulted in what early American educator Carter G. Woodson (1933/2016) calls the "miseducation" of Black students and other students of color. As Apple (1979/2019) notes, schools, especially through the curriculum, serve three primary functions – to assimilate immigrants and people of color into the "American culture," to prepare children for the industry, and to preserve conservative values. Schools are institutions meant to preserve "cultural hegemony" (p. 67). According to Apple, this mission of the school became more pronounced in the early 20th century as African Americans from the South migrated to the cities and the country became a beacon for immigrants, leading "native" white Americans more and more concerned as Eastern European and Asian immigrants settled down on the country's coast: "schools were seen as institutions that could preserve the cultural hegemony of an embattled 'native' population. Education was the way in which community life, values, norms, and economic advantages of the powerful were to be protected. Schools could be the great engines of a moral crusade to make the children of the immigrants and the Blacks like 'us'" (p. 67). Apple lays bare the political and social motivations for developing a curriculum based on Western European values and knowledge, a curriculum that still exists almost intact to this day, and when coupled with standardized testing on this curriculum, it begs the question – who is this for? And community colleges are no different; in fact, our adherence to the "official knowledge" of our disciplines is even more perverse because we opt into it – we aren't forced by laws and state assessments to teach certain content. To make this more concrete, consider my own institution, College of San Mateo (CSM). Students of color at CSM make up over 70% of the student body, yet the majority of the courses that they take will be steeped in Western European epistemologies and white supremacist beliefs. Furthermore, over 60% of all the faculty at CSM are white, and according to the U.S. Census Bureau, nearly 60% of San Mateo county's residents identify as white (38.7% identify as "white alone") (Campaign for College Opportunity, 2017; U.S. Census Bureau, 2019). Again, the question is, who does this curriculum benefit?

This power dynamic becomes clearer when we consider the *way* in which we offer our curriculum, all the way from primary school to college, and how the traditional methods of delivering the curriculum have been informed by the needs of industry and business (e.g., the "banking model"). In other words, the curriculum has been used as a way to promote conformity among the students, who will one day enter into the larger society and workforce, or as Apple notes, it "would adjust individuals to their respective place in an industrial society" (p. 68). This is what educator Sir Ken Robinson would refer to as the factory model of education. In a popular TED Talk, Robinson (2006) asks, "Why are we educating people out of their creative capacities?" As Robinson argues, creativity is an innate ability in all children that our public education system tends to eradicate through rote learning and the banking model of pedagogy, all in the service of an "output" that benefits the workforce. Furthermore, Robinson questions our use of terms like "academic ability," which at this point in the book we know to be coded, racialized, gendered, and classed language meant to separate the haves from the have-nots:

> Our education system is predicated on the idea of academic ability. And there's a reason. Around the world, there were no public systems of education, really, before the 19th century. They all came into being to meet the needs of industrialism. So the hierarchy is rooted on two ideas. Number one, the most useful subjects for work are at the top. So you were probably steered benignly away from things at school when you were a kid, things you liked, on the grounds you would never get a job doing that. Is that right? 'Don't do music, you're not going to be a musician; don't do art, you won't be an artist.' Benign advice – now profoundly mistaken. The whole world is engulfed in a revolution. And the second is academic ability, which has really come to dominate our view of intelligence, because the universities design the system in their image. If you think of it, the whole system of public education around the world is a protracted process of university entrance. And the consequence is that many highly talent, brilliant, creative people think they're not, because the thing they were good at at school wasn't valued, or was actually stigmatized. And I think we can't afford to go on that way.

In a separate presentation, Robinson (2010) explicitly critiques the education system's service to workforce preparation and how this vocational focus actually harms children. It is this education-industrial alliance that has resulted in the "production line" model of education. As he argues, the education system is modeled on the interests of industrialism and in the image of it. I'll give you a couple of examples of it. Schools are still pretty much organized on factory lines - ringing bells, separate facilities, specialized into separate subjects. We still educate children by batches. We put them through the system by age group... why is this there this assumption that the most important thing kids have in common is how old they are... I know kids who are much better than other kids at the same age in different disciplines, or at different times of the day, or better in smaller groups than in large groups or sometimes they want to be on their own. If you are interested in a model of education, you don't start from this production line mentality. It is essentially about conformity, and increasingly it is about that as you look at the growth of standardized testing and standardized curricular. And it is about standardization.

It is fairly easy to write this reality off as a characteristic of the K-12 system since we generally do not group our students by age (though this often is the result of our course sequences and demographics). However, we are complicit in reproducing the factory model of the K-12 system: we have carefully tailored course sequences and prerequisites; our students sit in rows of desks and are quiet until they politely raise their hands to speak; we tend to group our disciplines into divisions or schools whose administrations utilize formulae to determine their programs' *efficiency*; and we tend to undervalue the arts in favor of programs that are job oriented. Furthermore, this is all compounded by the Guided Pathways movement, which is literally an assembly line of courses with an "output" of transfer or a job, depending on the program. Exploration is not encouraged because these types of pathways are predicated on efficiency, and because students are steered away from the fine arts and humanities – since they have supposedly dreary job prospects – these critical programs are perpetually in danger of being cut. What is left is a vocation-focused curriculum that includes the most basic general education and major courses, which often exclude courses and programs where minoritized students can see themselves mirrored in the content.

It is also worth scrutinizing this education-industrial codependency for the ideologies that it produces through the curriculum. And to be clear, community colleges are not immune from reproducing these ideologies in the curriculum. Let's take, for example, the ideology of American individualism, and its concomitant values and beliefs, including the "pull yourself up by the bootstraps" mantra and the mythology of the American Dream. This ideology goes something like this: "In America, the land of opportunity, anyone can be successful, achieve the American Dream, and find happiness as long they have the motivation and a strong work ethic." Of course, in order for this to manifest, it must be undergirded by equal opportunity to resources and opportunities and by color-blindness, or the belief that all people, regardless of race, have the opportunity to accumulate wealth and knowledge. However, members of the African American and Latinx communities disproportionately experience unemployment, housing insecurity, and food insecurity, and they experience disproportionate barriers to quality education, technology, and financial resources (like mortgages and small-business loans). Under the ideology of American individualism and its belief in equal opportunity, the members of the African American and Latinx communities who aren't living the American Dream are seen as deficient in some way, and if they can't accumulate wealth and success, then it is their own fault. As a result, this ideology perpetuates the stereotypes that people of color are lazy and unmotivated and that they come from cultures of poverty.

As justice-minded, critical educators, we know these stereotypes to be untrue, and we know that people of color experience racialized barriers to accumulating wealth and power (see Chapter 2). We know that American individualism is a myth, and hopefully, by the end of this book, you will realize that it is a mythology that was constructed to perpetuate racism and a racial hierarchy. So if we know all this, why do we continue to celebrate the American Dream in the curriculum? Why do we continue to teach students about the Rockefellers, the Fords, and the Jobs of this country, or at least, why do we continue to teach our students about these so-called "rags to riches" white men without qualifying that they were able to find their successes precisely because they were white and male? Why do we perpetuate this myth that people of color have historically had equal access to resources and capital when we know that even today, this is not true? As a case in point, let's look at the U.S. government's economic response to the SARS-CoV-2 (COVID-19) pandemic. As part of the multitrillion-dollar stimulus package, Congress allocated billions of dollars to supporting small businesses. This was laudable considering these businesses didn't have the capital to stay afloat during a spate of lockdowns and shelters-in-place. However, it was later found that Black business owners were by and large excluded from these bailouts – why? To be utterly blunt, it was because they were Black, and they were discriminated against by the country's major banks. Lederer and Oros (2020) of the National Community Reinvestment Coalition conducted a matched-pair audit test, where Black and white researchers posed as business owners with similar businesses, similar credit ratings, and similar financial needs and where they sought loans through the federal government's Paycheck Protection Program, which was passed by Congress in order to help businesses stay afloat during the pandemic. They found that Black-owned business owners were given different "levels of encouragement" to apply for the PPP loans (the white testers were more often encouraged to apply for them), they were offered different products and loans (the female testers were given less information about PPP), and the Black testers were asked to provide more information for preapproval and were given less information about rates and fees (pp. 10–15). As the NCRC notes about the study, "White applicants were treated better than Black applicants, a pattern that was well documented in small business lending before COVID-19." This is just one example in a long list of historical examples of systemic racism, which has hindered the aspirations and dreams of so many people of color. The American Dream is not an equal opportunity, and as critical educators, we do our students a disservice in promoting that ideology and any other that centers Eurocentric norms and white privilege.

As alluded to above, ideology has a tremendous impact on the curriculum; for example, the American individualism/American Dream ideology manifests in a host of curricular decisions, whether imposed by policy or unconsciously by the educator, such as course content on successful businessmen like John D. Rockefeller and Steve Jobs, on theories such as those promoted by Adam Smith in *The Wealth of Nations*, and on the romanticization of post-WWII America and the concomitant rise of the middle class, suburbs, and materialism. And this not only canonizes problematic figures and white supremacist ideologies, but it also misrepresents the realities of people of color and omits the struggles of successful entrepreneurs of color, such as Oprah Winfrey and Madame CJ Walker, who found success despite systemic racism. This revisionist and exclusionary curriculum is a component of Apple's (1993/2014) "official knowledge" or official curriculum. Similar to Swartz's (1992) "master script," Apple theorizes that the "official knowledge" of the K-12 system, in particular, has been used both to propagate conservative, white nationalist norms and to perpetuate social and racial inequities. Consequently, the epistemologies, values, and voices of Western Europeans and White Americans are elevated, while the knowledge and cultural norms of people of color are marginalized and omitted, all of which is deemed natural by educators, parents, and the community.

However, this hidden curriculum is often unintentional. As Apple makes clear, most educators are not active perpetrators of some conspiracy to miseducate the nation's youth: "'naturally' generated out of many of educators' commonsense assumptions and practices about teaching and learning, normal and abnormal behavior, important and unimportant knowledge, and so forth are conditions and forms of interaction that have latent functions. And these latent functions include some things that many educators are not aware of" (p. 66). In other words, we are a product of our own environments and educational experiences, and many of us have been indoctrinated by the "official curriculum." As mentioned at the beginning of this chapter, most of us in higher education learned how to teach and what to teach by those who taught us.

Nonetheless, this problem is exacerbated by a textbook industry that is woefully behind in promoting texts written by justice-minded authors and authors of color, instead offering texts that skew or even exclude the contributions, knowledge, and voices of minoritized peoples. Donaldo Macedo (2000) argues that these "omissions" are "a more sophisticated form of censorship" (p. 16). And as Apple (1993/2014) writes, "texts are not simply 'delivery systems' of 'facts'. They are at once the results of political, economic, and cultural activities, battles, and compromises. They are conceived, designed, and authored by real people with real interests. They are published within the political and economic constraints of markets, resources, and power. And what texts mean and how they are used are fought over by communities with distinctly different commitments and by teachers and students as well" (p. 47). In other words, textbooks serve the agendas of those in power. Consider, for example, how textbooks are chosen in the K-12 system – through committees, which have often been politicized in order to promote a certain type of ideology. Different states want their students to have a different set of "facts," which has resulted in a textbook industry that has sold out to the conservative factions of state education departments across the country and has created different versions of the same textbook depending on the agenda of that state. Take, for instance, the case of a textbook that described slaves as "workers" in its Texas version, which departed from the more accurate (though still underwhelming) version in other states (Isensee, 2015). Apple argues of textbooks that "it is naïve to think of the school curriculum as neutral knowledge... [textbooks] signify, through their content *and* form, particular constructions of reality, particular ways of selecting and organizing that vast universe of possible knowledge" (pp. 47, 49, emphasis in original). Said another way, the reality that is constructed for our children is essentially a struggle between those in power and those who seek to liberate the curriculum of its oppressive and exclusionary roots. We saw this power struggle in 2020 when, during some of the most widespread and powerful protests for racial justice since the mid-20th century, President Trump denounced critical race theory (as if he knew what it was) and ordered the federal government to end any implicit bias trainings in its departments. Unfortunately, this mandate had very real consequences for academia, as it was intellectuals in these fields that provided these trainings, not to mention many colleges started to dissociate themselves from critical race fields for fear of losing federal funding.

Again, those of us in the community colleges are not immune from these power struggles and the unconscious reproduction of Eurocentric, white supremacist thought. Akin to Apple's "official knowledge," Swartz (1992) theorized a "master script" that highlights and elevates the achievements and knowledge of Western European and European American individuals and distorts or omits the struggles, achievements, and knowledge of people of color. She writes:

> the master script refers to classroom practices, pedagogy, and instructional materials – as well as the theoretical paradigms from which these aspects are constructed – that are grounded in Eurocentric and White supremacist ideologies. Master scripting silences multiple voices and perspectives, primarily by legitimizing dominant, White, upper-class, male voicings as the "standard" knowledge students need to know. All other accounts and perspectives are omitted from the master script unless they can be disempowered through misrepresentation. Thus, content that does not reflect the dominant voice must be brought under control, *mastered*, and then reshaped before it can become part of the master script. (p. 341, emphasis in original)

As Swartz notes, the master script is "monovocal" and the non-European content is often misrepresented as a means of stripping minoritized communities and non-European cultures of their agency.

Furthermore, thinkers and people of color are often tokenized in what Swartz calls "compensatory approaches," which relegates included people of color and women to "firsts" (e.g., the first Black scientist, the first female astronaut, etc.). Swartz uses the example of Crispus Attucks, who "is included only to tell students that he was a former slave who died in the Boston Massacre, rather than tell them that he was a symbol of both colonial independence and African American leadership and liberation" (p. 344). In comparing different history textbooks, Swartz found that Attucks was almost always defined by his identity as a "runaway slave." Similar misrepresentations have happened with Dr. Martin Luther King, Jr., whose socialist beliefs are often unacknowledged, and with Frederick Douglass, who is often marginalized in textbooks so that abolitionist William Lloyd Garrison can be "given the central position" (p. 348). David Ikard (2018) describes this same phenomenon almost two decades after Swartz's initial study in a story about his son's teacher. Ikard, in his TED Talk, *The Real Story of Rosa Parks,* shares that his fourth-grade son once came home from school to tell him that he had learned Rosa Parks was "this frail, old Black woman in the 1950s in

Montgomery, Alabama. And she sat down on this bus, and she had tired feet, and when the bus driver told her to give up her seat to a white patron, she refused because she had tired feet. It had been a long day, and she was tired of oppression, and she didn't give up her seat. And she marched with Martin Luther King, and she believed in nonviolence." This is the version of Rosa Parks that we often see in textbooks and in the media. As Ikard explains, "a story emerges in which somebody is telling the world that [Rosa Parks was] old and [she] had tired feet and that [she just was] an accidental activist, not that [she] had been an activist by then for twenty years, not that the boycott had been planned for months, not that [she was] not even the first or the second or even third woman to be arrested for doing that."

Ikard alludes to the power structure of these narratives and how the master script tends to strip activists and thinkers of color of their agency. As he points out, an elderly woman with tired feet (Parks was actually only 42 years old) is unthreatening to the status quo because her "accidental activism" is less inspiring – it is not "scary." However, as Ikard argues, "young, radical black women who don't take any stuff from anybody are very scary, who stand up to power and are willing to die for that – those are not the kind of people that make us comfortable." It is worth asking ourselves why we were given the sanitized version of Rosa Parks as children and why we aren't taught about activists like Kathleen Cleaver, Angela Davis, or Assata Shakur. Why is it that we are given the sanitized versions of Frederick Douglass and Dr. Martin Luther King, Jr., and why are we not taught about Nat Turner, Kwame Ture, or Huey P. Newton? As Swartz notes, "This compensatory approach only strengthens the grip of Eurocentrism on the construction of knowledge" (p. 344). Why do we refuse to teach about the contributions of people of color to our own disciplines, and when we do, why do we sanitize their contributions and tokenize their achievements as "firsts"? I argue that it comes down to two reasons: first, like Ikard argues, teaching about powerful activists is scary and uncomfortable. Strong men and women of color, especially strong Black men and women, are threatening to the racial order of the United States. And whether we recognize it or not, we do feel threatened by them, in part because what they say is uncomfortable but also because we feel as if what they want – justice – will somehow deprive us of some privileges (McGhee, 2021). Second, these powerful historical figures and activists are inspiring for our students of color, and when our students are inspired and empowered, they are more likely to speak up for themselves and their communities. Student activism becomes a threat to the order and "civility" of higher education. But as justice-oriented educators, we need, as I have argued previously, to embrace the discomfort and invite our students' activism. We should be equipping them with the tools to transform their communities and our collective society, no matter our discipline.

b. The "Triple Helix Dilemma" and Community College Curricula

Unfortunately, these types of self-sustaining systems allow little room for criticism. When a new scholar or educator enters into the discipline, the scholarship and values set forth by this "official knowledge" reign supreme, and all knowledge outside this framework is ignored and invisible. And even when a scholar or educator pushes back against this status quo, they are generally stonewalled by the establishment (e.g., journal editors, department chairs, etc.). This has resulted in what I call, borrowing the term from the pivotal critical race study by Delgado and Stefancic, the "triple helix of community colleges." In their study, Delgado and Stefancic (1989) scrutinized the homogeneity of legal studies and case law and how they seemed to continuously reproduce themselves within the Library of Congress cataloguing system and associated databases and periodicals. Delgado and Stefancic point to the three most widely used classification systems in the legal field – the Library of Congress Subject Heading System, the *Index to Legal Periodicals,* and the West Digest System. On the surface it would seem that access to three classification systems would provide legal scholars diverse arguments, precedents, case law, and knowledge, but they found that all three systems feed into and replicate the other two in what they term the "triple helix dilemma" (p. 216). In describing the legal research process, they write:

> Moreover, in many instances the researcher will not know what he or she is looking for. The situation may call for innovation. The indexing systems may not have developed a category for the issue being researched, or having invented one, have failed to enter a key item into the database selected by the researcher, thus rendering the system useless. The systems function rather like molecular biology's double helix: They replicate preexisting ideas, thoughts, and approaches. Within the bounds of the three systems, moderate, incremental reform remains quite possible, but the systems make foundational, transformative innovation difficult. Because the three classification systems operate in a coordinated network of information retrieval, we call the situation confronting the lawyer or scholar trying to break free from their constraints the triple helix. (pp. 216–217)

These constraints and systems are not unlike the college curriculum, which is developed and reproduced by discipline experts and institutional curriculum committees, and when coupled with the course materials created by the nation's leading publishers, it can be nearly impossible to create a curriculum that is inclusive and representative of the college's (and our country's) demographics and diversity. For Delgado and Stefancic, similar institutional barriers exist in disrupting the triple helix. As they note, changes to new headings in the Library of Congress are reviewed and approved by an editorial committee, and when these changes are approved, other libraries and classification systems follow suit. Delgado and Stefancic comment, "critics complain that the system of headings simply replicates majoritarian politics and thought and gives too little attention to new, marginal, or renegade ideas" (p. 211). Such was the case when critical race scholars pushed, unsuccessfully, the inclusion of "intersectionality" in the Library of Congress Subject Heading System.

The process for cataloguing legal scholarship and case law is outside the scope of this book, but the concept of the triple helix is quite relevant to higher education. In my conception of the triple helix of community colleges, the following three processes act together to reproduce and maintain Eurocentric thought and white supremacist beliefs – the curriculum development process, faculty hiring, and faculty evaluation processes. As mentioned in Chapter 1, the vast majority of college faculty are white, and this has been the case since the inception of the community college as an institution a century ago (and has been the case for universities for centuries). As a result, the college curriculum has overrepresented Western European knowledge and values, and as we will see later in this chapter, this has changed very little even with the rise of multicultural education. All of this is to say that the college curriculum has been firmly established and reproduced academic year after academic year with very few updates and very little changes to its representation. Furthermore, the college curriculum is protected from drastic changes through the other two college processes – faculty hiring and evaluation.

Let's take faculty hiring, for example. When our departments hire for adjunct and tenure-track positions, we often convene a hiring committee of discipline experts to screen applicants and conduct interviews. Since the vast majority of faculty are white, the vast majority of these committees are either all-white or predominantly white (there are exceptions of course). However, because we tend to hire colleagues who mirror us and our beliefs and values, and because we all have implicit biases about people who look and think differently than us, the odds are that we will hire another white colleague. That new colleague now goes through an evaluation process in which their pedagogy and curriculum are assessed, especially in how well they align with the pedagogies and curricula of the department's existing faculty. In other words, most evaluation processes in the community college gauge how well the evaluee adheres to the existing department curriculum (e.g., the student outcomes, course content, course objectives, assessment policies, etc.). And since this curriculum has been historically developed through a Eurocentric, white supremacist lens, our new white colleague is usually able to breeze through the evaluation because they had little to change in their existing pedagogy and curriculum, if any changes were needed at all. However, let's imagine that our department does hire a professor of color. What does that evaluation process look like? To be honest, in most cases, it is probably very similar to the white evaluee. Academics of color usually go through the same university graduate programs before entering the professoriate, so their pedagogies and curricula will look very similar to the established curricula.

But what happens when the evaluee – whether they are white or a person of color – tries to deviate away from the established curriculum or subvert it? This is where the evaluation process steps in, and they are brought back in line if that is the will of the committee. It looks like this: let's imagine that the evaluee decides to incorporate the knowledge and voices of people of color, and as a result, they must eliminate some of the Eurocentric knowledge and voices from the course, many of which have already been enshrined in the course outline. The evaluation committee is likely to admonish them for not covering the course outline as written, which can result in probation, an official reprimand, or even dismissal.

As mentioned in Chapter 2, I experienced very similar circumstances in my second year of tenure review when my curriculum was questioned by members of my evaluation committee. In Chapter 2, I described an experience with a member of my evaluation committee in which she expressed puzzlement about the class session's focus on racism, white supremacy, and state-sanctioned violence in the wake of several police-involved murders of Black men and boys. She also expressed concern for the one white student in the class. This meeting took place after a class observation, and this discussion – or rant – happened between the two of us. It was probably easy to explain away her reactions to my pedagogy and curriculum as the beliefs of a racist white woman. But as I would find out at the end of that semester, it was a belief held by the majority of my committee. In fact, rather than an indictment of one lesson plan, the committee questioned my entire curricula. In this particular semester, I was teaching a freshman composition class for the students of the CSM Umoja Community, an Afro-centric learning community tailored primarily for African and African American students.

My second class was a critical thinking and literature class that I had developed with three tenured colleagues as part of a loose learning community called "Voice of a Stranger," which strived to expose students to the struggles and stories of minoritized people. Authors for this second course included Ralph Ellison, Laila Lalami, Jimmy Santiago Baca, Brent Staples, Judith Ortiz Cofer, and David Carr, among others. If you are unfamiliar with some of these writers, Carr is the only white author among them. My evaluation took umbrage with the fact that I had only included one white author in the curricula of these two classes. Officially, it was stated in my evaluation report that I was "encouraged" to use "a variety of reading materials and writing prompts on themes other than those of exclusively social justice issues." Furthermore, they wrote that "genocide, racism, and slavery are fine topics, but students get no warning that [my classes] explore nothing but these topics." It is an interesting mind exercise to figure out which students they wanted to be warned of my curriculum and why they didn't propose curricular disclaimers for all courses in the department. Unofficially (i.e., verbally), I was told I needed more Emily Dickenson and that texts written after 1950 about social inequities were too limiting for students. And of course, I was told that if I didn't shape up for my next evaluation, my contract would be eliminated.

I recognize that not all committees are like this. Had my committee been comprised of different colleagues in my department – like the three who I had developed part of the curriculum with – I would have been given high fives and a pint of beer. The point isn't to argue over how widespread this type of behavior is; the point is to question why we have a process that lets a small number of bigoted educators derail the careers of evaluees who are trying to tailor their curriculum to the students sitting in their classrooms. And needless to say, I am a white man. Had an educator of color been sitting in my seat, the consequences likely would have been more severe. Indeed, I have colleagues of color who have been dismissed for not adhering close enough to the course outline. The point is that we need to change the evaluation processes for both tenure track and adjunct so that progressive, critical educators are not punished for creating curricula for the students sitting in their classrooms. However, even if the evaluation procedures are changed to be more equity and justice centered, the process will still be fraught with Euro-centric norms and standards until the official course outlines are changed. Disrupting the triple helix of community colleges is only possible when all three elements are replaced with hiring, curriculum, and evaluation processes that are antiracist, that are anti-oppression, and that are socially just. While changing one component helps weaken this cycle, it really takes an overhaul of all three to deconstruct the pedestal of white supremacy and Eurocentric thought. Ultimately, this type of change takes institutional changes, which is beyond the scope of this book (see Sims et al., 2020, for strategies for transforming the institution). The aim of this book is to help educators transform their classrooms (i.e., grassroots social justice), so the remainder of this chapter will focus on how we can reimagine our curricula and our classrooms.

c. Practicum: "The People's History": Revising the Curriculum

The political agenda of the official curriculum begs the question – who does it benefit? Instead of focusing on the curriculum as it exists, I find it useful to think about the curriculum as it could be. Let's imagine the hypothetical experience of a new student in one of our colleges. Based on the demographics of community college students, they are likely to be a student of color. They show up to the college on the first day of classes and walk in to their first college class – mathematics, let's say. The student finds out that they won't just be learning about formulae and equations, but the professor has infused the course curriculum with historical information about mathematics, including how it was used by the Africans and the Central and South American civilizations. The student will eventually learn about how modern scientists of color have used mathematics, some very similar to what they are learning in class, to save astronauts – like Katherine Johnson did – or about how Benjamin Banneker, a Black urban planner, designed Washington D.C. The student goes to their next class – English – and they find a reading list that includes authors from communities of color, immigrants, and members of the LGBTQ+ community. In their third class, U.S. history, they learn about not only the Founding Fathers, the white abolitionists like William Lloyd Garrison, and successful white entrepreneurs, like Rockefeller and Carnegie, but they also learn about the rich cultures, histories, and contributions of Indigenous people and the Black, Latinx, and Asian communities. This student learns about the Madame CJ Walkers of the nation, the true histories of the Black Panther Party and Third World Liberation Front, and the accurate stories of great leaders like Dr. Martin Luther King, Jr., Malcolm X, Ida B. Wells, Sojourner Truth, Cesar Chavez, and Dolores Huerta (and we're not talking about the watered down or whitewashed versions). In other words, imagine a world in which every course that this student enrolls in at your college has decentered whiteness and instead fully integrated the histories, knowledge, and values of communities of color. Furthermore, imagine that this student had this same experience throughout their K-12 education. Imagine that their worldview and identity are informed by a more inclusive curriculum that doesn't marginalize or skew the contributions of people who look like them. What does that do for this student? It is hard to know for sure, but I would guess that the student would feel more empowered and like they have more agency. Brilliance and accomplishment for people from their community would have been normalized, and they would be able to see themselves as a mathematician or a scientist or an entrepreneur.

This type of educational experiences is exactly what Howard Zinn (1980/ 2003) imagined with his groundbreaking text *A People's History of the United States*. The title of Zinn's book is brilliant, as it speaks to both the epistemologies that provide the foundation for the text and their interlocutor – the "people." Said another way, Zinn's book provides a look at history that is tailored to the majority of Americans – people of color, the Indigenous, immigrants, low-income and working-class people, and other marginalized, minoritized peoples. A historian by training and a longtime Boston University professor, Zinn felt obligated to write this book because he knew something was missing from his own education, noting that his own educational experience had been incomplete and politicized. He writes, "There were themes of profound importance to me that I found missing in the orthodox histories that dominated American culture. The consequence of those omissions has been not simply to give a distorted view of the past but, more important, to mislead us all about the present" (p. 526). *The People's History* was his response to the misrepresentations, omissions, and revisionist histories of traditional textbooks. In other words, Zinn sought to critique the official knowledge of the public education system and to dismantle the master script, as Apple (1993/2014) and Swartz (1992) theorized, respectively.

Ultimately, Zinn's scholarship and publications are in service to tradition started by educational stalwarts of the 19th and early 20th centuries, including George Washington Williams, Carter G. Woodson, and W.E.B. DuBois. In his pivotal book, *The Mis-education of the Negro*, Carter G. Woodson (1933/2016) railed against the public education system for its disservice to African American students, foreseeing the very arguments about ideology and conformity that Apple would write about decades later: "The so-called modern education, with all its defects, however, does others so much more good than it does the Negro, because it has been worked out in conformity to the needs of those who have enslaved and oppressed weaker peoples" (p. 4). In other words, Woodson is highlighting the fact that the curriculum was not only developed by European Americans for European American children, but that this curriculum was also used as a tool of orthodoxy and oppression. Indeed, as Apple argues, the curriculum's aim of conformity was always meant to "reduce their potential revolutionary threat" (p. 74). In one of his most famous passages, Woodson describes the consequence of the curriculum's mission to colonize the Black mind: "When you control a man's thinking you do not have to worry about his actions. You do not have to tell him not to stand here or go yonder. He will find his 'proper place' and will stay in it. You do not need to send him to the back door. He will go without being told. In fact, if there is no back door, he will cut one for his special benefit. His education makes it necessary" (p. 4). Woodson died in 1950, so he never saw the Supreme Court decisions that desegregated schools. However, if he was to visit us today, he would see that much hasn't changed. Schools are still segregated due to decades of housing and banking discrimination, many students of color – regardless of the socioeconomic status of the school – are taught by white teachers, and those students, again regardless of where the school is, are still taught a curriculum chock full of dead white men and devoid of any real content about their cultural heritages or their lived realities.

Instead, Woodson suggests an Afro-centric educational program that is tailored to the needs and experiences of African American students. As he envisions, "The program for the uplift of the Negro in this country must be based upon a scientific study of the Negro from within to develop in him the power to do for himself what his oppressors will never do to elevate him to the level of others" (p. 75). Woodson not only calls for more Afro-centric scholarship as a counterbalance to the "official knowledge" of the education system, but also for more Black teachers to deliver that scholarship in the form of curriculum. Furthermore, Woodson is not necessarily advocating for a curriculum devoid of Western European contributions, but instead for one that highlights African epistemologies and centers the African American experience. As he writes, "After Negro students have mastered the fundamentals of English, the principles of composition, and the leading facts in the development of its literature, they should not spend all their time in advanced work on Shakespeare, Chaucer and Anglo-Saxon. They should direct their attention also to the folklore of the African, to the philosophy in his proverbs, to the development of the Negro in the use of modern language, and to the works of Negro writers" (p. 78). Of course, Woodson's points about the education of African American student can be interpreted more broadly to encompass the educations of all minoritized students, from students of color to students with disabilities to LGBTQ+ students. Admittedly, this type of curricular transformation may seem daunting. For many us, it is a complete shift in what we teach and how we teach it. Fortunately, as we will see later in this chapter, this "scientific study" has been undertaken for decades by scholars in both the ethnic studies and multicultural studies disciplines, not to mention in many others, like sociology, composition, and STEM. In fact, Woodson would be a foundational leader in what we now call the ethnic studies movement, having co-founded the Association for the Study of Negro Life and History (ASNLH) and starting the *Negro History Bulletin,* which was an important pedagogical and curricular resource for elementary and secondary school teachers striving to accurately teach African American history and culture. Taken in a broader sense, we can take from Woodson the need for a multicultural education that decenters whiteness and elevates the epistemologies, histories, and experiences of students of color and other minoritized students. This type of curriculum includes what Swartz (1992) calls "emancipatory narratives," which "reflect the multiple and collective origins of knowledge, and correct sanitized, repressive, and monovocal textbook portrayals of historically cultures and groups. There narratives are reformative curricular interventions that strive to reflect the indigeneity of those involved. As such, they require the collective representation of diverse cultures and groups as significant to the production of knowledge" (pp. 342–343).

To borrow from Zinn, I am alluding to a sort of "people's curriculum." The fact is, as mentioned in Chapter 1, that more and more of our students are coming from minoritized communities. Not only are most students in community colleges across the nation students of color, but our colleges also have a larger share of students with disabilities, veterans, low-income students, and immigrants, among others. And if we walk into our classrooms with this beautiful diversity and we continue to teach the same Western European curricula and we continue to assess our students using the same white supremacist values and measures, we are doing our students a great disservice. Instead, we need to decenter white, heteronormative, nativist, misogynistic epistemologies and create curricula that are more inclusive and empowering. This will look different for every discipline, and it is far beyond the scope of this book, but examples might include acknowledging the ways in which science has been used to justify racism, anti-Semitism, and misogyny; critiquing the academy's – and composition studies' – idolization of "standard" English; highlighting the racialized capitalist system that is the foundation of American economics; admitting that modern business and financing practices and laws allow for de facto discrimination against minoritized peoples; and much more. It is simply not enough to add a minoritized voice or two to the curriculum; it needs a shift in perspective and worldview.

As Woodson (1933/2016) declared, this type of transformative curriculum would have great benefits for students of color and other minoritized students. For example, decades after Woodson's educational research and scholarship, the social psychologist Claude Steele and his colleagues would discover that the type of educational experience advocated by Woodson would actually reduce stereotype threat in African American students and other students of color. Steele (2010) writes about the power of "cues" in both perpetuating and alleviating stereotype threat. While much of Steele's research focuses on the demographics of the class (e.g., lone Black students are more likely to feel stereotype threat) and of the faculty (e.g., teachers and professors of color reduce stereotype threat for students of color), Steele also briefly examines the role of "environmental cues," focusing on the environment's inclusivity or hostility. In determining the role of environment, Steele asks, "Does [the] school value the experiencing of group diversity as integral or as marginal, to one's education? Is the school's leadership on the same page, or is there disagreement over this issue?... Is the expression of prejudice common, normative? Are some groups disdained...? Are people from different groups competitive with each other – on a group basis?" (p. 141). Steele admits that these environmental cues are often "incidental," meaning they are unconscious and usually natural to the environment. For example, if an English teacher hangs portraits of famous American authors in a classroom, and they are all white men, that could be a cue for the students of color and the female students in the class that their experiences, knowledge, and stories are not valued in that classroom. Many of these findings were confirmed in previous studies (see Inzlicht & Ben-Zeev, 2000; Murphy, Steele, & Gross, 2007; Purdie-Vaughns, Steele, Davies, & Crosby, 2008). In many ways, our curriculum acts as an environmental cue. If all of the readings we assign are written by authors of the same identity, students without that identity will not feel a sense of belonging and could instead feel stereotype threat (see Chapter 4). If all the topics in class are taught from a Western European lens, students who do not identify with the ethnic heritage might not feel a sense of belonging, and they will potentially feel stereotype threat. In sum, a "people's curriculum" could help alleviate the feelings of stereotype threat that so many of our minoritized students feel when coming onto our campuses.

Recently, I had the opportunity to discuss these very issues with a colleague in the biology department at my college. She was interested in creating a curriculum for her courses that covered the content as written in the course outline while also engaging in critical discussions about biology's complicity and even encouragement in promoting biological and cultural racism. It was an extensive discussion that cannot be covered here, but I'd like to highlight one example from our conversation – the biological classification system, or what is more accurately called taxonomy. When naming new species of living organisms, scientists rely on a Latin-based classification system that most of us simply refer to as an organism's "scientific name" (as opposed to its "common name"). For example – and in an homage to my home state – we are all familiar with the whiskered small mammal that frolics around kelp forests in California, the sea otter (which is its common name). Less of us may be familiar with its scientific name – *Enhydra lutris*. This scientific name includes the genus and species of the sea otter, or what is called binomial nomenclature, which are two components of a larger classification system that includes kingdom, phylum, class, order, and so on, and since the biological classification system is used globally, these Latin scientific names transcend any one language, making scientific research across the globe more efficient and consistent. Even less of us may know that this taxonomic system was the creation of a Swedish scientist by the name of Carl Linnaeus. The thing about Linnaeus, however, was that he was a raging racist who used his taxonomic system to, you guessed it, classify humans into different categories.

Ultimately, my colleagues in biology have to teach this classification system to their biology students, as it would be impossible for them to be successful not only in future courses but also in science careers without this knowledge. So what is a biology professor to do? First and foremost, biology professors need to be open to discussing not only the racist beliefs of the Linnaeus himself but also how he used his classification system to perpetuate racism and the American racial caste system. Many would argue that this is irrelevant to a science classroom and that taxonomy goes far beyond human classification. That is true – there are millions of species on Earth – but here's the most important consideration for biology professors – science, including the natural sciences, has historically and continues to be used to uphold and perpetuate racism, and if we are going to train a new generation of scientists who are able to disrupt this racism, we need their professors to be honest about the past and present vis-à-vis racism in the discipline. In other words, we can't eradicate racism in the sciences without first talking about it. Secondly, this discussion is one part of a much larger curriculum that not only exposes racism in the discipline and field but also celebrates and highlights the contributions of scientists and thinkers who come from minoritized communities. This discussion about Linnaeus can't stand alone; it must be part of a larger curricular transformation. With that, the next section of this chapter helps conceptualize that transformation, which includes a general introduction to the field of multiculturalism.

d. Practicum: "Folktales and Ethnic Foods" – Rejecting Tokenism and Embracing True Multiculturalism

Woodson and Zinn were essentially alluding to curricular decisions that we have come to term multiculturalism. Unfortunately, the term multiculturalism has gotten a bad rap in recent years after being co-opted and disfigured by policymakers, curriculum specialists, and well-meaning (and not-so-well-mining) educators. The problem is that people of color have been relegated to a slew of "firsts" (e.g., *first* Black astronaut, *first* Black president, *first* Black vice president, etc.) and to the role of tokens (e.g., "I'll add Toni Morrison to my curriculum to make it diverse"). Furthermore, as my colleague Jeremiah J. Sims (and editor of this book) argues, many well-meaning yet naïve, uninformed educators often do more damage under the guise of multiculturalism than they do with a purely Eurocentric curriculum. In one poignant example, Sims describes a math teacher who, in their attempt at multicultural education, asked her class of predominantly African American students to do mathematical word problems related to drug dealing. It should be pretty obvious that this exercise was highly problematic and inappropriate, and it speaks to harm that comes from the nexus of culturally relevant pedagogies and white ignorance of communities of color. True multiculturalism, however, rejects such trite curricular additions and misrepresentations and, instead, advocates for the inclusion of non-Western European peoples and knowledge that is at least on par with Eurocentric course content and its concomitant ideologies and norms. The remainder of this chapter will discuss multiculturalism in its true sense and how community college educators can remake their curricula in order to highlight and equally celebrate the knowledge, values, and achievements of people of color and other minoritized groups. Multiculturalism is not a "bad word"; it has just been used badly. If we return to the intent of multiculturalism as envisioned by educational pioneers like DuBois, Woodson, and Zinn, we can create curricula that empower our students of color in the same way as our European American students.

The multicultural education movement is over a century in the making, starting with the works of historian George Washington Williams in the 19th century (Banks, 1992). His early writings on African American history and culture would inspire educational theorists and practitioners, including Woodson and DuBois, to undertake a project of making teaching and learning more relevant and empowering for African American children. More recently, multiculturalism has taken on a more democratic project that strives to improve the schooling experience for all students. As James A. Banks (2004), one of the prominent thinkers of multiculturalism, writes, "A major goal of multicultural education... is to reform the schools and other educational institutions so that students from diverse racial, ethnic, and social-class groups will experience educational equality" (p. 3). For Banks and other educators, multiculturalism is a complete transformation – or "reform" – of the entire teaching and learning environment, extending from the classroom to the whole institution. Banks continues, "for multicultural education to be implemented successfully, institutional changes must be made in the curriculum; the teaching materials; teaching and learning styles; the attitudes, perceptions, and behaviors of teachers and administrators; and the goals, norms, and culture of the school" (p. 4). In other words, true multiculturalism is a total and holistic transformation of the classroom and institution.

Unfortunately, multiculturalism has been both co-opted and misunderstood. Many educators mistakenly believe that multiculturalism is akin to diversity and that adding a few writers of color to a curriculum makes it "multicultural." Even more problematic is the appropriation of multiculturalism for unscrupulous means, such as boosting enrollment or "checking the diversity box" on teacher evaluations or program reviews. As Banks (2004) notes, "many school and university practitioners have a limited conception of multicultural education, viewing it primarily as curriculum reform that involves only changing or restructuring the curriculum to include content about ethnic groups, women, and other cultural groups" (p. 4). As a result, authors of color and cultural artifacts from non-European communities are often "tokenized" or given the surface treatment mentioned previously by Swartz (1992). Ladson-Billings and Tate (1995) took such practices to task in their important article "Toward a Critical Race Theory of Education":

> Current practical demonstrations of multicultural education in schools often reduce it to trivial examples and artifacts of cultures such as eating ethnic or cultural foods, singing songs or dancing, reading folktales, and other less than scholarly pursuits of the fundamentally different conceptions of knowledge or quests for social justice. At the university level, much of the concern over multicultural education has been over curriculum inclusion. (p. 61)

In this critique, Ladson-Billings and Tate strengthen the notion that multiculturalism and critical pedagogy are intricately linked, and in order for the former to be effective, it must utilize the latter. In other words, multicultural education is about the transformational pedagogies discussed in Chapter 5. However, since many educators utilize one without the other, Ladson-Billings and Tate note that there is a "tension" between their conception of critical race theory in education and multicultural education. As they argue:

> Instead of creating radically new paradigms that ensure justice, multicultural reforms are routinely 'sucked back into the system' and just as traditional civil rights law is based on a foundation of human rights, the current multicultural paradigm is mired in liberal ideology that offers no radical change in the current order. Thus, critical race theory in education, like its antecedent in legal scholarship, is a radical critique of both the status quo and the purported reforms... we... underscore the difficulty (indeed, impossibility) of maintaining the spirit and intent of justice for the oppressed while simultaneously permitting the hegemonic rule of the oppressor. Thus, as critical race theory scholars we unabashedly reject a paradigm that attempts to be everything to everyone and consequently becomes nothing for anyone, allowing the status quo to prevail. (p. 63)

This is an important observation, and I concur with Ladson-Billings and Tate that multiculturalism can be used to maintain white supremacy and Western European hegemony in the classroom. Instead, justice-minded, critical educators must use multiculturalism in conjunction with a critical reality pedagogy in the pursuit of liberation. In other words, critical educators, by definition, must transform their curricula in a way that problematizes the status quo and promotes justice.

The reproduction of white supremacy and Western European hegemony is often the consequence of educators' incomplete understanding of what true multiculturalism is, especially as it was envisioned by its forebearers. Sleeter (1989) sees multicultural education as both "dynamic and growing" (p. 54). In her response to critics of multicultural education, Sleeter emphasizes its social justice component, or more accurately, the Multicultural and Social Reconstructionist approach of multicultural education, which "teaches directly about political and economic oppression and discrimination, and prepares young people in social action skills" (p. 55). More specifically, Sleeter views multicultural education "as a form of resistance to oppressive social relationships. It represents resistance on the part of educators to White dominance of racial minority groups through education, and also (to many) to male dominance" (p. 59). Sleeter suggests that true multiculturalism not only celebrates minoritized groups but also highlights the oppression that they experience. That means we can't, for example, water down the Civil Rights Movement by focusing only on MLK's "I Had a Dream" speech. King's other teachings and activism must be taught in conjunction with other activists, including Marcus Garvey, Malcolm X, the Black Panther Party, and, more recently, the Black Lives Matter movement. Indigenous American cultural practices have to be taught alongside the land theft committed by white Americans, including more recent Indigenous rights movements against injustice such as the water keepers and the protests of the Standing Rock Sioux Tribe. Similarly, critical educators must teach racism and white supremacy as a present danger – not something of the past – and they must go beyond the discredited belief that racism and white supremacy are problems of individuals and, instead, teach their institutional and systemic frameworks. Unfortunately, as she notes, the social reconstruction approach is often marginalized in favor of the overutilized Human Relations approach, which, as Ladson-Billings and Tate warned, emphasizes cultural celebrations. The unfortunate consequence of this approach is that "many who are relatively new to multicultural education do not see it as directly connected with political struggle" (p. 62). As such, oppression, resistance, and justice must be the foundation for a true multicultural curriculum.

To provide a general overview of the components of multicultural education as it has been conceived by its founder, I turn to Banks (2004), who describes the five dimensions of multicultural education. It will be easy to see that multicultural education goes well beyond curricular revisions.

Content Integration: Content integration is the most common dimension used in multicultural education, and it is the complete *overhaul* of one's curriculum. *Overhaul* is the operative word here, and this is where too many of us get into trouble. Too often, white educators try to make their curricula more inclusive or diverse by simply adding one or two authors of color or incorporating a few topics that they believe will be of interest to their minoritized students. Unfortunately, this easily leads to the tokenizing described by Ladson-Billings and Tate. Furthermore, these types of curricula continue to cling to the Eurocentric, white supremacist foundation of the course. Instead, we must reimagine our curricula and start from a place of pluralism. As Banks (2004) writes, "Content integration deals with the extent to which teachers use examples, data, and information from a variety of cultures and groups to illustrate key concepts, principles, generalizations, and theories in their subject area or discipline" (p. 4). The word "extent" here is ambiguous, but suffice it to say that it goes beyond the inclusion of a few authors or topics.

Furthermore, we must go beyond what Ladson-Billings and Tate call the "trivial examples and artifacts" of non-European cultures and communities. A true multicultural education adheres to the tenets of critical pedagogy as described in Chapter 5 of this book. For example, we need to engage in a dialogue with students on how people of color and other minoritized groups have been oppressed within our disciplines and because of our disciplines. As an English professor, for instance, I might open a dialogue about so-called "standard" English with my students and how this discourse has been used to oppress people of color. In my literature classes, we may critique the lack of Black and Brown voices in the canon and discuss how racism in education has not only prevented Black and Brown authors from telling their stories but also how discrimination in the publishing industry has kept those stories from the reading public for as long as mass publications have existed. In other words, we must discuss the legacy of racism and other forms of oppression in our curriculum. We can't talk about Carl Linnaeus and taxonomy without talking about how this system and its founders have used it to perpetuate white supremacy and to justify a racial caste system, a legacy that continues to this day. Our students live in a racialized world, and they will go out into a racialized workforce, and it is our responsibility – our obligation – to ensure that they are ready to disrupt the status quo – not propagate it.

Similarly, multicultural curricula empower students of color and other minoritized groups, but we also need to start recognizing that it is also of great value to white students and students that belong to other dominant groups. Racism, white supremacy, and even white privilege have negatively affected people of European descent. While we may enjoy many advantages and we may avoid race-based obstacles, these benefits come at a cost – our privileges create inequities for those who are denied such benefits, and such inequities are a blemish on our collective morality. To simply ignore the impact of whiteness – our whiteness – on people of color is wrong and immoral. We must teach our white students about the construction of race, including whiteness, and how it has created a racialized hierarchy based on white supremacy. And we can all do this in the context of our disciplines.

This is an important point. While ethnic studies and multiculturalism share the same roots, most of us are not ethnic studies professors. In other words, unless we teach in ethnic studies departments or disciplines (e.g., African American Studies, Asian American Studies, etc.), we are not teaching ethnic studies in our courses, as ethnic studies is a distinct academic discipline that scholars (mostly scholars of color) train for years in, which culminates in a graduate degree in that discipline. I write this because ethnic studies is continually under attack by other disciplines and from other colleagues who either don't see the value in the ethnic studies discipline (e.g., because these opponents promote color blindness) or believe they teach ethnic studies because they have a few authors of color in their curricula. Unfortunately, ethnic studies has been co-opted, appropriated, and gutted by ill-informed and sometimes malicious academics because of such views. Instead, we need to strive to create a curriculum within our own discipline that is multicultural and that utilizes the five dimensions as described by Banks. But ultimately, we must do so in the context of our own disciplines; we must, as the saying goes, "stay in our lane." Multiculturalism helps us do that.

The Knowledge Construction Process: Utilizing the content integration dimension alone has two fundamental problems: first, it tokenizes voices from non-dominant groups (e.g., adding one or two authors of color), and second, it presents these voices through a Eurocentric lens. In other words, we discuss these authors and topics in the context of European values, beliefs, norms, and knowledge. For instance, many educators in my discipline use Malcolm X's auto-biography in their courses, but often, Malcolm X is presented as a foil to Martin Luther King, Jr., or they may over-rely on humanistic discourses to condemn the actions of the racist individuals that tormented his family or to express sentiments that Malcolm X should not have had to change his appearance (e.g., straightening his hair). However, these perspectives normalize whiteness because they don't critique the structures and norms – that is, of Western Europe – that necessitated Malcolm X's decisions and activism. In a way, Western European hegemony becomes invisible, and as such, the oppression and marginalization experienced by communities of color remain unseen and unexamined or scrutinized. hooks (2015) can help us understand why this self-examination can be so difficult for us white educators in her writing about "whiteness in the black imagination." hooks describes, for example, classroom discussions where, during discussions about racism and whiteness, white students "respond with disbelief, shock, and rage, as they listen to black students talk about whiteness, when they are compelled to hear observations, stereotypes, etc., that are offered as 'data' gleaned from close scrutiny and study" (p. 167). As hooks suggests, these negative feelings are in response to a perceived betrayal of our country's investment in colorblindness and the "liberal belief in universal subjectivity (we are all just people)." However, I would contend that these feelings of "disbelief, shock, and rage" stem from anger over a breach of what Charles W. Mills (1997) calls the "racial contract," part of which allows whiteness and white supremacy to exist unacknowledged and unchallenged. For hooks, the origin of this invisibility dates back to the peculiar institution of chattel slavery (and even post emancipation), where Black folks were not allowed to walk on the same sidewalks as white folks or even to look at them, violations of which could result in physical harm and even death. Historically, Black people have been invisible to white people, and the latter, at least, believes that they are invisible to the former. hooks writes, "In white supremacist society, white people can 'safely' imagine that they are invisible to black people since the power they have historically asserted, and even now collectively assert over black people, accorded them the right to control the black gaze" (p. 168). I believe this dynamic is reproduced in our classrooms when we refuse to turn the gaze back on our curricula and teaching. As Derrick Bell (1992) insists, race and racism are ubiquitous and far-reaching, and each of our disciplines has and likely continues to perpetuate a racial caste system, both inside and outside our institutions. We need to make the invisible visible. We must have the courage to identify and scrutinize white supremacist values and beliefs in our curricula.

All of this is to say that our perceptions of reality are informed by Western European values, beliefs, taboos, norms, and mores, which are all borne from Western European epistemologies, or, more simply, Western European construction of knowledge. In multicultural education, the knowledge construction process helps us create a curriculum that critiques Eurocentric knowledge and highlights the knowledge production of minoritized communities and cultures. As Banks (2004) writes, "The knowledge construction process describes the procedures by which social, behavioral, and natural scientists create knowledge, and the manner in which the implicit cultural assumptions, frames of reference, perspectives, and biases within a discipline influence how knowledge is constructed within it. When the knowledge construction process is implemented in the classroom, teachers help students to understand how knowledge is created and how it is influenced by the racial, ethnic, and social-class positions of individuals and groups" (p. 4). Many critics might argue that the knowledge and content that they teach are absolutely necessary to their discipline, but it is worth asking, who decided which knowledge was required in our disciplines? In my own discipline – composition and literature – many would point to Matthew Arnold who is considered one of the forebearers of the English canon, coining the phrase "the best that has been thought and said." Said another way, the basis for how American literature teachers of all levels present their discipline to students from all backgrounds and walks of life has been based on the opinion of one British educator and literary critic. A critical educator, however, will acknowledge that the canon – or the privileging of any body of work or knowledge – is a by-product of those in power and the subjectivity of their tastes, values, and beliefs. A critical educator, "rejects the prevailing orthodoxy that scholarship should be or could be 'neutral' and 'objective'" (Crenshaw, Gotanda, Peller, & Thomas, 1995, p. xiii).

Banks theorized four approaches to curriculum reform – contributions, additive, transformation, and social action:

> The *contributions* approach focuses on heroes and heroines, holidays, and discrete cultural elements. When using the *additive* approach, teachers append ethnic content, themes, and perspectives to the curriculum without changing its basic structure. In the *transformation* approach, which is designed to help students learn how knowledge is constructed, the structure of the curriculum is changed to enable students to view concepts, issues, events, and themes from the perspectives of various ethnic and cultural groups. In the *social action* approach, which is an extension of the transformation approach, students make decisions on important social issues and take action to help solve them. (p. 15)

Banks is again speaking to the importance of critical pedagogy, specifically critical reality pedagogy. The first two approaches are uncritical, and they do little to challenge the status quo or prepare students to enter a society and workforce that is built upon racial hierarchies. The latter two, however, allow the students to see society through the lens of minoritized peoples and prepare them for identifying and challenging prejudice and oppression in the world. In many ways, the knowledge construction process dimension is all about the *lens* we use in the class or whose perspectives and knowledge we are privileging, and it becomes clear that true multiculturalism – the multicultural education that its founders envisioned – was intricately linked with critical pedagogy. As Ladson-Billings (2009) argues, when we decenter Western European epistemologies to make room for traditionally marginalized and omitted knowledge, "students real-life experiences are legitimized as they become part of the 'official curriculum'" (p. 117). Our students won't know that you read this books or books like it; they'll just see their experiences and their cultural heritages and ways of knowing normalized in the curriculum. That is powerful and empowering.

Prejudice Reduction: The prejudice reduction dimension focuses on students' racial identifications and their attitudes toward their classmates and teachers of color. This dimension is the work of antiracism. As Banks writes, "The prejudice reduction dimension of multicultural education describes the characteristics of children's racial attitudes and suggests strategies that can be used to help students develop more democratic attitudes and values... [and] help students develop positive racial attitudes and values" (p. 5). Multicultural research has been predominantly focused on how children perceive race and how they develop an awareness of race early in their lives. As Banks summarizes, many researchers over a period of seventy years have consistently found that children develop an awareness of race as well as racial attitudes as early as three years old.

While Banks notes that the research on prejudice reduction is often mixed, there seems to be one common thread among them – curricular interventions and antiracist teaching practices. An early study by McGregor (1993) found, for example, that intergroup interactions are simply not enough to eradicate personal racist beliefs. This makes sense – white folks and people of color have been in proximity to each other for centuries, and in theory, many schools have been desegregated for decades. Yet racist beliefs and prejudice still exist. Instead, McGregor notes that the curriculum must shine a spotlight on oppression, injustice, and the systems that propagate them, either through role-playing or curricular interventions like films, readings, and discussion. In other words, antiracist educators, as mentioned previously, must make the invisible visible. It is important to note that McGregor is arguing for pedagogies and curricula that go far beyond the "cultural information program": "Antiracist teaching confronts prejudice through discussions of past and present racism, prejudice, stereotyping, and discrimination in society. That approach differs from a cultural information program because it is not the understanding of cultural differences that is important, but the awareness of the economic, structural, and historic roots of inequality, for which racism is a justification" (p. 216). In fact, in the studies that McGregor reviewed, it was found that the "cultural information program" is highly ineffective in eradicating racist beliefs, a conclusion confirmed by Ladson-Billings and Tate (1995) in the admonition of privileging cultural artifacts over the lived realities and oppression of minoritized people.

Most of the research in this dimension is focused on children and the K-12 system, so what does this mean for community college educators? There are two primary takeaways from the literature on prejudice reduction. First, our students' racial attitudes and racial identities are deep-seated by the time they arrive in our classrooms. Nonetheless, many of our "traditional aged" students (and even many of our older students) are open-minded and curious. They want to learn from us, and it means a lot when they are learning about social justice in classes other than ethnic studies and sociology. While role-playing (one of McGregor's suggestions) might be less effective for our students, we can have real, deep discussions with them that serve the mission of antiracism and social justice. Second, we must go beyond individual racial beliefs and attitudes and focus also on institutional and systemic injustices. As McGregor notes, "education cannot be expected to alter the structure and balance of power in society" (p. 215). This may be true, but as college educators, we have a unique opportunity to impact the world outside our campuses, as we are training our society's future professionals, whether they are pursuing a terminal A.A. degree or transferring to a university. Our proximity to the students' lives as professionals and citizens creates some promising opportunities for disseminating antiracist values and activism.

Equity Pedagogy: An equity pedagogy is one in which community college educators see the students as unique individuals with unique needs and, as a result, educate the whole student. This type of pedagogy is opposed to one in which each student gets the same materials, the same teaching, and the same support – this is equality. Since equity-minded educators are concerned with the success of all their students and understand that students may be privileged in some ways and disadvantaged in others, they tailor their pedagogical approaches to the needs of their students. As Banks (2004) writes, "An equity pedagogy exists when teachers use techniques and methods that facilitate the academic achievement of students from diverse racial, ethnic, and social-class groups" (p. 5). Among other things, this dimension is cognizant of the students' learning styles, and equity-minded educators create lessons and discussions that account for the students' learning strengths. In many ways, an equity pedagogy is a critical pedagogy that engages the students on their own turfs. It invites students to bring their own interests and "funds of knowledge" into the classroom (Gonzalez, Moll, & Amanti, 2005; Moll, Amanti, Neff, & Gonzalez, 1992). But the bottom line – and this must be said – equity-minded educators are mindful of their students' struggles in the class, and they go out of their way to support that student (or find the right support with them). An equality pedagogy gives every student the same educational experience regardless of need; an equity pedagogy gives each individual student what they need to succeed and to find fulfillment in their education.

Empowering School Culture: Finally, multicultural education is the transformation of the whole college. As Banks (2004) writes, it is "the process of restructuring the culture and organization of the school so that students from diverse racial, ethnic, language, and social-class groups will experience educational equality and cultural empowerment" (p. 6). This dimension alludes to the elimination of what Delpit (1988) calls the "culture of power," which she argues makes such a transformation impossible. In her ethnographic study of white teachers and teachers of color, Delpit found that the latter were often excluded from discussions on how best to educate students of color, and when teachers of color were invited to the table, their contributions were often disregarded and even derided. Delpit describes five components to the culture of power: "1) Issues of power are enacted in classrooms; 2) There are codes or rules for participating in power; that is, there is a 'culture of power'; 3) The rules of the culture of power are a reflection of the rules of the culture of those who have power; 4) If you are not already a participant in the culture of power, being told explicitly the rules of that culture makes acquiring power easier; 5) Those with the power are frequently least aware of – or least willing to acknowledge – its existence. Those with less power are often most aware of its existence" (p. 282). See Sims et al. (2020) for institutional strategies for eliminating this culture of power and "empowering the college culture."

So what do these tenets look like from a curricular perspective? It may help to first think about whose epistemologies, beliefs, and values inform the basis of the curriculum – white, middle-class, heterosexual, cisgender males – and who controls the curriculum – individual members of the faculty, department chairs, and curriculum committees, who are, as mentioned in Chapter 1, predominantly middle-class, white folks. As a result, the culture of our classrooms, whether intentional or not, replicates the power dynamic between European American and people of color in society, writ large. As a result, we need to use the dual approaches of critical reality pedagogy and multicultural education to start dismantling the culture of power in the classroom. It is worth noting that classrooms and colleges that are inclusive of the knowledge, figureheads, values, and artifacts of minoritized students reduce the pernicious effects of stereotype threat (Steele, 2010).

As Banks (2004) notes, "The five dimensions are conceptually distinct but highly interrelated" (p. 6). And while Banks suggests that each dimension could function independently, I contend – as I believe Banks would – that a truly multicultural education utilizes all five dimensions. Any one dimension alone is not enough to transform a classroom or college in the pursuit of educational equity and social justice. In fact, we have seen this when teachers and professors over-rely on a dimension like course integration, which only tokenizes certain writers and thinkers and further marginalizes students of color. Furthermore, it is not enough to simply celebrate their cultures and heritages. Multicultural education, critical reality pedagogy, and social justice are not about diversity or even inclusivity. They are about power – who holds the power, how that power manifests, and how we can collectively dismantle that power.

Ultimately, this section was not meant to be exhaustive, but rather an introduction to multiculturalism, which hopefully provided some clarification on a scholarship and practices that have suffered from too much misinterpretation and misunderstanding. Like the rest of this book, this section and chapter are broad overviews that will hopefully inspire readers to continue to delve into the very robust corpus of knowledge about educational equity and justice in the curriculum. In the meantime, I'd like to suggest some quick strategies for an antiracist, truly multicultural curriculum:

- Discuss with your students what race and racism are and make sure you avoid the "race has no biological basis...we're all the same, so we should just get along" argument. This is akin to a colorblind pedagogy, which, as Bonilla-Silva (2017) has taught us, is just another form of racism. Instead, acknowledge that even though race may not be a biological fact, people are "raced" and that their racial identity either provides privileges or it subjects them to oppression, discrimination, violence, and trauma. Acknowledge that racial injustices and the American racial hierarchy are not the consequences of individual racists, but the intentional by-product of an economy and government that serves to protect white supremacy and Western European thought.

- Similarly, discuss how your discipline has perpetuated racist beliefs and racial hierarchies (and their intersections with gender, class, and sexuality). For example, in my composition classes, I openly discuss how our privileging of so-called "standard English" has resulted in what Baker-Bell (2020) calls anti-Black linguistic racism. Similarly, I openly discuss the exclusion of authors of color from the traditional English literary canon and how scholars and publishers have privileged the voices of white authors over authors of color. Likewise, if you teach economics, explain racialized capitalism. If you teach chemistry, explain why very few of the chemists you teach about are scientists of color. If you teach real estate, make sure the students understand housing discrimination and how it still exists today. Every discipline is culpable in perpetuating systemic and systematic racism, and we need to own up to that. Anything less is tacit endorsement of the racial hierarchy.

- Incorporate the epistemologies, values, and prominent individuals from communities of color that have contributed to your discipline. And while this may feel uncomfortable, it is important to unseat the Western European focus of your course and make it one small part of the overall course. That way, you can include the knowledge and achievements of non-European countries and non-European Americans. We have to end the "add-on" or "a la carte" approach of including a person or two of color in a curriculum and discussing them through the lens of Western European knowledge and norms.

- Introduce tools and practices in your discipline that can be used to eradicate racial injustice (and if there are none, come up with them). As mentioned previously, our students are on the precipice of starting their careers and adult lives. They will go out into a world that is organized by race, and they need the knowledge and tools to dismantle our American caste system in their spheres of influence and in their careers. For example, your real estate students should go into their careers as agents and brokers with the ability and desire to change their agency or professional organization. Your future chemists should ask why they don't have Black and Brown colleagues and fight for more inclusion.

e. Practicum: Broader Considerations for Equity-Centered Curricula

This book (and therefore, this chapter) is primarily focused on the classroom or on educators' courses as singular curricular units. However, the classroom as a learning space and singular unit is inextricably linked to the larger institution, from the department to which it belongs to the college, at large. And while my colleagues and I have written about equity and justice in community colleges as larger institutions (see Sims et al., 2020), I think it is worth mentioning two structures that inform the classroom unit – academic program development and the curriculum approval processes (e.g., course outlines).

First, we need to start having conversations as academic departments and degree programs about the type of educational experience and curricula that we are offering our students. While one or two equity- and justice-minded professors in a department are better than none, it is not good enough for a fraction of the program's students to get a nurturing, affirming experience. Department and program faculty and staff must convene and have the difficult conversations about Eurocentricity, white supremacy, anti-Blackness, and other forms of prejudice that exists within their curricula. This may require retreats or meetings facilitated by equity experts from outside the institution or a collective social justice inquiry project. However, it is important that there is action. Program requirements need to change. Student learning outcomes need to change. The department's culture and processes – from hiring to evaluations to curriculum development – need to change. The course outlines need to change. The faculty and staff need to decenter whiteness and European hegemony, and each educator needs to undergo the reflective practices described in Part I of this book, and the culture of power described by Delpit needs to be eradicated. Furthermore, we need to collectively heed the call by Ladson-Billings

Speaking of course outlines, our institution's curriculum committees have an important role to play in ensuring that the college's courses are appropriate and relevant to the student body being served. Indeed, curriculum is one-third of the triple helix that continues to perpetuate Eurocentrism and white supremacy. The curriculum committee, then, has two very important tasks: eradicating tokenism and promoting transformational curricula. In the former, curriculum committees should create rubrics, potentially using the five dimensions of multicultural curriculum, that will help committee members determine the extent of the course outlines' representations of minoritized peoples, epistemologies, histories, and values. If a course outline only adds them "a la carte," then the curriculum committee can provide feedback for revision. In the latter, curriculum committees can uphold standards for transformation courses that are, as Cohn and Mullenix (2007) call them, "diversity-rich." Diversity-rich courses "include other voices... communicate interconnectedness... value diversity and equity... [and] promote transformative thinking" (pp. 14–17). This final characteristic is key, and it separates a "diversity-rich" course from what Cohn and Mullenix call an "inclusive" course. Transformation is, of course, an important component of a classroom wherein critical pedagogy is used and where the student-teachers and the teacher-student collaboratively discuss real-world and community issues. Curriculum committees should consider including similar tenets in a rubric to be utilized by the course authors, those in the course approval workflow, and the members of the curriculum committee.

f. Chapter 6 Synopsis and Questions to Consider

Synopsis

Justice-centered curriculum development is the inseparable partner to critical reality pedagogy, but transforming one's curriculum can be a great deal of work since the college curriculum, or the "official knowledge" of the academy, at large, is steeped in centuries of Western European history, epistemologies, values, and norms. This Eurocentric tradition has created a system of higher education, including community colleges, that has perpetuated white supremacist beliefs and the otherizing of minoritized and traditionally marginalized communities. The question we need to ask ourselves is, "Who does this official curriculum benefit?" Instead, we need to replace this curriculum with a "people's curriculum" that decenters Western Europe and whiteness and that elevates the histories, epistemologies, and values of communities of color and non-European civilizations, and we can do this by adhering to a multicultural framework built on equity and social justice. Taken together, a critical reality pedagogy and a people's curriculum can empower students, engage them in the work of academia, and equip them to transform their communities and lives.

Questions to Consider

1. How does the history of American higher education help us better understand the types of curricula that are ubiquitous in community colleges?
2. What is the "official curriculum"? Who does this "official knowledge" (or official curriculum) benefit? Why?
3. How would you define a "people's curriculum"? How can your own curricula better align with this definition?
4. Why has multicultural education been taboo in educational circles in recent years? How can a multicultural curriculum go awry?
5. What is multiculturalism, and what are its five tenets? How is multiculturalism different from "diversity"?
6. How can you integrate discussions of race, racism, and Eurocentricity in your classroom, especially as they relate to your discipline?
7. What can academic programs and institutional curriculum committees do to promote antiracist, multicultural curricula?

Keywords: official curriculum, master script, triple helix dilemma, multicultural education, curriculum committees

g. References

Apple, M.W. (1979/2019). *Ideology and curriculum* (4th ed.). New York: Routledge.

Apple, M.W. (1993/2014). *Official knowledge: Democratic education in a conservative age* (3rd ed.). New York: Routledge.

Baker-Bell, A. (2020). *Linguistic justice: Black language, literacy, identity, and pedagogy.* New York: Routledge.

Banks, J.A. (1992). African American scholarship and the evolution of multicultural education. *Journal of Negro Education, 61*(3), 273–286.

Banks, J.A. (2004). Multicultural education: Historical development, dimensions, and practice. In J.A. Banks & C.A. McGee Banks (Eds.), *Handbook of research on multicultural education* (2nd ed.). San Francisco: Jossey-Bass.

Bell, D. (1992). *Faces at the bottom of the well: The permanence of racism.* New York: Basic Books.

Bonilla-Silva, E. (2017). *Racism without racists: Color-blind racism and the persistence of racial inequality in America* (5th ed.). Lanham, MD: Rowman & Littlefield.

Campaign for College Opportunity. (2017). *Left out report.* Retrieved from https://collegecampaign.org/left-out-tool/

Cohn, E.R., & Mullennix, J.W. (2007). Diversity as an integral component of college curricula. In J. Branche, J. Mullennix, & E.R. Cohn (Eds.), *Diversity across the curriculum: A guide for faculty in higher education* (pp. 11–17). Boston: Anker Publishing.

Crenshaw, K., Gotanda, N., Peller, G., & Thomas, K. (1995). *Critical race theory: The key writings that formed the movement.* New York: New Press.

Delgado, R., & Stefancic, J. (1989). Why do we tell the same stories?: Law reform, critical librarianship, and the triple helix dilemma. *Stanford Law Review, 42*(1), 207–225.

Delpit, L.D. (1988). The silenced dialogue: Power and pedagogy in educating other people's children. *Harvard Educational Review, 58*(3), 280–298.

Gerber, L.G. (2014). *The rise and decline of faculty governance: Professionalization and the modern American university.* Baltimore: Johns Hopkins UP.

Gonzalez, N., Moll, L.C., & Amanti, C. (Eds.). (2005). *Funds of knowledge: Theorizing practices in households, communities, and classrooms.* New York: Routledge.

hooks, b. (2015). *Black looks: Race and representation.* New York: Routledge.

Ikard, D. (2018, March). *David Ikard: The real story of Rosa Parks – and why we need to confront myths about Black history* [Video file]. Retrieved from https://www.ted.com/talks/david_ikard_the_real_story_of_rosa_parks_and_why_we_need_to_confront_myths_about_black_history/info-details?language=en

Inzlicht, M., & Ben-Zeev, T. (2000). A threatening intellectual environment: Why females are susceptible to experiencing problem-solving deficits in the presence of males. *Psychological Science, 11,* 365–371.

Isensee, L. (2015, October 23). Why calling slaves "workers" is more than an editing error. *NPR.* Retrieved from https://www.npr.org/sections/ed/2015/10/23/450826208/why-calling-slaves-workers-is-more-than-an-editing-error

Ladson-Billings, G. (2009). Just what is critical race theory and what's it doing in a *nice* field like education? In E. Taylor, D. Gillborn, & G. Ladson-Billings (Eds.), *Foundations of critical race theory in education* (pp. 17–36). New York: Routledge.

Ladson-Billings, G., & Tate, W.F. (1995). Toward a critical race theory of education. *Teachers College Record, 97*(1), 47–68.

Lederer, A., & Oros, S. (2020). *Lending discrimination within the Paycheck Protection Program.* Washington, DC: National Community Reinvestment Coalition. Retrieved from https://ncrc.org/lending-discrimination-within-the-paycheck-protection-program/

Macedo, D. (2000). Introduction. In P. Freire (Ed.), *Pedagogy of the Oppressed* (pp. 11–27). New York: Continuum.

Magee, R.V. (2019). *The inner work of racial justice: Healing ourselves and transforming our communities through mindfulness*. New York: TarcherPerigree.

McGhee, H. (2021). *The sum of us: Wht racism costs everyone and how we can prosper together*. New York: Penguin Random House.

McGregor, J. (1993). Effectiveness of role playing and antiracist teaching in reducing student prejudice. *Journal of Educational Research, 86*(4), 215–226.

Mills, C.W. (1997). *The racial contract*. Ithaca: Cornell UP.

Moll, L.C., Amanti, C., Neff, D., & Gonzalez, N. (1992). Funds of knowledge for teaching: Using a qualitative approach to connect homes and classrooms. *Theory into Practice, 31*(2), 132–141.

Murphy, M.M., Steele, C.M., & Gross, J.J. (2007). Signaling threat: Cuing social identity threat among women in a math, science, and engineering setting. *Psychological Science, 18*(10), 879–885.

Purdie-Vaughns, V., Steele, C.M., Davies, P.G., Ditlmann, R., & Crosby, J.R. (2008). Social identity contingencies: How diversity cues signal threat or safety for African Americans in mainstream institutions. *Journal of Personality and Social Psychology, 94*, 615–630.

Robinson, K. (2006, February). *Do schools kill creativity?* [Video file]. Retrieved from https://www.ted.com/talks/sir_ken_robinson_do_schools_kill_creativity?language=en

Robinson, K. (2010, October). *Changing education paradigms* [Video file]. Retrieved from https://www.ted.com/talks/sir_ken_robinson_changing_education_paradigms

Sims, J. J., Taylor-Mendoza, J., Hotep, L., Wallace, J., & Conaway, T. (2020). *Minding the obligation gap in community colleges: Theory and practice in achieving educational equity*. New York: Peter Lang.

Sleeter, C.E. (1989). Multicultural education as a form of resistance to oppression. *Journal of Education, 171*(3), 51–71.

Steele, C.M. (2010). *Whistling Vivaldi: How stereotypes affect us and what we can do*. New York: Norton.

Swartz, E. (1992). Emancipatory narratives: Rewriting the master script in the school curriculum. *The Journal of Negro Education, 61*(3), 341–355.

U.S. Census Bureau. (2019). *QuickFacts: San Mateo County, California*. Retrieved from https://www.census.gov/quickfacts/sanmateocountycalifornia

Warth, G. (2017, August 29). 'Black Minds Matter' under fire from conservative group. San Diego Union-Tribune. Retrieved from https://www.sandiegouniontribune.com/news/education/sd-me-black-minds-20170829-story.html

Woodson, C.G. (1933/2016). *The mis-education of the Negro* [ebook edition]. Digireads.com

Zinn, H. (1980/2003). *The People's History of the United States: Abridged teaching version*. New York: New Press.

7

The Time for Action is Now

In the aftermath of the George Floyd murder and during the nationwide (even global) protests for racial justice in the summer of 2020, many white folks were quick to express sympathy for and solidarity with their friends, colleagues, and family members of color. During one academic senate meeting in my district, we were discussing how we could leverage our purview over academic and professional matters to promote equity and achieve racial justice. For example, we were interested in revamping our faculty hiring and evaluation processes and in critiquing how our bylaws were barriers to participation in the senate, among other things (for more information about this type of institutional work, see Sims et al., 2020). Because of this meeting's timing and topics (and the fact that it was easily accessible on Zoom), we had several colleagues of color attend, and during the discussion, many of them shared their stories of racism both inside and outside the institution. There were tears, apologies, and likely a lot of guilt from the white folks in the "room." These types of discussions would span several meetings, and to make a long story short, several of my white colleagues professed that they were "allies." The problem is that this word – "ally," especially when coupled with "white" – is often hollow and facile. Unfortunately, I have seen too many white colleagues claim to be "white allies" in one moment and in the next say or do something overtly racist. In one instance, a colleague claimed to be an ally just to, months later, rail against the necessity or even legitimacy of ethnic studies and to perpetuate colorblind approaches to social justice.

This type of white allyship has been labeled as "performative allyship" (Phillips, 2020). In distinguishing between "true allyship" and "performative allyship," Phillips writes, "An ally is someone from a nonmarginalized group who uses their privilege to advocate for a marginalized group. They transfer the benefits of their privilege to those who lack it. Performative allyship, on the other hand, is when someone from that same nonmarginalized group professes support and solidarity with a marginalized group in a way that either isn't helpful or that actively harms that group" (par. 5). With this in mind, I'd like us to ask ourselves what we are doing to actively support our friends and colleagues of color when we say we're allies because simply stating that we are allies "isn't helpful." Even more pointedly, Phillips critiques the spike in white allyship just after an officer-involved killing, asking, "Where are you the other 364 days a year when anti-racism isn't trending?" (par. 3). And in the era of Zoom, we often see the wave of Black Lives Matter and #sayhername virtual backgrounds in the immediate aftermath of racial violence only to see them come down as the news – at least in our circles – dies down. Unfortunately, the word "ally" has simply become a way for us white folks to cut through the tensions of race during conversations and debates and is a modern form of saying "I'm not racist." Even more perverse, allyship has become a wicked form of voyeurism in which white folks are able to participate in the pain of their friends and colleagues of color without actually doing any work to alleviate that pain outside of apologies and hugs.

I have never once called myself an ally (though I have friends and colleagues who would call me this). This may be because of my upbringing in a multiracial family – I never once heard the word ally until I was in academia – or my general aversion to such labels (I don't call myself a feminist either, and it wasn't until the Jan. 6 Capitol riot that I joined a political party), but I think the primary reason is that it the word is hollow; it has never felt comfortable. I have witnessed so many so-called allies describe themselves as such while doing nothing to eradicate anti-Blackness or racial injustice, and I have seen too many white folks call themselves allies while simultaneously saying or doing things that are racist and that maintain the American racialized hierarchy. As a result, I have steered away from the term.

This book will conclude with a call to action, which starts with the rejection of the term "white ally," or at least the public utterance of it to describe ourselves. Ultimately, it comes down to what we do and how we act. Do we claim to be an ally just to turn around and promote some racist policy? Or do we call ourselves an ally and then work to dismantle that policy? And ultimately, why do we even bother with the declarative phase of this process – why not just dismantle the racist policy? The actions make the declaration obsolete because the actions demonstrate that we are antiracist. This is why others refer to me as an ally even though I do not identify as one myself – they see my actions, which speak for themselves.

So what does action mean for us? Well, it depends on our spheres of influence – a congressperson has a very different responsibility for eradicating racism and racist structures than a physician or a banker does, for example. Furthermore, this book is for community college educators, which comes with a whole set of antiracist responsibilities and obligations that these other folks do not have. We can't create legislation (though we can advocate to our elected officials), we can't dismantle the white body supremacy that exists in the medical field, and we can't eliminate racialized lending discrimination. But we can change our classrooms, our institutions, and our profession. We can disrupt the status quo in the community college. As Chapter 1 highlighted, little has changed for hyper-marginalized students in community colleges since 1960s despite numerous federal and state initiatives and billions of dollars; that is because top-down initiatives can rarely permeate the entire institution or even a substantial number of its classrooms, not to mention widespread feelings of initiative fatigue and the decontextualization of successful programs once they've been scaled up. The problem of educational inequity and the project of racial justice demands something closer to home. It demands a form of grassroots equity where educators identify the very unique experiences, knowledge, and needs of their very unique student body in order to recreate an institution that works for all students. In other words, community college educators must think more locally about who their students are, where they come from, and what they need from their professors and their colleges.

a. Practicum: Self-care for Antiracist Educators

Because this is such an exhausting personal and professional undertaking, it is important for antiracist educators to develop a strong self-care routine. With that being said, always remember that racism has been and will always be more exhausting for our colleagues of color, and in some instances, even detrimental to their health (James, 1994; James, Keenan, Strogatz, Browning, & Garrett, 1992). I'd like to conclude this chapter by offering some tips for dealing with the fatigue, overwhelm, and stress associated with this important work.

1. Keep work at work: I'm not talking about grading or lesson planning here! Rather, I am referring to your antiracist and social justice work. First, you are under no obligation to be available to colleagues or students after you go home for the evening or weekend, so feel permitted to turn off your email or to ignore text messages and phone calls until business hours. And if something happens at work that is related to this social justice project, leave it there, which leads me to my second recommendation.

2. Create a network of antiracist, equity-minded colleagues: If something happens at school, whether it is in the classroom, in a meeting, or in some other space, utilize your network for processing and reflecting on it. For example, imagine that you are having a class discussion on a racially charged topic, say the Colin Kaepernick/NFL controversy, and a student says something racially insensitive that sparks a tense, maybe even hostile, classroom exchange. A student of color approaches you after class and says that she felt unsafe and microaggressed during the conversation, which creates a great deal of guilt and stress for you. The antiracist, equity-minded colleagues in your network can help you process this situation and, yes, even critique and push you to take responsibility.

3. Know you have support: It can be quite uncomfortable to advocate for educational equity and social justice on campus, and it is certain that you will experience criticism from resistant colleagues. You will likely be called a "reverse racist" or accused of "playing the race card." However, there are likely other advocates on campus. Seek them out and build a network that will help you not only build a broader coalition but can also help you process the struggles that come with this work. Similarly, when you are promoting more equitable policies, curricula, and other departmental or institutional changes, it helps to have allies who can join you in this fight. Much of the equity work that my college's academic senate successfully undertook was only possible because there was a large contingent of equity-minded, antiracist senators on the committee.

4. In that same vein, know your mission: When you inevitably make a racial faux pas in class or when you are confronted with resistance from colleagues, remind yourself of why you are doing this work. Always keep in mind why you are fighting for justice. It has also been helpful for me to bring to mind my colleagues who are also doing this work, which is especially useful when anguishing alone. You are not alone in this journey, and there are colleagues and students who are looking to you to continue on even after you've stumbled.

5. Teachers are not therapists: One of the inevitable consequences of this type of work is a peek into the lived realities of our minoritized students, which means we will see the poverty, the emotional and physical trauma, and a host of other barriers and very personal issues. We will want to act as unofficial therapists to our students, and while there is nothing wrong with lending an ear or working with students to keep them current in their schoolwork, we need to avoid the temptation of offering advice for their personal situations, of diagnosing trauma, addiction, or disabilities, and of providing treatments for psychological or emotional trauma. Almost every institution of higher education either employs personal therapists or has the capacity to make referrals. In this way, we become resources for navigating students to the services they need, so if you don't know where students can go on campus to get help with mental or emotional needs, learning disabilities, housing, food insecurity, or the like, do your research!

6. Relinquish control: This is a hard one for many educators because we have been trained to be the leaders in the classroom and to always be prepared for the class (even for things we can't foresee). But overdependency on control will always lead us back to the safety of what we know and are comfortable with, which means we will revert to our old pedagogies and our old curricula. I'd like to argue that relinquishing control often leads to the most exciting, productive classes. One of the tenets of the Umoja Community, an Afro-centric student success program in California, is "live learning":

> Live learning is risky; it is freewheeling and open. The instructor yields control of meaning and understanding in the classroom while keeping a keen eye on learning as it is emerging. Live learning implies that the learning experience is generative and performative. In a live learning situation, the exact content and learning experience are not known before the class session begins. Surprise and original language burst out all over the classroom; the instructor facilitates and culls the learning that is happening. Live learning intentionally captures and documents learning in real time. It is a way of having a discussion that really flies, while focusing the insight, capturing it on boards and in notebooks, so the discussion does not disappear after the students leave the class session. It is democratic and analytically rigorous at the same time. Live learning demonstrates to the students through their own words that language is powerful; ideas and texts are rich and can be made their own. Most importantly live learning demonstrates to the students that they are smart, deep. ("Umoja Practices")

In other words, be prepared for class but let go of where the students take the course material. As mentioned earlier in this chapter, our students have a great deal of cultural capital to bring to the classroom, and an important component of critical thinking is making connections between course content and their existing schema and experiences.

7. Be genuine: In order for live learning to take place, you need to be "real." We can't get agitated or uptight when lesson plans don't go as planned, and we need to be genuinely excited when our students engage with the course materials, even if they may come to a wrong conclusion or veer off-topic. Furthermore, we need to not only be genuine as we give the students more agency in class, but we also need to be transparent. It is ok to share with our students that we are undergoing this transformational journey and that we are struggling to understand race, racism, and white supremacy better, especially as they shape institutions of higher education. In fact, this only helps us keep the class in the event that we commit a gaff or say something insensitive. I have yet to be in a class where the students were not forgiving and supportive when I have slipped up. If they know your heart is pure, they will always give you the benefit of the doubt.

8. Build your "racial stamina": In her book *White Fragility*, Robin DiAngelo (2018) emphasizes the importance of developing our abilities to continually engage in discussions of race and to continually critique our own privilege and power. This "racial stamina" is particularly important in situations where conversations about race become uncomfortable and, sometimes, quarrelsome. As DiAngelo (2018) writes, "An antidote to white fragility is to build up our stamina to bear witness to the pain of racism that we cause, not to impose conditions that require people of color to continually validate our denial" (p. 128). In other words, we need to be able to understand the violence that we inflict on people of color with our comments and actions without running away from the conflict. This is the only way that we can begin to mend the trauma of racism and to reclaim the humanity that racism has deprived us all of. But at the most fundamental level, this "racial stamina" requires us to "name our race" – we need to understand how white supremacy has created a racialized hierarchy in our country and how we both benefit from and perpetuate this system (p. 1).

b. Practicum: Radical Compassion

In her book *Radical Compassion,* Tara Brach (2019) discusses how awareness – or as she calls it, "clarity" – gives way, or makes room, for feelings of compassion. Brach's book is focused primarily on meditation and how mindfulness practices can lead to self-compassion and compassion for others. This book is not about meditation, and I am not advocating for a hybrid spirituality-antiracist framework, but I think some of her points are salient. Brach argues that many of us live life in a sort of "trance – a partially unconscious state that, like a dream, is disconnected from the whole of reality. When we're in trance, our minds are narrowed, fixated, and usually immersed in thought. Our hearts are often defended, anxious, or numb... You are in trance when you are living on autopilot, when you feel walled off and separate from those around you, when you are caught up in feeling fearful, angry, victimized, or deficient" (p. 4). Community college educators have a lot on their plate. When we aren't teaching and grading, we are serving on institutional committees, assessing our courses and degrees, serving on hiring and evaluation committees, advising student clubs and organizations, writing grants, creating new courses and curricula, and a host of other tasks. It is not surprising that we fall into the trance that Brach speaks of nor that we tend to ignore issues of racial justice and racial inequity. It is just so easy for us to put the blinders of white privilege on at will. Similarly, when we find ourselves in situations where race, racism, and white privilege are brought to light, we often react with the white fragility and white guilt theorized by Matias (2016), DiAngelo (2018), and Flynn (2018), respectively, both of which have many of the characteristics of Brach's trance.

If there exists a substantial overlap between the "trance" and racial ignorance, then Brach's solution for the former may be of use for the latter. Without delving into the intricacies of Brach's RAIN meditation practice, it is worth discussing her concept of "radical compassion," which she describes as an "awakening" that "frees us from this confining trance" (p. 42). To review Chapter 4, compassion is shown when one goes beyond the feelings of anguish and simple statements of sympathy to significant actions that not only eliminate another's suffering but also work to eradicate the root cause of that suffering. While Brach's conception of "radical" is elusive – it is never defined – one could take it to mean the rejection of the status quo. It is about becoming more aware of one's surroundings and the experiences of others. As Brach writes, the "basic elements of radical compassion [are] clarity, openhearted presence, and emotional intelligence" (p. 176). In a way, radical compassion is a call to "go against the grain," and in the context of this book, it is a *moral imperative* to wake up to the racialized experiences that all Americans experience (whether we recognize them or not), to understand and accept that white supremacy and its offspring white privilege actually harm and traumatize people of color (including friends, family members, colleagues, students, acquaintances, and strangers), and to *actively* work to eradicate the source of this violence within our spheres of influence.

I do not use the word "moral" lightly. However, if you have made it this far into the book, it is safe to assume that you accept this reality. You have "awakened" to the pain and suffering of racism, anti-Blackness, homophobia, transantagonism, nativism, white supremacy, misogyny, Islamophobia, and classism that exists all around us. And once we see it, can we truly unsee it? Not to overdo it on the *Matrix* citations, but there is a well-known scene in which the character Cypher sells Neo out to Agent Smith in exchange for being "plugged" back into the Matrix with no memory that it isn't real. In other words, Cypher, after seeing the suffering outside the Matrix, was willing to take the proverbial "blue pill" so that he may unsee it. After reading this book, I hope that you see that the veil of color blindness and post-racialism are, like the Matrix, simply not real and that the reality is that, as Cornel West (1994) argues, "race still matters."

Ultimately, the question is whether you are willing to "take the blue pill" and return to a state of ignorance about race, racism, and other forms of hatred. Are you ok with the continued suffering and trauma experienced by people of color? Are you ok in becoming, again, an agent of that suffering? Are you ok with blindly accepting the privileges of being labeled as white even though that means that your privileges take away opportunities and resources from people and communities of color? And since the blue pill doesn't exist and there is no magical remedy for "plugging" back into racial ignorance, are you willing to ignore the racial oppression around you knowing full well that it is happening?

Or instead, do you practice "radical compassion"? Do you go against the majority of white Americans and see what is really happening around you? Do you reject the nihilism of so many of our white peers that explains racism away as natural and unchangeable? Do you awaken and dedicate, at the very least, your professional life to eradicating the roots of white supremacy and racial violence in your spheres of influence? I argue that it is absolutely a *moral* imperative that we stop talking about race, racism, and allyship and that we start taking action, that we engage in radical compassion. Conversely, it would be absolutely *immoral* of us to retreat back into white ignorance or to accept racial oppression as the natural state of our society.

The time to act is now, and if the Trump era has taught us anything, it is that hatred, intolerance, and racial violence have never been relegated to the fringes of our society (and to be clear, our colleagues of color have been telling us this for decades). We can't get bogged down in the academic conversations about equity that end up stalling the fight for justice. We must heed Macedo's words about Paulo

Freire: "Freire's denunciation of oppression was not merely [an] intellectual exercise... [he] represented for those of us committed to imagine a world, in his own words, that is less ugly, more beautiful, less discriminatory, more democratic, less dehumanizing, and more humane" (pp. 12, 25).

Ultimately, it comes down to one final question: will we join the fight for racial justice or will we find a place on the sidelines... will we sit down or will we stand up?

c. Chapter 7 Synopsis and Questions to Consider

Synopsis

It is time to take action in the fight for racial and social justice!

Questions to Consider

Just one: will you join the fight or sit it out?

Keywords: performative allyship, radical compassion

d. References

Gujndjsdjsn *Iyubgsiasdb* Tubjjdsn

Brach, T. (2019). *Radical compassion: Learning to love yourself and your world with the practice of RAIN.* New York: Viking.

DiAngelo, R. (2018). *White fragility: Why it's so hard for White people to talk about racism.* Boston: Beacon Press.

Flynn, J.E. (2018). *White fatigue: Rethinking resistance to social justice.* New York: Peter Lang.

James, S.A. (1994). John Henryism and the health of African-Americans. *Culture, Medicine, and Psychiatry, 18*(2), 163–182.

James, S.A., Keenan, N.L., Strogatz, D.S., Browning, S.R., & Garrett, J.M. (1992). Socioeconomic status, John Henryism, and blood pressure in black adults: The Pitt County study. *American Journal of Epidemiology, 135*(1), 59–67.

Matias, C.E. (2016). *Feeling white: Whiteness, emotionality, and education.* Rotterdam: Sense.

Phillips, H. (2020, May 9). Performative allyship is deadly (here's what to do instead). *Forge.* Retrieved February 2, 2021, from https://forge.medium.com/performative-allyship-is-deadly-c900645d9f1f

Sims, J.J., Taylor-Mendoza, J., Hotep, L., Wallace, J., & Conaway, T. (2020). *Minding the obligation gap in community colleges: Theory and practice in achieving educational equity.* New York: Peter Lang.

West, C. (1994). *Race matters.* New York: Vintage.

The Epilogue: Love as Praxis by Jeremiah J. Sims

In this, the Epilogue, I am going to eschew tradition in some small measure. It has been held as taboo, in English classes far and wide, to introduce new information at the conclusion of a text. Nevertheless, in this text, I will do just that. I am not a betting man, but if I were, I feel it a safe wager that the vast majority of books are not written in one sitting. This book is no different. I have continued to teach community college students in a program titled: The Initiative in Diversity, Equity, Antiracism, and Leadership (IDEAL). In fact, we are in the process of developing a book proposal so that we can write about our experiences with love as praxis.

Praxis, as defined by Freire (2000), is a recursive process of understanding theory, then putting into practice said theory; then, finally, reflecting on both the theory and the practice to ensure that it achieved liberation. Reflection is key. John Dewey challenged a revered axiom when he argued that experience is not, in fact, the best teacher. Instead, Dewey argued that reflecting on experience is where real, potentially transformative learning takes place. This epilogue, then, is a reflection on what I learned from IDEAL and from the many opportunities, which I have been blessed with, to lead educators on conversations, workshops, and trainings on race, equity, inclusion, and justice (REIJ).

The Context

As I wrote earlier on in the introduction, regarding 2020, it has become abundantly clear that the events of 2020 will go down as a seminal year in the history of this country. Our so-called democracy was laid bare. We witnessed the differentiated ways that people—based on race, gender, and socioeconomic status—were forced to navigate all of the calamities that occurred in 2020 (civil unrest, protest, acts of state-sanctioned violence, natural and manmade calamity, all seemingly just below consciousness the exponential growth of the wealth gap). As you all know well, the year 2020 in many ways pulled back the proverbial curtain regarding the two interrelated pandemics that poor, ethnoracially minoritized people of color (PERMPOC) were forced to navigate. One pandemic, COVID-19, has fundamentally changed the way that society functions. Additionally, COVID-19 has, simultaneously, highlighted and worsened many of the systemic inequities that are baked into both our historical and extant sociopolitical realities. The other, much older pandemic, racialized capitalism working in the interest of white Supremacy, has been (disproportionately) wreaking havoc on Black, Indigenous, and Other Peoples of Color (BIPOC) for centuries.

We cannot lose sight of this fact: this shift, essentially, transformed the shape and function of education. Question began to bubble of regarding the efficacy and usefulness of traditional models of education. Phrases that seemed to signal a kind of melancholic resignation like "the new normal," began to be more and more prevalent in common parlance. This phrase worked to, simultaneously, announce an acceptance of the current state of affairs as informed by a seemingly never-ending global pandemic, and a pining lament for a return to the "normalcy" of pre-COVID America. It must be said that the old normal, the pre-COVID-19 normal, was still incredibly problematic for poor ethnoracially minoritized students of color.

In the name of public safety, precautionary measures developed to mitigate the spread of COVID-19, caused unprecedented, monumental shifts in educational spaces that, prior to COVID-19, functioned primarily in person. I saw firsthand on my college campus, and also heard stories from friends and colleagues, about newfound demands placed on school administration, staff, and, especially, faculty. Educators were being asked to transform courses that were developed to be in-person, to fully online courses, in less than a week. Many of these educators had never before taught fully online courses. Nevertheless, talented, committed educators did the work like they always do. In 2020, I was presented with the opportunity to continue on in this work in a way that was markedly different to the administrative work I had been involved in for nearly a decade. I was tasked to co-develop a program for community college students in the Pacific Northwest. This program, the Washington State Guided Pathways IDEAL Fellowship, welcomed its inaugural cohort in early 2021.

I have been blessed to lead conversations, nationwide, on the seemingly intractable institutionalized obstacles to realizing educational equity. Obviously, white supremacy, racialized capitalism, anti-blackness, and cis-heteropatriarchy form an intersectional nexus of oppression and harm. But what I want to take up here is what I have termed the Four A's. The first "A" is axiom. An axiom is a thought that is considered to be unquestionably true even without empirical substantiation. For example, if I ask someone what a Q-tip is, or what a Kleenex is, they can usually picture and subsequently describe it. But not all cotton swabs are q-tips; q-tip simply controls the lion's share of the market. And not all facial tissues are Kleenex, but like q-tip, Kleenex controls the lion's share its market.

In many circles, it is axiomatic that irrespective of the actual brand, all cotton swabs are q-tips. These examples are innocuous. But, according to the Italian Marxist philosopher, Antonio Gramsci, this is how hegemony works. Hegemony controls what is considered to be commonsensical or axiomatic. This is important because there are pernicious, stereotypical commonsensical/axiomatic ideas that claim that black students come from cultures that do not value education, or that students form whom English is not their first language are inherently deficient in some way. These axiom are not innocuous. They are dangerous because they inform both individual and institutional practices. When institutions do not radically analyze the institutionalized axioms that govern how they interface with students, they run the risk of becoming ambivalent.

The word ambivalence denotes an unwillingness to take a position (and, in this context, an unwillingness to wrestle with privilege). Ambivalent people are perpetual, professional fence-riders. The problem is that the proverbial fence, in our educational milieu, is an additional obstacle that poor, ethnoracially minoritized students of color have to overcome. So, when people are ambivalent, when they sit atop the fence, they are necessarily fortifying the weight of the fence so that it becomes more difficult to move. There is no liminal space in this work. If we're on the fence, we are contributing to oppression. So, we must eschew ambivalence at all costs. If we're not ready to fight for justice, because we have not been impelled by radical love, then we need to move out of the way. Because if ambivalence goes unchecked, it becomes apathy.

To be apathetic means to be beyond feeling. If axioms go unchecked, institutional ambivalence is soon to follow. If institutionalized ambivalence goes unchecked, institutional apathy is soon to follow. Institutional apathy can be characterized by an unwillingness or an inability to be moved by the human condition of hypermarginalized students. Of course, individuals can be apathetic; but individuals who are apathetic cannot subvert the work of a school that is empathic and compassionate. However, once the institution becomes apathetic, it is very difficult to move in a way that is justice-centered and equity-advancing. We cannot be beyond feeling. We must be motivated by a radical love for justice if we ever hope to achieve educational equity. I want to be clear on this point: if an institution becomes apathetic, this apathy will eventually transmogrify into an incurable institutionalized antipathy.

Antipathy is characterized and he would define by deep disdain. We see these types of things in greater society as well as in our institutions. People who complain about Black Lives Matter, for example, by lamenting the loss of property or the disruption convenience are actually blaming oppressed peoples for reminding them of their privilege. Instead of interrogating the macrostructural systems that privilege certain groups of people, strictly by virtue of the families that they were born into, antipathy employs a recriminatory strategy (Sims, 2018). Calls for real justice explode the mythology of meritocracy. The people that benefit from white supremacy (the peoples racialized as white) like to believe that their hard work and dedication is what has won their favor. Because meritocracy is not real, the tenuous arguments that hold these positions together fail under scrutiny.

When these faultiness are uncovered, the response has been the systemic and systematic blaming of people victimized by white supremacy, racialized capitalism, and cis-heteropatriarchy for their own (purported) cultural or gendered deficiencies. Antipathy leads to recrimination (i.e., blaming the victim). Institutional antipathy is the death knell of equity and justice efforts. This is why radical leadership, predicated on radical love, is integral. We have to avoid antipathy at all costs. In order to do that, we have to address the preceding three A's in a way that lays them bare so that they can ultimately be eradicated. These Four A's and their varied manifestations have been and continue to be the greatest obstacles in my work and the work of so many others who want to see real, transformative educational justice. I have been committed to leading brave conversations on the identify and call out institutional inequity. I have designed extended professional development programs that center race, equity, and inclusion. I have also developed a tool, the IMPACT (Innovative, Measurable, Purposeful, Antiracist, Caring, and Transformative) Equity Evaluation Toolkit (Gable, O'Sullivan, & Sims, 2021) and a concomitant training that helps my college and a number of other colleges audit their institutionalized policies, practices, procedures, and pedagogies in order to ensure that they are commensurate with justice. In order to achieve justice, we have to confront and, ultimately, overcome the abovementioned (institutionalized) Four A's. How can we counter the Four A's? In addition to functioning as indefatigable love and justice warriors, we must continue to empower, encourage, and equip our precious students to fight for justice. In the following section, I will speak to a program that was designed to serve this function with a diverse group of community college students in the Pacific Northwest.

Love as Praxis: The Initiative in Diversity, Equity, Antiracism & Leadership (IDEAL)

The goal of the *Initiative in Diversity, Equity, Antiracism and Leadership (IDEAL) Fellowship* is to encourage, empower and equip IDEAL Fellows to advocate for justice, not just in the classroom but also at the policy and procedural level. Fellows will be helped to understand what equity can look like in the community college system, as well as society writ large. We examine how community colleges can function as disruptive technologies that disrupt macrostructural inequity (Sims, et al., 2020). In order to do this, IDEAL Fellows spend time analyzing extant literature on educational equity and justice, and they become adroit in applying their knowledge to real-life situations by using the IMPACT Equity Toolkit in order to make recommendations to their respective colleges. By the end of the program, IDEAL Fellows present to their respective colleges regarding ways for their campus to become more equity-advancing.

Snapshot of IDEAL Cohort One

- More than 600 applicants for 30 spots
- Diverse in age, race/ethnicity, college, majors, employment, family status, knowledge, and experience in equity work
- Cohort 1 – 1 semester, 8 sessions; Cohort 2 – 6 weeks, 6 sessions
- Current topics, guest speakers, community, alumni network & IMPACT project
- Weekly office hours, but available 24/7
- $1000 stipend for fellows
- IMPACT Equity Practitioner Certificate
- Continued presentation and speaking opportunities

The IDEAL Approach

From its inception here in the United States, the institution of compulsory K-12 public education has been a tool to mechanically reproduce a certain type of student (Althusser, 1971). To be more precise, K12 schooling here in the United States is designed after a factory model that reproduces a Eurocentric, middle-class aesthetic. This is why our schools have failed far too many poor ethnoracially minoritized students of color (PERMSC). According to recent reports, 80 percent of America's teaching force self-identifies as European American and what is more, more than 65 percent of all teachers are, in fact, European American women. These demographic numbers hold true in higher education, too. European American teachers, whether female or male, are not incapable of teaching PERMSC simply by virtue of their differential ethnoracial identities. Nevertheless, the reality for the vast majority of PERMSC students is that they will encounter very few teachers who come from where they come from, and very few teachers who look like them.

Understandably, many instances of cultural dissonance are created by this dynamic. The IDEAL Fellowship Program was created as a space where the issues that spring out of this cultural mismatch can be addressed, and ultimately redressed by empowering IDEAL Fellows, via research based, agency-inciting pedagogical techniques, to work toward equity and justice in all aspects of their education. More simply put, IDEAL Fellows are encouraged, empowered, and equipped to advocate for themselves as well as other poor, ethnoracially minoritized students of color (PERMSCs).

Students Don't Care About What You Know Until They Know That You Care...

In IDEAL, we endeavored to engender a positive, and empowering atmosphere where students' identities do not have to be compromised in order to achieve academic success. We work to do this, at the curricular level, by providing space where I, as the program lead, work to carve out opportunities for students to discuss, interrogate, and disrupt the negative stereotypes that they feel have been sutured to their identities simply by virtue of who they are, where they were born, and to whom. Hypermarginalized students of color are rarely afforded these kinds of dialogic opportunities in traditional schooling. I have found that intentionally carving out spaces, within a given educational milieu, for hypermarginalized students to recognize, discuss, interrogate, and disrupt their marginalization has shown marked increases in student engagement. It is my view that student gains in competence and understanding are predicated on student engagement. And what is more, I have found that engagement, though sometimes hard-won, has everything to do with relationships (Sims, 2018).

Relationships

Relationships are key to the educative process; in fact, I have found that the educative process becomes less difficult when authentic, generative, and trusting relationships begin to develop between students and educators, irrespective of age (Mahiri & Sims, 2016; Sims, 2018). It is my belief that any students' cognitive and psychosocial growth, in large part, can be attributed to healthy, nurturing, and supportive relationships, which is why I work to ensure an atmosphere that is holistic. Holistic educational atmospheres, educational atmospheres that are radically inclusive, are conducive to growth intellectually, practically (as measured by empirical progress) and psychosocially. Radical love has to impel this work. Furthermore, for this to be realized, IDEAL Fellows were encouraged, empowered, and equipped to understand and demonstrate high-order empathy and, simultaneously, a form of cultural sensitivity (based on understanding) that is empowering as opposed to dismissive and disempowering. I wanted IDEAL Fellows to develop agency; however, the goal is not only to build them up individually. Rather, this Leadership Academy was designed to help IDEAL Fellows (students) commit to radical love as praxis. That is to say, the goal of the IDEAL Fellowship Program was to help students reimagine and fight for justice for themselves and for all of the students that have been systemically and systematically denied it.

Pedagogically, the goal of this program is to create agency-inciting opportunities for community college students to radically reimagine how they can commit to anti-racism and how they contribute to the transformation of the educational experiences for all students, especially hyper-marginalized students. Concomitantly, the goal of this program was to foster an inclusive and welcoming environments, predicated on radical love, that disrupt structural barriers and welcomes, validates, and celebrates all students. There can be no real, transformative equity work without radical love. We, were, working to develop a kind of Beloved Community in the spirit of the Beloved Community Rev. Dr. Martin Luther King, Jr., fought so hard for; the same community that he, unfortunately, died for.

This program for me, and my co-developer – in life and in love – Rachel Sims, was a labor of love. In fact, love, or more specifically radical love was and is central to the form and function of this program. Dr. Cornel West argues that "tenderness is what love looks like in private; justice is what love looks like in public." I think that Dr. West is essentially arguing that where tenderness is lacking, in private, interpersonal relationships, love is absent; and, concomitantly, where oppression – based on race, socioeconomic status, gender, religion, and/or sexual orientation (or the intersections thereof) – exists, love is absent. Radical love necessitates a radical reimagining of structures of power; it demands paradigm-shifting interrogation; it is proactive, holistic, transformative, and it is invested in treating chronic diseases like anti-Blackness, white supremacy, and racial capitalism, et al.

According to West (King, 2015) radical love is not possible without radical integrity, which means that we have to willingly sacrifice the cowardly self, which is cold, defensive, and selfish. The cowardly self resists love and is therefore incapable of reciprocating (philia) love, and is adversarial to real, radical unconditional (agape) love. In order to get to radical integrity, we must arrive at radical humility. Radical humility necessitates the daily dying of the cowardly self so that the courageous self can live, and love--without fear. Radical love has to be predicated on radical honesty, too. When truth is present, there is synchronicity between word and deed. This synchronicity results in radical integrity. In educational spaces, word and deed have match for individuals and institutions. For example, mission statement that speaks to a college's commitment to PERMSC and to equity and just must be accompanied by a budget that makes manifest the commitments offered in a mission statement, or vision and goals, or solidarity statement. Incommensurability between word, in this instance, some form of extrinsic commitment to justice, and the actual measures taking to bring these promises to fruition is not only bad faith – it's also dishonest.

The point of radical love, in our educational context, is to arrive at a radical (love-based) analysis of inequity, oppression, and injustice. Radical love will impel us to commit to radical analysis of our institutionalized and personal, idiosyncratic policies, practices, and pedagogies so that we can identify and root out the inequities baked within. Not only this, but our radical analysis must also result in action, action designed to first mitigate, and subsequently eradicate the inequities built into our institutional and personal ways of doing school. The IDEAL Fellowship was devised to create a safe space for community college students to radically analyze inequitable institutional policies, practices, procedures, and pedagogies. The goal of this analysis was to encourage, empower, and equip IDEAL

Fellows to develop and design ways to address and redress the harms caused by institutional (mal)practices that disproportionately impact PERMSCs. I will not go into great detail regarding the inner workings of the IDEAL Fellowship in this book, because I, along with several IDEAL Fellows, am working on a manuscript that speaks to the transformative efficacy of this innovative program. There is, however, an attached document in Appendix (1.1) that outlines the scope and sequence of the IDEAL Fellowship. That said, I will provide a high-level overview of this program, especially for educators interested in replicating this program in some measure. The educational transition catalyzed by COVID-19 left educational institutions and individual educators scrambling to create thriving online educational communities. There was a prevailing lamentation in educational circles that decried the loss of engagement and community due to the abrupt switch of educational modality. Quickly, the goal for committed educators inhered around creating and curating virtual communities of engaged meaning-making and knowledge creation. With IDEAL, we achieved this.

The Beloved Community: IDEAL

Radical love is necessary, even integral, in order to develop a beloved community as defined by Rev. Dr. Martin Luther King, Jr. Our goal was to create a program that is characterized by and built upon a foundation of inclusivity and belongingness. That said, we did not just want IDEAL Fellows to feel that they were included and that they belonged; rather, we wanted them to feel loved,

> Love is creative and redemptive. Love builds up and unites; hate tears down and destroys. The aftermath of the 'fight with fire' method which you suggest is bitterness and chaos, the aftermath of the love method is reconciliation and creation of the beloved community. Physical force can repress, restrain, coerce, destroy, but it cannot create and organize anything permanent; only love can do that. Yes, love – which means understanding, creative, redemptive goodwill, even for one's enemies – is the solution [...].– *Martin Luther King, Jr., 1957*

We wrestled with complex theoretical material, graduate-level critical and critical race theory, and we asked these undergraduate students to transform these theories into actual, measurable social change. The work was rigorous. But here is the thing about rigor: rigorous course content – with proper supports – helps students learn; rigorous course content without proper support is burdensome and stultifying. Some educators hide behind anachronistic conceptions of rigor in order to avoid doing educational/pedagogical work that centers equity and justice (Sims, 2018). This is unfortunate, and it is also wrong. Rigor and high expectations are components of good teaching; however, blind adherence to outdated concepts of rigor cause more harm than good. Rigorous course content has to be offered in a way that is culturally relevant (Smitherman–), culturally sustaining (Paris & Alim, 2017), and liberatory. Here is what I am really trying to say: transformative pedagogy – pedagogy that helps all students reach their fullest academic potential – must be predicated on and impelled by a radical love of justice. Otherwise, it is deadening and oppressive. IDEAL was an attempt to develop an educational program that instantiated this positionality. It was not perfect, but it was good. But thankfully, you do not simply have to take my word for it. This point is further elucidated by the responses of IDEAL Fellows to a post-program review survey:

What, if anything, was different about IDEAL vis-à-vis other justice-centered programs you have participated in?

- The community bonds are paramount. I have a hard time opening up and trusting folks when navigating a new space, and this space was a breath of fresh air. The speakers we listened to were passionate and willing and open to speak, and Jeremiah and Rachel made themselves available and accessible in the most nurturing of ways. With all that foundation and true expression of love in a "professional" space, I felt like I could take on anything. (Marissa, 29, IDEAL Fellow, Community College Student)
- THIS is IT! The most real justice centered program I've been a part of. (Hector, 32, IDEAL Fellow, Community College Student)
- I think being in a loving, nurturing, and accepting space was a little more of a shock for me than I was anticipating. I keep talking about how I have a hard time trusting new experiences and tend to take a long time to open up. And this was no different. A lot of the traumas of a system that does not center all of me or understand all that I am takes over. I tend to believe that people in this work say the talking points, but essentially don't mean it or are so invested in a certain system, that that gets in the way of authentic and true connection. The authenticity in constantly reassuring that this is for real, and the love is for real and centered in justice – really touched me in a way I didn't think it would. To be fully honest, I'm still processing all that I received during this short time. (Eve, 19, IDEAL Fellow, Community College Student)

- Once acclimated, I believe I was fully engaged – both in group time and in the lecture period. The chat where we students worked through and commented on the topics was a powerful way to build knowledge and understanding of the material and fostering a sense of community. I was a bit surprised by the strong sense of community built up – both in our groups and with the cohort as a whole. I have attended many Zoom meetings and classes, but none left me feeling a part of a community as much as IDEAL did. Further, it was a spot of encouragement to meet others interested in radical change as activist circles can be a bit fatalistic and draining. (William, 49, IDEAL Fellow, Community College Student).

What Do You Feel was the Main Strength of This Program (IDEAL)?

- The main strengths of the IDEAL fellowship are the accessibility of material, community building, individual empowerment, and personal interactions with experts in their relative field. The material provided, while on complex and nuanced topics, was presented in such a way that even those relatively inexperienced with equity work in an academic way could quickly be given the tools to understand and materially contribute to the discussions. In having a community of students from different backgrounds but interested in developing skills to do equity work, it fostered a strong sense of community – even over Zoom. Being able to take individuals' experiences with inequity and identify the way in which the system works to manufacture said inequity and discuss as a group how we can work together to tackle said inequity is a powerful bonding experience. Said system is a monstrous, many-headed hydra. At first, on an individual level, that feat – which we must accomplish – can be quite discouraging. But the seminars and presentations by those doing equity work and making real, material changes to combat the system show that progress is possible. In short, the IDEAL fellowship is a potent antidote to both the feelings of inadequacy those new to equity work often feel and to the fatalism that often pervades activist spaces. (Joel, 26, IDEAL Fellow, Community College Student).

Would You Recommend This Program to a Friend?

- Yes, absolutely. I was very presently surprised by the diversity of the group with regards to gender and sexuality. It was beyond a "safe space." It was an "affirming space" – where everyone's identity and experience was often celebrated and seen as a lens from which we all can learn from. (Lisa, 22, IDEAL Fellow, Community College Student)

Which Topic Covered, This Semester, was Most Eye-Opening?

- Racialized capitalism – I think typically racism and capitalism are presented as two separate systems of oppression/power, when in reality, they are inseparably connected. One doesn't exist without the other, particularly in America. Viewing them as the connected construct – racialized capitalism – allows us to work toward dismantling it. If one only works to dismantle one aspect – capitalism or racism -- the other aspect will keep the system entrenched. (Freedom, 25, IDEAL Fellow, Community College Student).

IDEAL is still going. We will soon welcome our third cohort. IDEAL is not perfect. We are constantly fine-tuning the program so that it does no harm. I am bringing it up here because this is a guide to equity. Equity cannot be realized without a radical love for justice. Like many of you, I knew this intuitively, and I have had glimpses of this in reality. However, IDEAL was different in that I got to see (and contribute to) critical transformations predicated on radical love as praxis. I would be remiss if I did not share this with you all.

Lessons Learned

Remember, radical love, which is made up by important components like radical integrity and radical humility (King, 2015) in the final stage, results in a radical analysis of inequity and justice from the vantage point of people systemically victimized by racial capitalism, white supremacy, anti-blackness, misogyny, homophobia, etc. When conducting research, researchers must wrestle with a key axiological question: will my findings simply describe phenomena, or will my findings allow me to address the phenomena uncovered. The analyses that are borne out of radical love are interested in the latter, not the former. Radical love catalyzes a radical analysis that seeks to fuel socially just societal change. What is more, a radical analysis makes this important point clear: equity is indispensable; however, it is not the end goal – justice is (Sims et al., 2020).

How can we move closer to this reality? I am glad that you asked. We must willingly walk the talk by deepening individual and institutional understanding of what it means to be justice-centered, so that we can insist on and, subsequently, catalyze institutional transformation. We must also demonstrate a commitment to justice by doing the work, not just reading, ruminating, and talking about it. We must deepen individual (and institutional) understanding of how disruption of current policies, procedures, practices, and pedagogies must be arrived at by working in solidarity WITH student. We must break down silos so that we, as committed educators/practitioners, can foster connections across a network of justice-centered community college/educational leaders and practitioners. We must be willing to function as conduits of justice-centered disruption, which means that we must question both our quotidian and anomalous policies, practices, procedures, and pedagogies. We must work to employ an intersectional analysis of inequity in order to arrive at solutions that empower, encourage, and equip all of our students to reach their highest human and academic potential.

Returning to the ethos of the first section of this book, if we hope to achieve educational equity and justice, we must tell the truth. The truth is that for PERMSCs, living in a country that normalizes racialized, macrostructural inequity – albeit while denying its very existence – is soul-crushing, spiritually-deadening, and potentially fatal (Sims, 2018; Sims, et al., 2020). There is no solidarity, no justice, without self-criticality. Everyone committed to justice work must account for how they show up to the work and how their privilege informs their positionality; this is self-criticality. Self-criticality requires unadulterated honesty. We are individually and collectively responsible to tell the truth. It is important to reflect on how far we have come. It is also equally important to continue to push against macrostructural white supremacy and anti-blackness and other forms of racism, so that we can continue to move forward toward a just society.

We have to challenge our individual and collective understanding of how things came to be. We must be willing to confront the lies that have become axiomatic. We must be willing to hold our institutions accountable. We must be willing to fully engage with Impactful work and to build solidarity by doing the work. We have to demonstrate radical humility and radical integrity so that radical love can take hold and grow. We have to be self-reflective and have grace for others. We must speak the truth in love! Educators working toward equity must work from an asset-based educational paradigm. Equity efforts must be intentional. Educational equity must be arrived at via a partnership between students and faculty, staff, community, and administration. This work must produce educational spaces that are predicated on radical inclusivity.

Radically Humanizing Pedagogy and Radical Inclusivity

Let's say that I built a beautiful banquet hall, which is filled to overflowing with the best foods. But, because I have my own insecurities, fueled by cultural ignorance--and these insecurities have led me to believe that human difference is hierarchical and that some people are better than others based on who they were born too--I do not allow people that are different for me into this space. This causes an uproar. People argue that my banquet hall is exclusionary. Then, based on the mounting societal pressure, I acquiesce. I agree to create space for people that are different than me. I even allow them to sit at my dining table. In this particular example, I, like all of my initial dining companions, have ready access to food and drink, and we have access to food outside of this banquet hall as well. But let's say, sticking to this metaphor, that I invite people in who do not have the same economic means. Well, they are in the banquet hall now, right? I let them in. They are even "at the table". They are, by definition, they are now "included". Surely, that's progress. We can even say that there's a kind of integration that has taken place. But, because I still have work to do on my understanding of equity and justice, I refuse to give them any food. Again, the fictive people in this example are in the banquet hall, they are "at the table". Ostensibly, they have been included; but, in reality, they have not been given what it is that they need to be successful. This is not real inclusion, even tough—for far too long—it has been celebrated as such.

Radical love produces radical inclusion

The above example illustrates what inclusion has looked like for the past 15 years. The focus has been on simply making space for people to sit at the proverbial table, without accounting for whether or not the table is socially, intellectually, and spiritually sustaining. This is the difference between inclusivity and radical inclusivity. With radical inclusivity, the goal is always to create a space that foments social, intellectual, and spiritual transformative opportunities, especially for hypermarginalized students. Precisely because they are in an environment where they feel affirmed, valued, and loved. What is more, an environment that is predicated on radical inclusivity should encourage, empower, and equip all students to reach their fullest academic and human potential. Pedagogy and programming that are built on a foundation of radical love as praxis are not simply interested in achieving traditional (Europocentric) student learning outcomes. Rather, this kind of work is interested in affording students every opportunity to realize their academic and human potential while also encouraging, empowering, and equipping them to contribute to a more just society. This is the standard for radical love as praxis. Are students growing academically? Are they growing humanly? And, are they interested in contributing to a more just society? These are the guiding questions for this kind of work.

Radical love is the catalyst for radical inclusivity. In classroom spaces, radically humanizing pedagogy functions as the bridge from radical love to radical inclusivity. According to dictionary.com, the definition of radical is: relating to or affecting the fundamental nature of something; Far reaching and thorough. The way that we operationalize "radical/radicality" builds on this definition. For Rooted in Love, the word radical means that a reimagining is going on so that current structures of asymmetrical power are being identified, interrogated, and interrupted. That is to say, for work to be radical, by our definition, this work has to shift paradigms so that what has been and what is currently acceptable, individually, and institutionally, is called into question. The goal of this work is to make that which is acceptable, again both individually and institutionally, commensurate with social justice. Every day we have an opportunity to redouble our efforts to achieve equity and justice for all of the people we serve. This is a really important point. The goal of this radical analysis is to audit our policies, practices, procedures, and pedagogies, so that our campus environments instantiate radical inclusivity.

For us, the inclusion that has been championed in many educational circles is anemic and powerless because it is not predicated on radical love. Instead, it is a move to simply make space for (other) people without accounting for how the space should be or is designed either to their benefit or, in the case of far too many hypermarginalized students, to their detriment (Sims, 2018). Radically inclusivity goes much further in that not only acknowledges human experience, but also affirms the variegated human experiences that poor ethnoracially minoritized students of color experience. And, this is crucial, it works to identify interrogate and ultimately interrupt policies practices, procedures, and pedagogy's that are incommensurate with justice. Radical inclusivity must be the goal. To get here we need to understand and ultimately employ a radically humanizing pedagogy that embraces radical love. In order to achieve radical inclusivity, we have to create an educational atmospheres that champion, affirm, and empower all of the students we serve to reach their fullest academic and human potential while under our care. Inclusivity is not a new concept for people who have been committed to the DEI work. Even people who are not, in fact, have heard about and even use rhetoric around inclusion. This anachronistic concept of inclusion is not enough. We have to fight for radical inclusivity.

Radical inclusivity is a byproduct of radical love. Within this orientation there is radical affirmation and radical (re)positionality. This means that we reposition ourselves vis-a-vis the students that we serve. It's not enough to just create spaces for students that are hypermarginalized, or in more common educational parlance, to provide "access" Instead, we need to make sure that the spaces that we create, and curate are culturally relevant, affirming, healing, and sustaining. More simply put educational spaces, in order to be equity-advancing, must be designed so that they feed the souls of our students. We must celebrate students' beautifully intersectional identities and carve out space for them to reach the fullest academic and human potential because this is what radical love does. What is more, an environment that is predicated on radical inclusivity should encourage, empower, and equip all students to reach their fullest academic and human potential. Pedagogy and programming that are built on a foundation of radical love as praxis are not simply interested in achieving traditional (Europocentric) student learning outcomes.

Rather, this kind of work is interested in affording students every opportunity to realize their academic and human potential while also encouraging, empowering, and equipping them to contribute to a more just society. Radical inclusivity should be the standard because it is liberatory, affirming, and agency-inciting. We need radical love to make this real. Radical inclusivity not only address harm; it also creates spaces to heal (Ginwright, 2022).

In Conclusion

This work is always multipronged. We have to commit to and work toward eradicating the underlying causes while, simultaneously, treating the pernicious symptoms of racism. In order to do this work, we have to commit to radically analyzing and, subsequently, improving our systems to root out systemic, institutionalized white supremacy and anti-blackness as well as other forms of racism. Anti-racism must be infused in every aspect of our work – such as but not limited to our mission statement, resource allocation, hiring practices, curriculum, and policies – to create a culture of equity. We have to acknowledge that racism is systemic and does not happen in a vacuum. Racism is both the offspring of and support for white supremacy and racialized capitalism (Sims, 2018). As such, we acknowledge that our institutions were designed to privilege certain groups and not others, and they are built upon a white supremacist framework that disenfranchises poor, ethnoracially minoritized students of color.

A radical analysis must see racism as a complex political system, not just individual, micro-aggressive acts. A radical analysis of race must be intersectional. Renowned professor, Robin D.G. Kelly, argues that race and gender are how capitalism is lived out. Therefore, any radical analysis of race must also investigate both gender and racialized capitalism. If we do this work individually and institutionally, we will improve our resource allocation decisions, systems, practices, and policies for our Black, Indigenous, and People of Color (BIPOC) as well as our entire campus communities. When we address these inequities, all of us benefit. We must be individually and institutionally invested in working to eliminate racialized injustices and inequities, and their byproducts, individual acts of racism. We are keenly aware that we must also work to eradicate the systems and structures that make racial microaggressions and other instances of anti-Black (and other forms of) racism normal in the first place. We recognize that we are a part of the white supremacist institution and must begin this work as administrators, faculty, and classified staff/professionals by examining our own roles in perpetuating a racist system.

Friends, in order to do this, in order to commit to love as praxis, we have to be honest about where we are individually and institutionally. And, we have to recognize that, by and large, our schools are not broken. In fact, they are working the way that they were designed. Education in this country is capitalistic, white supremacist, and cis-heteropatriarchal. Therefore, our educational system has always privilege cis-hetero, white (land-owning) males. We cannot continue to expend valuable time seeking to "fix" a system that is not broken. Instead, we have to commit to realizing radical love as praxis so that we can begin to radically reimagine the form and function of the educational spaces that we occupy. We cannot be bystanders anymore. Out PERMSC's are drowning because our institutionalized policies, practices, procedures, and pedagogies do not serve them. We cannot never become apathetic. This is a call to action. We have to be ready to not just jump in to save drowning students, we have to do the necessary work of changing our systems so that the drowning danger is no more.

References

Freire, P. (2000). *Pedagogy of the oppressed* (30th anniversary ed.). New York, NY: Continuum.

Gable, T, Holiday, T., O'Sullivan, P., & Sims, J.J., (2021). *Getting started with equity: A guide for academic department leaders.* Every Learner Everywhere.

Ginwright, S.A. (2022). *The four pivots: Reimagining justice, reimagining ourselves.* New York, NY: Random House.

King, M.L. (2015). *The radical King*. London: Penguin.

Mahiri, J., & Sims, J.J. (2016). Engineering equity: A critical pedagogical approach to language and curriculum change for African American males in STEM. *In Curriculum change in language and STEM subjects as a right in education*. Rotterdam: Sense Publishing.

Sims, J.J. (2018). *Revolutionary STEM education: Critical-reality pedagogy and social justice in STEM for Black males*. New York, NY: Peter Lang.

Sims, J.J., et al. (2020). *Minding the obligation gap in community colleges: Theory and practice in achieving educational equity*. New York:, NY Peter Lang.

Sims, J.J. (Forthcoming). *Love as praxis: Antiracism and justice*. New York, NY: Peter Lang.

Appendix A: Index of Practicums

Below, you will find a list of the tools and practices from throughout the book along with short descriptions and where you can find them in the book. It is important to note that this book, and the tools within, are not comprehensive, and it is really just a start in creating a classroom that is justice-advancing. The references throughout this book contain some amazing, foundational texts and scholars, and I would encourage you to continue your growth using those resources.

1. **Language and Equity (pp. 76–81)**
   This practicum helps clarify some of the terms and phrases often used in equity and racial justice work (e.g. minoritized), with an emphasis on the terms used for ethno-racial groups (e.g. Latinx vs. Latino vs. Chicano). It is important to understand that this language is fluid and constantly changing, so when in doubt, ask your student(s) how they identify.

2. **Antiracist Reflective Praxis (pp. 152–173)**
   Antiracist Reflective Praxis (ARP) is a heuristic meant to help white educators become more mindful of their actions and beliefs vis-à-vis race. As Kendi (2019) notes, "being an antiracist requires persistent self-awareness, constant self-criticism, and regular self-examination" (p. 23). And in a

world where we are constantly being exposed to racist ideologies, anti-Blackness, and other forms of prejudice, hatred, and violence, we need to have the tools to recognize how these ideologies inform our own beliefs and how they manifest in our actions and teaching. ARP is comprised of four steps:

a. **Step 1: Identification and Acknowledgement (p. 155)**

Antiracist educators must be able to identify racist thoughts, beliefs, and actions, which requires a great deal of knowledge and understanding of race, racism, and white supremacy. This also requires antiracist educators to be continually curious and mindful and to learn how racism and white supremacy are evolving over time. Ultimately, this first step is taking responsibility for our thoughts and actions.

b. **Step 2: Understanding (p. 162)**

Once we have identified the racist belief, thought, or action, we need to figure out where it originated from. We may ask ourselves, "why do I believe in [fill in the blank]?" or "Why did I think it was ok to say or act in that way?" These racist beliefs and actions will never go away if we don't understand where they came from.

c. **Step 3: Deconstruction (p. 165)**

Once we identify their source(s), we can understand that while it may be

impossible to eliminate racist beliefs and thoughts entirely, we can attenuate them. The less power we give these thoughts and beliefs and the more cognizant we are of their presence, the easier it is to eliminate them from our subconscious. Furthermore, deconstruction requires us to reflect and learn about why these beliefs and thoughts are patently false.

d. **Step 4: Antiracist action (p. 171)**

I can't say this enough but antiracism requires action, even when working on what

Magee (2019) calls the "inner work of racial justice." In this practice, we may need to apologize and make amends with those who we injure and traumatize with our actions. If we had a racist thought or we hold a racist belief, we need to commit ourselves to always being aware of such thoughts and to continually deconstructing them. And, of course, we need to be committed to calling out others for the same beliefs, thoughts, and actions.

3. **Social Justice and Disrupting the Status Quo (pp. 215–217)**

This practicum differentiates between empathy and compassion and asks readers to consider their own feelings when we witness or learn of racist abuse and violence against our students and colleagues of color. I contend that it is not enough to feel sympathy or even empathy, and while we cannot change what our students of color have experienced at the hands of white supremacy and racist ideologies, we can use our positions as educators to change our classrooms and even our institutions. In other words, we must feel compassion for our students, which compels us to disrupt the systems that have been complicit and even active in promoting racism, hated, and violence.

4. **Facilitating Sensitive Classroom Discussion (pp. 238–244)**

In a classroom that advances educational equity and social justice, the topic of race (as well as other forms of oppression, like sexism, homophobia, xenophobia, etc.) is bound to come up in class assignments and discussions. This practicum includes suggestions for how to facilitate these types of sensitive discussions, including a "norming" exercise that establishes guidelines early in the semester for these types of discussions (p. 134). Ultimately, I argue that we need to create "safe discourse spaces" where students know they can speak their mind, but where they also know they will be challenged – with love and compassion – when they say something inappropriate or problematic.

5. **You're Not a Therapist...But You Are a Navigator (p. 245)**

As community college educators, we work with some of the most vulnerable student populations in higher education, and when we do the work of social justice, we are almost guaranteed to hear about the struggles and horrors that some of our students experience, including physical, emotional, and sexual violence, homelessness, food insecurity, addiction, and mental health issues. But we are not therapists, and we should not, under any circumstances, try to "heal" our students or intervene on their behalf. It simply is not our job (and it can do more harm than good). However, as employees of the college, we should know which programs and services the institution offers to students. In fact, it is an obligation that we know. That way, when a student shares their struggles, we can walk them over to the appropriate service. Our only intervention is to connect our students with professionals who can assist them.

6. **The Syllabus and Course Policies (pp. 245–251)**

The course syllabus is often the first impression of you and your class, and in many ways, it sets the tone for the rest of the term. So if your syllabus starts with policies and penalties, your students will see your class as one in which they must keep their heads down and follow the rules. This type of class kills creativity, curiosity, learning, and compassion.

On the other hand, if your syllabus starts with your teaching philosophy, a statement that elevates their success and learning above all else, and student support programs and services that will help them succeed, the tone for the class is one of intellectual growth and student-centeredness (see Appendix B). This isn't to say that you are a "pushover" or "soft," it's just that you frontload your syllabus with student-centered statements and language. You can get to the policies and penalties afterward.

7. **"The People's History": Revising the Curriculum (pp. 271–276)**

Here's the reality of American community colleges – our student bodies are growing more and more diverse, but our curricula have generally stayed the same (maybe with a few women and people of color sprinkled in and tokenized for good measure). By and large, the curriculum of American higher education highlights and perpetuates Western European episte-mologies, social norms, and beliefs. This isn't inherently bad, as Western Europe has much to offer the world, but our near-exclusive focus on its knowledge and history excludes the myriad non-European epistemolo-gies and social norms that also have a great deal to offer to our students. Furthermore, we often present European history and knowledge uncrit-ically. For example, in the natural sciences, we often teach the biological classification system – or taxonomy – since it is used to name and classify every living organism on Earth. It is important. But we often don't teach our students that the man who created it, Carl Linnaeus, was an extreme racist and eugenicist who used his system to classify humans into a hier-archy where whites were at the top and Africans, and Indigenous folks were at the bottom. This information doesn't take away from the system's usefulness, but it is a lesson on how supposedly "objective" science can be used to perpetuate white supremacy and racist ideologies. Future scien-tists need to know this. This practicum discusses the problem with much of our curricula and how we can begin to create courses that are critical and inclusive.

8. **"Folktales and Ethnic Foods": Rejecting Tokenism and Embracing True Multiculturalism (pp. 277–289)**

In a follow-up to "The People's History" practicum, this section provides the theoretical background for multiculturalism and how to integrate it into one's curriculum. Multiculturalism, unfortunately, has been deeply misinterpreted and misused in our classrooms, which has resulted in tokenism and false narratives. Too many of us have not only added a Latinx author or Black activist to our course content, but we have also misrepresented their contributions and activism. For example, Martin Luther King's entire life is distilled down to one speech – "I Have a Dream" – which is then used to justify colorblindness and meritocracy without any exploration of King's other speeches or sermons or even his evolving views of capitalism. We have to do better, which means we can't take thinkers and authors of color, women, and other minoritized people and try to fit them into the larger patriarchal, Eurocentric narrative of American history, economics, and art. As institutions of higher education, we should be asking our students to look at the latter critically using the knowledge of the former.

a. **Content Integration (p. 280)**

This tenet of multiculturalism calls for the complete overhaul of the course curriculum, not just the addition of a few minoritized authors and thinkers (i.e. tokenism). True multiculturalism uses the tenets of critical pedagogy where the students are asked to look at historical inequities and injustices, how they manifest in their own communities, and what they can do to promote change. In this way, a multicultural education rejects the "banking model" and instead utilizes "problem posing" and praxis.

b. **The Knowledge Construction Process (p. 282)**

This tenet of multiculturalism helps us rebuild our overhauled curriculum. The "Knowledge Construction Process" dethrones Eurocentric epistemologies and social norms and places it on equal footing with Indigenous, African, Middle Eastern, Asian, and other ways of knowing and existing. James A. Banks describes four forms of curriculum reform – contributions, additive, transformation, and social change. The first two would be akin to "tokenism," as they simply sprinkle non-Western European people and knowledge into the existing course. However, the transformation tenet is used to help students understand *how* knowledge is constructed and to "view concepts, issues, events, and themes from the perspectives of various ethnic and cultural groups." The social action approach is the natural follow-up to transformation, as it compels students to identify social injustices and to create solutions.

c. **Prejudice Reduction (p. 284)**

Prejudice reduction is the work of antiracism, as this teaching practice is used to investigate students' awareness and beliefs around race and other marginalized identities. Traditionally, this practice has been used by educational researchers to investigate how students' awareness of race evolves during their lifetime, which informed the belief that if students just knew more about their classmates of color, their prejudices would dissipate. However, research has shown that simply being around students of color and learning more about their histories and cultures was not enough to reduce prejudice and eradicate racism. Instead, intentional discussions about race, racism, and racial ideologies and how they impact the lived realities and well-being of people of color are much more effective. As a result, prejudice reduction – or antiracism – requires a shift in pedagogy (e.g. critical reality pedagogy) and curricular interventions that don't tokenize communities of color but instead center their histories, epistemologies, and social norms.

d. **Equity Pedagogy (p. 286)**

An equity-centered pedagogy is one in which educators see their students as unique individuals with unique needs. The notion of "equality" – treating all students as equal and therefore providing equal support and materials – is problematized and rejected. Since equity-minded educators are concerned with the success of all their students and understand that students may be privileged in some ways and disadvantaged in others, they tailor their pedagogical approaches to the needs of their students. This could include individualized materials, regular one-on-one meetings, and loaner equipment and books. Unsurprisingly, this approach requires educators to get to know all of their students, so individual check-ins, reflective assignments, and students' needs surveys are crucial. Equity-minded educators must know their students and their educational needs.

e. **Empowering School Culture (p. 286)**

The final tenet asks educators to reimagine the entire institution, which means critiquing policies and procedures (including curriculum approvals and faculty hiring), budgeting, and student support services. This tenet extends beyond the scope of this book, but see Sims, Taylor-Mendoza, Hotep, Wallace, and Conaway's (2020) book *Minding the Obligation Gap in Community Colleges and Beyond* for more information on how community college leaders can transform their colleges.

9. **Broader Considerations for Equity-Centered Curricula (p. 289)**
   While institutional changes are beyond the scope of this book, there are two structures worth noting that impact the classroom – academic program development and the curriculum approval process. In the case of the former, we need to start having difficult conversations with our department colleagues about our programs' offerings, curricula, and student learning outcomes and how our departments hire new faculty and evaluate them. More specifically, we must start interrogating how our programs and department processes perpetuate white supremacy and privilege Western European thought and social norms. In the case of the latter, our curriculum approval processes need to change, which means that our curriculum committees need to change how they critique and approve courses. For example, curriculum committees could use rubrics that determine whether a course's content perpetuate white supremacist ideologies and privileges European norms and knowledge or whether a course's content is "diversity-rich," meaning that the course utilizes a critical pedagogical approach, it uses activities and assessments that invite students into the knowledge creation process, and it decenters Western European epistemologies and integrates those of other cultures and ethnicities.

10. **Self-care for Antiracist Educators (pp. 297–300)**
    This is hard work. While it may be relatively easy to transform your classroom, it is not an insular space. Our societal pathologies will make their way into the space, and you will have to contend with them, and at times, it may feel like you are losing an uphill battle. As a result, this section contains practices for self-care so that you can maintain the work of antiracism and thrive while doing so. The pernicious and unfortunate fact is that we live in a country so entrenched in racism and white supremacist ideologies that it is far too easy for us white folks to retreat back into blindness and ignorance. If we get overwhelmed, it is far too easy to just throw our hands up and give up (a luxury that our colleagues and students of color do not enjoy). So take care of yourself, so you can continue to fight.

11. **Radical Compassion (pp. 300–303)**

Radical compassion, using the work of Tara Brach, is the rejection of the status quo. She argues that many of us exist in a "trance – a partially unconscious state that, like a dream, is disconnected from the whole of reality." Community college educators, like all higher education professionals, have a lot on our plate outside our teaching, and it becomes easy to fall into this trance and to "fall back" on comfortable pedagogical techniques and curricula without realizing that much of it is problematic. Radical compassion, to Brach, includes "clarity, openhearted presence, and emotional intelligence," meaning that when we get overwhelmed, and we fall into a trance, we are mindful of that reaction and that we wake up to the reality of the world around us. As antiracist educators, we have to remain vigilantly aware of the racialized experiences of our students and colleagues of color, even as our minds (and bodies) tell us to seek our old, comfortable rhythms.

References

Kendi, I.X. (2019). *How to be an antiracist.* New York: One World.

Magee, R.V. (2019). *The inner work of racial justice: Healing ourselves and transforming our communities through mindfulness.* New York: TarcherPerigree.

Sims, J.J., Taylor-Mendoza, J., Hotep, L., Wallace, J., & Conaway, T. (2020). *Minding the obligation gap in community colleges: Theory and practice in achieving educational equity.* New York: Peter Lang.

Appendix B: Sample Syllabus

Instructor: Jeramy Wallace
MWF 11:10 am – 12:30 pm
Central Hall, Building 16, Room 206
College of San Mateo
Fall 2021

email: wallacej@smccd.edu
Phone: (650) 574 - 6355
Office: Building 15, Room 103
Office Hours: M/W, 1-2 &
T/Th,11-12, & by appointment

English 100 Course Syllabus

"Tell your story. Otherwise, others will tell it for you."
  – Dr. Jennifer Taylor-Mendoza, President, College of San Mateo

"We have to take time to tell stories. Storytelling is such an important part of liberation."

– Lama Rod Owens, author of *Love and Rage*

Welcome to English 100, *Composition and Reading*, at the College of San Mateo! As the quotes above attest, we will be focusing primarily on storytelling this semester. And I am *not* talking about cheesy stories, like fairy tales or self-help memoirs, or tales of glory in battle or on the field. I am talking about *real* stories – the stories about what it's like to live in America, to attend its schools, to live in its neighborhoods. I am talking about people's lived experiences. I am talking about *the people's stories.*

This is, of course, a reading and composition course, and many people may look at this course and argue that storytelling isn't really rhetoric or composition; they may say it's the soft side of writing or non-academic. However, this course will be informed by a field of study called Critical Race Theory (CRT), which is a scholarly framework that seeks to identify and eradicate racism in American society and its institutions. One of CRT's primary tenets is majoritarian storytelling and counterstorytelling (the former being oppressive and the latter being liberating). It is under this *academic* theory and practice that we will engage in a scholarly discussion about the power of stories and counterstories, which will be the basis for our reading and writing.

I am looking forward to undertaking this journey with you this semester!

Student Learning Outcomes

Upon successful completion of this course, you will meet the following outcomes:

- **SLO1**: Enter into written, academic discourse with course readings by presenting ideas of others in relation to ideas of your own.
- **SLO2**: Write text-based expository essays unified by a thesis and by an organizational strategy that reflects the assignment's task and purpose.

- **SLO3**: Write clearly focused, complex sentences using coordinating and subordinating conjunctions, concession, noun phrase appositives, verbal phrase modifiers, and correct parallel structure.
- **SLO4**: Proofread effectively for grammar and usage errors, including correct application of MLA document format.
- **SLO5**: Effectively evaluate and fluidly integrate relevant sources, using appropriate research strategies and tools and documenting them according to MLA guidelines.

Course Prerequisites

ENGL 838 with a grade of C or higher; OR ESL 400 with a grade of C or higher; OR appropriate skill level as indicated by the English Placement Test

Books and Materials

Required

- Coates, Ta-Nehisi. *Between the World and Me* (2015)
- Martinez, Aja Y. *Counterstory: the Rhetoric and Writing of Critical Race Theory* (2020)
- A binder for class materials
- A two-pocket folder for essay packets
- A composition notebook
- Google Drive (included with your SMCCCD online account)

Note: e-books are totally ok! They are usually cheaper and instantly available.

Recommended

- A College Dictionary (online is ok – just bookmark it. I recommend Merriam-Webster)
- An MLA Handbook (again, online is ok. I recommend Purdue OWL)

Educational Equity at College of San Mateo

The faculty at the College of San Mateo affirm that students are entitled to an equitable learning environment that celebrates their voice, fosters their agency, and develops their capacity for self-advocacy and that is free of unfair practices.

If you feel you are in an environment that is not conducive to your learning, or you want to learn more about educational equity, please come talk to me. You may also contact CSM's Director of Equity (collegeofsanmateo.edu/equity) to explore your options.

CSM Student Support Services

- CalWORKS
- o CalWORKs assists students receiving cash aid (TANF) with a variety of coordinated support services such as academic and personal counseling, work-study, priority registration, assistance purchasing required textbooks and supplies, assistance applying for financial aid and scholarships, help with child care costs, transportation assistance, enhanced job skills, workshops, trainings, and computer access as they pursue training to increase employment opportunities that lead to self-sufficiency.
- Career Services
- o The mission of Career Services is to assist students in developing career awareness, exploring related employment options, and outlining career pathways.
- Counseling Services
- o CSM's academic counselors are available to help you understand your educational options, to help you explore and establish educational and career goals, to help you develop your Student Education Plan (SEP), and to help you identify and overcome any personal issues that may be impeding your personal and academic success. Counseling Services is located in Bldg. 10, Third Floor. (650) 574-6400.
- Disability Resource Center (DRC)
- o If you have a documented disability and need accommodations for this class, please see me as soon as possible or contact Disability Resource Center (DRC) for assistance. The DRC is located in Bldg. 10, First Floor. (650) 574-6438; TTY (650) 574-6230.
- Extended Opportunity Programs and Services (EOPS) & CARE
- o EOPS and CARE are committed to providing access to higher education for students who face significant academic and socioeconomic barriers. They provide an array of student support services and academic resources. EOPS/CARE is located in Bldg. 10, First Floor. (650) 574-6154.
- Financial Aid

o Financial aid is also a partnership between you as the student and the college that provides the money to help pay your college costs. If you receive financial aid, you are expected to enroll in courses needed to complete your chosen program, work hard at learning, and move responsibly toward the successful completion of your educational goal.

• Multicultural Center/DREAM Center

o the Multicultural/DREAM Center can help you with AB540 admissions, DACA, the California Dream Act, and similar issues. They also provide a safe and nurturing space for AB540 and DACA students. The DREAM Center is in Bldg. 10, First Floor. (650) 574-6120.

• Learning Support Centers

o CSM has several learning centers on campus to help you succeed in many disciplines. CSM has a Learning Center, which offers multi-disciplinary tutoring, computer access, and group study rooms, among other services. The college also has discipline-specific centers, including the Writing Center, the Math Resource Center, the Business Lab, and the Integrated Science Center. Finally, CSM, of course, has an amazing library, which is staffed by library faculty ready to help you access the information you need for your studies and assist you in evaluating that information. The library also has computers, study spaces, and a MakerSpace area.

• Learning Communities

o CSM is home to several learning communities, including the MANA program, Project Change, the Puente program, the Umoja Community, and the Honors Project. For more information, visit www.collegeofsanmateo. edu/learningcommunities.

• Personal Counseling and Wellness Services

o the personal counseling center provides free, confidential counseling to students enrolled at CSM. The personal counseling center is located in Bldg 1, First Floor. (650) 574-6396.

• SparkPoint

o SparkPoint serves students and other San Mateo County resident with individualized financial coaching, public benefits enrollment, and access to the on-campus food pantry. SparkPoint is located in Bldg. 1, First Floor. (650) 378-7275.

• Transfer Services

o Transfer Services provide important services to assist students in planning for transfer to a four-year college or university. Information and workshops are offered on transfer requirements, transfer planning, writing the application essay, choosing a college, and completing transfer admission applications.

- Veterans' Services
- o We can assist you in starting, continuing, or resuming your education. We have experience and knowledge of the Post-9/11 GIB, MGIB-SR, Voc Rehab, CalVet Fee Waiver, VA Work Study, GI Bill Payment Rates, and Post-9/11 BAH rates. We can help you navigate through the VA system as well as connect you to your local county veteran services office.
- The Writing Center
- o The Writing Center provides one-on-one writing conferences with English instructors; computers, printers, DVDs, and VHS equipment; a library of literature, film, textbooks, and reference materials; and tutorials on specific writing skills.

Title IX Policy Addressing Sexual Misconduct, Harassment, and Assault

"The San Mateo County Community College District is committed to maintaining safe and caring college environments at Cañada College, College of San Mateo, and Skyline College. The District has established policies and procedures regarding Sexual Misconduct, Harassment, and Assault. A District website has also been developed, which provides you with important information about sexual misconduct and sexual assault. http://smccd.edu/titleix/"

Grading Policies

For this course, we will be using self-assessments to determine your final grade; in other words, you will be determining your own final grade, which will be based on your homework completion (including turning in all essays), your participation in class, and the quality of your final portfolio (we'll go over this later). As a result, in the gradebook, I will simply be marking homework assignments and essays as "complete/incomplete," and in the case of the latter, I will be providing feedback only on your final drafts (which I expect you to use in completing your final portfolio). Please note that completion does not simply mean turning in your work. All your coursework and participation must be of the quality and depth expected of a college student. We will, of course, discuss what this means throughout the semester. Furthermore, we will meet during finals week to discuss your self-assessment (note: if I think your final grade self-assessment is wildly off,

I reserve the right to assign a different grade, but don't worry, students tend to underassess themselves).

See the "Final Grade Self-Assessment" page for more information. Finally, it is a course requirement that ALL essays are turned in (which means you can't pass the class with missing essays).

Participation and Homework

As you will soon find out, becoming an effective writer does not require you to merely *write*. You must be able to actively and critically read a text, articulate your ideas while speaking in class or participating in a discussion forum, and thoughtfully listen and respond to your peers' comments. As such, your participation in class is imperative to your success in this class because you must "test" your ideas in an open forum before writing about them, not to mention that your classmates are depending on your participation in order to complete their work (e.g. in discussion forums, peer response, group projects, etc.). Over the course of the semester, we will strive to build an academic community that is inclusive and supportive, and your participation in the class is necessary to the success of the entire community.

Late Policy

I know that most of you, if not all of you, are juggling family responsibilities, work, other classes, and, of course, trying to survive a global pandemic. I am committed to your success, and I want to be as supportive as possible, so if you are struggling with the work, let me know as soon as possible. With that being said, falling behind can have an adverse impact on your coursework, and late work can stack up and make your workload even more difficult to handle. To that end, please turn in your work on-time, and if something comes up, let me know as soon as you can. Generally speaking, I do not accept late work, but I realize that emergencies do come up – the key is open and honest communication about your needs.

Essays

You will write five essays through the course of the semester (two of which will be collaborative). Essay topics will vary and will be based on the assigned readings. **All essays must be typed, double-spaced, with 1-inch margins, and in 12-point Times New Roman**. Because your final grade will be determined in part on your final portfolio, I will provide feedback only on your essays, and in the gradebook, they will show up as "complete/incomplete," which translates to "turned in/not turned in or incomplete. Like mentioned above, a "completed" essay fulfills all the assignment requirements and is of the quality expected of a college writer.

All essays must be turned in on Canvas at the posted time on the due date – no exceptions. If you are out of town, you get sick, etc., make sure your essay is turned in on Canvas by the deadline (again, I do not accept essays through email). **Late essays will not be accepted.**

I grade your essays on Canvas, so that is where you will see your feedback (Canvas uses a complete/incomplete system, so complete = turned in and incomplete = not turned in or incomplete draft). We will go over how to see your specific feedback in class.

Finally, you must turn in all essays to pass the class.

Peer Response

Prior to turning in your essays, we will engage in a peer response activity. These workshops are extremely important for getting feedback on your essay and for asking questions (this is why it is such an important part of your final grade). It is important that you complete these activities on time because your classmates are relying on your feedback to revise your essay. In order to get credit for peer review activities, your rough draft must meet the page requirement, you need to submit your rough draft to Canvas by the due date (so your peers have access to it and time to provide you with feedback), and you need to provide feedback to your peers by the deadline.

Revisions

Since I provide feedback only on essays, your revisions will be due in the final portfolio. Please note that there is no such thing as a perfect draft, which means that every single essay that I read will need to be revised in some way. More on the portfolio later.

Plagiarism

"Plagiarism" means submitting work that is someone else's as one's own. For example, copying material from a book or other source without acknowledging that the words or ideas are someone else's, and not one's own, is plagiarism. If a student copies an author's words exactly, he or she should treat the passage as a direct quotation and supply the appropriate citation. If someone else's ideas are used, even if they are paraphrased, appropriate credit should be given. Also, it is possible to plagiarize yourself by turning in essays from previous courses, which also counts as cheating. Please bring only new and original work to class. Lastly, a student commits plagiarism when a term paper is purchased and/or submitted that he or she did not write.

Cases of plagiarism will be reported to the Dean and Vice President of Instruction, which could result in consequences up to expulsion.

Here's the bottom line: if you are having so much trouble that you feel you need to cheat, please reach out to me for help – that's what I'm here for:)

Final Grade Self-Assessment and End of Semester Portfolio

Overview

First and foremost, I want to start by emphasizing that college (and schooling, writ large) is about learning and growth, and study after study indicates that traditional assessments (e.g. tests, letter grades, etc.) actually inhibit real learning. This shouldn't be surprising when you think about it. Just ask yourself, when you have a midterm or final exam coming, are you studying to pass the test or because you are genuinely curious about the course material? Admittedly, for many students, it is both, but the point I am trying to make is that high-stakes assessment takes mental resources away from true learning. And just as an aside, I haven't found one research article that argues that traditional, high-stakes grading is good for learning.

As a result, I try to eliminate as much high-stakes assessment as possible. In fact, I have eliminated it all, with the exception of the final course grade, which I legally have to assign to every student. However, during the semester, your homework assignments will simply be marked as "Complete" (meaning you turned in a completed assignment) or "Incomplete" (meaning the assignment is missing or it isn't complete). Homework assignments, including essays, will not be given actual grades (they will be assigned 1 pt. in the gradebook to show completion), but they will be given feedback because, again, this class is about growth and learning, and I want you to learn from the assignments.

So how will your final grade be determined if I'm not assigning grades to individual assignments? The answer is that each of you will conduct a self-assessment at the end of the semester, which will be based on your final portfolio, the percentage of assignments you completed, and how much you participated in class. Let's dive into this a bit further.

Self-Assessment

At the end of the semester, you will complete a guided self-assessment, which will be based on three things – your essay portfolio, your completed assignments, and your participation in class – and this self-assessment will include a series of questions (both quantitative and qualitative) that will help you determine your final grade. This self-assessment and portfolio will be due to me the week before finals, and during the week of finals, each of you will schedule a meeting with me so that we can discuss your self-assessment and your final grade. This will be an opportunity for me to give you my feedback and for us to discuss your final grade, and by the end of this meeting, we will assign you a final grade. These meetings usually take around ten minutes.

Final Portfolio

I can't say this enough: I am more concerned with learning than with assessment. This portfolio is how you demonstrate your growth. In your portfolio, you will include your self-assessment along with three (3) **revised** essays, one of which will be your publication-ready autobiography and the other, your group research project. You will choose the third essay from Essay 1 and Essay 2 to be included. Note that the essays must be REVISED – this is where you demonstrate what you have learned and how you have grown as a writer. In other words, you will use the feedback I provide you on the original drafts to create final drafts for the portfolio (with the exception of the final group essay, which I will not have looked at yet). As mentioned previously in this syllabus, there is no such thing as a perfect final draft, so each of you will have something to revise in each of your essays, and it should go without saying that a portfolio with un-revised essays will not be reflected kindly in your final grade.

Disclaimer

I firmly believe that self-assessments work, and I trust all of you to accurately represent your level of learning and mastery in this class. In fact, in my experience (and the research bears this out), students tend to *under*-assess themselves. With that being said, if I feel like you have wildly misrepresented your learning and mastery in your self-assessment, I do reserve the right to assign a different grade that I believe more accurately represents your work. Rest assured, this is very rare!

Appendix C: Classroom Norms

Purpose: to create a classroom where students can freely express their views and experiences without fear of reprisal or judgment, but where students also know they will be challenged by classmates and instructors

Objectives:

- Reflect and draw on past experiences discussing sensitive topics in academic and non-academic spaces.
- Create a set of guidelines – or "classroom norms" – that are generated by the students and facilitated by the instructor.

Lesson Plan:

1. Freewrite: ask the students to reflect on the following questions:
   a. How would you feel most comfortable approaching topics like racism, racial inequity, and other injustices? How do we, as a class, discuss these topics in an insightful and productive way? You may draw on examples from previous classes where these types of conversations were positive or negative.

2. Group discussions
   a. Students should introduce themselves to the rest of the group.
   b. Ask the students to share their free-writes in their small group.
   c. Once everyone has shared out, the group should create at least two "guidelines" for class discussions based on the group's share-out.
3. Class discussion
   a. Each group will share at least one of their guidelines with the class, but the instructor should ask for volunteers first.
   b. Instructor should project a Word document where they will record the groups' guidelines. Instructor should facilitate the discussion by asking clarifying questions, pushing back against problematic guidelines, and word-smithing the guidelines as they are added to the list.
   c. After each group has shared, ask the students for any guidelines that haven't been added. Instructor can also suggest any that haven't been added to the list.

Next Steps:

- Print a copy of the classroom norms for each student and/or post it to the Course Management System (e.g. Canvas).
- Revisit classroom norms frequently, especially when sensitive discussions happen.
- Revise the guidelines, as needed, by adding new ones or changing/deleting existing ones.

Educational Equity in Community Colleges

Jeremiah J. Sims and Lasana O. Hotep
GENERAL EDITOR

This series centers theory and practice in enacting educational equity, and, ultimately, educational justice at the administrative, institutional/programmatic, governance, and pedagogical levels of community colleges and other institutions of higher learning (Woods & Harris, 2016; Nevarez & Wood, 2010). There is a corpus of literature on the pernicious effects of oppressive pedagogy at the K–12 level, especially for traditionally marginalized, minoritized students (Nasir, 2011; Delpit, 2012; Leonardo, 2010). However, this is not the case at the community college level even though these same traditionally marginalized, minoritized students overwhelming start their college careers in two-year community colleges. Frankly, though there are many valuable contributions to community college education, overall there is a dearth of literature on critical, justice-centered pedagogy, theory and practice (i.e., praxis) within community college administration, governance, programming, and pedagogy. Community college practitioners are interested in enacting educational equity. However, there is little community college-specific literature for them to use to reimagine and, ultimately, reconstruct their administrative, programmatic, and pedagogical practices so that these institutionalized practices become commensurate with educational equity and justice (Tuck & Yang, 2018). Therefore, the goal of this series is to blend the work of university researchers and community college practitioners to illuminate best practices in achieving educational equity and justice via a critical-reality pedagogical framework (Giroux, 2004; Emdin, 2017; Sims, 2018). This series aims to highlight work that illuminates both the successes and struggles in developing institutionalized practices that positively impact poor ethno-racially minoritized students of color. Therefore, we will be looking at pedagogies, policies, and practices that are intentionally developed, curated and sustained by committed educators, administrators, and staff at their respective college campuses that work to ensure just learning conditions for all students.

To receive more information, please contact:

editorial@peterlang.com

To order books, please contact our Customer Service Department:

peterlang@presswarehouse.com (within the U.S.)
orders@peterlang.com (outside the U.S.)

Visit our website at WWW.PETERLANG.COM

Made in the USA
Las Vegas, NV
19 January 2024

84617910R00203